Don Rittner

WATERVLIET
THE CANAL DAYS

Copyright 2021 by Don Rittner

All rights reserved. International copyright secured. No part of this book may be reproduced, stored in a retrieval system, or transmitted in any form or by any means electronic, mechanical, photocopying, recording, or otherwise—without the prior written permission of New Netherland Press and Don Rittner, except for the inclusion of brief quotations in an acknowledged review.

ISBN: 978-0-937666-65-4

Dedicated to
Tom & Marylou Ragosta
Stewards of Watervliet History

Book design by Don Rittner

New Netherland Press
Schenectady, NY

First Edition

Introduction

This is Volume Two in a series about Watervliet, NY, and its earlier villages of Washington, Port Schuyler, Gibbonsville, and West Troy.

This collection of images deals with the time that the Erie Canal went through the city and allowed it to prosper as a canal town. West Troy was created by businessmen of Troy, NY, across the Hudson River. Troy was Albany's old rival and they competed for everything from who would get the first bridge, turnpike, and any other economic incentive. History tells us Albany was awarded the terminal city of the canal, but Trojans did not sit idle in defeat. The purchased the land and created West Troy and made sure it had a suitable size lock so products could enter/exit giving Troy an economic advantage over Albany. It worked. Why this area? Location! The Hudson-Mohawk Valleys were the only natural east-west break between the Appalachian Mountains.

When the canal was completed it went through the villages of Port Schuyler, the US Arsenal, Gibbonsville, then located between 9th and 15th Sts., and West Troy, located north of 15th to 27th Streets. By 1836 business was so good that the three villages incorporated into the Village of West Troy. On May 26, 1896, it became the city of Watervliet.

The 23rd Street Side Cut was usually the last stop before entering the Hudson into the canal, even though technically Albany was the last stop. Every type of business or service was located here. Hotels, saloons, butchers, carpenters, grocers and more. It was called the *"Barbary Coast of the East."* In a two block area there were 29 bars. The side cut from the Hudson River is now buried under I-787. Watervliet looked quite different when the canal was in use. There were several bridges over the canal. Port Schuyler: road bridges at 5th, 7th and 8th Sts and foot bridges at 6th and 8th Sts. Arsenal: two road bridges and one railroad bridge. Gibbonsville: Road bridge at 13th, 14th and 16 Sts and a foot bridge at 15th St. West Troy: Road bridge at 23rd and 25th Sts, and a change bridge for mules (tow path on west side until 23rd St) at 23rd St, and lift bridge at 19th St. A basin was a pool or wide spot connected to the canal for docking, loading, unloading and turning of boats. On the original Erie there were two basins: Gibbonsville along 2nd Ave between 13th and 14th Sts and West Troy along 2nd Ave between 19th and 23rd Sts. Enlarged basins followed: West Troy along the Hudson (lower basin) south of 23rd St. Mohawk Basin north of 23rd St. Use this book to walk the original canal path.

Originally there were three canal stages with the original completed October 26, 1825, followed by the enlarged on September 1, 1862, replaced by the Barge Canal in 1918 that utilized the rivers more and bypassed cities like Watervliet. It was the end of a 93 year run of profits for the city and would change the nature of Watervliet for many years after.

As a result of the side cut, West Troy was a main starting point for emigration to the West. NY Harbor, because of the Erie, surpassed all others in traffic along the Eastern Seaboard. Emigrants travelled up the Hudson and entered the canal at West Troy on their way to the West and a new life.

In 1918 the new Barge Canal opened at Waterford and the Erie between Albany and the Mohawk River closed. On January 8, 1924, Watervliet paid $39,874.93 for land and rights to the previously owned and used canal through the city. They started filling in the canal marking the end of an era for the city. This volume will show you what it looked like during the canal days along with interesting sidenotes. Special thanks to Tom and Marylou Ragosta, stewards of Watervliet's history.

Don Rittner
As always comments and suggestions are welcome at drittner@aol.com

Canal Boats in river by the 23rd Street Side Cut. Barges awaiting the opening of the canal in the spring time. Many canalers wintered in the East River area of New York City. The horses and mules were kept on local farms during winter. A paddle wheel steamboat is on the Troy side of the Hudson. Watervliet on the left and Center (Starbuck) Island is in the center.

View of canal boats outside the 23rd St Side Cut. Lyon Shirt factory can be seen across in Lansingburgh. In 1871 the West Troy upper Side Cut lock did more business than any lock from New York to Buffalo except for New York City itself. Earnings in tolls was second only to NYC. West Troy had 11,000 people at the time.

23rd Street Side Cut and future Hudson Shore Park from Congress Street Bridge. Large culvert still there. Historic flood levels can be seen on the bridge abutment on the right.

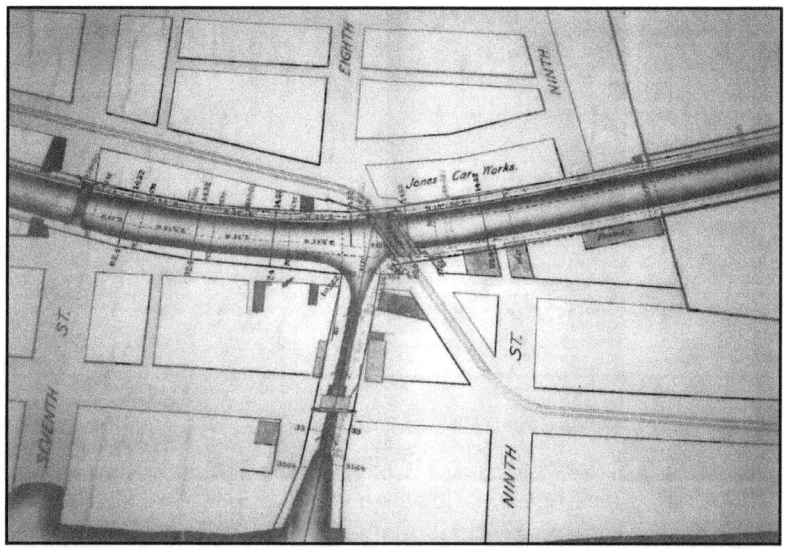

Lower Side Cut Park. In 2011, the lower Side Cut near the arsenal became a park. Some of the walls and entrance to the lock are visible. Photo below shows the entrance lock and canal now buried under the highway. Lock entrance portions still visible from the river. VFW building is built on top of the lock and you can see some of the blocks today.

1850-1915. Greek-revival style weigh station. One of several weigh stations along the Canal used to levy the tolls for barges carrying goods. Until 1850 freight cargoes were measured by the displacement theory, but this hydraulic type worked with scales rather than displacement. After a boat entered the lock it came to rest on a wooden cradle. Then certain rods transferred the weight along a series of levers to the beam of the scales inside the building. The Weigh Master moved a center balancing weight along the beam which determined the weight of the loaded boat. Writing on the East wall: "Canal Tolls and Weigh House." North wall: Collector's Office. BELOW: Maplewood Weighlock in 1900.

The location of the old weighlock is near 2607 2nd Ave and is now a park. There were seven weighlocks on the Erie Canal. Weighlocks were abandoned in the late 1800s because the State abolished tolls in order to compete with the railroads. This weighlock was built in 1853 when the canal was enlarged in West Troy. It replaced the original one that was at 23rd St until 1915. Weighlocks were abandoned in the late 19th century when tolls were abandoned to compete with the railroads. The original weighlock originally at the 23rd St Side Cut was one of the first three constructed on the canal and only seven total on the canal.

The Weighlock before it became a park in the 1950s.

The Weigh Lock today is a park.

14th Street Bridge over the Erie Canal. The former United Methodist Church and the current Civic Center is in the foreground.

23rd St Upper Side Cut. Most canalers were paid in West Troy at the end of their trips. Most boats loaded or unloaded here before entering or exiting the Hudson River. West Troy had one of 13 collectors offices on the canal. Tolls stopped in 1882.

Upper Side-Cut lock for entrance to canal at 23rd street. The river was 11-15 feet lower than the canal depending on the tide. This was one of two locks to raise or lower boats to and from the Hudson. Note the indentation in the wall for the gates. 1950s view. Looking west.

Abandoned Erie Canal Side Cut at 23rd St before fill in. 1950s. Taylor Apartments can be seen in Troy and old Congress St bridge. Looking southeast.

This is the entrance to the canal at Eighth Street prior to construction of I-787. The houses were removed. It's still visible on the Hudson at 7.3 mile of I-787 but hard to get to.

The canal boat *Licoheja* moored across from the West Side Foundry north of the weighlock. According to Mary C. Brown on the historical society Facebook page this is Mr. and Mrs. J. Augustus De Long and Mr. and Mrs. Henry De Long and maid leaving for a three week cruise on Lake Champlain in their new 30-foot gas powered boat built by De Long in 1908.

The amount of tolls received by the West Troy Canal Collector during the month of September, 1870, is $27,212,20.—Troy Daily Whig, Oct. 3, 1870

This is 23rd St between Broadway and 2nd Ave, circa 1920s. Filling in the Side Cut entrance to the canal on 23rd street. Bridge over the Side Cut at Broadway in the foreground and DiNuzzo's store on the left. The cobblestone entrance to the alley is visible.

DiNuzzo Gas and Store. 217 23rd Street. Circa 1930. All these buildings are standing.

Today

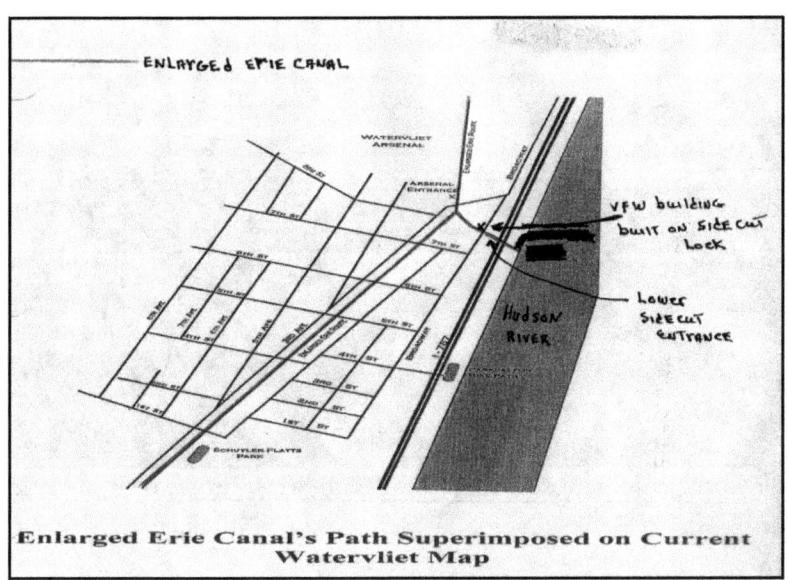

Erie Canal, Watervliet South. Circa 1860s.

"A. Wilcox & Son are cutting q third crop of ice on the West Troy canal basin this season." — The Daily Times, March 5, 1896

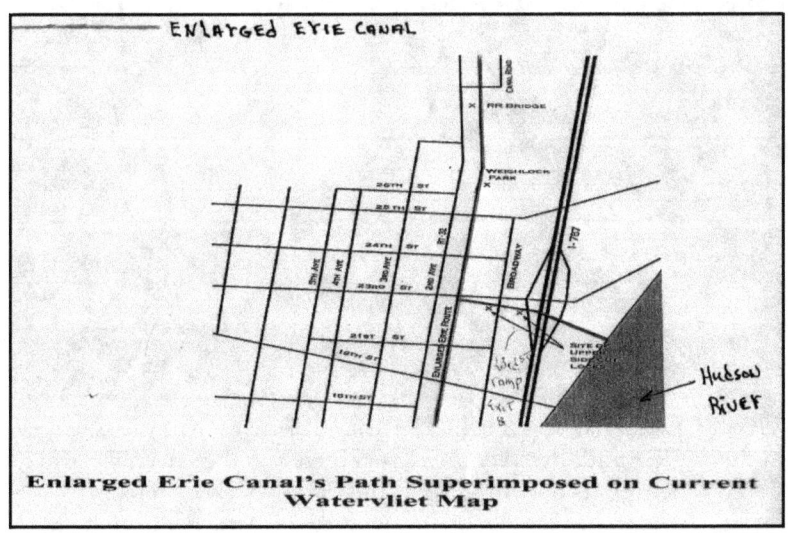

Erie Canal, Watervliet North. Circa 1860s

The bridge in the foreground is the 25th Street bridge over the Erie Canal in Watervliet.

View of Canal looking north. The 13th St Bridge over the Canal in the foreground. Between the Canal boat and the Arsenal north wall on the right is the entrance to the dry dock (boat repair facility), where the city garage is now located. Tow Path on the left side of the Canal. See page 78.

Andrewsville near 14th St and 2nd Avenue on left. The Dome, old State Bank of Albany and swimming pool are now located on the Erie Canal bed. While the entire canal was not finished until October 1825, the section from Rochester to West Troy opened in October 1823. A Troy canal boat was the first to go west on the canal.

This is 2nd Ave and 13th St in 1950. Same view as top photo.

THRILLING SCENE AT WEST TROY.

Canal Boat and Skipper at the Mercy of the Waves.

RESCUED AT LAST BY A TUG BOAT — *A Canal Driver Robbed.*
Great excitement was caused yesterday afternoon on both sides of the river at West Troy by what nearly terminated in a "shipwreck." A Delaware and Hudson "coal plug," moored to the wharf at the foot of Liberty street, West Troy, broke loose from Its fastenings. The wind was blowing; a gale from the south and the "white caps" were rolling quite high. The captain of the boat was asleep on top of the cabin, and did not discover that he was adrift until the boat, getting into the "trough of the sea " nearly went over on its side. As the craft rolled, the navigator was thrown from his resting place to the deck, and nearly into the river. That awakened him. Grasping an iron cleat he saved himself from going into the water. Then he began to shout for assistance. His cries attracted the attention of persons on both sides of the river, and the wharves were quickly lined with people. All kinds of suggestions were advanced as to how a rescue should be effected. Soon several row boats put out from the shore. Then the tug boat James Morris came to the rescue, and the boat was secured. When the "coal plug" was made fast to the propeller, a sigh of relief went up from the multitude that had been worked up to a high pitch of excitement. Several old river men said they did not remember ever to have witnessed such excitement during the long years they followed the water. Between Buffalo and West Troy there are en route about 500 canal boats. During yesterday and up to 8 o'clock last night more than fifty arrived at the side cut. They were locked into the river as fast as possible and made up into tows which proceeded at once to Albany to be forwarded to New York. One of the noticeable features this fall is that the tug boat owners' association has not advanced the price of towing to the Capital city. The bill of George Flannigan, as tender of the lift bridge on Nineteenth street, 112 days at $2.25 per day, was agreed to in full for the amount of $492,75. Eugene Woodward reported to Justice Grogan yesterday, that while he was asleep on the canal boat Edward Burke on which he was employed as a driver, Sunday night, he was robbed of $25 by two other employees on the boat. He said he had the money in the hip pocket of his trousers. The money was the hard earned savings of two months, and the man sobbed as if his heart would break. The captain of the boat, Edward Burke, owed enough in wages to the accused men to make good the loss of Woodward, if the Justice would rule he should pay it over to Woodward. As no positive proof could be produced that the men really stole the money, the justice could not advise the captain to Withhold the amount.

— Albany Morning Express, Wednesday, November 27, 1895.

Erie Canal Side Cut at 23rd St. The lower lock looking east towards Troy. West Troy was usually the last stop before entering the Hudson to the canal. Every type of business or service was here. Hotels, saloons, butchers, carpenters, grocers and more. Called the *"Barbary Coast of the East."* In a two block area there were 29 bars. At the *"Bird at Hand,"* 300 wallets were found behind the mirror when it was being torn down. Get drunk, lose your money!

Passing through the locks opposite Troy

Passing through the 23rd St lock to enter or leave the canal.

Erie Canal. Side Cut at 23rd St. Looking northwest from the Congress Street Bridge. The large culvert is for the dry river bed outflow and is still visible.

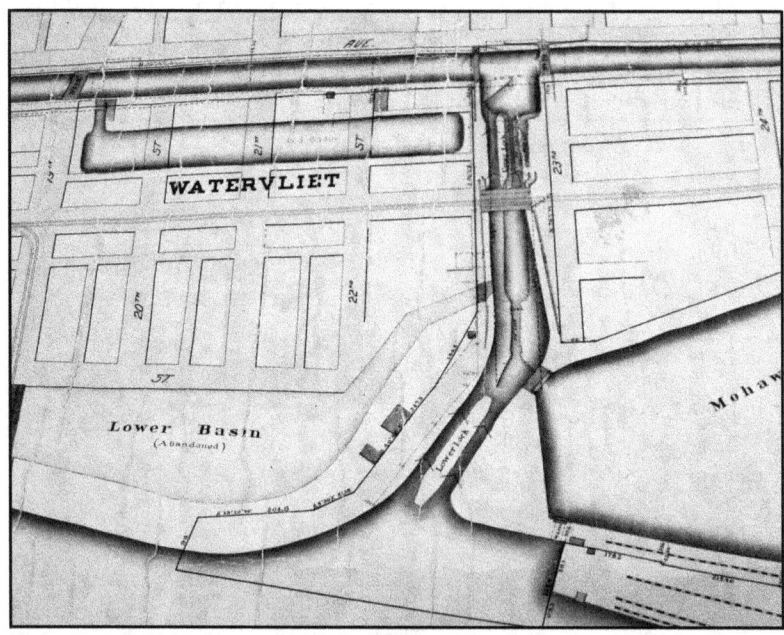

Erie Canal. Side Cut at 23rd St. The old basin between 19th-23rd streets can be seen (now filled in).

A view of the canal on September 3, 1916.

Erie Canal Whipple Bridge (Tow Bridge) at 23rd Street. Side Lock is to the right. Toe path to the left. Looking north. Oct. 23, 1921.

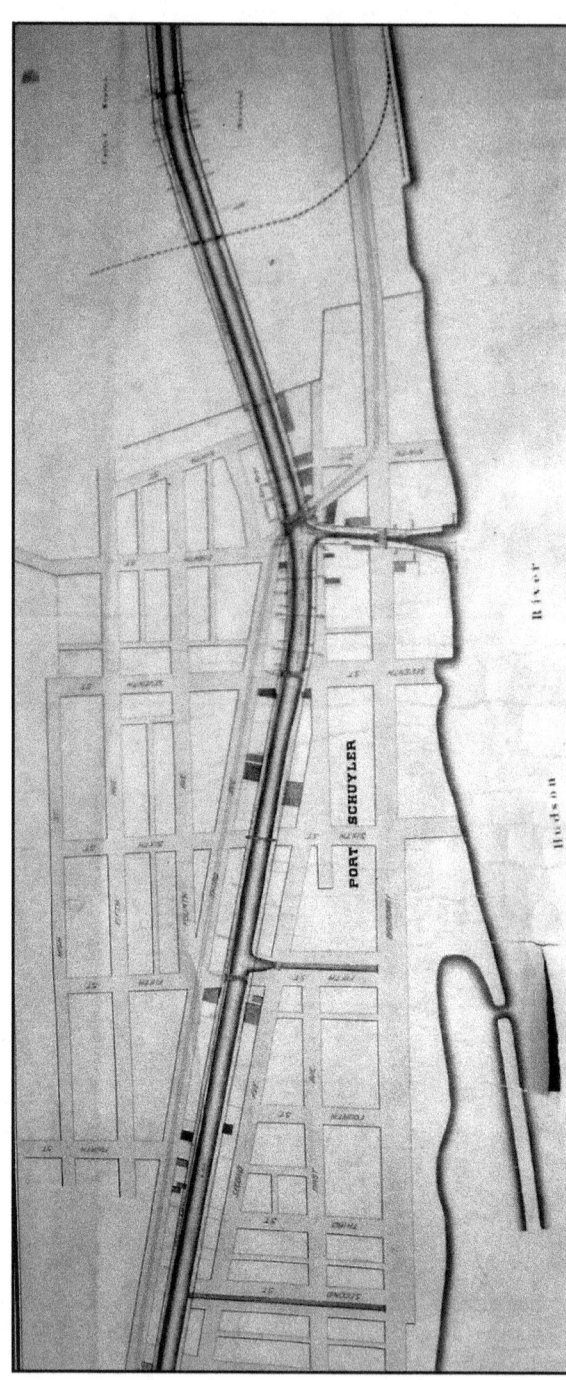

Map showing the Lower Side Cut at Port Schuyler. 1896 Schillner #1 Survey Map. Parts of the side cut entrance can be seen along I-787.

Lower Side Cut entrance at Port Schuyler. Parts still visible from the I-787 highway, southbound.

"The ice in the West Troy canal basin is five Inches thick. Good skating can be had near the West Troy bridge."—Troy Daily Times, Jan 11, 1892.

Women riding in a canal boat in winter.

Viking boat waiting to enter the 23rd St Side Cut. Humphrey's Harness Shop at left. The Viking ship was on its way to the Chicago World Fair in 1893. The ship survived the Fair and is now preserved and exhibited in Geneva, Illinois. It is the replica of the *Gokstad*. It was piloted by Captain Magnus Andersen and sailed across the Atlantic from Bergen, Norway to New York and sailed to Chicago via the Erie Canal and Great Lakes.

"The West Troy canal basin is frozen over, the ice being nearly two inches thick." — Troy Daily Times, Nov 30, 1891

Another view of the Viking boat waiting to enter the 23rd St Side Cut in 1893. *"T. I. Hardin of West Troy, is the superintendent of the West Troy canal section. Will receive appointment of deputy superintendent under Superintendent of Public Works Hannan in 1889-90."* — Troy Daily Times, Jan 30, 1889

The canal at Port Schuyler looking south Between 5th and 6th Street. 1910. House on right is Lamb & Lamb.

Canal boat parked along the canal.

Remains of the West Troy Side Cut lower locks being filled in. West view.

Barge being pushed by a tugboat along the canal.

Filling in the canal and removing the bridge.

Side Cut off 23rd St. On August 26, 1863, Albert G. Sage of Watervliet was contracted to remove the benches and slope wall and the construction of a vertical wall from the Upper Side Cut at West Troy to Lock Number 3.

Panorama of the Upper Side Cut in 1888 showing state and lower basins. Bridges can be seen along the canal.

Panorama of the Side Cut in 1877 showing basins.

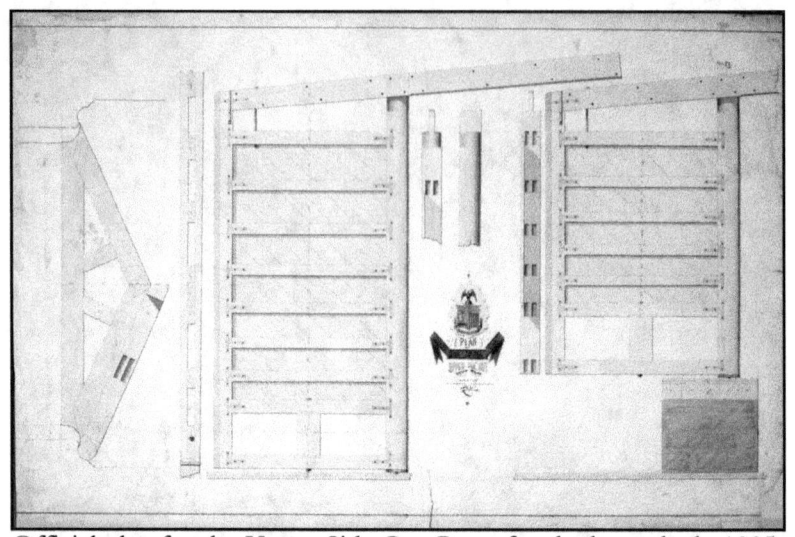

Official plan for the Upper Side Cut Gates for the lower lock. 1835. When closed, these lock gates met at an angle pointing upstream, and were braced against a triangular-shaped mitre sill at the bottom of the lock.

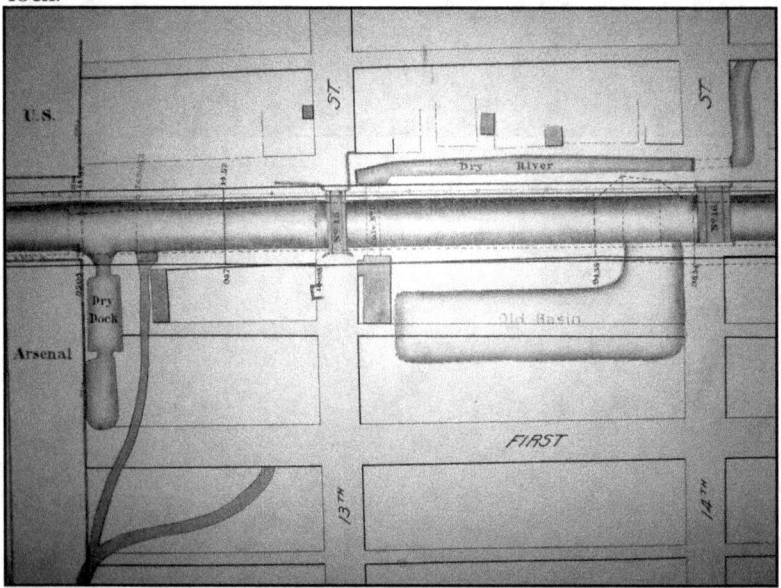

View includes the area between 13th and 15th Sts. Note vehicle/pedestrian bridge crossing canal at 14th St (#16) and that the Dry River runs parallel to the canal along 2nd Ave between 13th and 14th Sts.

TOP & BOTTOM. Filling in the canal and locks. Originally three canal stages with the original completed October 26, 1825, followed by the enlarged on September 1, 1862, and replaced by the Barge Canal in 1918 that utilized the rivers more and now bypassing cities like Watervliet. It was the end of a 93 year run of profits for the city and would change the nature of Watervliet for many years after.

West Troy 1891. Shows canal running through the U.S. Arsenal.

"A Whig reporter visited the West Troy canal barns on Saturday, and found few horses or mules suffering. It was in these barns where the disease was the most severe. All the horses and males used on the canal have been worked daily notwithstanding their sickness; still but few deaths have resulted." — Troy Daily Whig, Nov. 18, 1872

Aerial view of Watervliet north of the Arsenal in 1952.

Watervliet Aerial photo in 1968.

Barge along the Upper Side Cut. Broadway bridge and locks evident. On Nov. 3, 1883, the canal boats *C.A. Blake* & *O. W. Horton*, lying in the canal near the canal collector's office, was to be sold to the highest bidders. They were seized under a chattel mortgage by F. P. Wadhams, temp administrator.

This is 23rd Street and Broadway. Filling in the side cut from the Hudson River to the Erie canal. Circa 1920s.

A view of Troy from the Watervliet Side Cut. The power pole is located where the Taylor Apartments are today. The National Guard Armory on Ferry St is the large structure in the middle.

Canal boats line up near the Arsenal. West Troy was a main starting point for emigration to the West. NY Harbor, as a result of the Erie, surpassed all others in traffic along the Eastern Seaboard. Emigrants travelled up the Hudson and entered the canal at West Troy on their way to the Western United States.

Canal near the Arsenal. Bridge and Stone Mansion visible. On May 14, 1900, William F. Lenway, collector at the West Troy collector's office got swindled out of a $50 check. A young man named Fred Harrison said the check was from his uncle.

A view of the canal walls directing the Erie through the arsenal. The arsenal used canal water to power their machinery. The wall is still visible at the arsenal though the public is not allowed on site.

Canal boat with Whipple Bridge behind it. On Feb, 28, 1896, a rumor circulated that the level of the canal between West Troy and Albany would be abandoned.

Looking south at 13th St and Second Ave. Canal bridges are in the Arsenal grounds. April 12, 1938. The image shows where work was going to start on the proposed extension of the Second Ave pavement (on the right). The highway has been constructed from the North City line south to 13th St. The new section was placed atop the abandoned canal bed. The Thomas M. McCormack Fire Headquarters is now on the left on top of the filled in canal.

Canal and Side Cut filled with some of the stones showing, near the Upper Side Cut.

"The removal to the river of about 190 cribs of spruce and pine spars lying in the West Troy canal basin will be begun on Monday. A clear field will then be left for the winter work of ice harvesters. The timber belongs to West Troy and Albany dealers." —Troy Daily Times, Oct 2, 1890

Canal and Side Cut filled with some of the stones showing, near the Upper Side Cut.

Canal and locks in the Upper Side Cut idle and abandoned.

On August 15, 1876, the body of Mrs. Sarah Dickson was found floating in the basin in the upper locks. She was a domestic employed at the Arbor Saloon. Was last seen alive Sunday night in the company of an unknown man. She was drunk.

A Wife Drowned While In Search of Her Husband — A Remarkable Case.

A despatch was received at the West Troy Canal Collector's office Saturday requesting the collector to notify William Miles, of the canal boat Putnam of the death of his wife at Utica. The circumstances of the case are a little singular. Miles, who is from Oriskany Falls, telegraphed his wife to meet him at Utica. While waiting for her at that place, he entered a saloon near his boat, and during a quarrel between the bar-tender and a customer was struck accidentally on the head by a large stone. The blow rendered him insensible, in which condition he remained three days. When he recovered, his wife not having arrived as he was informed, he started for West Troy. Meanwhile his wife arrived at Utica, and while searching for her husband's boat, during the time he lay insensible, fell in the canal and was drowned. — Albany Morning Express, Wednesday, May 24, 1876.

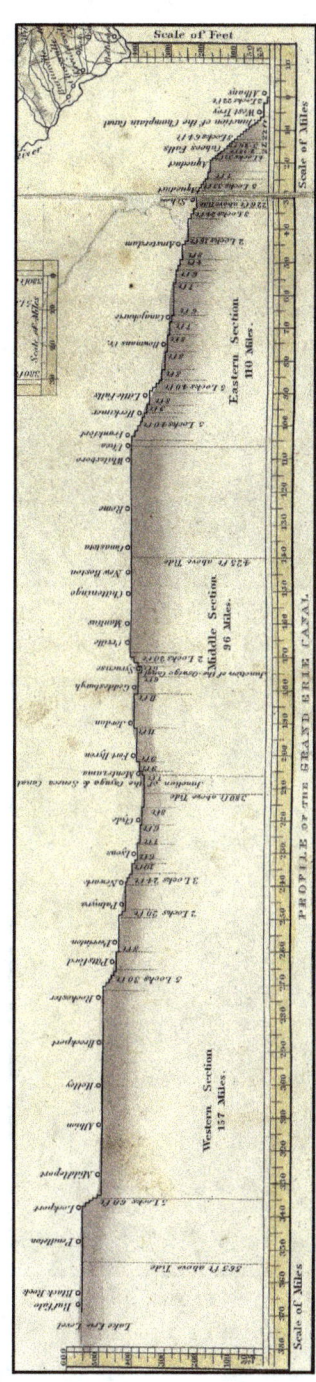

Profile of the original Erie Canal, 1832

Welcoming a boat in the Side Cut. Troy is visible opposite side. This may be the Viking boat entering the lock in 1883 headed to Chicago.

1921 Canal Boat School. Children of boatmen were often born and raised on canal boats. Often kids were taught by a parent if they were educated. Many were not.

1924. Kids on canal boat. Children did not have their own bedroom so often slept with parents or on a mattress or straw on the floor. Parents did not have enough money to buy shoes so usually they walked the towpath without them.

Upper Side Cut. Oil tanks on Centre Island (now called Starbuck Island from the old iron foundry that use to be there). Oil tanks have been removed and replaced now with apartments.

Another view of the abandoned lock. There were two side cuts (entrance & exits to and from the Hudson at West Troy). One located in the vicinity of the Arsenal's South Gate (lower side cut) and the other at 23rd St (upper side cut). Two locks at each side cut lowered or raised the canal boats to and from the Hudson River.

The Upper Side Cut view from Troy. Lock is on the left with the bulkhead wall and waste weir (4 small rectangles of the Mohawk Basin).

The Upper Side Cut being filled in. The original canal had 83 lift locks and 13 guard locks and was 363 miles long. The enlarged canal in 1862 had 72 double lift locks and 3 guard locks. The enlarged canal was 350 ½ miles long. On February 16, 1894, a bill was introduced by Assemblyman Douglass in the NY Assembly providing for the cleaning out of all old wrecks, bars and shoals in the canal harbor at West Troy, lying between the upper side-cut draw bridge and Harps ice house dock, and to deepen the harbor to not less than seven of water at an expense of $10,000.

More filling in the canal.

On November 15, 1893, the newspaper reported *"Business on the canals has been remarkably good this year and the boatmen have had no cause for complaint. More money has been made by the boatmen during the present season than in several years before. In West Troy Canal Section Superintendent Boyland has worked Zealously."*

Pay receipt to E. H. Powell for being a collector of tolls at West Troy.

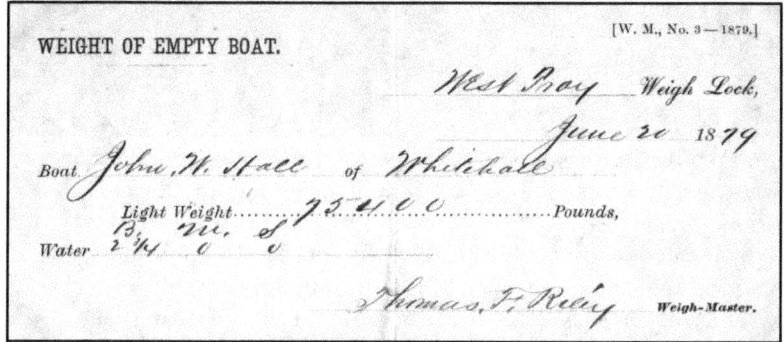
Weight receipt of empty boat to John W. Hall on June 20, 1879.

Garbage where formerly a mighty canal stood.

An arch of limestone blocks. When the canal was completed it went through three villages of Port Schuyler and the Arsenal, Gibbonsville, then located between 9th and 15th Sts and West Troy located north of 15th to 27th Streets. By 1836 business was so good that the three villages incorporated into the Village of West Troy. On May 26, 1896, it became the city of Watervliet. Green Island incorporated on May 21, 1896. There was no more "Town" of Watervliet.

Two 1950s view of entrance to the Erie Canal at 23rd Street on the left. This side cut from the Hudson River is now buried under I-787. There were several bridges over the canal. Port Schuyler: road bridges at 5th, 7th and 8th Sts and foot bridges at 6th and 8th Sts. Arsenal: two road bridges and one railroad bridge. Gibbonsville: Road bridge at 13th, 14th and 16 Sts and a foot bridge at 15th St West Troy: Road bridge at 23rd and 25th Sts and a change bridge for mules (tow path on west side until 23rd St) at 23rd St, lift bridge at 19th St.

Abandoned 23rd St Side Cut lock. Indentation area is where the lock gates were located. A basin is a pool connected to the canal or a wide place in the canal for docking, loading, unloading and turning of boats. On the Original Erie there were two basins: Gibbonsville along 2nd Ave between 13th and 14th Sts. West Troy along 2nd Ave between 19th and 23rd Sts. Enlarged basins followed: West Troy along the Hudson (lower basin) south of 23rd St. Mohawk Basin north of 23rd St.

Lower lock of 23rd St Side Cut, looking west.

Upper Side-cut looking north. Oil tanks on Centre Island (now called Starbuck Island from the old iron foundry that use to be there). In 1918 the new Barge Canal opened at Waterford and the Erie between Albany and the Mohawk River closed. On January 8, 1924, Watervliet paid $39,874.93 for land and rights to the previously owned and used canal through the city.

Upper Side Cut at 23rd St carried more freight and passengers than any other lock on the canal system. No wonder there were so many saloons in the area.

You would never know a canal and locks were here at 23rd Street.

"The Oswego Times charges member of Assembly Willard Johnson with transferring his real estate in that city to avoid attachment in the suit now pending against him for frauds on the West Troy Canal contract." — Hudson Weekly Star, September 9, 1875

Upper Side Cut entrance at 23rd St. Buttress in the Hudson River.

The area just north of the 23rd St Side Cut being filled in. Many of the buildings are no longer here. The next four pages show the area from different angles.

State Engineer Adams and Deputy State Engineer Kobens have a scheme for canal improvement which will, if put into execution, practically dispense with the series of sixteen, locks on the Erie canal between West Troy and Cohoes, familiarly known as "the sixteens." — The Argus, November 20, 1894.

The Troy View. The demonstration in this city last Thursday evening, in favor of improving the canals, has caused a great deal of excitement in the editorial department of the Troy Press. That newspaper is an advocate of canals and canal improvement; but it is possessed of the idea that the eastern terminus of the Erie canal is West Troy rather than Albany. — The Albany Express, March 27, 1888

The claim of Christopher Splittor, administrator, for loss of life of William H. Splittorf, by falling from swing bridge over the Erie canal near West Troy, for $23,000, was put on the calendar. — The Argus, April 14, 1886.

Canal Captain Downed. Troy, N. Y., Aug. 14.—Captain Charles Young, of the canal Isiats Thorndyke *and* Chattie, *was drowned in the Erie canal at West Troy this morning.* —August 15, 1893

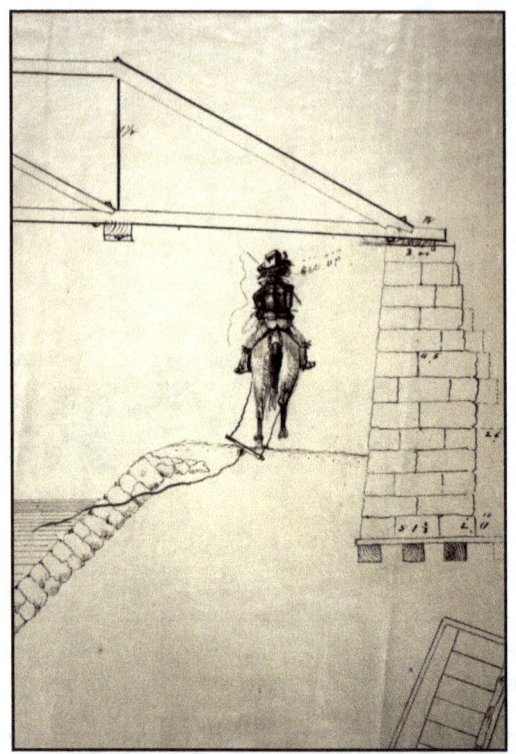

Drawing of a mule and his handler from a map of the enlargement of the canal in 1854.

Icemen harveted ice from the canal locks during winter time. Not sure if I would use that in my drink though since there were little hygienic laws during this time.

A view of 2nd Ave after the canal was filled. Switchmans Tavern on the right end of building. Cartwright's auto was to the left of building.

"From April 17, when boats first entered the canal, to April 30, the number of clearances at the West Troy canal collector's office was 751, the total number of miles of travel represented by the clearances being 161,546. The amount of tolls collected was $1,750.52. The vessels clearing carried 15,000 tons of coal, 10,000 tons of merchandise and 3,000 tons of pig iron." — Troy Daily Times, April 24, 1880. Pig iron was used heavily in the Troy iron foundries.

Electrical reuse of the canal bed.

D&H Railroad bridge north of the Upper Side Cut with canal being filled in. Located between Cohoes and Watervliet in 1921. Route 32 (2nd Ave) on left. Nothing remains in this picture. See page 119.

Abandoned 23rd St lock with water and debris.

"The icemen of Troy have commenced to cut ice in the West Troy Canal Basin. It is only five or six inches." —Albany Argus, January 24, 1863.

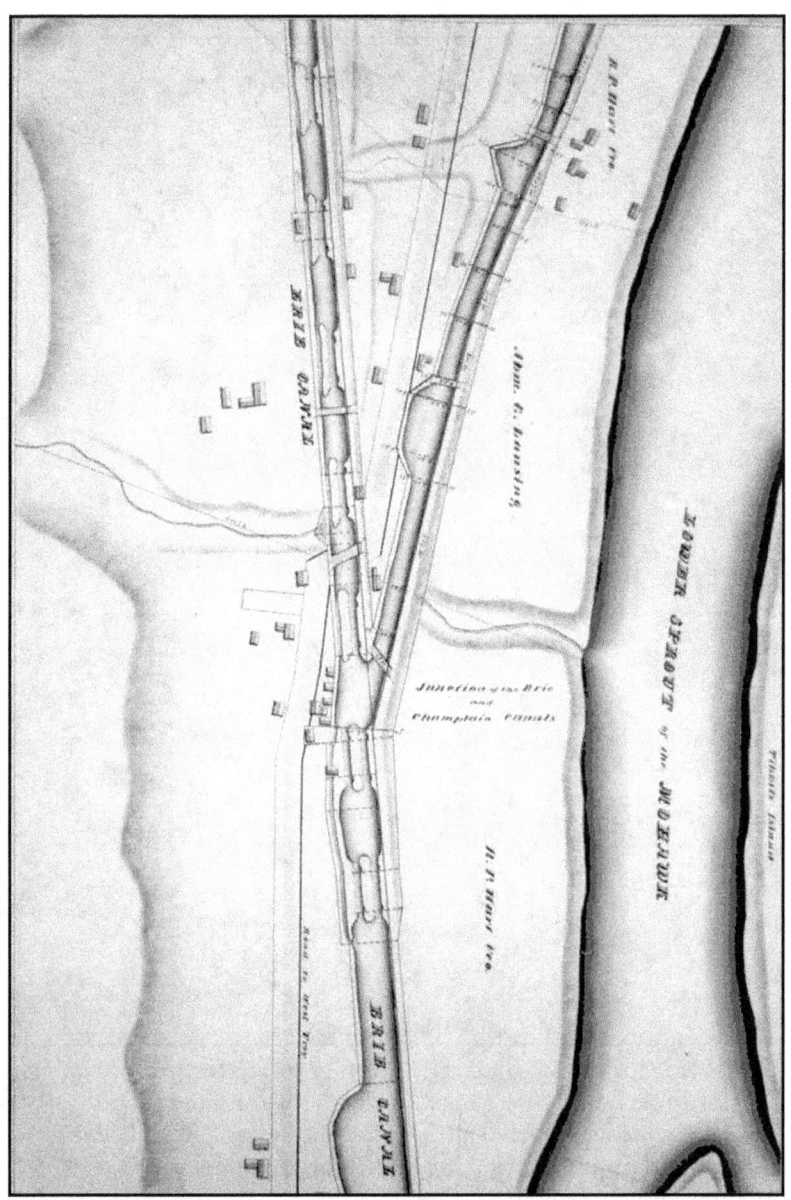

The Juncta. Where the Champlain and Erie Canals met. It is the area near the southern ends of Saratoga St and Main St in Cohoes where the canals met to continue the route through Watervliet to Albany, New York south or Lake Champlain north. Stores sold all the materials necessary to a canal man here at this junction.

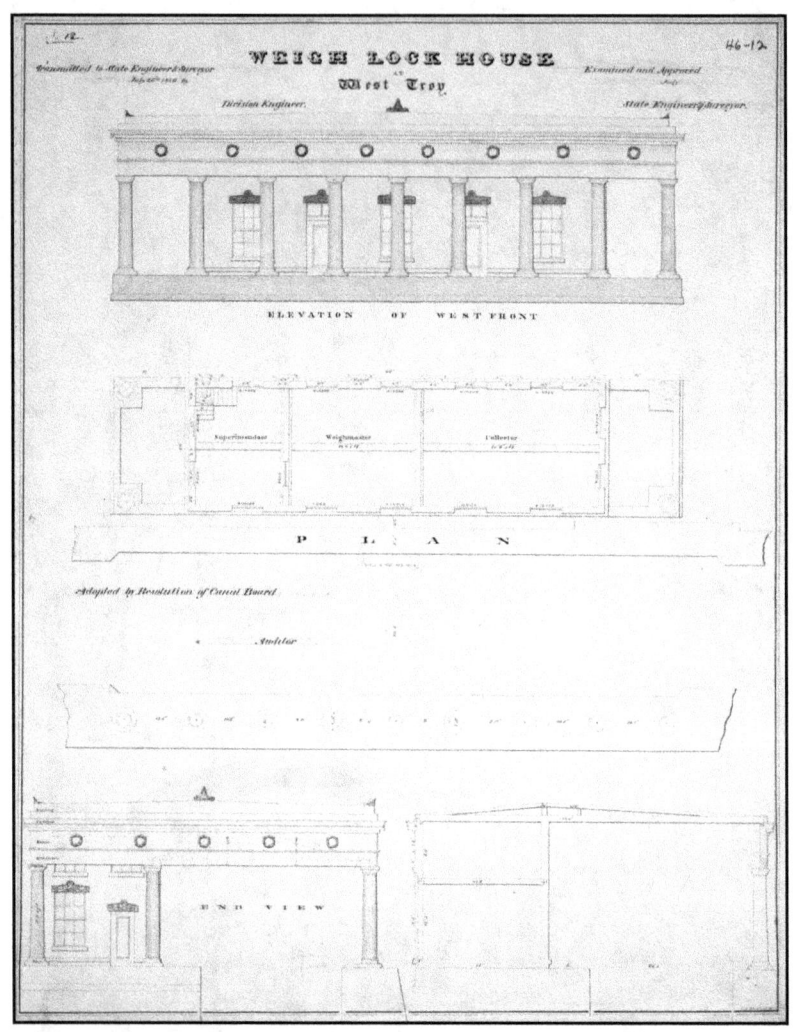

1850. Plans for the Weigh Lock House in West Troy. In the top drawing, boats would pass between the house and the Doric columns, which supported a roof over the scale. The scale itself, not pictured in this drawing, occupied the space between the columns and the building.

"A dead man was found floating in the West Troy canal locks Saturday evening." — Albany Evening Times, July 9, 1888.

There was a job hauling dead bodies out the canal for $5 a body.

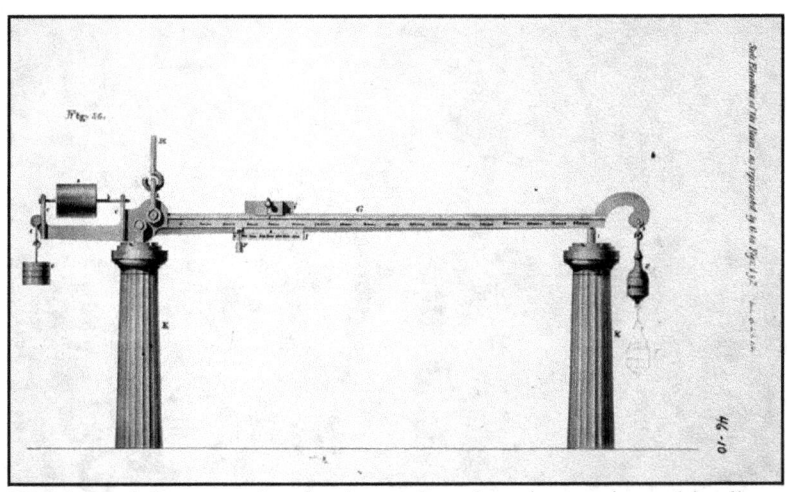

Weigh Lock beam and scale. A good explanation on how this all works is located here: https://www.eriecanal.org/UnionCollege/The_Weigh_Lock.html

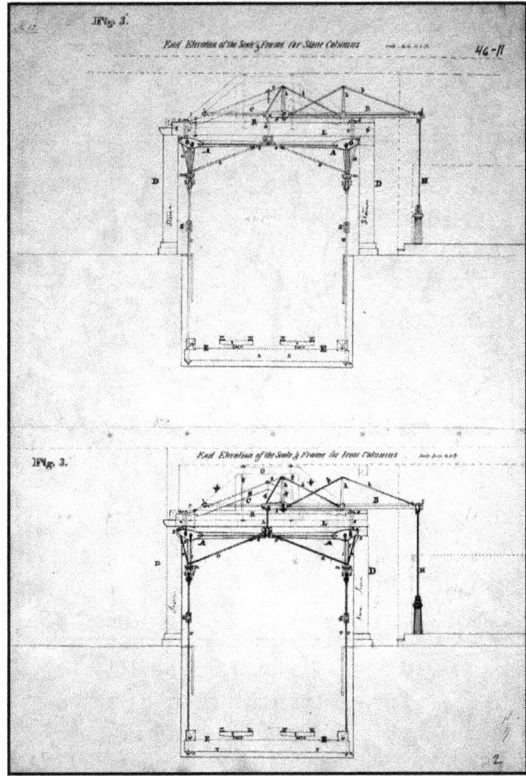

"The remains found in the West Troy canal lock on Monday have been identified as those of Dennis Hayes of Milford, Mass. He is said to have been an amateur detective, and at the time of his death was on the trail of a man who committed a murder in Chicago four or five years ago. The murder is believed to have been committed by the murderer or his confederate." — Daily Saratogian, Oct 28, 1881.

Canal boat near the Side Cut.

"About $8,000 has been received at the West Troy Canal Collector's office, thus far this season." — Daily Saratogian, May 25, 1874.

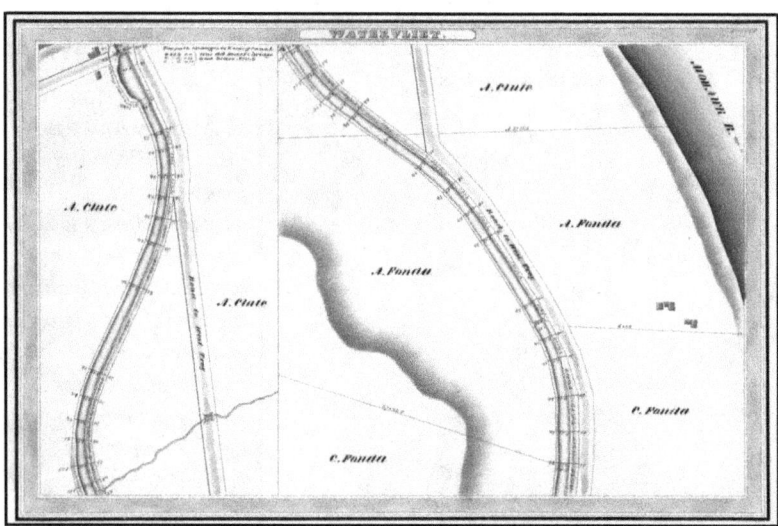

Canal Map 1834. First view: a stream, a basin, a bridge, two buildings and the Road to West Troy. A towpath changes to the East side of the canal. Second view: Mohawk River, a bridge, three buildings and the Road to West Troy.

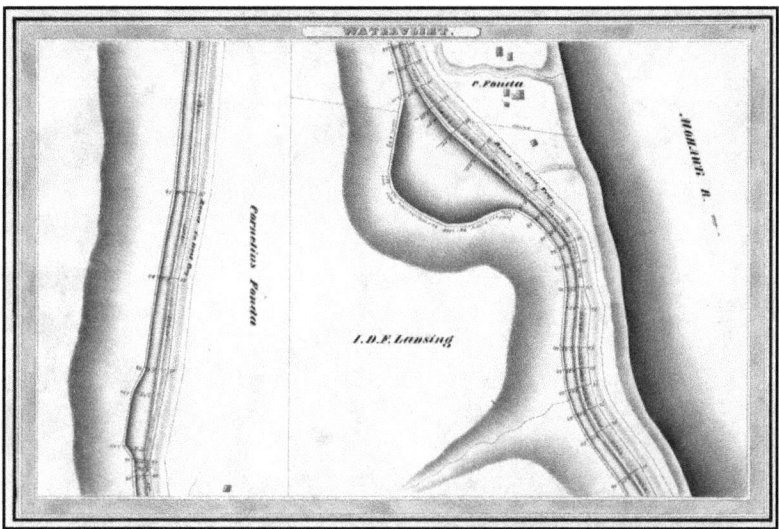

1834. First view: a bridge, a long basin, building and the Road to West Troy. Second view: Mohawk River, a large pond or basin, six buildings and the Road to West Troy.

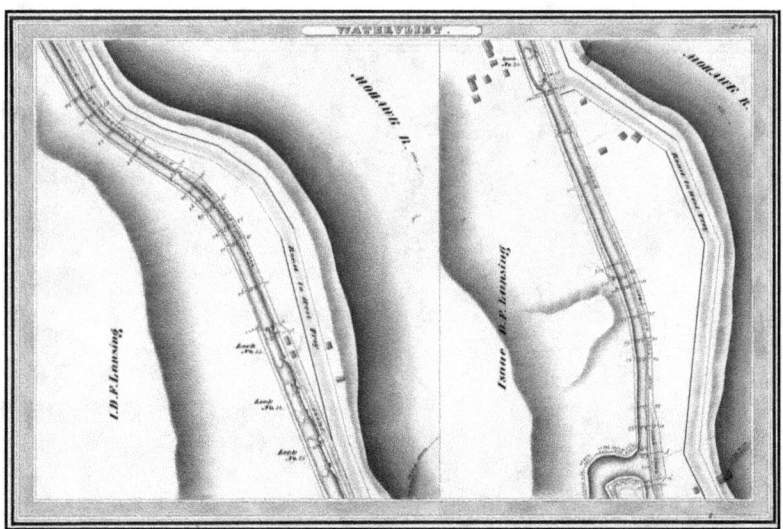

1834. First view: Mohawk River, Lock No. 33, 34 and 35, four buildings and the Road to West Troy which runs between the canal and the river. Second view: Mohawk River, Lock No. 36, two bridges, thirteen buildings, Road to West Troy, and the canal splitting into two channels.

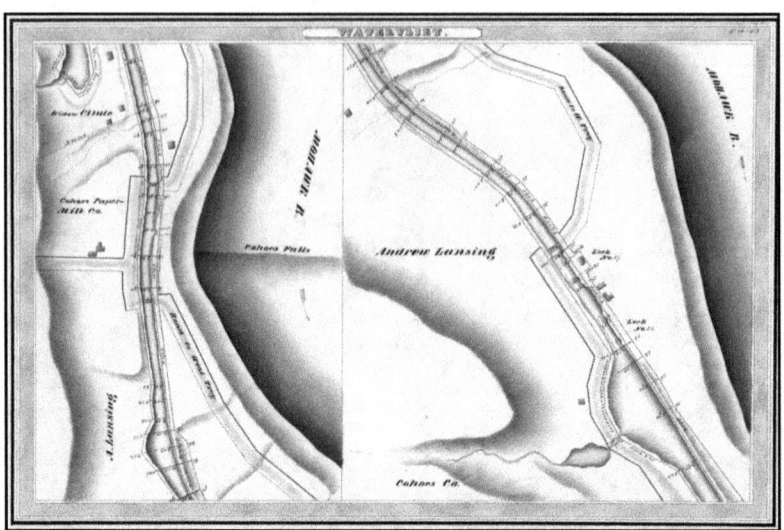

1834. First view: Mohawk River, Cohoes Falls, three bridges, six buildings and the Road to West Troy which crosses the canal at two points. Second view: Mohawk River, Lock No. 37 and 38, a large basin and pond, five buildings and the Road to West Troy.

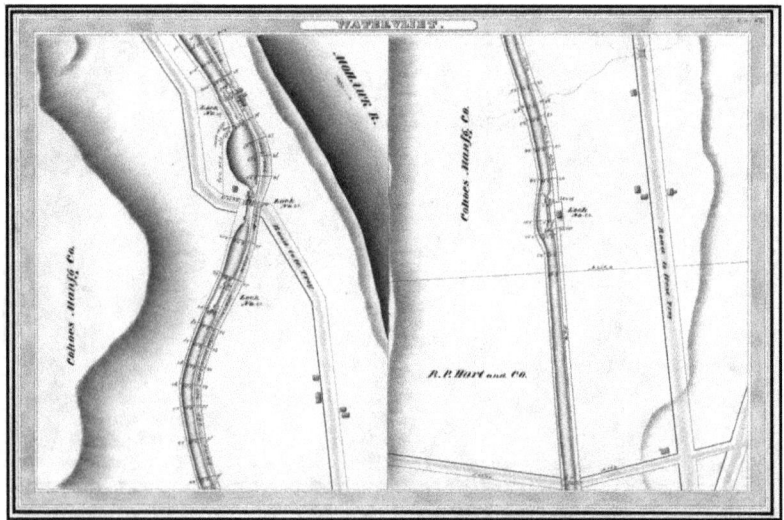

1834. First view: Mohawk River, Lock No. 39, 40, 41 and 42, two bridges, five buildings and the Road to West Troy. Second view: Lock No. 42, a bridge, six buildings, the Road to West Troy and an unidentified road.

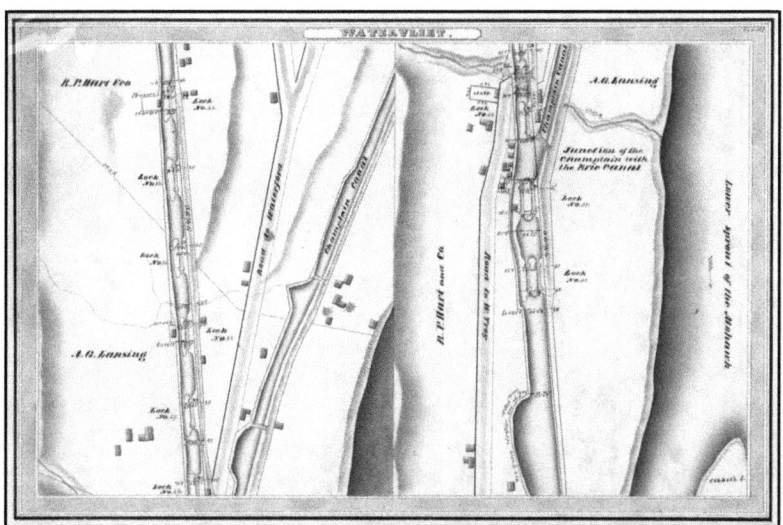

1834. First view: the Erie and Champlain Canal, Lock No. 44, 45, 46, 47 and 48, three bridges, twenty-three buildings and the Road to Waterford. Second view: the lower sprout of the Mohawk River, Tibbits Island, junction of the Champlain and Erie Canal, Lock No. 49, 50 and 51, two bridges, sixteen buildings and the Road to West Troy.

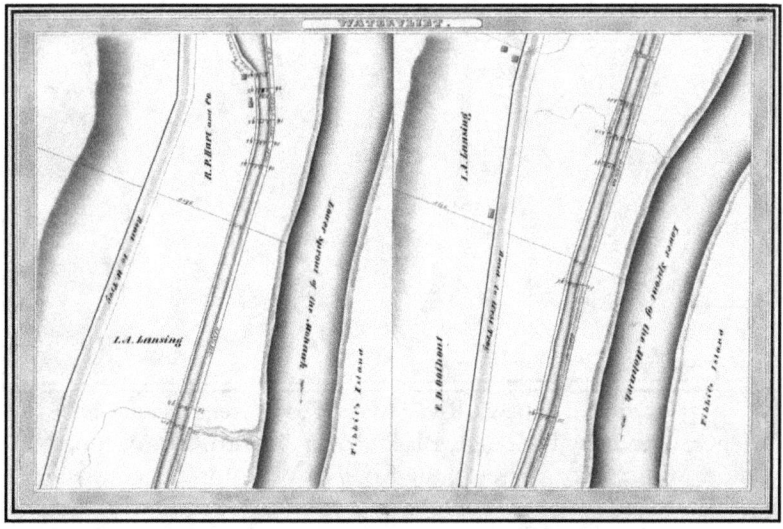

1834. Both views show the Mohawk River, Tibbits Island, a bridge, a few buildings and the Road to West Troy.

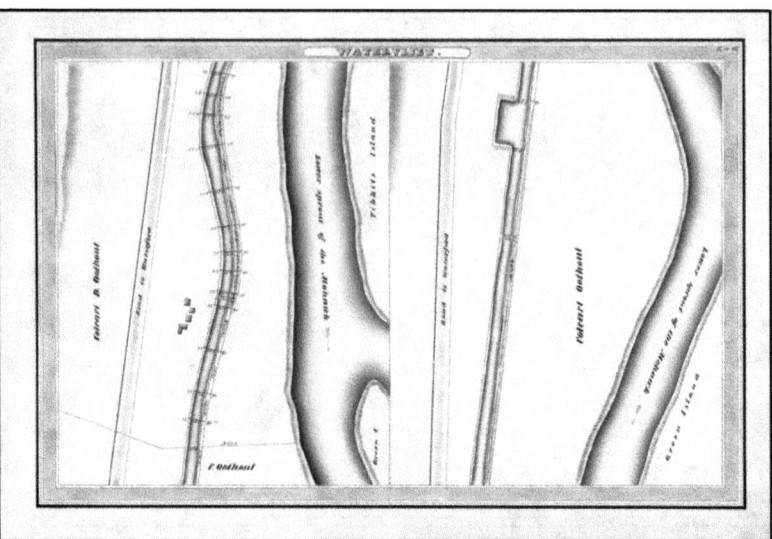

1834. First view: Mohawk River, Tibbits Island, Green Island, a bridge, four buildings, Road to Waterford. Second view: Mohawk River, Green Island, a bridge, the Road to Waterford.

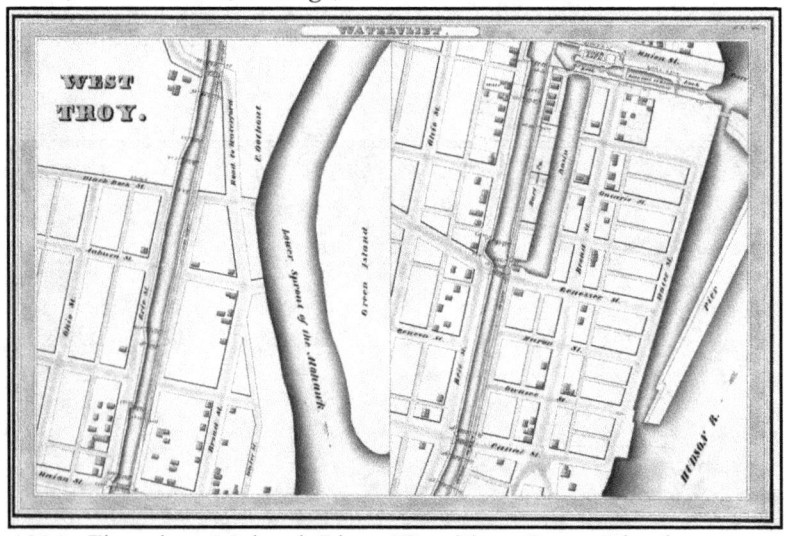

1834. First view: Mohawk River, West Troy, Green Island, two bridges, over forty buildings, Black Rock, Auburn, Erie, Ohio, Union, Water, Broad Streets, the Road to Waterford. Second view: Hudson River, long pier, long basin, series of locks, five bridges, over 50 buildings, Union, Ontario, Genesee, Owasco, Canal and Geneva Streets.

1834. First view: Hudson River, the area called Washington formerly known as Gibbonsville, an L shaped basin, four bridges, over 100 buildings, US Arsenal, Buffalo, Albany, Montgomery, Ferry, Washington, River, and Schenectady Streets and Shaker Road. Second view: Hudson River, a stream, two bridges, twenty-three buildings, Saratoga, Steuben and Rensselaer Streets.

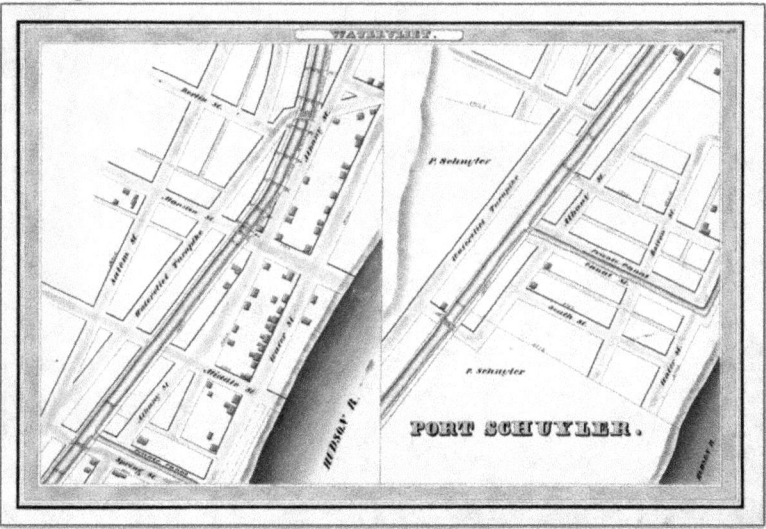

1834. First view: Hudson River, a private canal, three bridges, forty-nine buildings, Berlin, Albany, Mansion, and Salem Streets, Watervliet Turnpike, Spring and Middle Sts. Second view: Hudson River, Port Schuyler, two bridges, seven buildings, South, Canal, Boston and Water Streets.

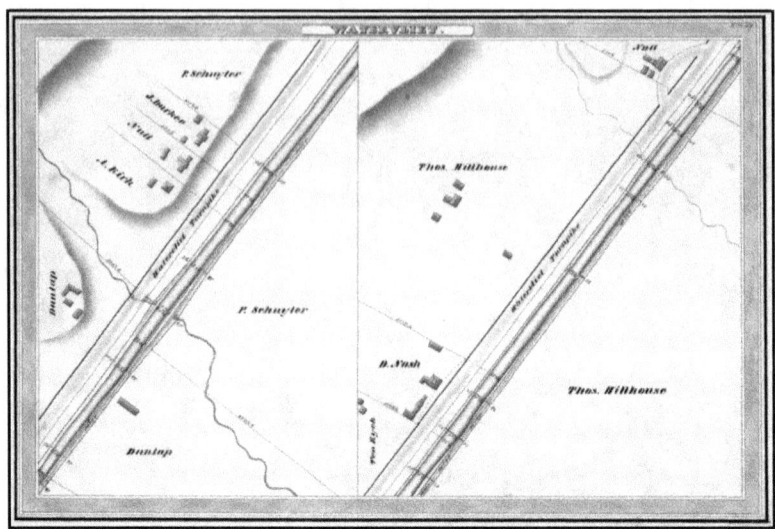

1834. First view: a stream that runs under the canal through a culvert, a bridge, eleven buildings and the Watervliet Turnpike. Second view: a bridge, thirteen buildings and the Watervliet Turnpike.

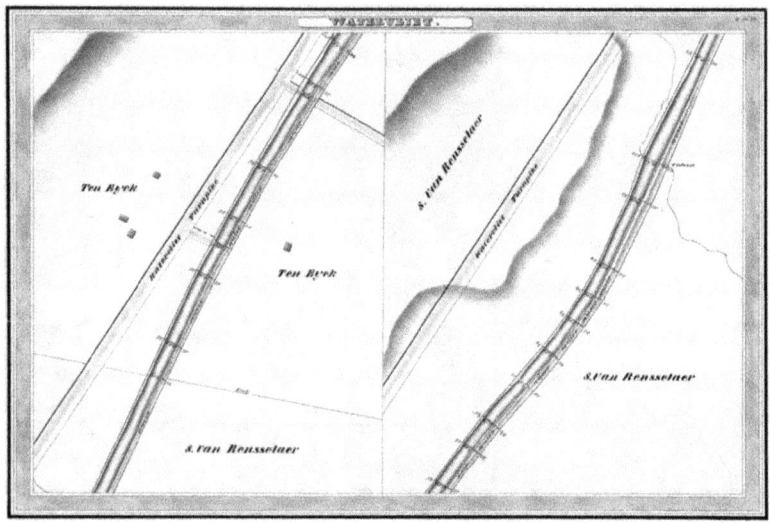

1834. First view: two bridges, four buildings, Watervliet Turnpike and an unidentified road. Second view: a culvert and the Watervliet Turnpike.

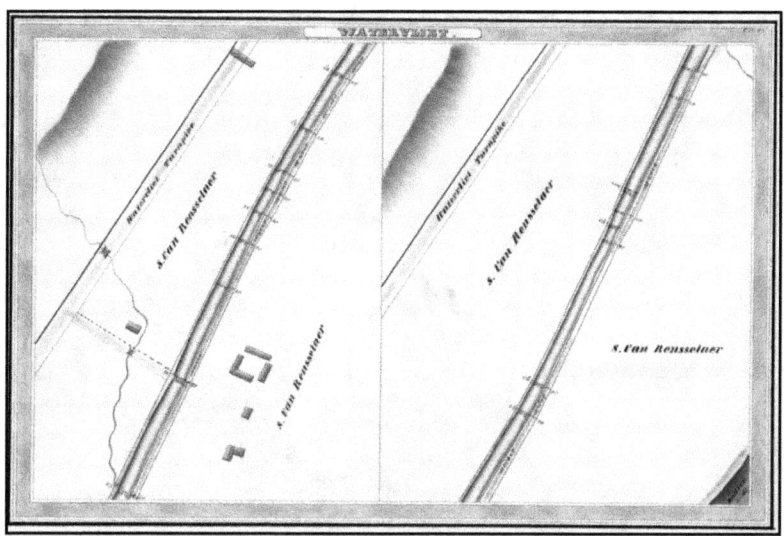

1834. First view: three bridges, seven buildings and the Watervliet Turnpike. Second view: Hudson River and the Watervliet Turnpike.

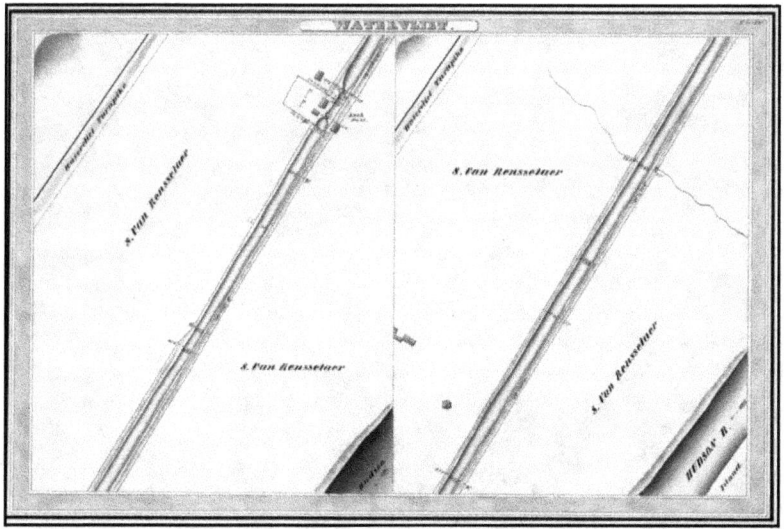

1834. First view: Hudson River, Lock No. 52, a bridge, four buildings and the Watervliet Turnpike. Second view: Hudson River, an island, four buildings and the Watervliet Turnpike.

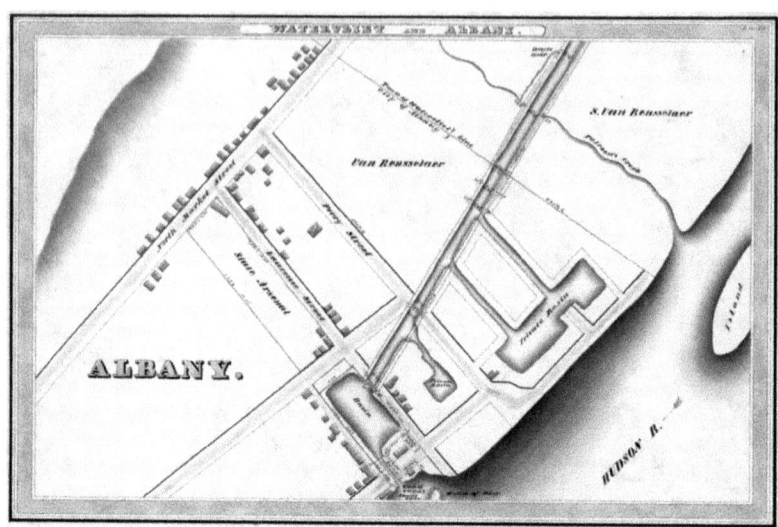

1834. Shows the Watervliet and Albany Town Line, Hudson River, an island, Lock No. 53, Patroons Creek, waste weir, three basins, three bridges, 69 buildings, State Arsenal, Ferry St, Lawrence St, North Market St and the end of the Erie Canal.

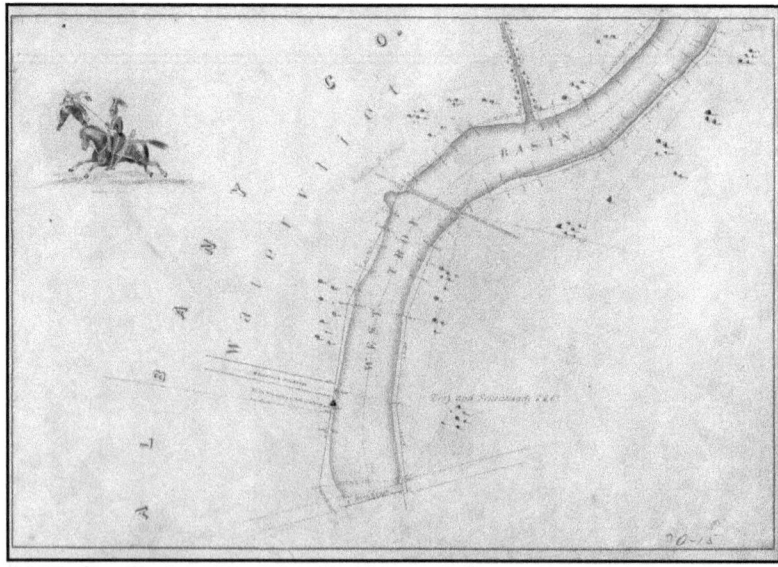

1857. Shows the West Troy Basin. Includes a sketch of a soldier on horseback with a captive suspended from his lance, labelled "Catching a Tartar." Shows cross of the Troy & Schenectady Railroad and discharge location for the Weighlock.

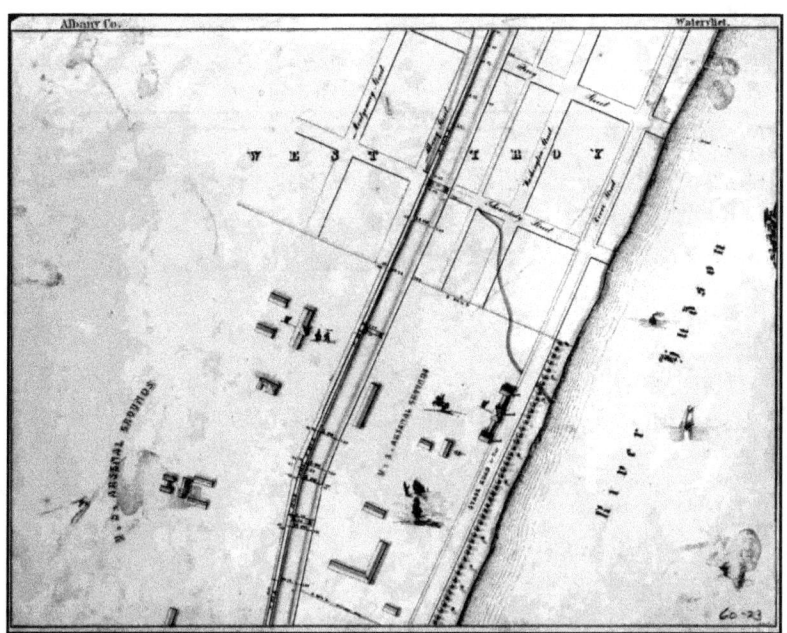

1857. Plan shows the US Arsenal and includes sketch of an officer on horseback watching troops at drill.

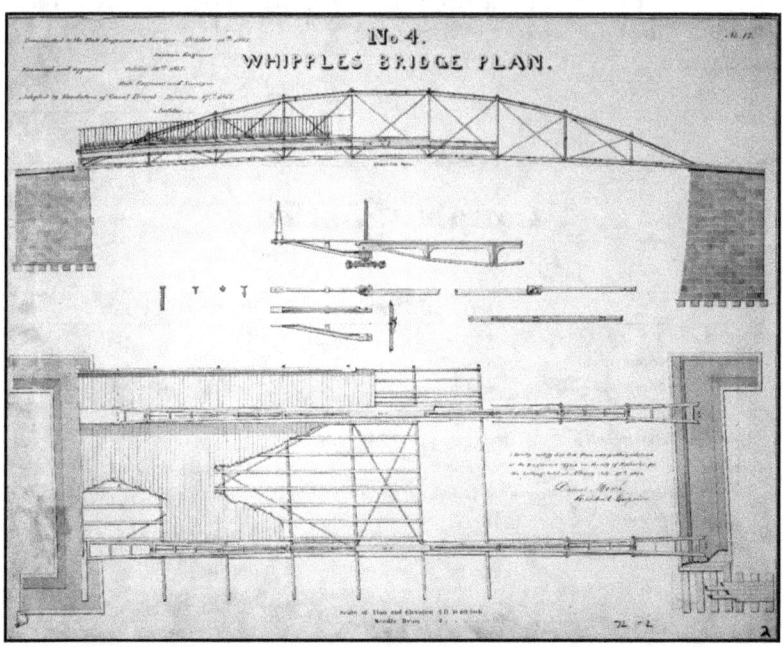

1851. Design of the Whipple bridge to be built over the Erie Canal. Whipple was a Union College graduate. This plan was shown at the Rochester engineer's office on November 18, 1851.

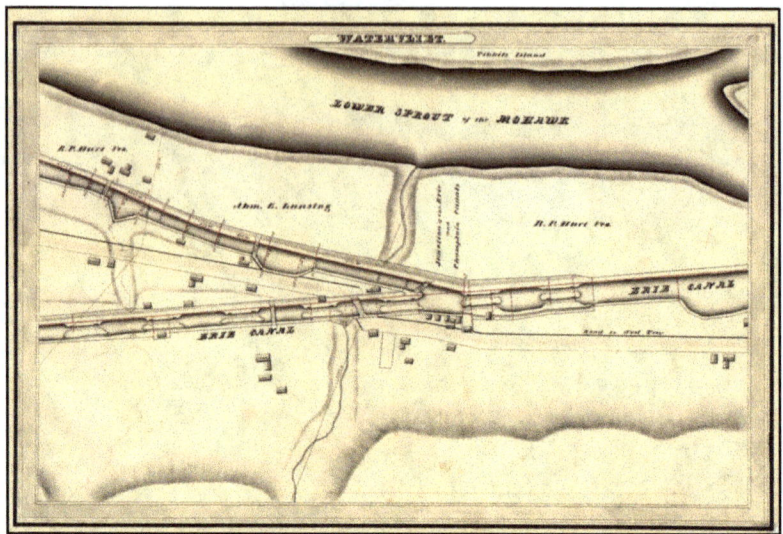

Juncta 1830. A section of the Champlain Canal in Watervliet. It shows the Lower Sprout of the Mohawk River, the junction of the Erie Canal and the Champlain Canal, five bridges, thirty-three buildings and the Road to West Troy.

Canal Statistics:

	Original Canal:	Enlarged Canal:
Construction Authorized	April 15, 1817	May 11, 1835
Construction Commenced	July 4, 1817	August 1836
Construction Completion	October 26, 1825	September 1, 1862
Engineer's Estimate of Cost	$4,881,738	$23,402,863
Actual Cost of Construction	$7,143,789	$31,834,041
Length	363 Miles	350.5 Miles
Size of Prism	40' and 28'x 4'	70' and 56'x 7'
Number of Lift Locks	83	72
Number of Guard Locks	13	3
Size of Locks	90' x 15'	110' x 18'
Total Lockage	675'	654.8'
Material in Locks	Stone	Stone
Tonnage of Boats	75	210-240

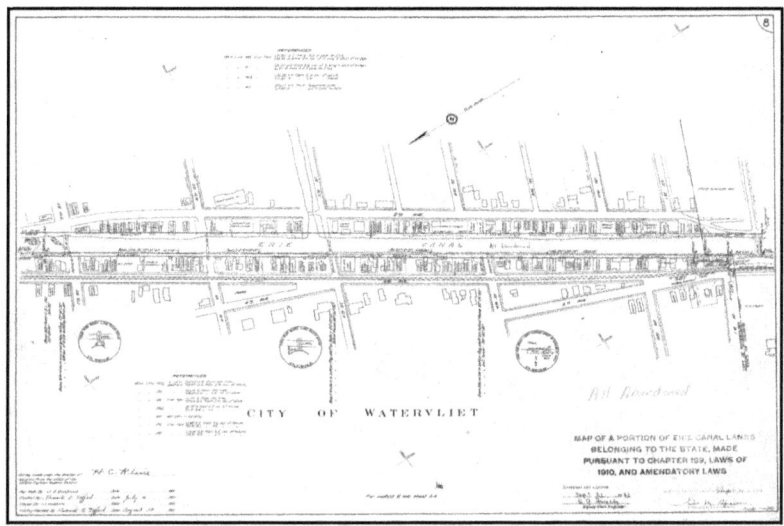

The following four canal maps of 1921 showing the abandonment of the Erie Canal system in Watervliet being replaced by the Barge Canal. The State of New York commissioned the maps. Titled: *"Map of a Portion of Erie Canal Lands Belonging to the State, made pursuant to Chapter 199, Laws of 1910, and Amendatory Laws."*

In the old days, James Burns, superintendent of the Albany Rural Cemetery use to race horses on the canal during winter.

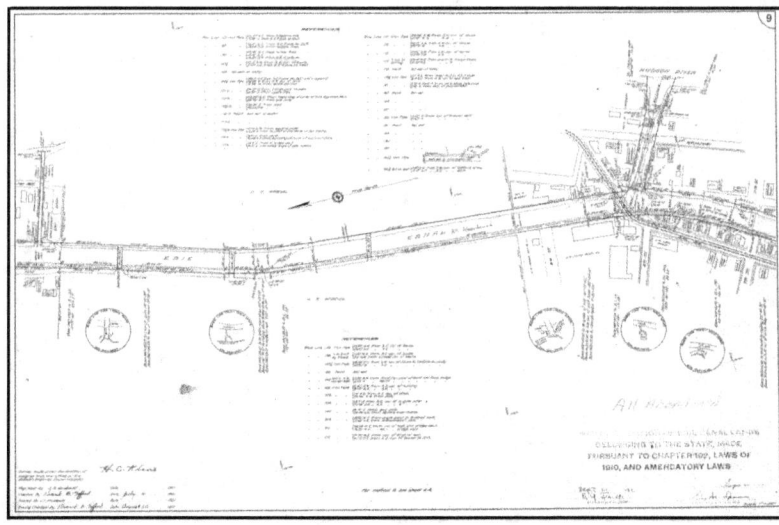

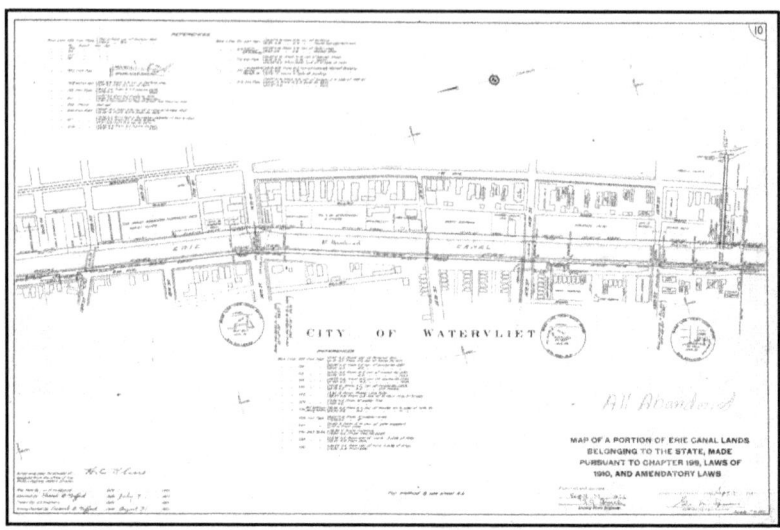

"GATHERING AT WEST TROY. Canal Boatmen, and Canal Mules Arriving in Large Numbers. An influx of canal horses and mules is expected this week in West Troy from winter quarters along the line of the canals; The extensive canal stables in that village have been put in readiness for the reception of the army of animals that trudge the "big ditch" during the canal season. A large force of men will be put to work this week under the direction of Supt. Hardin cleaning the Erie and Champlain canals in this section. Just at present the boat captains are busy repainting and making improvements to their crafts. It is said that about forty new boats have been built during the past winter, including a number of steam canal boats. At present West Troy is flooded with boatmen who are awaiting the opening of navigation." — The Argus, April 20, 1891.

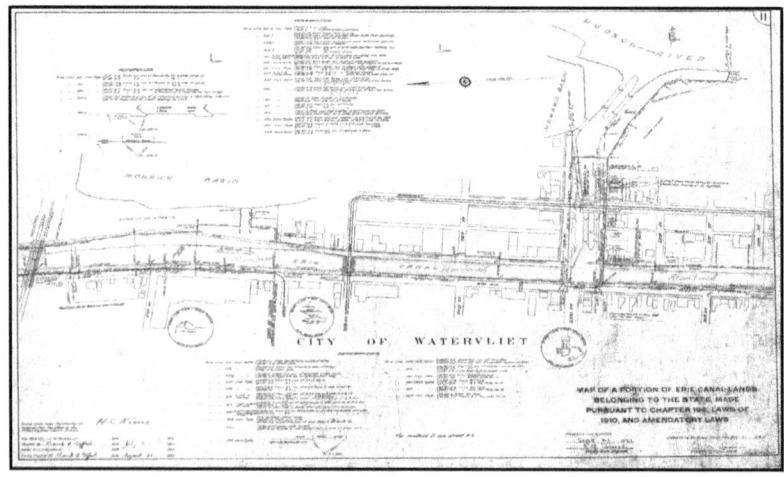

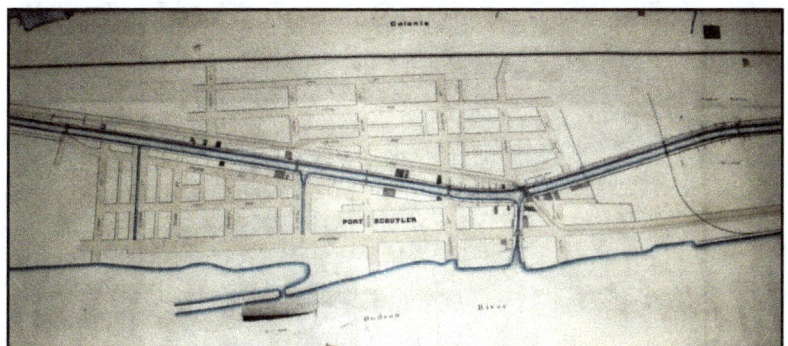

1896 Schillner #1 Survey Map. The Erie Canal route through Watervliet from Schuyler Flats to and including Watervliet Arsenal. The lower Side Cut can be seen along with the Jone Car Works, makers of carriages and later trolley cars that were sold around the country due to their reputation for elegance and workmanship.

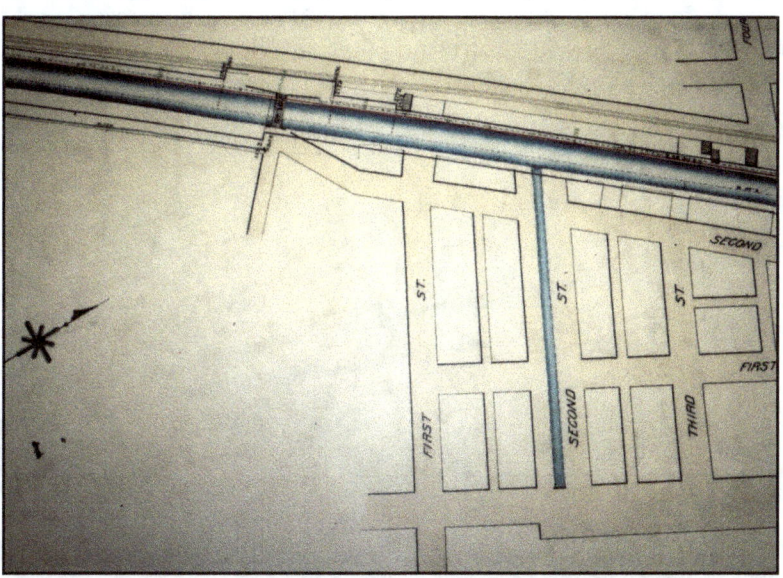

1896 Schillner #1 Survey Map. Enlarged view of the area between Schuyler Flats to between 3rd and 4th Streets in Port Schuyler. Vehicle/pedestrian bridge west of the Flats labeled #10. Waterway perpendicular to the canal most likely supplied water to the factories on the banks of the Hudson River, which ran the machinery using steam power (Roy Mills, for example).

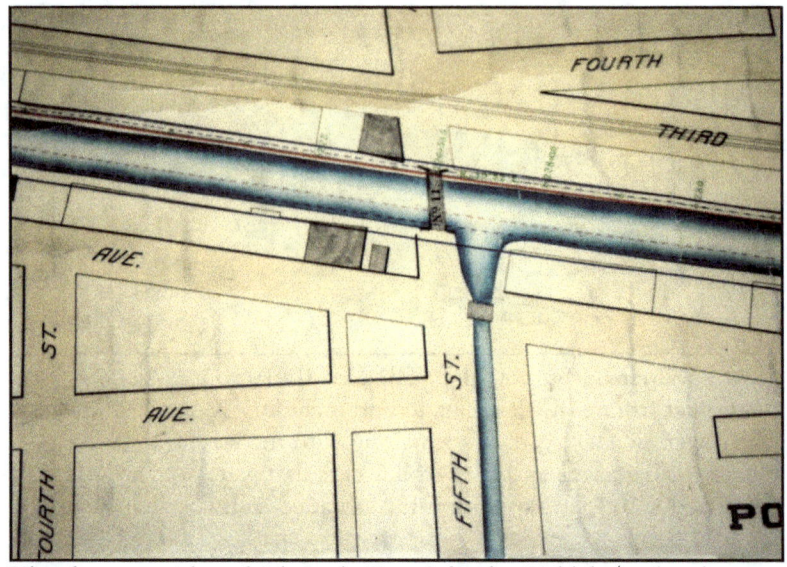

View between 4th and 6th Sts in Port Schuyler. Vehicle/pedestrian bridge (#11) over the canal at 5th St. Waterway with the bridge over 2nd Ave most likely supplied water to manufacturing companies along the Hudson. Most large industries operated machinery with steam power then.

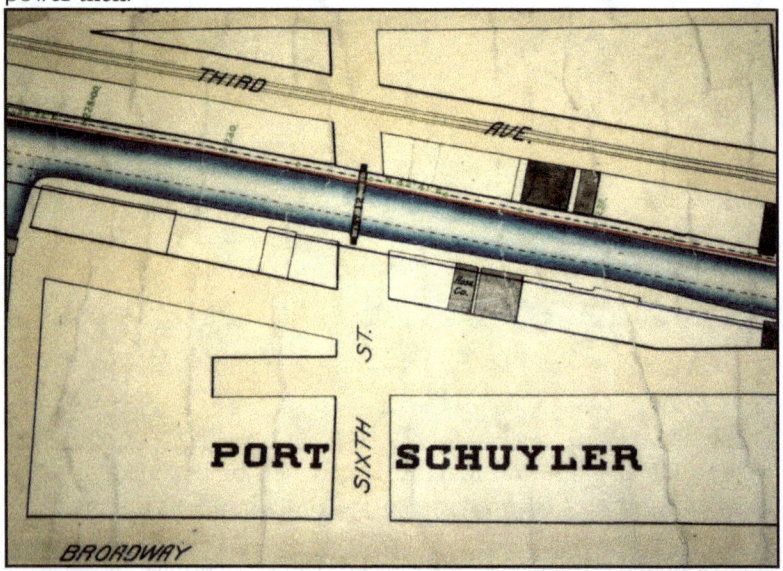

View of the area between Fifth and Seventh Sts in Port Schuyler. Pedestrian Bridge (#12) over the canal at Sixth St. The Hose Company is the MacIntyre Hose Co., built in 1873 (Steamer #3) at 609 2nd Ave. Building still exists.

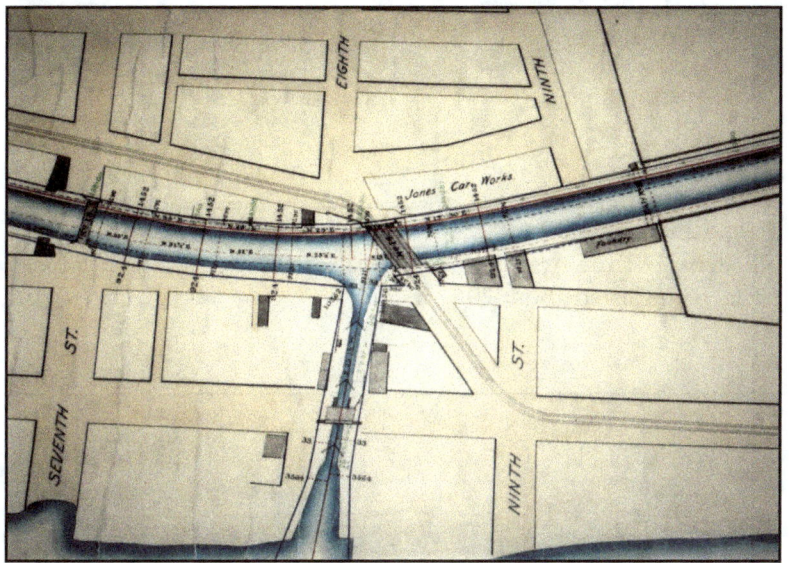

Between 7th St & south portion of the Arsenal in Port Schuyler. Vehicle/pedestrian bridge (#13) crosses canal at 7th St. Trolley tracks run along 3rd Ave cross the canal on the trolley bridge (#14), continue on Broadway north. Lower Side Cut joins the Hudson with the canal including two locks (upper/lower) raising lower Hudson level to the canal. J. M. Jones Car Works (trolley car maker) between 8th & 9th Sts. west of canal.

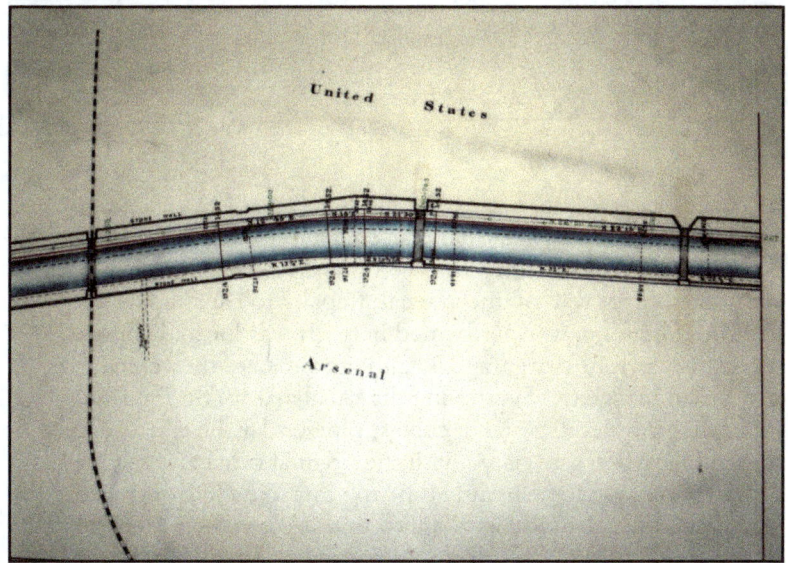

View of the canal through arsenal. RR bridge crosses and two vehicle/pedestrian bridges left to right. Stone walls on both sides of canal. Approval to build through arsenal only if walls built and approval to take water from the canal to operate machines.

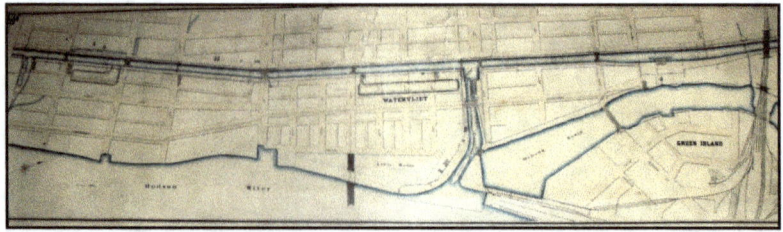

1896 Schillner #2 Survey Map. View includes the area between the North wall of the Arsenal and the Railroad Bridge in Maplewood. Canal boats lasted about 20 years.

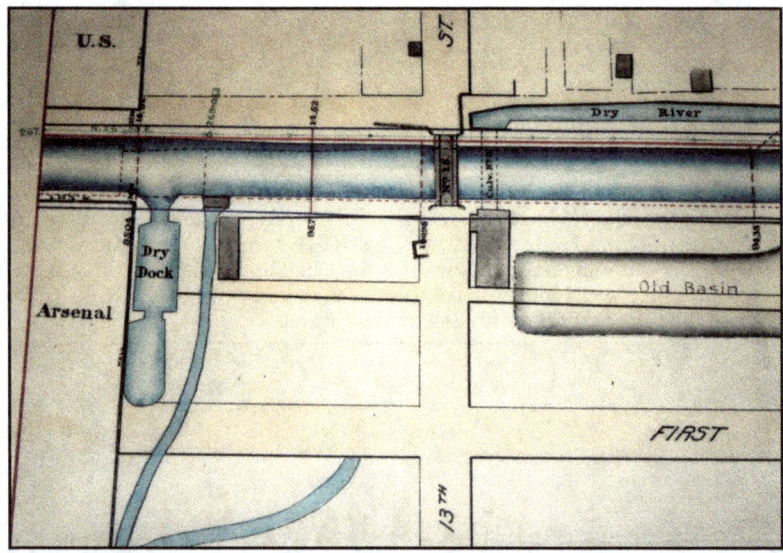

View between north wall of the arsenal and just shy of 14th St. Note West Troy Dry Dock between First Ave and the Erie Canal along the North wall of the arsenal. Repairs to canal boats and light boat building was performed here. It was located about where the current city garage is. Other points are the vehicle/pedestrian bridge (#15) crossing the canal at 13th St, the Dry River that traveled through a culvert pipe under the canal at 13th St, the Old Basin associated with the original canal and the Dry River connecting to a stream emptying into the Hudson River. The Dry Dock also discharged into this stream when canal boats were being repaired. Dry docks were used to repair canal boats below the water line. This dry dock shown on the map between 1st Ave and the canal is where the present city garage is located.

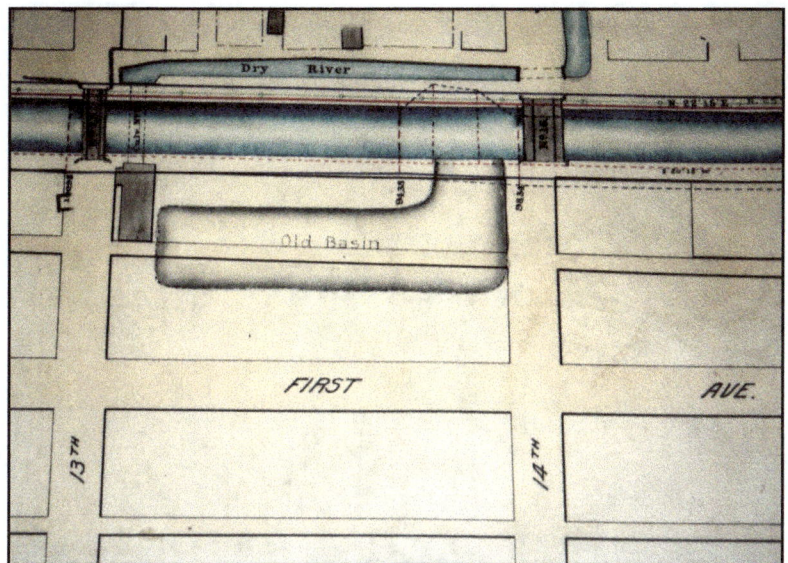

Schillner #2 Survey Map. View includes the area between 13th and 15th Sts. Note vehicle/pedestrian bridge crossing canal at Fourteenth St (#16) and that the Dry River runs parallel to the canal along 2nd Ave between 13th and 14th Sts.

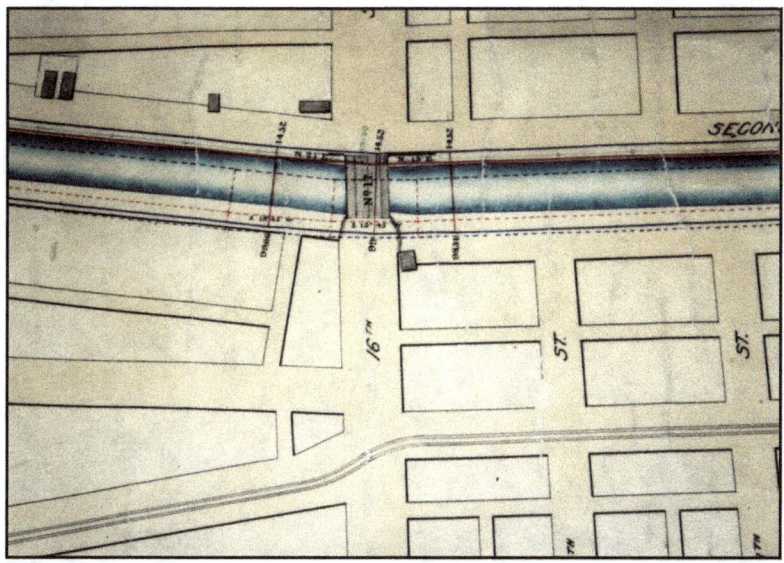

View includes the enlarged area between 15 and 18th Sts. Note the vehicle/pedestrian bridge crossing canal at Sixteenth St.

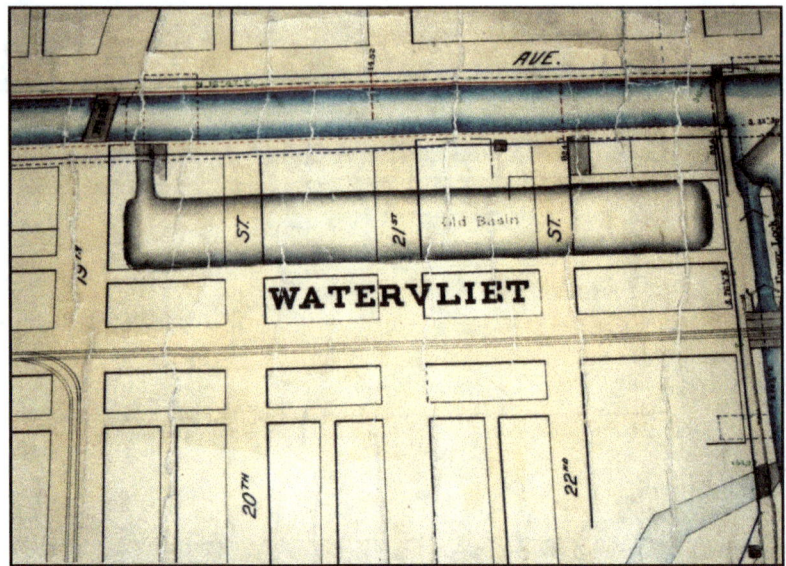

View between 19th St and the Upper Side Cut at 23rd St. Items of interest include vehicle/pedestrian bridge crossing the canal at 19th St and another old basin associated with the original canal used prior to the canal enlargement. Also note Trolley tracks along Broadway and then running east on Nineteenth St.

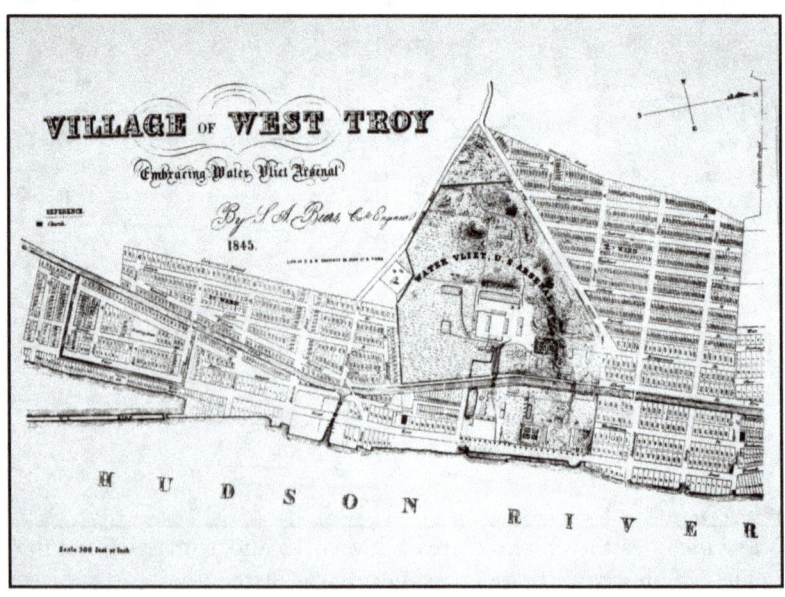

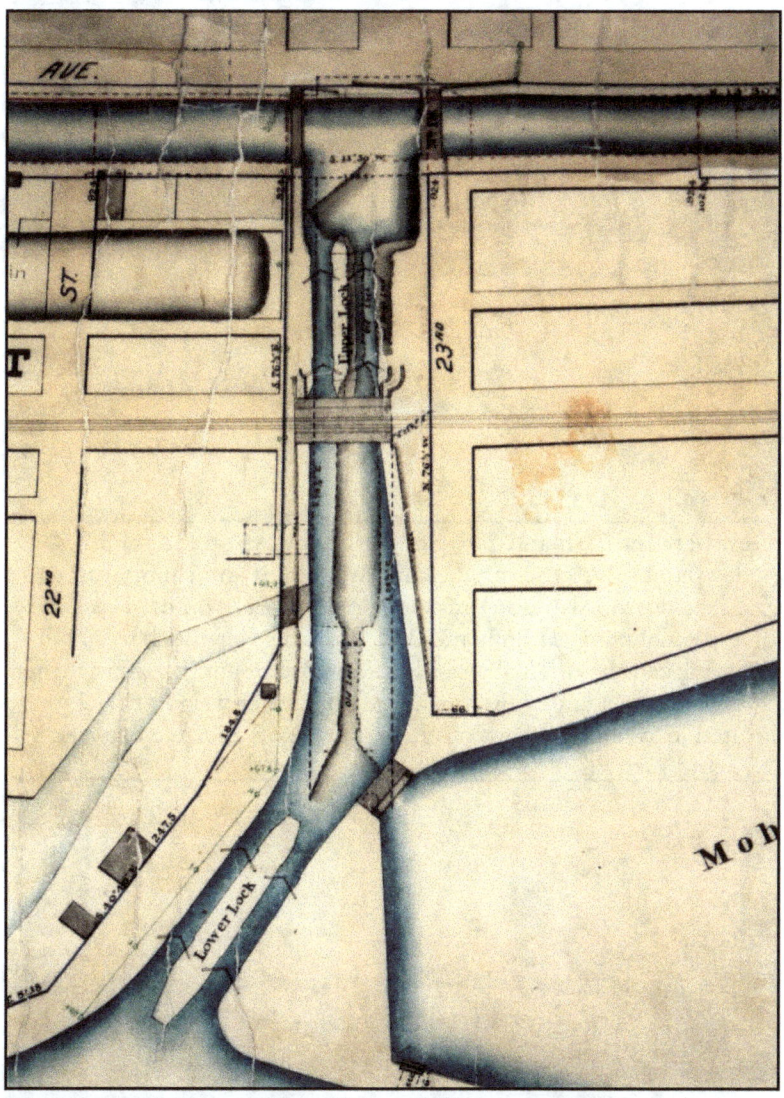

View between Twenty-Second St and Twenty-Fourth St outlining the upper Side Cut. In the center is a good view of the upper Side Cut showing the upper and lower locks connecting the Erie Canal to the Hudson River. Note the pedestrian bridge on the South side and the vehicle/pedestrian bridge on the North side of the Side Cut crossing over the Erie Canal. Note the trolley bridge crossing the Side Cut at Broadway.

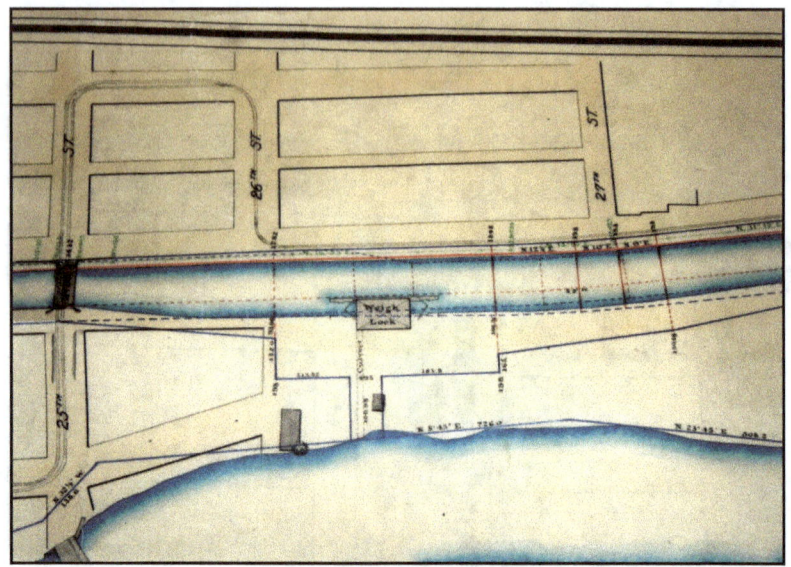

View between 25th and 27th Sts. Trolley tracks on the vehicle/pedestrian bridge crossing the canal at 25th St and running along 2nd Ave north. Also note the weighlock building on the East side of the canal between 26th and 27th Sts. This weighlock was built and replaced the original weighlock on 23rd St and Broadway when the canal was enlarged. Remnants of the newer weighlock are located in Weighlock Park on the East side of 2nd Ave between 26th and 27th Sts.

Old canal boat rotting away near the Mohawk or dry dock.

West Troy/Watervliet Erie Canal Statistics

October 8, 1823

The Erie Canal was not fully completed from Buffalo to Albany until October, 1825, yet in October 1823 it was completed enough to allow the running of boats from West Troy to Rochester. The "Trojan Trader", a western freight boat, came from the West to the bridge near the Gibbonsville (West Troy) basin and took on board the first load of merchandise sent from the Hudson, West on the Erie Canal. As the upper side-cut into the canal was not yet completed it became necessary to transport the goods from Troy on wheels across the river to the place of embarkation on the main trunk of the canal. Several of West troy citizens lent their assistance to load the boat and at two o'clock, the "Trader' having on board upward of twenty-five tons of merchandise started for the West.

November 15, 1823

The upper side-cut opposite to Troy was completed on Saturday, November 15, 1823. In the afternoon the locks were ready, the water was let in, and the packet boat "Superior", with a large party of citizens on board, passed through and crossed the river to Troy. Two freight boats followed the Superior, and unloaded their cargos at the river wharves of Troy, one laden with staves, and the other with wheat.

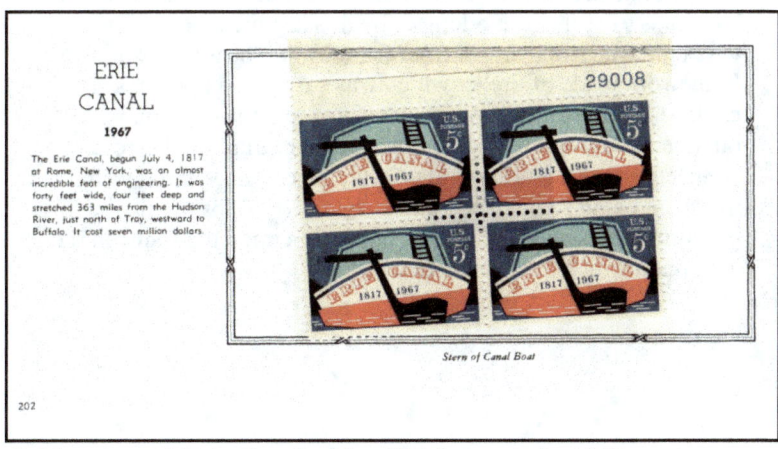

Celebration of Erie Canal with official stamps in 1967.

September 18, 1824

Another interesting event in connection with the Erie Canal took place in the village in 1824, a visit or rather the passing through the village, of General Lafayette. The General, accompanied by his suite, the Governor of the State of New York and his suite, and the Mayor and Corporation of the City of Albany, came up from Albany on the Canal, in the Packet-boat "Schenectady".

1825

The original weighlock was located on the South side of Union Street (23rd), a short distance West of Broadway. The weighlock building was a small wooden structure, and the mode of ascertaining the weight of a boat was to run the same into a large stone reservoir, or lock, which was connected with the Canal by means of a Gate, and then close the gate, when the water which was then in this large reservoir or lock was drawn off into a small reservoir, located below the level of the large lock, and the water thus drawn off was measured, and from the measurement, the weight of the boat and cargo was ascertained. This mode of weighing did not prove a success, as it was very inaccurate, and a few years, thereafter it was abandoned and the mode of weighing by means of scales was adopted; by this last mentioned mode, when the water was drawn from the lock, the boat rested upon a framework made of timber which was suspended upon heavy chains, and these chains were connected to an iron beam, which ran overhead from the lock in the office or building, where it was connected with a platform, upon which were placed iron weights, the beam being so balanced that a wgt of 31 #2 lbs upon this platform represented the weight of one ton upon the frame in the lock upon which the boat rested.

1837

The enlargement of the Erie Canal was made in the Village of West Troy. Its depth was increased to seven feet by means of removing eighteen inches of earth from the bottom, and raising the banks b the same number of inches. The width was also increased to seventy feet, by removing thirty feet of earth from the East side of the original bank.

1853

The weighlock at weighlock Park on the West side of Rte 32 between 26th & 27th Street was built as part of the Canal Enlargement and replaced the wooden structure on Union (23rd Street). The mode of weighing by means of weights sliding upon scale beams replaced the cumbersome method used in the earlier weighlock.

1840

Dry Docks were used to maintain, repair and alter a ship below the waterline. One such dry dock was built by John Lamport and Jim Barnard between 1st Avenue (Washington Street) and the Erie Canal.
Population in West Troy – 4500

1850

Wilbur McDonald has a mule/horse canal stable at the rear of the Jones Car Works. Edward Wight had one on Second Avenue.

1855

The number of canal boats at the upper locks with those moored to the Troy docks extended out so far that the tow from Albany passing up the channel between
formed a bridge and Captain James Oliver crossed from West Troy to Troy, utilizing boats of tow to perform the tick.

1863

The Auburn Street (25th Street) Canal Bridge fell October 1863. Cattle killed and one man injured. New upper side-cut bridge (23rd Street) built August 23, 1863.

1871

The 23rd Street West Troy lock did more business than any other lock along the route from New York Bay to Buffalo, except New York itself. This data was compiled by the State of New York Department of Commerce. In 1871 the lock carried 20,000 tons of iron ore, 31,000 tons of other metals, 15,000 tons of wheat, 35,000 tons of coal and 158,000 tons of flour. Its traffic totaled 281,000 tons of freight for the year and its earnings in tolls was second only to New York City.

1880

Population in West Troy was 11,000

1923

By the time of World War One the sidecut of Watervliet had become a shadow of its former self. During the latter part of the 19th centruy, the railroads speed freight and passengers throughout the site in a fraction of the time it took by Canal boat. In 1923 when the state opened a new Barge Canal at Waterford they closed the section between Albany and the Mohawk River.

WEST SIDE FOUNDRY Co., TROY, N. Y.

The West Side Foundry was just one of many industries that utilized the canal in West Troy during the 19th century.

"About 100 boats a day pass the West Troy canal lock." — New York Evening Express, May 20, 1870.

Patrick Henry "Paddy" Ryan
(March 15, 1851 – December 14, 1900)

A saloonkeeper and bare knuckle American boxer from Troy who won the worlds heavyweight-boxing championship from Joe Goss in 1880. Lost his title two years later fighting John L. Sullivan. Known as the Trojan Giant he owned a saloon in the famous Watervliet "Sidecut," a section of the Erie Canal in Watervliet across from Troy, and a location for many drinking holes. Jimmy Kiloran, who was the Athletic director for Rensselaer Polytechnic Institute trained Paddy. Paddy and Sullivan fought a dozen times more but he never won. He was elected into the Boxing Hall of Fame in 1973.

Businesses, Bars and Brothels: A list of famous and Infamous establishments in the Watervliet Sidecut Neighborhood.

The sidecut neighborhood of West Troy in the 1860's and 1870's was full of hotels, saloons (29) and brothels – every kind of service a recently paid canaller on a layover could possibly need or want. It was because of this abundance of temptations that there existed many services a canaller hoped he wouldn't need, such as funeral parlors and churches. Most establishments have been lost to history. The approximate locations of some of the more famous ones were traceable. It is perhaps a fitting legacy to the neighborhood that the only ones from that period remaining today are several churches and the Parker Funeral Home.

The People of the State of New York, by the Grace of God, Free and Independent,

TO ALL TO WHOM THESE PRESENTS SHALL COME, GREETING:

Know ye, That Whereas at a meeting of the Commissioners of the Land Office, held January 8, 1924, it was ordered that letters-patent issue to the City of Watervliet for certain abandoned Erie canal lands hereinafter described; and Whereas, the Council of the City of Watervliet, at a meeting of said Council held February 8, 1924, adopted the following resolution: "RESOLVED: That the Council of the City of Watervliet hereby accept said amended resolution of said Commissioners of the Land Office of the State of New York with all the stipulations therein contained and hereby approves of same and authorizes the City of Watervliet to make payment contained in said resolution and accept the title to said lands in accordance therewith."; ―――――
―― NOW, KNOW YE, That pursuant to an amended resolution of the Comtiesioners of the Land Office adopted January 8, 1924, and in consideration of the sum of thirty-nine thousand eight hundred seventy-four dollars and ninety-three cents ($39,874.93), lawful money of the united States paid by the City of Watervliet, County of Albany and State of New York, and upon the conditions hereinafter expressed, we have granted, released and quit-claimed, and by these presents do grant, release and quit-claim unto the CITY OF WATERVLIET, in the County of Albany and State of New York, all the right, title and interest of the State of New York in and to the abandoned Erie canal Lands and structures in the said City of Watervliet, bounded and described as follows:

Hotels

Trumble Hotel – Seneca (22nd Street)
Jacob Wagner's Pleasant Retreat – Cohoes Road
The Collins House – Canal (16th) and Broadway
The Farmer's Hotel – Genesee (19th Street)
Jack Folley Hotel (and brothel) – Broadway
Tom Coggins Metropolitan hall - Union (23rd Street)
Nelson Carter's Riverview Hotel – Seneca (22nd Street)
The Lansing House – on Broadway and Union (23rd Street) on the Riverbank
Union House _ Broad Street (Broadway)
Greenman Hotel – Albany Road
Ed Corbett's Boarding House (and brothel) – Broadway and Union (23rd Street)
Larken House – Broadway and 16th Street (Canal)
Exchange Hotel – Canal (16th Street) and Broad Street (Broadway)
Rouse's Hotel – River Street & in Washington (Broadway)
Ferry House – 23rd Street (Union Street)
    Robert Morrison, proprietor of the Ferry House, was the owner of some pet bears. A man one night went to sleep in their den and was hugged to death by one of them.

Saloons and Bars

Pat Halpins – Seneca (22nd Street)
Bird-In-Hand Tavern – Ohio (3rd Avenue)
    Once a popular bar in the sidecut in its hey-day, was torn down and during the demolition, three (300) hundred empty wallets were found behind a huge mirror behind the bar.
Pemberton's Saloon – Seneca (22nd Street)
Martin Long's Long Inn – Union (23rd Street)
Ed Grogan's Place on Union – Union (23rd Street)
Peg Leg Pete's Bar – Utica (24th Street)
    (Pete lost his leg in a canal lock)
Tom & Jerry (Paddy Ryan's bar)
The Black Rag –
Tub of Blood
Peter McCarthy's the Bank –
The Friendly Inn –
Rath Tavern
John Wald's Sidecut Bar – Union (23rd Street)
Pete Wolk's Boggie Rest – Ohio (3rd Avenue)

Funeral Parlors

The crime in the sidecut area supported no less than ten different undertakers between 1840 and 1910)
Carey and Bortolo – Washington (1st Avenue)
Cartin's – Broadway
J. I. Connel's – Broadway
Hastings – Ohio (3rd Avenue)
Lou Rock's – West (5th Avenue)
Touhey and Parker – E. Ontario (21st Street)
    (Now just Parker's)
Pat Nealon – Groton (5th Avenue)

"A Buffalo Canaler Killed at Troy. Albany, Sept 17 —At West Troy last night as a canal boat Leo of Buffalo was passing through the lock the steersman was knocked overboard by the tiller and drowned. Name unknown."—Buffalo Evening News, September 17, 1883

Miscellaneous and House of Worship

Bethel Mission (Rev. Marcus Smith – Union (23rd Street)
Trinity Mission Church (Rev. Davis Butler)
St Patrick's (father James Quinn) - Union (23rd Street)
    (later Our Lady of Mount Carmel)
Gospel Temperance Lodge #728 – Broadway

Brothels

Kevin Corbett's Rooming House – Utica (24th Street) and Broadway

Broadway bridge over the canal.

Canal Glossary

Aqueduct – A conveyance system, which carried canal boats over rivers, streams, etc. They were usually stone piers with a wooden structures to hold the water.

Bank Watchman or Inspector – Men who walked along canal banks to check for any leaks that might grow larger and cause breaks or washouts in the canal banks. He usually carried a shovel to repair small leaks and or reported large leaks.

Bow Lamps – There were no lights or channel markers along the Erie canal. A pair of bow lamps, one on each side of the bow deck, were standard equipment. The bow lamps were rather large and heavy being made up of metal and glass and about sixteen inches square containing a large kerosene lamp and reflectors, which lit up the shadowed, canal banks.

Canal – Man-made waterways came to be known as canals, a word derived from the Latin "canalis", meaning "pipe"or "channel".

Change Bridge – These brides allowed the mules/horses to cross the canal when the towpath changed from one side of the canal to the other due to terrain change, etc.

Double Locks – Locks built between 1835 and 1863 to allow for two-way traffic on the canal.

Drivers or Hoggees – They were usually young boys who walked or rode the animals on the towpath towing the canal boats. They worked six hours on and six hours off similar to the steersmen, night and day, in all kinds of weather.

Dry Docks – Areas connected to the canal used to repair or build canal boats. They were usually built near a stream lower than the canals so that when emptying the Drydock, the water drained by gravity through an opened valve into the stream.

Feeders – Water conveyed into the canal to maintain the proper level (lakes, streams, etc.)

Fog Gang – They were workers who cleaned out the canal on an annual basis to maintain the proper depth and remove garbage disposed into it during the year.

Gall Marks – The action of mule's forelegs caused the collar to move slightly on the animal's breast as he pulled steadily on the boats towline. The collar movement chafed some of the hide off the mule's breast under the collar, causing large sores or raw spots. The canallers called them "gall marks'.

Guard Gates - These are retractable dams that can be lowered quickly to stop the flow of canal waters.

Grog – A name used by the canallers for alcoholic beverages of various kinds.

Horse or Mule Bridge – A bridge run out between the canal boat and shore to change the team of animals towing the boat.

Hurry Up Boats – These were State Repair Scows who rushed to the scene of damaged earthen banks of the canal to stop washouts.

Levels – The distances between locks. These were level stretches of canal between locks, each one a different height above sea level.

Locks – They were structures, which raised or lowered canal boats from one level to another. The original locks were ninety feet by fifteen feet.

Lock Tenders – Opened and closed the gates to let traffic pass from one level to another. He used his shanty as a kind of combination office and home.

Long Eared Robins or Hay Burners – Mules used on the Erie Canal for towing.

Low Bridge – This was an expression used for bridges crossing over the canal. Many were built low to the canal in by the State in an effort to save money, hence the expression "low bridge".

Manure Box – A box about sixteen inches square, fastened to a pole about twelve feet long filled with manure and litter from the bow stable floor. With the open side of the box held tightly to the side of the boat, it was shoved under the water, just below the bottom of the boat near the leak. The contents of the box floated up the bottom of the boat and was pulled into the leak by the action of the water. This method of repairing small leaks was known as "Puddling".

Mudlarked – The term used for grounded or mudstuck canal boats because of insufficient water level in the canal.

Rhino – The term used for ready money or cash.

Side-cut – A lateral canal connecting the main channel with adjacent river, stream, or other canal. Probably the most famous side-cut of all, that which connected the Erie Canal in Watervliet to the Hudson River, gave its name to the area. To all canallers it was known as "The Side-cut".

Snubbing – To stop moving canal boats (Animals could not be reversed to stop boats) at a certain place, a line was made ready and fastened to a post or cleat on the dock or shore. A few turns were then taken and the boats were stopped by maintaining sufficient tension to bring the boats to a stop.

Snubbing Posts – Posts which were located about twenty-five feet apart along the length of a lock. When the moving boats entered the lock, the boatman stepped ashore with the line and began snubbing the headway from the boats, moving from post to post as he did so.

Steersman – He operated the rudder when the boat was moving. Meeting and passing, he steered and guided the boats around crooked bends, across aqueducts, and in and out of locks, where he handled lines while passing through. He also helped to put the horse bridge ashore and assisted in getting the mules on and off the boats. When not steering he would often use the two tin hand pumps to remove water accumulating from leaks in the boats. Working six hours on and six hours off, he most always had the 1-7 trick, night and day, in all kinds of weather.

Swelling – A term used for swells caused by the sudden opening of the paddle valves in the lock gates, by emptying the lock when boats were locking down or by emptying the lock to get it ready for an approaching tow. Many times it was used to unstuck or move boats from the locks.

Towpath – A ten-foot wide section along side of the canal for the horses or mules to walk as they towed the canal boats. It consisted of a mixture of clay and gravel, hard packed and its surface sprinkled with small stones.

Towpath Bridges – These were bridges across the canal placed where the towpath changed from one side of the canal to the other. It allowed the animals to switch to the opposite side of the canal. These changes were necessary due to engineering difficulties and changes in terrain. The mules and driver crossed the canal on these bridges especially designed for this purpose.

Waste Weirs – Structures designed to dispose of excess Water from the canal.

Another Glossary

AQUEDUCT — A structure which carries a canal over a river, stream or valley.

BARGE — A large flat-bottomed boat for cargo, usually referring to boats on the New York State Barge Canal System.

BERM — A side bank of the canal, usually the one opposite the towpath.

BILGE PUMP — Used to pump out the water which leaked into a canal boat.

BOATER — Term used by man on canal to describe himself.

BOATHOOK — A long pole with a hook to pull or push objects toward or away from the boat.

CANAL — An artificial waterway for transportation, irrigation, or drainage.

CANAL BOATS — Proper general term for cargo boats used on the original and enlarged Eries.

CANAL TOWN — A town along the canal that grew with the use of the waterway.

CLINTON'S DITCH — A derogatory term for the original Erie Canal (40 feet wide and 4 feet deep). Later, an affectionate name for the Old Erie.

CUDDY — Sleeping bunk on a canal boat.

DAM — Structure used to maintain water levels on the rivers, creating level pools which could be used by the canal boats.

DRYDOCK — A basin where the water level can be controlled; used in the construction or repairing of canal boats.

FEEDER — Diverted stream water to supply water which maintain the canal level.

FLYING LIGHT — Term used to describe boats travelling empty.

FREIGHTER — Canal boat that carried only cargo.

GANGPLANK — A wooden plank for boarding a canal boat.

GUARD LOCK — A lock for the purpose of controlling the water flow in the canal; usually where a canal and natural waterway joined.

HEELPATH — The side of the canal bank opposite the towpath; see berm.

HOGGEE — A driver; could be boy or man.

HOODLEDASHER — Empty canal boats were tied to loaded boats so a team could pull them all.

LEVEL — A stretch of canal between locks. The nearly 70 miles from Frankfort to Syracuse was known as the Long Level.

LOCK — An enclosure with gates at each end used in raising or lowering boats as they pass from one level to another.

LOCK-KEEPER — The lock-keeper opened and closed the gates of a lock, working seven days a week, with a shanty for home and office and $25-a-month pay.

MUD-LARKED — When boats got stuck in the mud due to low water or a break in the canal.

MULESKINNER — A mule driver

PACKET — Passenger boat on canal, usually travelling about four miles per hour.

PATHMASTER — The official in charge of inspecting the canal banks and structures.

SCHOHARIE CROSSING — Aqueduct over Schoharie Creek, where Erie Canal crossed.

SCOW — Most common canal boat type, comprised cargo of almost any description.

SEA LEVEL — Level of water at Atlantic Ocean; canal heights calculated from this base.

SLACK WATER — River level used for canal navigation, where canal used both artificial cut and natural waterways.

SNUBBING POST — Post along canal berm used to tie up canal boat.

SPILLWAY — A passage of excess water to run over or around a dam.

TILLER — The bar at the stern of the boat by which the boater turned the rudder and guided the boat.

TOWPATH — Path along one bank of canal where the teams walked pulling the boats.

TOW-ROPE NEWS — Word-of-mouth news which followed the canal.

TRICK — A hoggee's tour of duty; a driver boy walked two six-hour tricks a day, each about ten miles long.

TUGBOAT — Steam, Diesel, or electric boat used to push/pull tows on Barge Canal System.

WASTE WEIR — A dam-like structure along the canal berm with openings for controlling the water level.

WHIFFLETREE — Also whipple tree — A pivoted bar to which the mules were harnessed, linking the boats and their motive power.

"The cleaning of the Albany and West Troy canal levels was begun this morning." — Albany Evening Journal, April 11, 1881

Going through the Watervliet Arsenal. The wall is still there.

"Tolls received at the West Troy Canal Collector's office- last mouth, $7,786 10; clearance issued to date, 5,553." — New York Evening Telegram, November 5, 1875

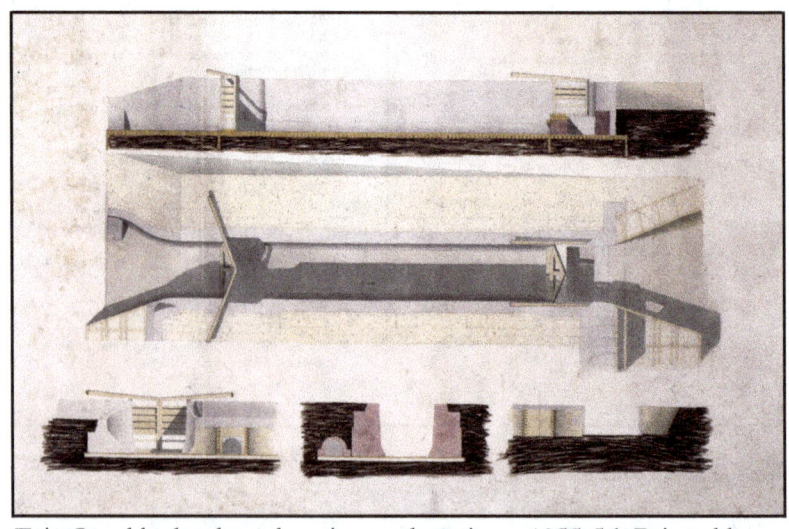

Erie Canal lock, plan, elevation and sections. 1855-56. Painted by Orlando Poe Metcalfe.

The following biographies of the builder of the lower side-cut was supplied by Tom Ragosta, City Historian.

Stillman Witt
1808-1875

He was born in Worcester County, Massachusetts, January 4th, 1808, and died at sea, April 29th, 1875. When only thirteen years old, he was taken with the family to Troy, New York, where he was employed to run a skiff-ferry at $10 a month. Mr. Canvass White, of the United States Engineer Corps, frequently crossed the ferry, and finding the lad eager to learn, Mr. White obtained permission of the elder Witt to educate him in his own profession. He applied himself with so much zeal that he was not long in mastering the principles of the profession and to apply them practically, when he was sent by his friend and employer to take charge of the Cohoes Manufacturing Company. He surveyed and laid out the village and arranged the waterpower, and from the beginning thus made has been developed one of the most important manufacturing points in the country. This work accomplished he returned, and was again dispatched to construct the bridge across the Susquehanna at the mouth of the Juniata River. Thence he went to Louisville, where he spent a year and a half in building the Louisville and Portland canal. Still retaining his connection with Mr. White, he removed to Albany, where he assumed the duties of agent of the Hudson River Steamboat Association. The Albany and Boston Railroad Company invited him to become manager of their line and he accepted the position, where he remained eight years. At the end of that time he was induced to visit Cleveland by the efforts that were making for the construction of a railroad to Columbus. The Cleveland, Columbus and Cincinnati Railroad Company had been organized, but there was difficulty in finding experienced builders who would contract for the construction of the road and take the greater part pay in stock. The ground was looked over, the propositions considered, and finally the firm of Harbach, Stone & Witt was formed for the building of the road. The work was completed and the road opened in 1851. A contract for the construction of the Cleveland, Painesville and Ashtabula Railroad was then made and the road finished by Stone & Witt, after the death of Mr. Harbach. The same firm next constructed the Chicago and Milwaukee Railroad and operated it for some time after its completion. He now turned his attention to the management of the large interests he had acquired in railroads and other property. He was at different times chosen director in the Michigan Southern; Cleveland, Columbus, Cincinnati and Indianapolis; Cleveland, Painesville and Ashtabula; Chicago and Milwaukee, and Bellefontaine and Indiana Railroad Companies. Besides his position on the directory of the different railroads in which he was interested, he was director of the Second National and Commercial National Banks of Cleveland, and president of the Sun Insurance Company, Union Steel Screw Company, and Cleveland Box Machine Company. In June 1834, he married Miss Eliza A. Douglass, of Albany. Of his two surviving daughters, Mary married Daniel P. Eells, of Cleveland, and Emma, Colonel W. H. Harris, of the United States army.

The Lower Side-Cut and docks on the Erie Canal at Port Schuyler was built under his management.

He died while on his way to Europe for the benefit of his health.

Second Bio

The Lower Side Cut was built by Stillman Witt sometime during the years 1836-1840 when the Erie Canal was enlarged from forty feet wide to seventy feet.

Mr. Witt was born in Worcester, Massachusetts, January 4th, 1808. His parentage was humble, and, in consequence, his facilities for obtaining an education very limited. When about thirteen years old, his father moved with his family to Troy, New York, where young Stillman was hired by Richard P. Hart to run a skiff ferry, the wages being ten dollars per month, which the lad thought a sum sufficient to secure his independence.

Among the passengers frequently crossing the ferry was Mr. Canvass White, U. S. Engineer, at that time superintending the construction of public works in various parts of the country. Mr. White took a strong fancy to the juvenile ferryman, and was so much impressed by the interest the boy manifested in construction, that he applied to Stillman's father for permission to take the lad and educate him in his own profession. The permission was granted.

Young Witt was greatly pleased with his new profession, and devoted himself to it with such zeal and faithfulness that he grew rapidly in the esteem of his patron. When he had sufficiently progressed to be entrusted with works of such importance, he was dispatched in different directions to construct bridges and canals as the agent of Mr. White. In this manner he superintended the construction of the bridge at Cohoes Falls, on the Mohawk River, four miles above Troy, where, in conjunction with Mr. White, he laid out a town which has since grown to a population of thirty-thousand. The side cut on the Erie canal, at Port Schuyler, was dug under his management, and the docks there, since covered with factories, were built by him.

Then, still connected with White, he became an agent of the Hudson River Steamboat Assoc. in Albany. With the emergence of railroads in the 1840s, Witt became manager of Albany & Boston Railroad Co. In the late 1840s, Witt moved to Cleveland, forming the firm of Harbach, Stone & Witt which built the Cleveland, Columbus & Cincinnati Railroad, completed in 1851. The firm then constructed the Cleveland, Painesville & Ashtabula Railroad, and the Chicago & Milwaukee Railroad. Witt managed the large interests he had acquired in railroads and other properties, becoming director of the above railroads and others. In 1863, Witt was an incorporator of Cleveland Rolling Mill Co. He also helped build the Cleveland & Newburgh Railroad in 1868 .

Witt's home was moved to Waterford.

In 1869, Witt bought and donated a boarding home for the Women's Christian Assoc. (later YWCA); in 1873, donating money for a second home, later known as the Stillman Witt Boarding House. Witt was active in many other Cleveland charitable and educational organizations, especially those for women. Witt married Eliza A. Douglass in 1834. They had 4 children: Emma, Eugenia, Giles, and Mary. He died on April 29, 1875, while at sea on the Steamship *Suevia* he hit his head and died in his sleep. Buried in Albany Rural Cemetery.

Man and his boat on the canal in Menands.

Witt Obituary from New York Times, May 10, 1875.

THE LATE STILLMAN WITT.

It is very seldom that we are called upon to record the death of a man more widely known, more universally esteemed, and whose life was more useful, than that of Mr. Stillman Witt, of Cleveland, Ohio, who died at sea, on his voyage to Europe, a few days ago. For a number of years the condition of Mr. Witt's health has been such as to cause much anxiety among his friends, but his naturally vigorous constitution and his habits of temperance have carried him through many severe attacks of sickness, and hope would take possession of his heart, and he thought he could look forward "to length of days." It was thought that a change of air and climate, and the waters of some of the celebrated springs in Europe, would prove greatly beneficial to him. But, alas, he was not spared to reach the shores of the Old World. On the great sea his spirit went up to the Father whom he worshiped and adored.

The life of such a man as Mr. Witt is full of instruction to young men, as it was a life of honest industry, of persevering effort, of highest rectitude of conduct, and of trusting Christian faith.

He was one of the many of the sons of New-England, born of respectable parents, but whose only inheritance was that of toil, and the necessity of making his own way onward and upward in life as best he could, without the advantages of liberal education and pecuniary assistance at the start. He early believed and acted upon the opinion that the man of labor and of integrity is the man that is sure to win in the battle of life; that success is always certain to come to him that is industrious, economical, and persevering.

In his early life his father kept the Half-way House between Troy and Albany, and Mr. Witt used to drive the hack that carried passengers between the two cities. The "Old Patroon" was frequently a passenger in this hack, and the young driver, by his quiet deportment, pleasant manner, and general good conduct, attracted the attention of this distinguished citizen of Albany, and on one of the trips he asked the young coachman if he would not like some other business. He replied: "Yes, sir, if my father can spare me, and if he is willing." He gave the "Patroon" the name of his father, and in a few days was informed by his new friend that he was wanted in the new iron-works at Cohoes. He commenced his clerkship by keeping the pay-rolls of the workmen and in paying them their wages. As this was a new business he was taught how to keep his books by a young friend who was a clerk in one of the Troy banks, where he took lessons in book-keeping and accounts in the evenings. From this place he was sent to Harrisburg, Penn., to perform about the same duties there as Paymaster General. When the large bridge over the Susquehanna was finished he went to Louisville, Ky., and was paymaster there on the canal work. Upon the completion of that canal, he returned to Albany and was employed as the agent of the People's Line of steamers on the Hudson. Here he became well known to business men, made troops of friends, and was next engaged as General Freight Agent of the Western Railroad from Albany to Boston. We once heard an old engineer on that road say "that Mr. Witt could get more work out of the men than any other man, as it was always with him, 'Come, boys, the work must be done.'" If the road was blocked with snow, he would provide beer and crackers, and always treated the men kindly. He was a very popular agent, and became known to capitalists who were engaged in new enterprises of railroad making. In 1848, in company with F. Harback and Amasa Stone, Jr., the contract was made to build the Cleveland and Columbus railroad. It was a very large undertaking, by men whose united fortunes did not amount to $125,000. These new contractors had the confidence of "moneyed men," and one of them was an accomplished engineer, whose "estimates" were relied upon as mathematical certainties.

The contractors put their work through, and the road was handed over to the officers of the company before the contract time was up, and the Legislature of Ohio and the people celebrated the opening in February, 1851, at Cleveland, with guns, bells, dinner, and speeches, and an eloquent and appropriate sermon by Rev. Dr. S. C. Aikin, from Nahum ii., 4: "The chariots shall rage in the streets; they shall jostle one against another in the broad ways; they shall seem like torches; they shall run like the lightnings."

These contractors organized a new era of railroad building in the West. Their credit was established, and the Cleveland and Columbus contract had proved a remunerative one. They entered into a contract to build the Cleveland and Erie Railroad. This was satisfactorily performed, with increased gains to the enterprising young railroad kings of the West. Mr. Harback died early. For several years past, Messrs. Stone and Witt, of Cleveland, could probably raise more money in Wall street than any two men in the West, as their large fortunes consisted of bonds and stocks readily used as collaterals in loans.

From Ohio they went to Chicago, and built about half of the Chicago and Milwaukee Line. Mr. Witt was interested in the Bellefontaine and Indianapolis Road, and in many other large enterprises, in which he was successful. He was President of the Cuyahoga Valley Railroad, a work now in progress, reaching from Cleveland into the coal fields of Ohio. He was President of The Union Steel Screw Company, of Cleveland, one of the most prosperous manufacturing enterprises of the time, making woodscrews from Bessemer steel wire. He was President of the Sun Insurance Company, a director in banks, and interested in almost every industry in his adopted city. His name in any undertaking always carried with it confidence from his known integrity and good judgment in business affairs. Mr. Witt was a benevolent man. He lived not for himself alone. He was generous to kindred and friends. He contributed liberally to his church (the Baptist.) It was a pleasure to him to give. He liked to do good, and in making others happy he was happy himself. He was a warm, steadfast friend, and ever honest, frank, outspoken. He knew not how to deceive. He loved his country, and during the rebellion was one of the most true and loyal of men, and contributed largely of his means to the needs and wants of the time.

"The Home," near his own beautiful residence, will remain a monument of his liberality. It was built for women, where they could have comfortable and pleasant rooms and board for a reasonable price. He took great interest in this noble charity, and the thousands it cost were most cheerfully expended.

The life and the work and the good deeds of such a man as Stillman Witt are worthy of imitation. He was an example for all, in his public as well as in his private life. He was, indeed, a model man in his love of home, where there was ever largehearted hospitality and never-ceasing love and devotion to his family. He has gone from among us as he had reached the promised bound of life, but his name will long remain "a holy and a treasured thing" in hearts by whom he was appreciated and beloved for all that ennobled man.

Table of new rates in 1846.

357	West Troy,	30	8 4.4.8	14 2	8	10 7	1	7 1	4	357	3
358	Gibbonsville,	30	9 3.1.2	14 3	2	10 7	4	7 1	6	358	3
359	Port Schuyler,	31	0 1.7.6	14 3	6	10 7	7	7 1	8	359	3

Erie and junction canal guide. Containing a list of distances on said canals, rates of toll, toll on 100 lbs per 100 miles at the different rates; also extracts from the canal law and regulations ... For sale at the Weigh Lock, Utica [c. June 10, 1833].

"By Mr. Culver—In relation to the enlargement of the Junction Canal, and upon the petition of the citizens of West Troy. The Report concludes with a resolution instructing the Canal Commissioners to deepen the bed of the Canal two feet and raise the surface of the same one foot on the West Troy Canal."— Evening Journal, April 9, 1838.

John Morey, the little boy who was drowned in the Erie Canal at West Troy on Thursday made a desperate struggle for life. Miss Sarah Becker, on the Central avenue bridge, saw the child go through the ice and called the attention of several persons. A plank was thrown into the canal, and the little fellow grasped it firmly. Other planks were thrown in, and ten minutes were passed in futile efforts to effect a rescue. The boy soon lost strength and held to the plank from the under side, his head being under water most of the time. At last Addison Becker went into the canal and brought the body ashore. When he took hold of it the arms still clutched the plank, but the boy was dead. More than thirty persons witnessed the drowning. —Argus, Mar. 4, 1882.

The Traveller's pocket map of New York: from the best authorities. Williams, William, 1787-1850. Stiles, S., 1826.

Broke Through the Ice. Troy, N. Y., Dec. 20.—*Henry Ferrett, a boy was drowned to-day in the Erie canal at West Troy. He was skating and broke through the ice.* — Rochester Democrat, December 27, 1894.

1825

ODE

FOR THE

CANAL CELEBRATION,

WRITTEN AT THE REQUEST OF THE PRINTERS OF NEW-YORK

By Mr. SAMUEL WOODWORTH, Printer.

'Tis done! 'tis done!—The mighty chain
Which joins bright ERIE to the MAIN,
For ages, shall perpetuate
   The glory of our native State.

'Tis done!—Proud ART o'er NATURE has prevail'd!
   GENIUS and PERSEVERANCE have succeeded!
Though selfish PREJUDICE assail'd,
   And honest PRUDENCE pleaded.

'Tis done!—The monarch of the briny tide,
   Whose giant arm encircles earth,
To virgin ERIE is allied,
   A bright-eyed nymph, of mountain birth.

To-day, the *Sire of Ocean* takes
   A sylvan maiden to his arms,
The goddess of the crystal lakes,
   In all her native charms!

She comes! attended by a sparkling train;
   The *Naiads* of the West her nuptials grace:
She meets the sceptred father of the main,
   And in his heaving bosom hides her virgin face.

   Rising from their watery cells,
      Tritons sport upon the tide,
   And gaily blow their trumpet shells,
      In honour of the bride.
   Sea-nymphs leave their coral caves,
      Deep beneath the ocean waves,
   Where they string, with tasteful care,
      Pearls upon their sea-green hair.
   Thetis' virgin train advances,
   Mingling in the bridal dances;
   Jove, himself, with raptured eye,
   Throws his forked thunders by,
   And bids Apollo seize his golden lyre,
      A strain of joy to wake;
   While Fame proclaims that *Ocean's Sire*
   Is wedded to the goddess of the *Lake*.
      The smiling god of song obeys,
      And heaven re-echoes with his sounding lays.

"All hail to the ART which unshackles the soul!
   And fires it with love of glory!
And causes the victor, who reaches the goal,
   To live in deathless story!

"Which teaches young Genius to rise from earth,
   On Fancy's airy pinion,
To assert the claims of its heavenly birth,
   And seize on its blest dominion.

"The ART which the banner of Truth unfurl'd,
   When darkness veil'd each nation,
And prompted Columbus to seek a new world
   On the unexplored map of creation.

"Which lighted the path of the pilgrim band,
   Who braved the storms of Ocean,
To seek, in a wild and distant land,
   The freedom of pure *devotion*.

"Which kindled, on Freedom's shrine, a flame
   That will glow through future ages,
And cover with glory and endless fame
   Columbia's immortal sages.

"The ART which enabled her FRANKLIN to prove,
   And solve, each mystic wonder!
To arrest the forked shafts of Jove,
   And play with his bolts of thunder.

"The ART, which enables her sons to aspire,
   Beyond all the wonders in story,
For an unshackled PRESS is the pillar of fire
   Which lights them to Freedom and Glory.

"'Tis this which call'd forth the immortal decree,
   And gave the great work its first motion;
'Tis done! by the hands of the brave and free,
   And ERIE is link'd to the Ocean.

"Then hail to the ART which unshackles the soul,
   And fires it with love of glory,
And causes the victor who reaches the goal,
   To live in deathless story."

Such strains—if earthly strains may be
   Compared to his who tunes a heavenly lyre—
Are warbled by the bright-haired deity,
   While list'ning orbs admire.

Such strains shall unborn millions yet awake,
   While, with her golden trumpet, smiling Fame
Proclaims the union of the Main and Lake,
   And on her scroll emblazons CLINTON's name.

The foregoing ODE was printed on a moveable stage, on the 4th day of November, 1825, during the Procession in honour of the completion of the Grand Western Canal.

Clayton & Van Norden, Printers.

It's all his fault. DeWitt Clinton (March 2, 1769 – February 11, 1828) was an American politician. He was a United States Senator, Mayor of New York City, and the sixth Governor of New York. Clinton was Governor from 1817 to 1822 and from 1825 to 1828, presiding over the construction of the Erie Canal.

He believed that infrastructure improvements could transform American life, drive economic growth, and encourage political participation. DeWitt Clinton was the nephew of Governor George Clinton of New York. DeWitt Clinton served as Mayor of NYC from 1793 to 1815. During his Mayoral position he promoted public education, city planning, public sanitation and relief for the poor. While Mayor he also organized the Historical Society of New York in 1804, and served as its president. He also organized the Academy of Fine Arts in 1808.

> West Troy Jan 5 1848
>
> Hon. Hugh White
>
> Sir
>
> excuse me for the liberty I have taken to adress you I am about to apply for the office of Inspector of canal for this distric and not knowing any of the canal board. I take the liberty to ask of you the favour of a letter in my favor to them.
>
> I was formely a resident of Saratoga town of Greenfield, were I had the honor of an introduction to you in the fall of 1844
>
> I have the honor to subscribe myself your humble servant
>
> William. B. May
>
> pleas take the erleyest oppertunity to answer this

William B May from West Troy trying to get a job as a canal inspector from Honorable Hugh White, Canvas White's brother. He created the Rosendale Cement Works and "White's water-proof cement" with his brother that was used on the canal. His house was moved to Waterford and is now a museum. It was built in Waterford with brick and wood from Chittenango and brought to the village over the Erie Canal. He was president of the Saratoga County National Bank. White was elected as a Whig to the 29th, 30th and 31st United States Congresses, holding office from March 4, 1845, to March 3, 1851. He was Chairman of the Committee on Agriculture (30th Congress).

Receipt for lumber sale from Saxe Bros wholesale lumber at 144 Broadway. Lumber was a large commodity shipped over the canal.

Receipt for weighing the boat *S Bing* of Fort Edward at the West Troy Weigh-Lock on May 17, 1848.

Receipt for lumber sale from Harmon & Gillespie, wholesale lumber at 11 Canal St, shipped over the canal to Jersey City, NJ.

Receipt for lumber sale consigned to Conde Bros (George, James & Sanford), lumber dealers shipped on the boat "*A A Tessr.*" Aug 11, 1871.

Old Street Names

The present City of Watervliet at one time consisted of three villages which eventually merged into the city as we know it. From First Street to the south wall of the Arsenal was the village of Washington. From the north wall of the Arsenal to 15th., Street was the village of Gibbonsville, and from 15th., Street to 27th., Street was the village of West Troy. In the year 1888 the City of Watervliet, then known as West Troy drew up the Street plan as it is today. In this plan the streets running East and West were designated as STREETS. Those running North and South were listed as AVENUES. The only exception was Water Street, which ran North and South was allowed to remain a Street. Water Street is now completely covered by Route 787. In 1888 the present house numbering system was also inaugurated. The renaming and renumbering of Streets, Avenues and houses became an absolute necessity for the operation of an efficient Fire Department and Postal Service. Listed below are the present Streets and Avenues and their former names.

PRESENT NAME	FORMER NAME
1st. Street.	South Street.
2nd. Street.	South Canal Street.
3rd. Street.	Athol Street.
4th., Street	Earl Street.
5th. Street.	Mill Street.
6th. Street.	Spring Street.
7th. Street.	Middle Street.
8th. Street.	Mansion Street.
9th. Street.	Berlin Street.
10th. Street.	Shaker Road.
11th. Street.	Charlotte Street.
12th. Street.	George Street.
13th. Street:	Schenectady Street.
14th. Street.	Ferry Street.
15th. Street.	Buffalo Street.
16th. Street.	Canal Street.
17th. Street.	Owasco Street. East of Canal (2nd.Ave.) only
18th. Street.	Huron Street, East of Erie Canal (2nd.Ave.)
18th. Street.	Geneva Street. West of Erie Canal (2nd.Ave.)

The amount of tolls received at the West Troy Canal Collector's office, last week, was $1,477.35. — Albany Morning Express, Monday, July 3, 1876

[This return is to be made by the Collectors at New-York, Albany, West Troy and Waterford, and is to correspond with and accompany each weekly abstract.]

WEEKLY STATEMENT

Showing the quantity of the several articles First Cleared on the Canals at, and the quantity Left at *West Troy* during the *1st* week in *October* 1866.

MERCHANDISE CLEARED.

ARTICLES.		ON ERIE CANAL.	ON CHAMPLAIN CANAL.	TOTAL.
Sugar, at 4 mills,	pounds,	317,400	204,800	522,200
Molasses,	"	141,300	38,500	179,800
Coffee,	"	300	400	700
Nails,	"	40,900		40,900
Iron,	"	66,200	10,300	76,500
Railroad Iron "		3,774,000		3,774,000
All other merchandise at 4 mills,	"	2,292,300	175,800	2,468,100
Total,		6,632,400	429,800	7,062,200

		LEFT FROM ERIE CANAL.	LEFT FROM CHAMPLAIN CANAL.	TOTAL.
Flour,	barrels,	6,437	599	7,036
Wheat,	bushels,	51,963		51,963
Corn,	"	8,936		8,936
Barley,	"	29,967		29,967
Rye,	"			
Oats,	"	12,200		12,200
Bran and Ship Stuffs,	pounds,	11,000		11,000
Ashes,	barrels,			
Beef,	"			
Pork,	"			
Bacon,	pounds,			

Weekly statement showing the amount of goods that crossed the canal at West Troy during the week of October, 1, 1887.

"The Canals.
Boatmen are anxiously awaiting the opening of the canals, which has been officially announced to take place May 7th. Over a hundred boats are at the West Troy side cut in readiness to be locked into the canals on that date, and the lock tenders, who, by the way, are to be appointed in a day or two, will have more than they can attend to for a short time in working the gates fast enough for the impatient army of boat captains. The rumor that many of the West Troy canal barns are to be removed to Albany by their owners seems to be unfounded." — Albany Morning Express, Wednesday, May 2, 1883.

[W. M. No. 4, 1876.]

[Weigh-Masters are required to send abstracts of light weights taken during each week of navigation, ending respectively on the 7th, 14th, 21st and last days of each month, immediately after the close of each week, to the Canal Department and every Weigh Master in the State. Be careful to write full name of Boat, as registered.]

WEIGH-MASTER'S WEEKLY ABSTRACT

Of all the Boats weighed light at the _West Troy_ Weigh-Lock, from the _23_ to the _31st_ day of _Oct_ 188_0_ both days inclusive.

Date	Name of Boat	Hailing Place	Light Weight	Water in Boat B.	M.	S.	Articles on Board
Oct 23	John Ammon	Oswego	105700	trace			WB&Bx
" 25	John Vedder	Granby	112700	dry			
" 29	Toledo	Utica	123000	2	½	1	
" "	Matt & Jess	Lyons Falls	55000				
" 31	Bartlett Nye	Champlain	107700			1	
" "	Sneed & Anston	New York	105700		0	0	
" 18	John M. Burt	" "	53000	2½	½	0	

Date	Name of Boat	Hailing Place	Light Weight	Water in Boat B.	M.	S.	Articles on Board

new
new
retained
new

new

new Built on the same Principle as the Planet Line

STATE OF NEW YORK, _Albany_ COUNTY, ss.

West Troy Nov 1st 1880

I, _L. Taylor_ Weigh-Master at the _West Troy_ Weigh-Lock, being duly sworn, do depose and say that the foregoing is a true list of all the boats weighed light at this Lock during the week commencing with the _23_ and ending with the _31_ day of _Oct_ 1880 and that all the entries on this abstract are correct, as appears from the Register of Light Boats kept at this Weigh-Lock; and that said Register exhibits the true light weight of each of said boats, according to the best of his knowledge and belief.

Sworn to before me, this _1st_ day of _Nov_ 187_

L. Taylor Weigh-Master

Weekly weigh masters report for October, 1880 in West Troy.

```
The Places a long the Erie Canal
              commenceing at Albany
 & the number of miles
 Albany to        miles
 west Troy          7      number of miles
 Junction to        0      from Albany
 Cohoes         ..  4       .. ..   11
 Crescent       ..  3       .. ..   14
 upper aqueduct 12          .. ..   26
 Schenectady    ..  4       .. ..   30
 Hoffmans ferry 10          .. ..   40
 Fort Jackson   ..  6       .. ..   46
 Schoharie creek 5          .. ..   51
 Aurisville     ..  2       .. ..   53
 Fultonville    ..  3       .. ..   56
 Yatesville     ..  6       .. ..   62
 Smiths         ..  3       .. ..   65
 Canajoharie    ..  3       .. ..   68
 Fort Plain     ..  3       .. ..   71
 St Johnsville  ..  5       .. ..   76

 Minderville    ..  2       .. ..   78
 East Canada creek 4        .. ..   82
 Little falls   ..  5       .. ..   87
 Mohawk         ..  8       .. ..   95
 River          .. 30       .. .. 100
 Frankfort     ..   3       .. .. 101
 Fergusons     ..   5       .. .. 106
 Utica         ..   4       .. .. 110
 fork mills    ..   3       .. .. 113
 Whitesboro    ..   1       .. .. 114
 Oriskany      ..   3       .. .. 117
 Rome          ..   8       .. .. 125
```

Portion of a hand made list of places and miles from Albany on the Erie Canal.

In answer to your inquiries for the cause of the extensive flats opposite and immediately below the entrance of the side cut from the Erie canal into the Hudson River — In what manner the Boats pass these flats that are bound for Troy — The difficulties that into attend keeping this navigation open and the remedy Third &

1st. These flats extend to about the extent of the alluvial triangle from the lower spruit of the Mohawk & the Hudson River and commence at those points where the water of those two Rivers first check each others velocity and continue downwards as far as the eddies extend

2d. A canal is extended from the lower lock of the Side cut across the flat to the City of Troy and has been executed at considerable expense by the Troys mechanics — through this canal the Boats pass into the Hudson R.R.R. —

3d. The difficulties that attend keeping this navigation open across the flats — are the continued operation of the same causes which originally produced those flats — which must gradually operate to fill up the canal now made —

4. The remedy is to remove the cause which first produced these flats & it will continue to embarrass the navigation so long as it is permitted to [continue] — And which can only be done by turning off the waters of the lower spruit of the Mohawk — This can be effected by throwing a dam across the head of said spruit from the main to Green Island — turning the water down the middle spruit into the Hudson —

The formation & views of the proprietors of west Troy — The advantages to western & northern inhabitants in having [immense] markets at the entrance of the canal into the Hudson — Competition &c — advantages of bringing foreigners with their capital into this State —

within the flats now formed — how to be improved and the improvements by basin & circle —

See Mr Young's certificate — Batteaus cannot get rid of the water of the spruit soon to discharge it below the canal across the flats —

Name the various propositions that have been made to bothers to use the water solely if we would make the pier to Green Island — to use it jointly by paying his proportion of the expenses &c —

Argument to create a damn across the Mohawk River. Unknown author or date. See next page.

116

In answer to your inquiries for the case of the extensive flats opposite and immediately below the entrance of the side cut from the Erie Canal into the Hudson River. In what manner the boats pass these flats that are bound for Troy - The difficulties that will attend keep for this navigation open and the remedy.

1st. These flats extend to about the center of the river and are formed by alluvial brought down the lower spout of the Mohawk and the Hudson and commence at these points where the waters for these two rivers first check each others velocity and continues downward as far as the eddie's extend.

2nd A canal is extended from the lower lock of the sidecut across this flat to the city of Troy and has been excavated at considerable expense by the dredge machine though this causes the boats pass into the channel of the Hudson.

3rd The difficulties that attend keeping the navigation open across the flats — are the continued operation of the same causes which originally produced these flats which must gradually operate to fill up the canal now made —

4 The remedy is, to remove the cause which first produced these flats and which will continue to embarrass the navigation so long as it is permitted to remain and which can only be done by turning off the waters of the lower spout of the Mohawk. This can be effected by throwing a dam across the head of the said spout from the main to Green Island turning the water across the middle spout into the Hudson.

The formation and views of the properties of West Troy. The advantages to western and northern inhabitants in having minimum markets at the entrance of the canal into the Hudson — competition &-advantages of bring foreigners with their capital into this state —

Within the flats how formed — how to be improved and the improvements of basin & lock —

Say no young's certificate — Oathouts comment, get rid of the water of the spout so as to discharge it below the canal across the flats —

Name the various properties that have been made to Oathout to use the water solely if we would make the pier to Green Island, to use it privately he pay his properties of the expenses, etc.

Lock #	Location	Elevation (upstream/west)	Elevation (downstream/east)	Lift or Drop	Distance to Next Lock (upstream/west)
Troy Federal Lock *	Troy	15.3 ft (4.7 m)	1.3 ft (0.40 m)	14.0 ft (4.3 m)	E2, 2.66 mi (4.28 km)
E2	Waterford	48.9 ft (14.9 m)	15.3 ft (4.7 m)	33.6 ft (10.2 m)	E3, 0.46 mi (0.74 km)
E3	Waterford	83.5 ft (25.5 m)	48.9 ft (14.9 m)	34.6 ft (10.5 m)	E4, 0.51 mi (0.82 km)
E4	Waterford	118.1 ft (36.0 m)	83.5 ft (25.5 m)	34.6 ft (10.5 m)	E5, 0.27 mi (0.43 km)
E5	Waterford	151.4 ft (46.1 m)	118.1 ft (36.0 m)	33.3 ft (10.1 m)	E6, 0.28 mi (0.45 km)
E6	Crescent	184.4 ft (56.2 m)	151.4 ft (46.1 m)	33.0 ft (10.1 m)	E7, 10.92 mi (17.57 km)
E7	Vischer Ferry	211.4 ft (64.4 m)	184.4 ft (56.2 m)	27.0 ft (8.2 m)	E8, 10.97 mi (17.65 km)
E8	Scotia	225.4 ft (68.7 m)	211.4 ft (64.4 m)	14.0 ft (4.3 m)	E9, 5.03 mi (8.10 km)
E9	Rotterdam	240.4 ft (73.3 m)	225.4 ft (68.7 m)	15.0 ft (4.6 m)	E10, 5.95 mi (9.58 km)
E10	Cranesville	255.4 ft (77.8 m)	240.4 ft (73.3 m)	15.0 ft (4.6 m)	E11, 4.27 mi (6.87 km)
E11	Amsterdam	267.4 ft (81.5 m)	255.4 ft (77.8 m)	12.0 ft (3.7 m)	E12, 4.23 mi (6.81 km)
E12	Tribes Hill	278.4 ft (84.9 m)	267.4 ft (81.5 m)	11.0 ft (3.4 m)	E13, 9.60 mi (15.45 km)
E13	Yosts	286.4 ft (87.3 m)	278.4 ft (84.9 m)	8.0 ft (2.4 m)	E14, 7.83 mi (12.60 km)
E14	Canajoharie	294.4 ft (89.7 m)	286.4 ft (87.3 m)	8.0 ft (2.4 m)	E15, 3.35 mi (5.39 km)
E15	Fort Plain	302.4 ft (92.2 m)	294.4 ft (89.7 m)	8.0 ft (2.4 m)	E16, 6.72 mi (10.81 km)
E16	St. Johnsville	322.9 ft (98.4 m)	302.4 ft (92.2 m)	20.5 ft (6.2 m)	E17, 7.97 mi (12.83 km)
E17	Little Falls	363.4 ft (110.8 m)	322.9 ft (98.4 m)	40.5 ft (12.3 m)	E18, 4.20 mi (6.76 km)
E18	Jacksonburg	383.4 ft (116.9 m)	363.4 ft (110.8 m)	20.0 ft (6.1 m)	E19, 11.85 mi (19.07 km)
E19	Frankfort	404.4 ft (123.3 m)	383.4 ft (116.9 m)	21.0 ft (6.4 m)	E20, 10.28 mi (16.54 km)
E20	Whitesboro	420.4 ft (128.1 m)	404.4 ft (123.3 m)	16.0 ft (4.9 m)	E21, 18.10 mi (29.13 km)
E21	New London	395.4 ft (120.5 m)	420.4 ft (128.1 m)	−25.0 ft (−7.6 m)	E22, 1.32 mi (2.12 km)
E22	New London	370.1 ft (112.8 m)	395.4 ft (120.5 m)	−25.3 ft (−7.7 m)	E23, 28.91 mi (46.53 km)
E23	Brewerton	363.0 ft (110.6 m)	370.1 ft (112.8 m)	−7.1 ft (−2.2 m)	E24, 18.77 mi (30.21 km)
E24	Baldwinsville	374.0 ft (114.0 m)	363.0 ft (110.6 m)	11.0 ft (3.4 m)	E25, 30.69 mi (49.39 km)
E25	Mays Point	380.0 ft (115.8 m)	374.0 ft (114.0 m)	6.0 ft (1.8 m)	E26, 5.83 mi (9.38 km)
E26	Clyde	386.0 ft (117.7 m)	380.0 ft (115.8 m)	6.0 ft (1.8 m)	E27, 12.05 mi (19.39 km)
E27	Lyons	398.5 ft (121.5 m)	386.0 ft (117.7 m)	12.5 ft (3.8 m)	E28A, 1.28 mi (2.06 km)
E28A	Lyons	418.0 ft (127.4 m)	398.5 ft (121.5 m)	19.5 ft (5.9 m)	E28B, 3.98 mi (6.41 km)
E28B	Newark	430.0 ft (131.1 m)	418.0 ft (127.4 m)	12.0 ft (3.7 m)	E29, 9.79 mi (15.76 km)
E29	Palmyra	446.0 ft (135.9 m)	430.0 ft (131.1 m)	16.0 ft (4.9 m)	E30, 2.98 mi (4.80 km)
E30	Macedon	462.4 ft (140.9 m)	446.0 ft (135.9 m)	16.4 ft (5.0 m)	E32, 16.12 mi (25.94 km)
E32	Pittsford	487.5 ft (148.6 m)	462.4 ft (140.9 m)	25.1 ft (7.7 m)	E33, 1.26 mi (2.03 km)
E33	Rochester	512.9 ft (156.3 m)	487.5 ft (148.6 m)	25.4 ft (7.7 m)	E34/35, 64.28 mi (103.45 km)
E34	Lockport	539.5 ft (164.4 m)	514.9 ft (156.9 m)	24.6 ft (7.5 m)	E35, adjacent to Lock E34.
E35	Lockport	564.0 ft (171.9 m)	539.5 ft (164.4 m)	24.5 ft (7.5 m)	Black Rock Lock in Niagara River, 26.39 mi (42.47 km)
Black Rock Lock *	Buffalo	570.6 ft (173.9 m)	565.6 ft (172.4 m)	5.0 ft (1.5 m)	Commercial Slip at Buffalo River, 3.89 mi (6.26 km)

Current locks of the Barge (Erie) Canal. From Wikipedia.

The First Railroad Iron Bridge.

The old iron truss bridge over the Erie canal between West Troy and Cohoes, which the Delaware and Hudson Canal Company is removing to replace with a double tracked one, has somewhat of an interesting history in more points than one. In passing over it, last Saturday, an Argus reporter's attention was called to it by Mr. Peter Hogan, civil engineer, who stated that it was the first iron bridge of any account in length of span that was ever constructed in this country, and now, after a continuous use for thirty years, it is removed for the above stated cause in as firm and strong state as when it came from the hands of its builders. It was erected in 1852, for the Albany Northern Railroad Company, by Squire Whipple, C. E., of this city, who has since become widely known at home and abroad as an inventor, architect and builder of iron bridges, and who is recognized as an expert authority on the subject in the courts of America and England, and was the first man who reduced bridge building to a science. Its pattern was that known as the Whipple trapezoidal truss bridge. The contract price for which he erected the bridge was $4,000, but it is a fact that it has been used for thirty years, is now being displaced and its builder has never received one cent for his work upon it. This is owing to the fact that the Albany Northern railroad early became bankrupt and its roadbed, track and franchises were foreclosed at mortgage sale; thus destroying all claims that Mr. Whipple had upon it and hope of payment from that source. The bridge, with the road, then became the property of the Albany, Vermont and Canada railroad and next passed, by lease, into the possession of the Resselaer and Saratoga Railroad Company, and, by a subsequent lease, into the hands of the Delaware and Hudson Canal Company, before whose strides in the march of improvement it gives way to a broader, but not more substantial, successor.

The Argus, March 21, 1882

J. M. Jones & Co.

Several industries grew up along the canal in Watervliet. One of them is J. M. Jones & Co founded in 1839 for the manufacture of wagons and carriages. In 1864 the company began also the manufacture of horse drawn street railway cars and eventually electric trolleys well into the early 1900s. Was located where Valente's Restaurant and Red's field is now situated between 8th and 9th streets. The Jones Works was amply attested to by the international volume of its business. Established by J. M. and Richard Jones as successor to the family wagon company. It was reorganized in 1886 as the J. M. Jones' Sons Car Co. and began building electric streetcars, some 300 per year. The J. M. Jones Car Works Company incorporated in 1911. It went out of business about 1912. It appears that for a short time they were in Schenectady. Following are some of the products they made as well as some advertisements and published mentions of them in various trade journals.

J. M. JONES & CO.'S STREET CAR MANUFACTORY, WEST TROY, NEW YORK.

This trolley ran from Albany to Warrensburg New York. Trolley has "Hudson Valley Railway" and "43" written on the side. Resting on the ground in front of the trolley is a sign that says, "Built By J. M. Jones' Sons West Troy N.Y." Watervliet Library.

J. M. Jones' Sons of West Troy, N.Y. use Josephine D. Smith's lamps exclusively on the cars built by them, they say, *"for the reason they are the best in the market, the lamps continue to give our customers very good satisfaction and we are yet to record the first complaint."* — The Street Railway Journal, June 1885.

Jones car number 308.

HV Railway 20 at Jones Shop.

Walter Jones, of the Jones Car Works, West Troy, N.Y. has returned from an extended European trip, much improved in heath. — The Street Railway Journal, Dec. 1885.

Jones open trolley Consolidated car 403.

Jones 601.

J. M. Jones' Sons turn over their Schenectady shops to the New York Central Sleeping Car Company July 1, having sold them to that company some weeks since. — The Street Railway Journal, July 1885.

J. M. Jones's Sons, West Troy, have just delivered to the Brooklyn City Railway four elegant cars for the Fort Hamilton steam road. These care have improved tracks, vacuum brakes and all the modern improvements. — The Street Railway Journal, July, 1885.

Jones 702 in 1906.

Jones 690 Suburban.

The Woodland Ave & West Side St. RR Co of Cleveland, Ohio have recently completed a slated roofed frame barn for one hundred horses; and added three open cars to their rolling stock. The cars are twenty-four foot length, manufactured by J. J. Jones's sons, West Troy, N.Y. The Street Railway Journal, June 1885.

Jones Open Trolley. HV Railway #23 in front of the plant located near Red's Field, Port Schuyler.

shown the change from wild life to manufactures, commerce, science, sculpture, painting, music and mining. In the dome is represented the discoverer of the New World with an olive branch, and a Goddess of Plenty with roses.

The seats and backs of the car are covered with old gold color silk plush, upholstered with the finest quality of curled hair. The curtains are of ivory and gold satin damask, and the sides of the car contain mirrors in white

FIG. 7.—JONES CLOSED CAR—WORLD'S FAIR.

and gold hand carved frames. The doors are of choice selected mahogany, and the floor is covered with wooden slat, flexible, roll up mats. The trimmings are of gold plate, and the car is lighted with two three light, combination oil and electroliers with two electric lamps. For summer use the doors can be removed, and storm curtains, operating on spring rollers, be employed, giving all the advantages of an open end summer car.

The roof is of the Brownell improved, patented truss form, the outside side sections being made of three ply veneer in one piece, glued and screwed to the carlines, making, it is claimed, the lightest and strongest roof possible. The roof is also equipped with the Brownell patented trolley bridge.

The platforms are circular with a wide nose piece, and the steps are of solid wrought metal with rubber pads. The drawbars are of the Brownell improved radial pattern with I beam slider, and the truck the Brownell improved non-oscillating electric motor truck. The exterior of the car is finished in cadmium yellow and white, with the lettering of gold in pure Empire design, harmonizing with the patterns of the curtains, rugs and carvings.

The manufacturers have taken special pains to prevent glaring incongruities in details and have certainly secured elegance of appearance.

EXHIBIT OF J. M. JONES' SONS COMPANY.

The exhibit of J. M. Jones' Sons, West Troy, N. Y., is located in the street railway department in the Transportation annex. The space is designated as L. N. 14.15. The exhibit comprises a closed and an open car of the company's standard types. The former is an eighteen foot car body framed and wired for electric service, and is mounted on a Taylor improved electric truck with seven foot wheel base. There are six mahogany window frames on each side, the windows being French plate glass. The interior is honestly constructed in solid mahogany throughout, without any special attempts at ornamentation, as the car is meant for regular service. The ceiling is quartered oak decorated with colors, and, divided into three sections by mahogany moulding, has an extremely handsome appearance. Hand carved and well finished mouldings combine to enhance the general effect. The seats and backs are upholstered in blue plush with hair filling, making them exceedingly comfortable for the passengers. Burrows curtain fixtures are used, and the curtains are blue and gold. Willson ventilators, which enable the conductors to adjust the openings of the vents in accordance with the requirements, are employed. Light russet hand straps on bronze poles enable the unfortunate standing passengers to maintain their equilibrium when the car is rounding curves. Double doors, so arranged that both are opened or closed as the case may be when either is moved, provide ample exit and entrance. The platforms are commodious, and are designed to carry a large number of passengers. The main body panels on the sides and ends are finished in blue with bronze borders, and gold striping. The bottom panels, of orange, harmonize with excellent effect. The contrast with the mahogany sash and blue panels is very effective. The trimmings of the car inside and out are of solid bronze polished. Fittings include radial drawbars, wall iron buffers, Willson's improved sand box, Jones' ratchet brake handle, Jones' window strips, West End trolley, foot gongs and signal bells, Smith electric lamps and shades, the shades being so attractive that some kleptomaniac with an eye to the beautiful could not resist the temptation of confiscating them recently.

The open car has five reversible and four back to back seats. It and wired for electric service, and is mounted on a Bemis truck, with seven foot wheel base. The interior is finished in natural wood, making it appear light and summer like. The ceilings are white birch decorated with cherry mouldings. The reversible seat backs are maple with maple spindles, while the back to back seats are paneled in cherry. There are three drop sashes with French plate glass at each end. Leather covered link chains extending from pillar to pillar resist the efforts of the passengers who insist upon leaving the car at the wrong side. Snaps in the center disjoin the chains when necessary. There are brown roller curtains, which are adjustable and run in guides, so that they do not flap in the wind. There are seven stationary vents on each side enclosing glass with a white and orange design, the center and end vents, as in the head bearing the words: "The Jones Car." The panels are painted a medium tan with gold edging and design. The sills are painted olive. Solid bronze trimmings are used inside and out.

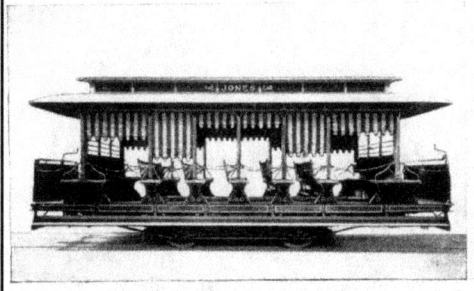

FIG. 8.—JONES OPEN CAR—WORLD'S FAIR.

The Troy City Railway Company has applied for permission to change its motive power to electricity on its White Line branch between this city, Green Island and Cohoes. The company also has ordered from the Jones Car Works, West Troy, fifteen closed cars, to be delivered by September 1. — The Street Railway Journal, International Edition, Volume 11. 1909.

Examples of advertisements from the Jones Car Works. These usually appeared in city directories.

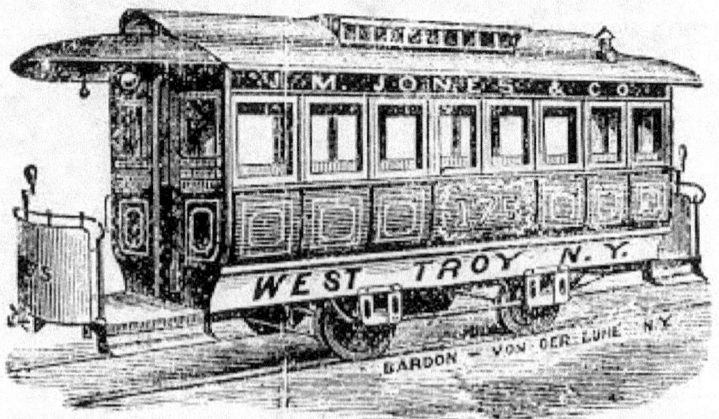

1884

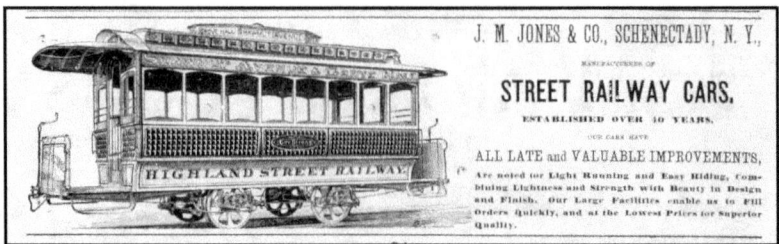

Advertisement in the National Car Builder Journal, 1870. March 1881 v.12: no.03 (1881-03).

According to the Schenectady Historical Society, *"The Jones Mfg. Co. came to Schenectady from West Troy (now Watervliet) in 1875, renting the premises of the Schenectady Car Co. for the manufacture of street cars. Soon after, the works were enlarged and they began the manufacture of drawing—room cars and sleepers, when E. Nott Schermerhorn was appointed Receiver and for eight months the business was continued by him. About the beginning of 1885 they were released to the New York Sleeping Car Co. which is at the present time the controller of the works (1886). The plant was located on Mill Lane. According to J. D. Thompson, The above account is not real clear as to what went on circa 1885, but apparently the Jones Co. in Schenectady was in financial trouble and in receivership. It's conceivable that Walter Jones could have gone back to Watervliet and reopened there under a slightly different name, or even that J. M. Jones Son's Co. could have stayed in Watervliet while J. M. Jones & Co. went to Schenectady, later changing its name to Jones Car Manufacturing Co. as in the ad of 1883. There are three different names that appear to be involved, so there might have been more than one company going concurrently."*

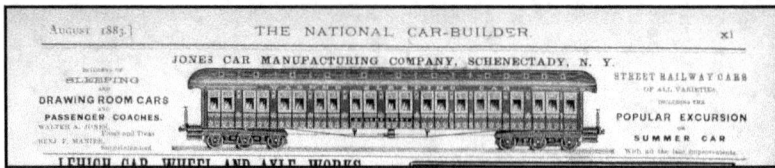

Advertisement in the National Car Builder Journal, 1883. v.14: no. 08 (1883-08).

This car was built by J. M. Jones Son's Co. of West Troy (now Watervliet) in 1893 and was awarded a prize at the conclusion of the World's Columbian Exposition held at Chicago, Ill May 1 to Oct 21-1893 Exposition. The Troy City Railway bought it and numbered it 222. When the United Traction Co absorbed the Troy City Railway it retained No 222. On June 30-1917 it was found with the former Cohoes City Ry #52 and became UT Center Entrance Car #922.

Jones Car 61 built in 1893.

Established 1839.

J. M. JONES' SONS,

Street Railway Car Builders, West Troy, N. Y.

Hudson Valley Railway #23. Waterford NY Covered Bridge.

HV Railway 115.

The Consolidated Street Railway Company, of Boston, are having built at the Jones car works, West Troy, N.Y., a few *specially* fine cars for their Back Bay series. *"The cars,"* says the Boston Herald, *"are to be of the most elegant design, and to surpass in workmanship and finish, any cars ever before built in this country."* The cars will be delivered on or about November next. — The Street Railway Journal, October 1885.

Troy Car - Hudson Valley Railroad - John L. Loughlin, conductor; Tim Sweeney, motorman.

Page 716 of *Electric Railway Journal* (1908). Pittsburgh Exhibit—View Showing Old-Style Car, Samples of Track Construction and Moving Picture Cabinet long was the average ride ten years ago and how long is the average ride now? A 5-cent fare in hilly Pittsburgh amounts to only one-half as much per passenger mile as a5-cent fare in most level cities. The well-known low-floor car of the Pittsburgh Railways.

Pittsburgh Exhibit—View Showing Steel Trail Car and Various Types of Motors and Controllers Fourteen obsolete types could not be found. Can you think of any other business requiring a change in the type of its equipment twenty-nine times in twenty-five years? Over an old-time horse car was a sign reading: How we rode twenty-five years ago and forgot to kick. Method of heating, straw to knees; method of lighting, tallow was included in the exhibit, and on it were signs reading:Fifty new motor cars are ordered like this except that they will have cross seats and front door exits. These will be the lightest single-deck motor cars ever built per seated passenger. Take a look at the Pittsburgh Railways Company's baby controller inside and note the seating space saved. 694 ELECTRIC RAILWAY JOURNAL [Vol. XLII, No. 15. CONVERTIBLE CAR WITH STEEL UNDERFRAME J. M. Jones Sons Company, Watervliet, N. Y., announces a new convertible car which it asserts has all the advantages and none of the disadvantages.

The plant of the Jones Car Company, at West Troy, N.Y., is to be increased by a large addition. This will double the capacity of the works, which are now overtaxed. The new plant will be in readiness for use by spring. — The Iron Age, 1891.

Advertising page in the December 1893 issue of The Street Railway Journal.

UTC 340 at Jones Car builders in Watervliet.

The Jones Car Works, West Troy, are building ten cars for the Rochester City (N.Y.) & Brighton R.R.; 16 for the Detroit (Mich.,) Ry. Co, and five for the Charles River Railway Co., of Boston, all of which are equipped with Lewis & Fowler's Randall gear. — The Street Railway Journal, Feb., 1885.

Mr. J. E. Rugg, Superintendent Highland Street Railway, Boston, Mass., writes us that "the Highland Street Railway Co. have added eight new cars to its different lines during the past winter, all having the Higby gear and Everett sash, and made by J. M. Jones' Sons, West Troy, N.Y." — The Street Railway Journal, Apr., 1885.

The Toronto (Can) Street Railway Co. is extending its line and has ordered a lot of American cars, we understand, of West Troy make. The consolidation of the West Side and Woodland Ave roads in Cleveland has been consummated, and a number of cars are being added. They are built by Jones, West Troy. — The Street Railway Journal, Apr., 1885.

The J. M. Jones' Sons. of West Troy, New York, are continuing to carry on the building of all kinds of street cars in the same conscientious manner which has always characterized an establishment which has been in operation over fifty years. The quality and finish of their work is too well known to require other mention than it is "Jones," of Troy." — The Street Railway Review, 1891.

The street car works of John M. Jones' Sons, at West Troy, N.Y., has shut down, and 350 men are idle. — Iron Trade Review, 1894.

Jones horse-drawn streetcar, about 1875. Maker: J. M. Jones and Sons, West Troy (Watervliet), New York.

Height is 120 inches. Width: 83 inches. Wheelbase: 97 inches. Overall length: 213 inches. Number of horses: 1. Number of passengers: seats 16. New York's Brooklyn City Railroad ran this car on its line between Hunters Point in Long Island City, and Erie Basin in South Brooklyn. From the Collections of The Henry Ford. Gift of the Brooklyn City Railroad Company.

Jones horse-drawn streetcar, about 1875. Maker: J. M. Jones and Sons, West Troy (Watervliet), New York.

"Burlington Traction Company" and "50" written on the side. Resting on the ground in front of the trolley is a sign that says, "Built By J. M. Jones' Sons Company." Watervliet Library.

J. M. JONES' SONS, car manufacturers, Circle Street, north of Berlin Street. John M. Jones, the father of the members of the firm, with Henry W. Witbeck, under the name of Witbeck & Jones, in 1839, began the manufacture of carriages and wagons, in a frame building, afterward burned, on the site of the present works. During the first years of gold mining in California, the firm made and shipped a great number of lumber and express wagons around Cape Horn to San Francisco. On Henry W. Witbeck's withdrawal in 1863, George H. Lawrence became associated for a short time with J. M. Jones in the business. In 1864, the firm of Jones & Co. was formed by J. M. and Richard W. Jones. In 1874, it was succeeded by that of J. M. Jones & Co.; the two sons John H. and Walter A. Jones engaging in the business with their father. In 1879, the business was discontinued in West Troy. In the spring of 1882, John H. and Walter A. Jones resumed in West Troy the manufacture of street-cars begun by Jones & Lawrence in 1864. Thousands of street-cars have been made at these works for different railway companies in the United States, South America, Australia, England, Germany, India, and other distant countries. In 1870, two hundred were made for the Bombay Tramway Company. During the civil war many gun carriages were made for the United States government. About 300 street-cars are now annually made by the firm, which employs about 200 skilled workmen.

The City of Troy and its Vicinity. Arthur Weise, 1886.

Electric freight locomotive.

J. M. Jones & Company

Jones car 838 postcard.

THUMBNAIL SKETCH of the HUDSON VALLEY RAILWAY COMPANY
Contributed to CERA Data Sheet Series
by James M. Slattery, Albany, N.Y.

For 43 years a most important transportation service for Glens Falls and surrounding communities and a favorite means of travel from the capital area (Albany) into the lower Adirondacks is the concise description of the Hudson Valley Railway given by the Glens Falls Times in an article published in 1939 reviewing that city's growth over the past century. The Hudson Valley Railway was formed of the consolidation of the Glens Falls, Sandy Hill and Fort Edward St. R.R. Co., the Saratoga Northern Ry., the Warren County Ry., the North River R.R. Co., the Stillwater and Mechanicsville St. Ry. Co., the Greenwich and Schuylerville Else. R.R. and the Saratoga Traction Company.

The original company, the Glens Falls Sandy Hill and Fort Edward, began operation with horse cars on narrow gage track in 1885. In 1891 the line was electrified and extensions. made, but it did not become the Hudson Valley Railway until 1901. In this year the line to Lake George was opened and extended to Warrensburg. The next extension was to Waterford. In 1903 Saratoga Springs was reached and a belt line and additional city lines were opened in Glens Falls. The final extension was from Saratoga Springs to the main line at Mechanicsville via Ballston Spa, and paralleling the Schenectady Railway line for part of this distance. In 1906 the system was acquired by the Delaware & Hudson Railroad, a prominent steam road operator of traction properties. The Company had 128 miles of track, 4' – 8 ½" gage, 150 cars, and employed 500 persons at its peak. By trackage rights south of Waterford on the United Traction Company its cars reached Troy, where connections were made with the Schenectady Railway for Schenectady, the UT to Albany, and thence via Albany Southern to Hudson. Hourly service was operated with single cars during the winter, with half-hourly and even 15 minute service on some lines during the summer peaks. crowds flocking to see the battlegrounds at Saratoga and Lake George t the Schuylerville monument and the many other points of scenic and historical interest along the road.

POWER SYSTEM:
The Hudson Valley Railway operated on the usual 625 v. direct current system and had power stations at Stillwater, Saratoga, Middle Falls and Warrensburg. Substations were located at Queensbury, Lake George, Wilton, Round Lake, Thomson and Saratoga, and were operated from a 22, 000 v. transmission line at the uncommon frequency of 40 cycles per second.

ROLLINGSTOCK:
The cars used on the interurban lines were mostly light suburban types, built chiefly by Jones Car Co.
and other nearby builders, but there were several large heavy cars, like #50 illustrated on the opposite side of this data Sheet. This car was built by Niles Car Co. Car shops were located at Queensbury, Stillwater and Saratoga.

FREIGHT SERVICE:
A general freight business was done by the company, for which it had 3 box and 3 flat cars of 50,000 lb. capacity and had interchange connections with steam roads as follows: Boston &Maine, Saratoga and Stillwater Jct.; Delaware & Hudson, Bloody Pond, Glens Falls and Saratoga Springs; Greenwich & Johnsonville, at Thomson.
At Left: Car 66 at Sarat068- Springs terminal of Hudson Valley
Railway and Schenectady Ry. on the last day of operation of the Hudson Valley line. Dec 1, 1928

CERA Data Sheet
March 15, 1940

UTC (United Traction Company) 803, Watervliet. Albany-Cohoes.

Jones car number 191.

At the Jones car works, four new electric cars are being constructed for the Watervliet Turnpike and Railroad company.

Four new electric cars are being built at the Jones car works, West Troy, for the Troy and Lansingburgh Street Railroad company. They will be used on the Green line road.— The Argus, November 18, 1889.

Jones car United Traction Co, Number 505.

Albany-West Troy Turnpike Jones trolley.

"The Jones Mfg. Co. came to Schenectady from West Troy (now Watervliet) in 1875, renting the premises of the Schenectady Car Co. for the manufacture of street cars. Soon after, the works were enlarged and they began the manufacture of drawing—room cars and sleepers, when E. Nott Schermerhorn was appointed Receiver and for eight months the business was continued by him. About the beginning of 1885 they were released to the New York Sleeping Car Co. which is at the present time the controller of the works (1886). The plant was located on Mill Lane." — SCHS, 1968

Car Number 5 for the Herkimer, Ilion, & Frankfort El. RY.

Car Number 180, 9 Watervliet, Troy and Albany. "Have Correct Fare Ready."

After an idleness of about seven weeks the Jones car works at West Troy partly resumed operations yesterday. In the neighborhood of 230 men were put back to work and, it is expected, that in a few weeks the plant will be in full operation. The Jones car works is one of West Troy's leading industries and the resumption of business will be good news to many. About five hundred men will be at work again in a short time. — The Argus, March 13, 1894.

The National Car-Builder, March, 1881. Ad when Jones was in Schenectady for a few years.

A Car Company's Probable Purchase.

Yesterday's Schenectady *Union* says:

Edward G. Gilbert and another gentleman, representing the Gilbert car company, arrived from Troy on the 3:30 o'clock train this afternoon, and were met by the owners of the Jones car works, who immediately went with them to the works for further inspection. The Gilbert car company have offered to buy the Jones car works, but they have not, so one of the owners said this afternoon, made a definite proposal. The owners of the Jones car works held a meeting this afternoon, but took no action relative to selling to the Gilbert company. The owners received the deed of the property and thereby took formal possession. The Gilbert car company have procured materials for building an extension to their works, and it is said they will immediately build at Green Island or buy or lease the Jones car works.

The Schenectady *Star* adds:

Mr. Gilbert arrived here this afternoon, and was met at the law office of A. P. Strong by Edward Ellis and Garrett Veeder, representing the bondholders of the Jones works. Their business was conducted in secret, and reporters were informed that they could obtain no information until a settlement was arrived at. At 4:30 o'clock no result had yet been reached. One of the trustees of the Jones works told a *Star* reporter, however, that at a meeting held last evening the affairs of the works were so arranged that the representatives could "talk business" to-day, and he thought a sale would be effected.

The negotiations for the lease—with the privilege of purchasing—of the Jones car works at Schenectady by the Gilbert manufacturing company of Green Island will probably be concluded to-day. The proposition of the Gilbert company yesterday was satisfactory to the representatives of the bondholders of the Jones car-works, and will probably be approved by all the bondholders, which will complete the lease. The establishment of a branch manufactory at Schenectady by the Gilbert company will not decrease the volume of business at the Green Island establishment, which would have been enlarged had the Jones works not been leased or purchased.

Troy Daily Times, November 17, 1886

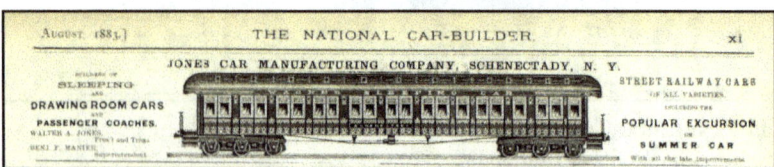

PIONEER CAR MAKER.

John H. Jones of Watervliet Is Dead—Builder of Horse Cars Crosses Into Great Beyond—Had Long Been Prominent in the Civic Affairs of Watervliet.

John H. Jones, Vice President of the Watervliet National Bank and one of the pioneer builders of horse cars in the United States, died yesterday afternoon at the Samaritan Hospital, where he had been undergoing treatment for the last three weeks. For the last few months Mr.

JOHN H. JONES.

Jones had been in failing health, but his condition did not become alarming until three weeks ago.

Mr. Jones was born in the old village of West Troy December 2, 1842, and had always been a resident of Watervliet, where during his entire life he had always taken an active part in that city's welfare. Mr. Jones was educated in the public schools in the old village of West Troy, and when a young man started in the business of building horse cars. A company was organized as the J. M. Jones Car Works, of which company he was elected President and Treasurer. For more than fifty years cars made at the Jones Car Works were known throughout the world. Ten years ago the plant was closed, and since that time Mr. Jones retired from active business. In the early history of the Jones Car Works stage coaches were first made, while during the Civil War the concern received an order from the War Department at Washington to manufacture gun carriages. During Mr. Jones's connection with the car-building industry, he became identified with many street railway corporations in various parts of the state, and for many years was a Director of the National City Bank of Troy. Mr. Jones traveled extensively during the early car-building days at his plant, visiting practically every large city in the United States and Canada. Mr. Jones was also identified with The Averill Park Land company and The Quedar Park Land Company of Watervliet. When the South Dutch Reformed Church was located in Port Schuyler Mr. Jones took an active interest in the affairs of the church. In politics Mr. Jones was a Republican, and forty-five years ago was elected a Trustee in the old village of West Troy. At one time Mr. Jones was also a member of the Electric Light Commission of Watervliet.

The survivors include his wife, who was formerly Miss Ella C. Miller of Niskayuna; three sons, John M. Jones of Washington, D. C.; Floyd R. and Paul Jones of Watervliet; two daughters, Miss Anna W. Jones and Miss Ella Jones, and a grandson, Paul Jones, Jr., all of Watervliet.

The funeral will take place Friday afternoon at 2:30 o'clock from his home, 734 Fourth Avenue. The service will be conducted by Rev. John G. Menges of Schenectady, a former Watervliet pastor. Burial will take place in the Albany Rural Cemetery. The flag on the Watervliet National Bank was placed at half staff yesterday afternoon.

During the erection of the new bank, Mr. Jones took an active interest, daily visiting the building, supervising the construction of the building. Mr. Jones for many years was a member of the Troy Club.

A new sixty-horse power engine has been placed in the Jones car works. Harry Peobles, superintendent at the Jones car works, has resigned his position to accept a similar one in a western car works — The Argus, April 25, 1887.

The Troy Times, January 17, 1923

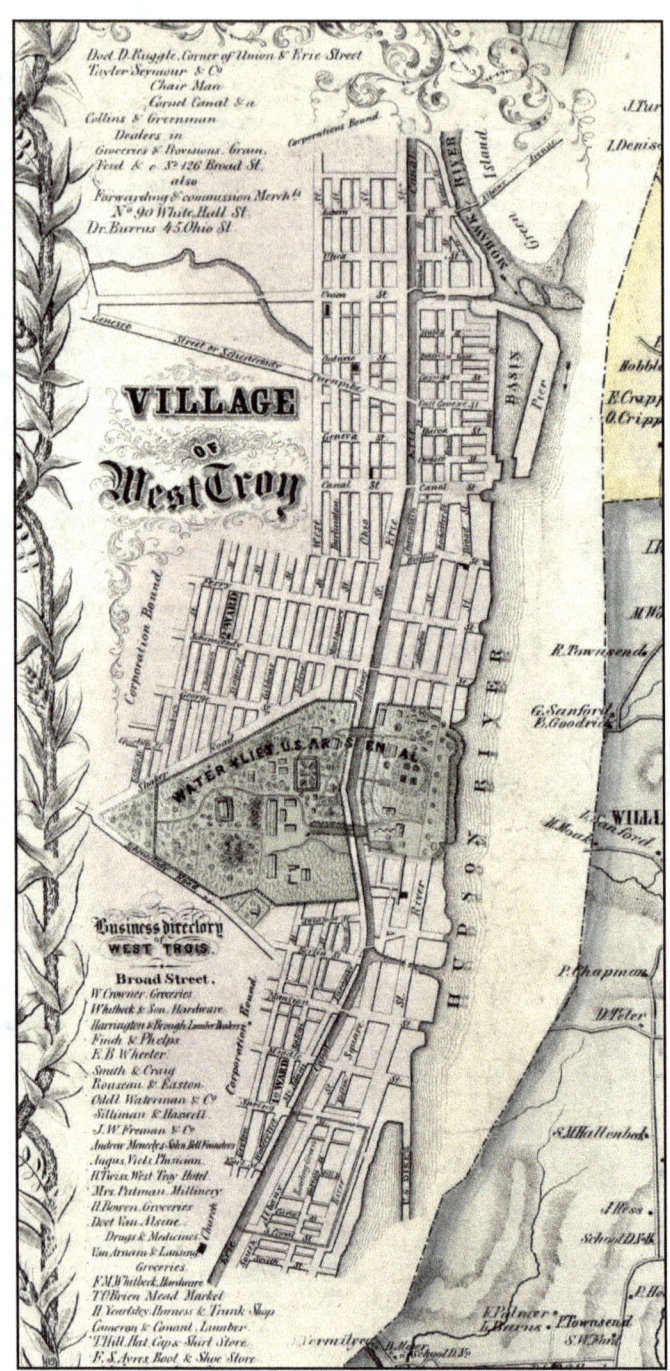

Floods

The name Watervliet is of Dutch origin from water and *vlakte* meaning level plains or flats. The level lands or flats along the Hudson River were and are subject to overflowing in time of freshets. The two reasons for flooding in our area and specifically to Watervliet in the early years was the overflowing of the Hudson River and overflow of a generally dry stream called the Dry River which ran diagonally through what we call uptown Watervliet. This stream meandered from northwest of 23rd Street to the Hudson River in the vicinity of the Northeast corner of the Arsenal (see map on previous page). This dry river drained much of the North slope of the Town of Colonie, including much of Latham east of Route 9 north to Boght Road. During heavy rain fall events water flowing down the hill would cause flooding several times a year. The solution to the Hudson River Overflow?

The main tributary to the Hudson River is the Sacandaga River which carries drainage from the North Country. Heavy rains and rapid snow melts during the course of the year caused major flooding of the Hudson. In 1930 this river (Sacandaga) was damned at Conklingville creating a huge reservoir now called "The Great Sacandaga Lake." The Hudson River Black River Authority regulates the level, lowering in the fall of the year to accommodate the surge of flow in the spring months. They can then release water through the dam maintaining a safe level during the summer months, Cities in our area to this day pay a stipend to the HRBR for their service. Solving the Dry River overflow Problems? Completion of the Dry River System to alleviate flooding occurred in 1912. This system is a storm water detention system, that detains storm water safely outside the city and releases it slowly after the rains have stopped. Two dams were constructed west of the City. An earthen dam and a concrete one to pool and distribute the surge from the high grounds and discharge at a rate to eliminate flooding in the city. Secondly the Dry River was eliminated by installation of an underground conduit system that carried the controlled flows from the dams and eventually runs under 21st Street to a concrete outfall at the Hudson River. This discharge structure is visible from the Congress Street Bridge located in the vicinity of Hudson Shore Park. Both the dams and conduit system are continually monitored by the City of Watervliet.

Major Floods in the Northeast and Capital District occurred many times from the 17th Century to modern times and many affected our area. Here are a few:

January 1949. A New Year's Day storm resulted in flooding principally in the Hudson Valley. In Troy it rose over 11 feet. Over 20 feet in Cohoes. No date for Watervliet but flooded nonetheless.

March 1936. Heavy Rain and melting snow caused major flooding throughout the Northeast and Middle Atlantic states.

November 1927. Significant flood on the Hudson River at Albany, 15.96 feet. Flooding was the result of rains from the remains of a late season hurricane.

March 24-29, 1913. Major flooding in the Northeast. Troy at 29.7 feet on the Hudson River. In Albany, 21.53 ft. In Watervliet, the angry waters reached five feet deep in some streets and some 1780 acres were flooded. In Troy, burst gas lines ignited fires that raged through downtown, leaving smoking ruins after flooding 500 acres and in Albany some 530 acres were flooded.

Overall major floods occurred in Watervliet in 1857, 1886, 1900, 1902, 1913, 1936, 1949, and 1977.

March 28, 1913, flood. Top photo marked. 14th Street and Second Avenue looking west in an area known as "Andrewsville" (It is incorrect on the photo). Notice the boat pulled up to the bridge with two people in the boat and one on the bridge perhaps stranded and waiting rescue. Andersonville was named after William Andrews, Jr., who created a settlement of ninety cottages where a person could lease a home at a reasonable rent with no other tenant to bother them. His father was a school teacher in Gibbonsville in 1824 and had a grocery store corner of Water and Ferry Sts (Broadway & 14th St.)

Unknown date and location. Probably the flood of 1913.

FLOOD SCENE ON THE HUDSON RIVER
THE FLOOD AT WATERVLIET, NEW YORK, SHOWING BUILDINGS TORN FROM THEIR FOUNDATIONS FLOATING DOWN THE RIVER

The Watervliet basin, 23rd St from Ferry house and many buildings under water. Some buildings and boats swept away. More than a quarter of million people were left homeless due to the 1913 flood. It ranks second to the Johnstown Flood of 1889 as one of the deadliest.

March 28, 1913, Flood. Intersection of 14th Street and 1st Ave. At the end of the block is the Troy Cold Storage building.

Unknown date and location.

1913 Flood. 16th Street and Broadway. American Grocery Co. store shown. Notice the submerged horse head hitching post at the curb of the submerged street.

March 28, 1913, flood. Intersection of 19th Street and Broadway. Irving C. Dater as a salesman who lived in Lansingburgh at 242 Second Ave. He sold flour, feed, grain, hay, and straw. Looking west from Congress St Bridge. A party on April 10, 1913, for flood victims in Watervliet where 400 people showed up raised $1,300 for flood sufferers.

1913 Flood. 23rd St looking east and canal flooded.

March 28, 1913, Flood. Looking east on 19th Street from top of canal bridge. Congress Street bridge in the center at the end. T. Richardson's Sons Coal on the right.

There are 461 properties in Watervliet that have greater than a 26% chance of being severely affected by flooding over the next 30 years. This represents 14% of all properties in the neighborhood.

In addition to damage on properties, flooding can also cut off access to utilities, emergency services, transportation, and may impact the overall economic well-being of an area.
Overall, Watervliet has a major risk of flooding over the next 30 years, which means flooding is likely to impact day to day life within the community — FloodFactor

1913 Flood. Unknown location.

1913 flood. Bridge over the Erie Canal.

'The greatest freshet 'since the time of Noah,' swept through West Troy, flooding the streets... — The Advocate, February 11, 1857

March 28, 1913, Flood. Looking south from 15th St and 1st Ave. The second house from the North Reformed Church with extended window was the residence of the Meneely Bell family.

March 28, 1913, Flood. Looking east on 16th Street. The Sans Souci Theater (later Family Theater), "The Strand of Watervliet" and Rowell Groceries is on the right. Bottom photo is the same view but showing the North side. The expression on the man's face tells it all.

The Flood. 16th Street. Unknown street but stranded trolley cars are on the right.

March 28, 1913, Flood. 16th Street. The Collins House on the right. The Collins House was the former Exchange Hotel. From 1838 Cloe Powell was manager. The Collins house became property of John A. Patten's sons, Joseph E and Mark Patten around 1860.

March 28, 1913, Flood. 16th Street. Top and bottom view of the Collins House (former Exchange Hotel). The bar on the left sold Boulton's Ale and Beverwyck beer, both locally brewed. In early November 1927 more than 300 dwellings and places of business on Broadway from 23rd Street on the North to the extreme lower section of Broadway were damaged by a flood. Arsenal City saw the roadway and sidewalk in front covered with three feet of water.

Notice the men on the second floor porch of the Collins House.

Dec. 31, 1948 flood. The peak stage at Albany was 17. 9 Ft, which was slightly lower than in 1936 and 3. 6ft lower than in 1913. The newly constructed Sacandaga Reservoir (1930) helped prevent larger floods. Troy saw a flood of 27.05 feet. Previously on March 19, 1936, flood water inundated the Port Schuyler section at the southern end of the city and more than a score of families abandoned their homes. Police or other officials were not called for aid in evacuating.

Coast Guard Station on Broadway near Arsenal. Dec. 31, 1948.

Watervliet Arsenal 1913 flood. View from bridge over the Erie Canal. Buildings 40 and 41 are to the left.

1913 flood. Hudson River flood in March of 1913. Looking north. Erie Canal is on the left. Building 41 and a shed are on the left. Three wings of building 40 are on the right. Horse near bridge.

1913 flood. Bridge over the canal. On February 18, 1884, a Kentucky paper reported that people of West Troy, on the East side of Broadway were flooded out.

Flood. No date.

Flood. No date.

Flood. No date.

Flood. No date.

Flood. No date. Young girl's expression is priceless.

www.ingramcontent.com/pod-product-compliance
Lightning Source LLC
Chambersburg PA
CBHW050732240426
43665CB00053B/2215

CAPT. ROBERT McCLURE'S COMPANY

Of Mounted Volunteers, belonging to the 5th Regiment, commanded by Col. James Johnson, of the Brigade of Mounted Volunteers of Illinois Militia commanded by Brig.-Gen. Samuel Whitesides. Mustered out of service of the United States, at the mouth of Fox river, Illinois, on May 27th, 1832; distance 130 miles from the place of enrollment.

Name and Rank.	Residence.	Enrolled	Remarks.
Captain.		1832.	
Robert McClure	McLean Co.	May 4.	
First Lieutenant.			
John H. S. Rhodes	"	"	
Second Lieutenant.			
Thomas Glenn	"	"	
Sergeants.			
Chaney Thomas	"	"	
Charles S. Dorsey	"	"	
Eli Frankeberger	"	"	
James G. Reyburn	"	"	
Corporals.			
David Maxiell	"	"	
Levi Danley	"	"	
John W. Brown	"	"	
Owen Chaney	"	"	
Privates.			
Ashburn, Jesse	"	"	
Benson, John	"	"	
Benson, James	"	"	
Baker, Elliott H	"	"	
Barr, James	"	"	
Baker, Jonathan	"	"	
Bemington, Joseph	"	"	
Burns, Wm	"	"	
Bowman, Thadius	"	"	
Ball, Henry	"	"	
Blair, Wm	"	"	
Copes, Jacob	"	"	
Chaney, Ebenezer	"	"	
Damal, Dundren	"	"	
Davis, Davis	"	"	
Dixon, Elisha	"	"	
Davidson, John E	"	"	
Ewing, Phineas	"	"	
Fordico, John	"	"	
Hamley, Henry	"	"	
Hamilton, Absalom	"	"	
Howard, Madison	"	"	
Harrison, Henry H			Served 5 days, pilot, Dixon to mouth of Fox.
Lane, Harrison	McLean Co.	May 4.	
Lundy, Nicholas	"	"	
Miller, Anderson	"	"	
McCord, Thomas A	"	"	
Moore, Josiah	"	"	
Martin, Mathew	"	"	
Oatman, Jesse	"	"	
Patrick, Allen	"	"	
Rogers, Thomas	"	"	
Ruth, Nathan	"	"	
Scott, Martin	"	"	
Wright, William G	"	"	

Capt. I. C. Pugh's Company

Of Mounted Volunteers, belonging to the 5th Regiment, commanded by Col. James Johnson, of the Brigade of Mounted Volunteers of Illinois Militia commanded by Brig.-Gen. Samuel Whitesides. Mustered out of the service of the United States, at the mouth of Fox river, in the State of Illinois, on May 27, 1832; distance 150 miles from the place of enrollment.

Name and Rank.	Residence.	Enrolled	Remarks.
Captain.	Macon Co.	1832.	
James Johnson	Decatur, Ill.	April 24.	Promoted May 16, 1832, to Colonel
First Lieutenant.			
William Warnick	"	"	Absent with leave
Second Lieutenant.			
I. C. Pugh	"	"	Promoted to Captain May 16, 1832
Sergeants.			
John D. Wright	"	"	Absent on extra duty
James A. Ward	"	"	Promoted to 2d Lieutenant May 16
Walter Bowles	"	"	Absent with leave
Joseph Hauks	"	"	
Corporals.			
Henry M. Gorm	"	"	
Stephen R. Shepherd	"	"	
Geo. Copperberger	"	"	Absent with leave
James Milton	"	"	Killed in battle
Privates.			
Adams, William	"	"	Absent with leave
Bell, Alexander W.	"	"	
Black, Abraham	"	"	
Butler, Elisha	"	"	Absent with leave
Black, Jacob	"	"	
Clifton, John	"	"	" " "
Cox, William	"	"	
Clifton, Josiah	"	"	" " "
Dickey, Jesse	"	"	Wounded
Dewees, Sam. B.	"	"	
Davenport, Thomas	"	"	Absent with leave
Ennis, James	"	"	
Hauks, John	"	"	
Henderson, John	"	"	Absent with leave
Herrod, James	"	"	
Hooper, Obediah	"	"	" " "
Hauks, William	"	"	
Hooper, William	"	"	" " "
Ingram, Kinian	"	"	
Lane, Jacob	"	"	Absent on extra duty
McCall, Daniel	"	"	
Miller, James	"	"	
Miller, Sam	"	"	
Miller, William	"	"	
Manley, John	"	"	
Murphy, John	"	"	
Querry, James	"	"	
Simpson, Asher	"	"	
Steward, David H.	"	"	Absent on extra duty
Smallwood, Geo. D.	"	"	
Smith, Robert	"	"	
Troxel, Sam	"	"	
Williams, John	"	"	Absent with leave

Capt. John G. Adams' Company

Of Mounted Volunteers, belonging to the 5th Regiment, commanded by Col. James Johnson, of the Brigade of Mounted Volunteers commanded by Brig.-Gen. Samuel Whitesides. Mustered out of the service of the United States at the mouth of Fox river, in the State of Illinois, on May 17, 1832.

Name and Rank.	Residence.	Enrolled	Remarks.
Captain.		1832.	
John G. Adams	Pekin, Ill	April 27	Killed in battle May 14, 1832.
First Lieutenant.			
Benj. Briggs	"	"	Absent on escort of family
Second Lieutenant.			
Jno. O. Hyde	"	"	Able for duty
Sergeants.			
Micheil Reeder	"	"	Able for duty
James Wright	"	"	Escaped in battle, by orders
Seth Wilson	"	"	Able for duty
John Ford	"	"	"
Corporals.			
Henry Cline	"	"	Able for duty
Conaway Rhodes	"	"	On duty
Hurtside Hittle	"	"	
D. Hanger	"	"	On escort of family
Privates.			
Alexander, David	"	"	On duty
Alexander, David	"	"	Appointed Paymaster
Berry, Phenis	"	"	On duty
Ballard, Jacob	"	"	
Briggs, Thomas	"	"	
Bomis, Eli	"	"	On furlough
Baxter, Samuel	"	"	On escort of family
Barlow, Jno. M.	"	"	On furlough
Council, Redick	"	"	On duty
Cullum, Green	"	"	
Cline, William	"	"	
Coffey, John	"	"	
Craig, Orison	"	"	
Conner, James	"	"	
Carter, Daniel	"	"	On furlough
Crain, Jas. W.	"	"	Appointed Adjutant
Dunbough, Pinkney	"	"	On duty
Drum, Abner	"	"	
Date, Jesse	"	"	On furlough
Evans, D. S.	"	"	Deserted May 16, 1832
Gordon, Geo.	"	"	On duty
Hughes, Geo. W.	"	"	
Haynes, Jonathan	"	"	
Hendricks, Wm. A.	"	"	
Henson, Samuel	"	"	
Harper, William	"	"	
Helme, Jonathan	"	"	On furlough
Judy, Jas.	"	"	Deserted May 16, 1832
Kreeps, David	"	"	Killed in battle May 14
Lewis, Bazwell	"	"	On furlough
Laudes, Joseph	"	"	On duty
Morgan, Reese	"	"	
McJenkins, Hugh	"	"	On escort of family
Maxwell, Ferdinand	"	"	On duty
McCann, Stephen T.	"	"	On furlough
Mendinall, Zadock	"	"	Killed in battle May 14, 1832
McKnight, Alex	"	"	Furlough
Orendorff, Benj	"	"	On duty
Paisley, Robt	"	"	
Paul, John	"	"	On escort of family
Perkins, Isaac	"	"	Killed in battle May 14
Ryon, Will	"	"	On duty
Reeder, Joseph	"	"	
Rickey, Samuel	"	"	On furlough
Ramsey, Wm	"	"	On duty
Summer, Jas	"	"	On furlough
Shoemaker, Elmore	"	"	On duty
Stout, Samuel	"	"	"
Williamson, Chapan	"	"	

SPY BATTALION.

Capt. John Dawson's Company

Of Mounted Volunteers, composing one of Spy Battalion, commanded by Major James D. Henry, in the service commanded by Brig.-Gen. Samuel Whitesides. Mustered out May 28, 1832.

Name and Rank.	Residence.	Enrolled	Remarks.
Captain.		1832.	
John Dawson.........	Sangam'n Co.	April 21.	
First Lieutenant.			
Wm. Dickroll	"	"	
Second Lieutenant.			
John Hornback......	"	"	
Sergeants.			
Corbin C. Judd	"	"	
Harrison McGary ...			
John Brewer.........			
John Retherford			On parole
Corporals.			
Thos. J. Knox........			
John Wright.........			
Seymour Vanmeter.			
Hugh McGary			
Privates.			
Brown, James........			
Bracken, John.......			
Black, Joseph........			
Bridges, John			
Burch, Benjamin....			Promoted to 2d Surg. Mate of Batt. April 26.
Barney, Lewis.......			
Burrett, Hugh			On parole
Brundage, Solomon.			
Clark, William.......			
Cherry, Benjamin...			
Churchill, Lewis			
Crane, William			
Dernon, Archelas ...			
Dickerson, David ...		April 21.	Trans. from com'y of Capt. Goodwin May 1.
Evans, Samuel			In place of John Critz
Foster, Squire			
Green, George........			
Glasscock, Geo. W..		April 21.	Trans. from com'y of Capt. Goodwin May 1.
Garrard, Joseph F..		"	"
Hornback, Jesse			
Harrison, Jesse M...			Promoted to Paymaster's Sergeant April 26.
Hughes, Robert			
Iles, Elijah			Trans. from Capt. Goodwin's com'y May 1
Jones, Edward		April 21.	
Killyon, Michael....			
Kelly, Jeremiah			
Killyon, Jacob.......			In place of Wm. Johnson
Keys, John		April 21.	Trans. from com'y of Capt. Goodwin May 1.
Kelly, Wm.			
Lucas, Geo. B.			
Lobb, Wm.			
Martin, John.........			
Monland, Zachariah.			
Minor, Joel			
Martin, Jacob........			

Name and Rank.	Residence.	Enrolled	Remarks.
		1832.	
Musick, John.........			
Martin, Jefferson....			
Morgan, Zaduck......		April 30.	
Matheny, Lorenzo D.		" 21.	Trans. from com'y of Capt. Goodwin May 1...
Oliphant, Ethelb'rt J.		" 21.	
Powell, Alphred......			
Potts, Wm. L.........		April 21.	Trans. from Capt. Goodwin's com'y May 1...
Pugh, Jonathan H...		" 30.	
Roger, John..........			
Reulno, John.........			
Ridgway, John.......			Discharged May 3............
Read, James M.......			
Reid, James F........		April 21.	Trans. from com'y of Capt. Goodwin May 1...
Reyborn, Joseph.....			
Strader, John C......			
Strickland, Clemons.			
Smith, James........			
Stone, Culohill......			
Short, Wm. B........		April 28.	
Stewart, John........		" 21.	Trans. from com'y of Capt. Goodwin May 1...
Sanders, Presley A...			
Scoggins, John.......			
Turley, Charles......			On parole...........
Taylor, James........		April 21.	Trans. from com'y of Capt. Goodwin May 1...
Venus, Adam.........			
Wade, Samuel........			
Williams, Jacob......			
Wages, Joseph.......			
White, Wm...........			
Ward, John..........			Discharged at Beardstown April 30.........
Warwick, Jacob G...			On parole............
Warwick, Montg'm'y			Promoted to Q. M. April 26, and on parole....

Capt. Thomas Carlin's Company

Of the Odd Battalion of Spies, commanded by Major James D. Henry, of the Brigade of Mounted Volunteers of Illinois commanded by Brigadier-General Samuel Whitesides. Mustered out of the service of the United States of America at the mouth of Fox river of the Illinois river on May 27, 1832; distant 230 miles from place of enrollment.

Name and Rank.	Residence.	Enrolled	Remarks.
		1832	
Captain.			
Thos. Carlin.........	Carrollton....	April 20	.............................▲...
First Lieutenant.			
Jesse V. Mounts.....	"	"	
Second Lieutenant.			
George D. Laurens..	"	"	
Sergeants.			
Mearel E. Ruttan....	"	"	Appointed Sergeant-Major April 28, 1832......
David Thurston.....	"	"	
James Gilliland.....	"	"	Attached to Capt. Chapman's Co. about Apr. 28
Harrison Boggess...	"	"	Lost horse night of May 22, 1832, by stampede
Corporals.			
Lewis B. Edwards...	"	"	
Josiah Ashlock.....	"	"	
William Cook.......	"	"	
William Finley	"	"	
Privates.			
Abner, Joshua......	"	"	
Ashlock, John......	"	"	
Banning, Williamson	"	"	
Bogers, Preston.....	"	"	Appointed 3d Sergt. April 28, 1832...........
Courtney, John.....	"	"	
Cook, John	"	"	
Carlin, James.......	"	"	
Crabb, Edward	"	"	

Name and Rank.	Residence.	Enrolled	Remarks.
Crane, Silas	Carrollton	April 20	
Dulaney, William H.	"	"	Appointed Surg. 2d Regt. April 30, Col. J. Fry
Dawdy, Howell	"	"	
Eldred, Elan	"	"	Appointed 1st Sergt. April 28, 1832
Eldred, Silas	"	"	
Edwards, Talbert	"	"	
Finley, Zuriah	"	"	
Gilliland, William	"	"	Attached to Capt. Chapman's Co. April 20, '32
Gibbs, Valentine A.	"	"	
Hoskins, William	"	"	
Hill, Jonathan	"	"	
Huitt, John, Jr.	"	"	
Huss, Samuel	"	"	Lost horse May 16, after forced m'ch to Dixon's
Herrick, Rheuben	"	"	
Hopper, Thomas	"	"	
Jackson, John	"	"	
King, Robert	"	"	
Linder, Joseph	"	"	
Linder, George	"	"	
Moore, James	"	"	
Moore, David	"	"	
Pinkerton, William	"	"	
Pinkerton, John F.	"	"	
Pinkerton, Henry B.	"	"	
Rattan, Larkin	"	"	
Reno, Philamon	"	"	
Reddish, John	Rock Island	May 10	
Short, James	Carrollton	April 20	
Scott, John W.	Beardstown	" 26	Det'hed on Exp. April 21; rejoined Co. May 15
Scott, Thomas D.	"	" 26	
Spencer, Roswell H	Rock Island	May 8	
Tunnel, Luther	"	" 10	Lost horse night of May 22, affright of horses
Tunnel, William	"	" 10	
Thackston, Sturlin	Carrollton	April 20	
Whiteside, William H	"	"	
Whiteside, John B.	"	"	
Williams, John C.	"	"	Never appeared after enrollment
Woodson, Joseph	Beardstown	April 26	App. Surg. to Spy Bat., Maj. Henry, April 28

CAPT. JOHN DEMENT'S COMPANY

Of the Odd Battalion of Spies, commanded by Maj. James D. Henry, of the Brigade of Mounted Volunteers of Illinois Militia commanded by Brig.-Gen. Samuel Whitesides. Mustered out of the service of the United States, at the mouth of Fox river, near Ottawa, on the 28th of May, 1832; distant from the place of enrollment 240 miles. Organized in Fayette county.

Name and Rank.	Residence.	Enrolled	Remarks.
Captain. John Dement	Fayette Co. Vandalia, Ill.	1832. April 20.	
First Lieutenant. Dem's'y Yarborough	"	"	
Second Lieutenant. Abraham Starns	"	"	
Sergeants. William Bradford	"	"	
Jos. Hickman	"	"	
Henry B. Roberts	"	"	
Joel Thomas	"	"	
Corporals. Wyatt B. Stapp	"	"	
T. N. Gains	"	"	
Isaac D. Taulbee	"	"	
Amos Eakle	"	"	

Name and Rank.	Residence.	Enrolled	Remarks.
Privates.	Fayette Co.	1832.	
Alley, James	Vandalia, Ill	April 20.	
Allen, Madison	"	"	
Blackwell, Robert	"	"	Sent on express May 15, 1832
Conner, Edward	"	"	
Coventry, John W	"	"	
Cole, Eldridge	"	"	
Duncan, Thomas	"	"	
Doolin, Daniel	"	"	
Dimond, G. W	"	"	
Duncan, Matthew	"	"	Promoted April 26, 1832, to Surg. Foot Bat'llon
Evans, Horatio	"	"	
Enos, Josiah	"	"	
Ewing, John	"	"	Sent on express May 15, 1832
Glass, Rody	"	"	
Ginger, M. C	"	"	
Green, Robert	"	"	
Hockett, Wm. I	"	"	
Harrington, John	"	"	
Hawkins, John B	"	"	
Hickerson, Geo. W	"	"	
Jones, Thomas	"	"	
Johnson, Henry	"	"	
Lee, Wm. H	"	"	
Leak, James P	"	"	
Moore, Benj. D	"	"	
Morrison, Wm. L. E	"	"	Appointed Adjt. of Spy Battalion April 26, '32.
Noris, Coleman	"	"	Sick, and sent to Rock Island
Posey, John F	"	"	Appointed Q. M. Sergt. Spy Bat. April 26, 1832.
Phelps, A. J	"	"	
Patterson, Jas	"	"	
Ryal, Nelson	"	"	
Sanburn, Nathl	"	"	
Shrader, L. O	"	"	
Snyder, John	"	"	
Shirley, John	"	"	
Smith, Wm	"	"	
Smith, John, Jr	"	"	
Scroggins, Henry	"	"	
Stapp, James T. B	"	"	
Whitfield, Bryand	"	"	
Wiley, Henry	"	"	
Wakefield, John A	"	"	Sent on express May 15, 1832
Whitlock, James	"	"	Appointed Q. M. to Maj. James' Odd Bat.
Walker, Harvey H	"	"	
Yarborough, E	"	"	

I certify that the above roll, with the annexed remarks, is correct, to the best of my knowledge, upon honor. (Signed.) JOHN DEMENT, Capt.

ODD BATTALION.

Capt. Daniel Price's Company,

Belonging to an Odd Batallion of Mounted Vonunteers, commanded by Brig.-Gen. Samuel Whiteside. Mustered out of the service of the United States, at the mouth of Fox river, Illinois, on May 28, 1832; distance from place of enrollment 275 miles.

Name and Rank.	Residence.	Enrolled	Remarks.
Captain.	Shelby Co	1832.	
Daniel Price.........	Shelbyville...	April 24.	Elected April 24, 1832; on John Sacket's horse
First Lieutenant.			
William Williamson	"	"	On furlough; elected April 24, 1832............
Second Lieutenant.			
Hiram M. Trimble..	"	"	Elected April 24, 1832...........................
Sergeants.			
Len Mosley.........	"	"	Elected April 24, 1832...........................
Elizer Briggs.......	"	"	" " " ....
William Price.......	"	"	
Mathew McNear.....	"	"	
Corporals.			
Gideon Walker.....	"	"	On Pleasant Gordon's horse...................
Isaac Daniel........	"	"	On furlough; on Beelin's horse...............
John Green..........	"	"	On Ben Walden's horse.......................
William Moore	"	"	
Privates.			
Austin, Hugh........	"	"	
Ball, George	"	"	Lost his horse; on Pleasant Dotson's horse..
Cochran, John......	"	"	
Daniel, William.....	"	"	On Daniel Price's horse......................
Daniel, Amon.......	"	"	John Reise's horse...........................
Daniel, Wiley B	"	"	On I. T. Sandford's horse....................
Daniel, Jeremiah ...	"	"	On I. B. Henry's horse; on furlough..........
Douthat, David......	"	"	On John Renshaw's horse
Elliott, David.......	"	"	
Frazer, Gran B.....	"	"	On Francis Gordon's horse...................
Green, Washington.	"	"	
Green, William......	"	"	
Howard, Jonathan B	"	"	
Harper, William....	"	"	
Hoosong, James	"	"	
Johnson, Isaac M...	"	"	On S. Scribner's horse.......................
Lee, George.........	"	"	
Mosley, John........	"	"	
McLavi, Joseph.....	"	"	
Poo, Abner..........	"	"	
Pardue, John	"	"	On S. Sherrill's horse........................
Richardson, Wm. A..	"	"	Appointed Asst. Q. M., May 5, 1832, to Odd Bat.
Scribner, Thomas...	"	"	
South, James........	"	"	
Smith, William......	"	"	On Witt Robinson's horse....................
Smith, Wesley......	"	"	On Mr. Graves' horse........................
Smith, David.......	"	"	His gun stolen; on Allen Bent's horse........
Strong, Solomon S..	"	"	On Absalom Hezzer's horse..................
Sherrill, William....	"	"	On Thomas Stutz's horse ....
Templeton, William	"	"	
Welch, Charles......	"	"	On Francis Jordan's horse...................

Capt. Peter Warren's Company

Of the Odd Battalion of Mounted Volunteers commanded by Brig.-Gen. Samuel Whitesides. Mustered out of the service of the United States, at the mouth of Fox river, Illinois, on May 28, 1832; distant from the place of enrollment, 275 miles.

Name and Rank.	Residence.	Enrolled	Remarks.
Captain.	Shelbyville,	1832.	
Peter Warren........	Shelby, Co ..	April 24	Elected April 24, 1832; on I. Culter's horse....
First Lieutenant.			
Archibald Wynns...	" "	"	Elected April 24, 1832 ....
Second Lieutenant.			
Robert T. Brown	" "	"	Elected April 24, 1832 ....
Sergeants.			
Isaac M. Shell	" "	"	Elected; on I. Culter's horse—pressed.........
John McGuire	" "	"	" horse gave out, l'ft on Gen. Daisey's
Levi Gorles...........	" "	"	" ....(horse.
John Perryman......	" "	"	" on Isaia L. Kortman's horse.........
Corporals.			
Thomas Hall.........	" "	"	Elected.................
William Headen.....	" "	"	App'd Surgeon of the Odd Battal. May 5, 1832.
John Abbott..........	" "	"	Elected 2d Corporal May 6, 1832; on furlough.
Thomas Lay	" "	"	App'd 2d Corporal May 22, 1832; E. Ellis' horse
James Davis.........	" "	"	On G. Todd's horse ....
Enos Ellis.............	" "	"	On John Smith's horse ....
Privates.			
Bergerman, John ...			
Bell, Alfred			On furlough; on G. Todd's horse.............
	Shelbyville,		
Casey, Levi	Shelby Co ..	April 24	
Curry, Nathan.......			
Cuink, James........			On furlough; lost horse; on J. Reese's horse.
Dowthat, James.....			
	Shelbyville,		
Dixon, Lawson	Shelby Co ..	April 24	On John Patub's horse.................
Dixon, Robert S.....	" "	"	
Elam, Joel			On John Storm's horse...................
Frazier, Albert			On furlough........................
Fleming, John......			
	Shelbyville,		
Fleming, Jacob L...	Shelby Co ..	April 24	On Abraham Teluck's horse.................
Graves, William.....			On Free Sexton's horse ....
	Shelbyville,		
Greer, James	Shelby Co ..	April 24	On Thomas Puiz's horse...............
Graham, Mortilus...	"	"	App'd Surg'n's Mate May 5, '32; lost his horse
Gorden, George	"	"	
Hale, John	"	"	On Barkley Lottz's horse ....
Hill, John	"	"	On G. Stucker's horse............
Hall, John P.........	"	"	On John Hale's horse..............
Johnston, James W.			
	Shelbyville,		
Johnston, Isaac O...	Shelby Co ..	April 24	
Johnston, Henry....	"	"	On John Hill's horse................
May, Thomas........	"	"	
More, Peyton.......	"	"	
Owens, William P...	"	"	
Penyman, Jacob	"	"	On furlough; on William Harrison's horse...
Parks, Samuel.......			
Rankin, Samuel			
Robinson, David M.			Horse left; on Mr. Young's horse; on furlo'gh
	Shelbyville,		
Ruther, James.......	Shelby Co ..	April 24	On furlough, lost his horse.................
Roberds, William D.	"	"	
Simpson, John			On Jas. Cockran's horse............
Smith, James........			On furlough; lost his horse ....
	Shelbyville,		
Sulivan, Dempsey F.	Shelby Co ..	April 24	On Peter Warren's horse..............
Stamp, Annias......	"	"	On John Rice's horse................
Vaughan, George A.			On Jacob Elliott's horse............
Vaughan, James W.			Appointed Armorer Odd Battalion May 5, 1832
	Shelbyville,		
Woolen, Edward....	Shelby Co ..	April 24	On Richmond Web's horse................
Williams, Thomas H.	"	"	....

CAPT. THOMAS HARRISON'S COMPANY.

Of the Odd Battalion commanded by Thomas James, Major, composing part of the Brigade of Mounted Volunteers commanded by Brig.-Gen. Samuel Whitesides. Mustered out of service of the United States, at the mouth of Fox river on the Illinois river, on May 28, 1832; distance 350 miles from the place of enrollment.

Name and Rank.	Residence.	Enrolled	Remarks.
Captain, Thomas Harrison...	Waterloo, Monroe Co....	1832. April 28	Entit'd to pay 1st Lt. April 19-28; app'd Capt..
First Lieutenant, Edward T. Morgan..	"	April 19	Entit'd to pay private Apr. 19-28; elect'd 1st Lt.
Second Lieutenant, Thomas McRoberts.	"	"	Entit'd to pay private Apr. 19-28; elect'd 2d Lt.
Sergeants.			
James Moor............	"	"	Entit'd to pay private April 19-28; app't'd Adjt.
Thomas Taylor......	"	"	
Felix Clark............	"	"	
John Strong..........	"	"	
Corporals.			
William McMoore...	"	"	
Pendleton Hill.......	"	"	
Wm. McNabb.........	"	"	
Henry Hartlin.......	"	"	
Farriers.			
Johnston, Nathan C.	"	"	App. Farrier Apr. 19; May 18 app. Sergt.-Maj.
Miller, William......	"	"	
Whitelock, James...	Beardstown..	April 30	
Cornelius, J. M. Mc..	Waterloo, Monroe Co.,...	April 19	Tr. May 9 another Reg.; Surg's Mate 1st Reg.
Privates.			
Bond, Shadrach B..	"	"	
Baird, Scipio..........	"	"	Appointed Quartermaster May 18, 1832........
Birch, John............	"	"	
Birch, Fielder.......	"	"	
Brooks, Stephen....	"	"	
Clark, George........	"	"	
Carr, Solomon.......	"	"	
Easton, Stephen....	"	"	
Fisher, Gramer......	"	"	
Haskins, Moses......	"	"	Entit'd pay priv. Apr. 19-28; app. Brig. Trump'r
Horin, Michael......	"	"	Appointed Paymaster April 28, 1832...........
James, John...........	"	"	On furl.;app. Sergt.-Maj. Apr.28; resig'd May18
Kidd, John.............	"	"	
Lacey, Caleb..........	"	"	
Livers, Joseph.......	"	"	
McDaniel, John......	"	"	Appointed 1st Sergeant April 28, 1832.........
Morgan, William....	"	"	
Moor, J. Milton......	"	"	Appointed Brigade Color Bearer April 28, 1832
Modglin, John........	"	"	
McNabb, James......	"	"	
McCulah, James.....	"	"	
Nowlin, Henry.......	"	"	
Neff, Henry...........	"	"	
Needles, James B. ..	"	"	
Preston, James......	"	"	
Ramsey, William ...	"	"	
Rogers, John..........	"	"	
Right, John............	"	"	
Snider, Solomon R..	"	"	
Smith, Calvin........	"	"	
Shook, Michael......	"	"	
Starr, Ashbridge....	"	"	
Todd, Edward........	"	"	
Trail, Xerxes F......	"	"	
Triplett, Nimrod....	"	"	
Wyatt, R. M...........	"	"	

ODD BATTALION.

Capt. Jacob Ebey's Company

Of Mounted Men (detached for foot purposes). One of the companies of the Odd Battalion, commanded by Major Thomas Long, now in the service of the United States, commanded by Brig.-Gen. Samuel Whitesides. Mustered out of service on May 25, 1832, at the mouth of Fox river, 175 miles from Springfield.

Name and Rank.	Residence.	Enrolled	Remarks.
Captain.		1832.	
Jacob Ebey...........	Sangamon Co	April 21	
First Lieutenant.			
Edward Shaw........	"	"	In hospital..........
Second Lieutenant.			
Winslow M. Neal....	"	"	
Sergeants.			
Thomas I. Marshall.	"	"	Appointed Q. M. Sergt. April 29, 1832.........
Davis Meredith......	"	"	
James B. Goble......	"	"	
David S. Collins......	"	"	
Corporals.			
Reese Williams......	"	"	
James E. Haws......	"	"	
Harmon Renshaw...	"	"	Promoted to 1st Sergeant April 29, 1832........
Wiley Blunt..........	"	"	
Privates.			
Attwood, Wm. C.....	"	"	
Bashaw, Jackulin...	"	"	
Byers, James D.	"	"	
Boyd, John	"	"	
Brown, Joseph	"	"	
Byer, Jesse..........	"	"	
Carver, James.......	"	"	
Clark, Philip........	"	"	
Clark, Isaac.........	"	"	
Catha, George.......	"	"	
Collins, John........	"	"	
Deimin, Joseph.....	"	"	
Dickson, Henry.....	"	"	Promoted 3d Corporal April 29, 1832..........
Davis, John.........	"	"	
Ferril, Milton.......	"	"	
Foster, George W...	B e dstown..	April 29	
Graham, Samuel....	Sangamon Co	April 21	
Graft, John.........	Rock Island..	May 10	Entered as mark'd; never afterw'ds appeared
Harper, James......	Sangamon Co	April 21	
Hamilton, Fred'k A..	"	"	
Hatan, Daniel......	"	"	
Hillis, John.........	"	"	
Hazlet, William.....	"	"	
Hinkle, Jacob.	"	"	
Hedrick, Stephen...	"	"	
Herndon, Felix.....	"	"	
Hash, Alfred........	Beardstown..	April 28	Entered as mark'd; never afterw'ds appeared
Jones, Granbury B..	Sangamon Co	April 21	
Milton, George......	"	"	
McClies, Daniel.....	"	"	
Martin, William.....	"	"	

8

Name and Rank.	Residence.	Enrolled	Remarks.
		1832.	
McMenus, Lawrence	Sangamon Co	April 21	
Nowhouse, John G..	"	"	
Rusett, William D...	"	"	
Rutlege, James......			
Rittenhouse, Obed'h	Beardstown..	April 29	Absent without leave, May 17, 1832.
Sherril, Thomas.....	Sangamon Co	April 21	
Stout, Thomas,.....			
Scovie, Samuel B...	Beardstown..	April 29	
Taylor, James......			
Vancel, Adam.......	Sangamon Co	April 21	In hospital.
Woolverton, Ulrich.			
Whitmore, John.....	"	"	In hospital.
Wright, John H.....	Beardstown..	April 28	Entered as mark'd; never afterw'ds appeared

CAPT. JAPHET A. BALL'S COMPANY

Of Mounted Men (detached for foot purposes), one of the companies of the Odd Battalion commanded by Major Thomas Long. Mustered out of the service on May 28, 1832.

Name and Rank.	Residence.	Enrolled	Remarks.
Captain.		1832.	
Japhet A. Ball......	Sangamon Co	April 21.	
First Lieutenant.			
Alexander D. Cox...	"	"	
Second Lieutenant.			
John McCormack...	"	"	
Sergeants.			
Joseph W. Duncan..	"	"	
James McCormack..	"	"	
Wm. F. Cox.........	"	"	
Charles Day........	"	"	
Corporals.			
Harvey Graham	"	"	
John M. Barns......	"	"	
Thos. I. Clark.......	"	"	
Richard Cox........	"	"	
Privates.			
Averill, Henry......	"	"	
Brunsfield, John....	"	"	In hospital.
Blue, Barnabas M...	"	"	
Ball, John..........	"	"	
Bagley, John D.....	"	"	
Coleman, Jonathan.	"	"	
Cook, Thomas......	"	"	
Donner, William....	"	"	
Galton, Thomas.....	"	"	
Gatlin, William.....	"	"	
Gately, John........	"	"	
Hazlet, Joseph......	"	"	
Hulton, John.......	"	"	
Hause, Salmon W.,.	"	"	
Hampton, Samuel C	"	"	On extra duty.
Howard, Abram.....	"	"	
Jones, Lewis C.....	"	"	
Ketchum, Daniel....	"	"	
Kendall, John.......	"	"	
Lanterman, Abram..	"	"	
McKinney, Thos. L.	"	"	
Massee, Elder.......	"	"	
Mitts, William......	"	"	
Menicks, Morris R..	"	"	
McCormack, Wm...	"	"	
Mitts, Jesse........	"	"	
Patton, Robert......	"	"	

Name and Rank.	Residence.	Enrolled	Remarks.
Spears, Nathan H	Sangamon Co	1832. April 21	
Smith, Charles	"	"	
Sexton, Robert B	"	"	
Swearingter, Thos	"	"	In hospital
Tempe, Garret	"	"	
Terry, John	"	"	In hospital
Vincent, John	"	"	
Ward, James	"	"	
Wright, Moses	"	"	
Waters, Daniel	"	"	

COMPANIES NOT ATTACHED TO REGIMENTS.

Capt. William Moore's Company

Of the Brigade of Mounted Volunteers commanded by Brig.-Gen. Samuel Whitesides. Mustered out of the service of the United States at the mouth of Fox river, Illinois, on May 28, 1832; distant from place of enrollment, 330 miles.

Name and Rank.	Residence.	Enrolled	Remarks.
Captain.		1832.	
William Moore	St. Clair Co.	April 18.	
First Lieutenant.			
Isaac Griffin	"	"	
Second Lieutenant.			
A. T. Fike	"	"	
Sergeants.			
Aaron Land	"	"	Sick; absent
Pleasant N. Dupee	"	"	
Nehemiah McMillion	"	"	
Elijah Herring	"	"	
Corporals.			
John Land	"	"	Absent; with the sick
Jonathan Crane	"	"	On furlough
Jarvis M. Jackson	"	"	Absent with leave
George Land	"	"	
Privates.			
Angle, David	"	"	Absent
Alexander, Julius	"	"	
Brown, Wm. G.	"	"	Appointed Paymaster to 1st Regt., on Apr. 28.
Brooks, Benjamin	"	"	
Baker, John T.	"	"	
Cunningham, Wm. J.	"	"	
Chisney, Benjamin	"	"	
Campbell, Wm.	"	"	
Cook, James	"	"	
Cook, Wm.	"	"	
Edwards, John	"	"	
Everett, Jesse J.	"	"	
Fike, Nathan	"	"	
Gaskill, Samuel	"	"	
Jackson, Lorenzo D.	"	"	
Johnson, John	"	"	
Hickman, George	"	"	
LaCroix, Rene M.	"	"	
Moore, Jonathan	"	"	
McDaniel, Benjamin	"	"	
Pate, Jeremiah	"	"	
Reynolds, Thomas	"	"	
Taylor, Charles	"	"	
Thompson, L. D.	"	"	
Tracewell, Edward	"	"	
Vodon, Harrison	"	"	
Wright, Wm.	"	"	
Ward, Henry	"	"	
Whitesides, John	"	"	

Capt. John Winstanley's Company

Of the Brigade of Mounted Volunteers commanded by Brig.-Gen. Samuel Whitesides. Mustered out of the service of the United States, at the mouth of Fox river, Illinois, on May 28, 1832; distant from the place of enrollment 330 miles.

Name and Rank.	Residence.	Enrolled	Remarks.
Captain. John Winstanley	St. Clair Co. Belleville	1832. April 18	
First Lieutenant. Aaron Stookey	"	"	
Second Lieutenant. David Snier	"	"	Absent sick
Sergeants.			
Thomas H. Kimber	"	"	Absent with leave
Joseph McAdams	"	"	
James W. McMurty	"	"	Absent with leave
George Higgins	"	"	
Corporals.			
Narcisse Pincinneau	"	"	
Joseph McMurty	"	"	
James R. Grigory	"	"	
George P. Dyke	"	"	
Privates.			
Brumly, Thomas	"	"	Absent sick
Barthume, Alexis	"		
Brock, Bayley			
Blackwell, John A			Appointed Quartermaster April 29
Coon, Thomas	Belleville	April 18	
Carr, Joseph			Absent with leave
Carr, James			
Decoto, Jno. Baptiste	Belleville	April 18	
Eastwood, Jacob Q.	"	"	
Hendricks, Elijah A.	"	"	
Hughes, Watson	"	"	
Hay, Richard			
Jarrot, Vital	Belleville	April 18	
Jarrot, Francis			
Leaird, Jarrot	Belleville	April 18	
Long, Thomas			Absent with leave
LeCompte, Louis			
McBride, Thomas	Belleville	April 18	Absent with leave
Macomson, Wm. B.	"	"	
Mitchell, Wm.			Appointed Surgeon's mate April 29
Menard, Peter			
Mecker, Ambrose			
Orr, William			
Pincinneau, Laurent	Belleville	April 18	Interpreter
Pincineau, Louis			
Roach, David			
Smith, Samuel	Belleville	April 18	
Smith, Valentine	"	"	
Snyder, Adam W.			April 29, appointed Adjutant 1st Regiment
Stubblefield, John	"	"	Armorer
Tetter, Philip			
Tetter, Solomon			
Walker, Gilla			Absent with leave
Woods, John			
Whiteside, Joseph			
Wildy, Rudolph			
Wemet, Louis			Appointed interpreter

Capt. William T. Givens' Company

Of the Brigade of Mounted Volunteers commanded by Brig.-Gen. Samuel Whitesides. Mustered out of the service of the United States of America, at the mouth of Fox river, on the 27th day of May, 1832, being 220 miles from place of enrollment.

Name and Rank.	Residence.	Enrolled	Remarks.
Captain. William T. Givens	Franklin, Morgan Co.	1832. April 21.	
First Lieutenant. Walter Butler	"	"	
Second Lieutenant. Thomas Wright	"	"	
Sergeants.			
Jacob Talkington	"	"	
James Pryon	"	"	
Joseph Reynolds	"	"	
Asa Johnson	"	"	
Corporals.			
James Thomas	"	"	
James Bryan	"	"	
John Null	"	"	
Jasper Roland	"	"	
Privates.			
Buchanan, Reuben	"	"	Furloughed and sent back on April 28; sick
Burnett, Freeman	"	"	
Clayton, William C.	"	"	
Clayton, John	"	"	
Clayton, William H.	"	"	Furl. and returned home April 28; sick
Deatherage, George	"	"	
Greer, Robert	"	"	
Gibson, William	"	"	Detailed as wagoner on April 20, 1832
Haynes, Lewis	"	"	
Jackson, Brice B.	"	"	
McDonnell, Fredrick	"	"	Detailed into service of Q. M. April 27, 1832
Reynolds, Samuel	"	"	
Sollers, William	"	"	
Smith, Jacob	"	"	
Tannohill, Alford	"	"	
Thomas, Joseph	"	"	
Van Winkle, Hiram	"	"	
Vickers, Henderson	"	"	
Wiggs, Daniel	"	"	[on April 29, 1832.
Weatherford, Wm.	"	"	Elected and appointed Lieut.-Col. 3d Regt.

Capt. Erastus Wheeler's Company

Of the Brigade of Mounted Volunteers commanded by Brig.-Gen. Samuel Whitesides. Mustered out of the service of the United States, at the mouth of Fox river, Illinois, on the 28th day of May, 1832; distance from place of enrollment, 295 miles; enrolled for 60 days

Name and Rank.	Residence.	Enrolled	Remarks.
Captain. Erastus Wheeler	Troy	1832. April 18	
First Lieutenant. John W. Lusk	"	"	
Second Lieutenant. Richard R. Randle.	"	"	

WHITESIDES' BRIGADE.

Name and Rank.	Residence.	Enrolled	Remarks.
Sergeants.		1832.	
William Tindall	Troy	April 18	
W. Torrence	"	"	On furlough
John Montgomery	"	"	
Wm. G. Martin	"	"	
Corporals.			
Josiah T. Randle	"	"	
Milton Gingles	"	"	
Henry H. West	"	"	
Benj. Stephenson	"	"	
Privates.			
Adams, O. M.	"	"	
Beers, Henry	"	"	
Carey, Thomas	"	"	On furlough
Cochran, Hugh E.	"	"	
Cleveland, Lorin	"	"	
Cason, John	"	"	
Dugger, Alfred	"	"	
Gracey, Jas. T.	"	"	
Gillespie, Joseph	"	"	
Herrington, Charles	"	"	
Holman, Nathaniel	"	"	
Hamilton, Samuel	"	"	
Howard, Abraham	"	"	
Journey, Ninian E.	"	"	
Lusk, Marquis	"	"	
McCullock, Samuel	"	"	
McElroy, James	"	"	
McMahan, Robert	"	"	
Montgomery, Wm.	"	"	
Owens, John	"	"	
Otwell, Ceylon Y.	"	"	
Pritchett, John	"	"	On furlough
Pearce, Robert B.	"	"	
Powell, Arkansas	"	"	
Robinson, Allen	"	"	
Randle, Peter W.	"	"	App'd Surg's Mate in Spy Bat., April 26, 1832
Shields, G. R.	"	"	
Shields, Alexander	"	"	Appointed Sergeant-Major April 28, 1832
Stice, Chas.	"	"	
Steele, Jesse	"	"	On furlough
Starr, Wm. F.	"	"	Appointed Brigade Paymaster April 26, 1832
Vanhouser, Valent'e	"	"	
Voyles, Abel	"	"	
Walker, John L.	"	"	
Yates, Elijah	"	"	

Capt. Samuel Smith's Company,

formerly

Capt. Jacob Fry's,

Of the Brigade of Mounted Volunteers commanded by Brig.-Gen. Samuel Whitesides. Mustered out of the service of the United States, at the mouth of Fox river, Illinois, on the 27th day of May, 1832; distant 230 miles from the place of enrollment.

Name and Rank.	Residence.	Enrolled	Remarks.
Captains.	Carrollton,	1832.	
Jacob Fry	Greene Co.	April 20.	Elected Col. April 30, 1832
Samuel Smith	"	"	
First Lieutenants.			
Samuel Smith	"	"	Elected Capt. April 30, 1832
E. D. Baker	"	"	
Second Lieutenant.			
E. D. Baker	"	"	Elected 1st Lieut. April 30, 1832
Mathias S. Link	"	"	

Name and Rank.	Residence.	Enrolled	Remarks.
Sergeants.		1832.	
Mathias S. Link	Greene Co.	April 20	Elected 2d Lieut. April 30, 1832
Frederick Atchison	"	"	
David Miller	"	"	
T. J. Brown			
Corporals.			
Martin Rigsby			Absent with leave
John Miller			
Abner P. Hill			
David Buson			
Privates.			
Atchison, Fielden			
Adcock, Isam			
Burton, Lemuel			
Brown, Erving D			
Crane, Harvy			
Campbell, Nicholas			Appointed 1st Corporal May 8
Deeds, Philip			
Emerson, Henry			
Goan, Shedrick			
Hobson, John			
Lee, Archibald			
Lee, Richard G			
Link, David	Greene Co.	April 20	
Lee, William			
Milton, David			
Miller, Lemuel			
Medkiff, David			
Nix, Elisha			
Nix, Joseph			
Powell, Dempsey			
Poindexter, Harris'n	Greene Co.	April 20	
Piper, Israel			
Renna, Wm. C			
Smith, Aaron			
Sanders, George			
Samuel, Thomas			Deserted
Scott, Benj. F			
Scott, James D			
Thomason, Spencer			
Thomason, William			
Tucker, James			
Tunnel, Luther	Greene Co.	April 20	
Tunnel, William	"	"	Transferred to Spy Battalion May 10
Trearney, James			In the staff
Vandiver, Ervin			
West, T. A			
Watton, Thomas R			
Whittle, Wyatt			Absent with leave
Wallace, Wm. P			
Wood, Squire	Greene Co.		Elected 1st Sergt. May 13

Capt. Thomas McDow's Company

Of the Brigade of Mounted Volunteers commanded by Brig.-Gen. Whitesides. Mustered out of the service of the United States, at the mouth of Fox river, Illinois, on May 27, 1832; distant 250 miles from the place of enrollment.

Name and Rank.	Residence.	Enrolled	Remarks.
Captain.		1832.	
Thomas McDow	Greene Co.	April 20	
First Lieutenant.			
James Whitlock	"	"	
Second Lieutenant.			
Silas Crain	"	"	Absent on furlough

WHITESIDES' BRIGADE.

Name and Rank.	Residence.	Enrolled	Remarks.
Sergeants.		1832.	
Thos. Briggs	Greene Co	April 20	
B. F. Massey	"	"	
Jas. Burke	"	"	Absent on furlough
Jas. Whitehead	"	"	
Corporals.			
Josiah Dunn	"	"	
Wm. Phillips	"	"	
Jas. Walden	"	"	
Privates.			
Brown, Hezekiah	"	"	
Boren, Daniel	"	"	
Clifton, Thos	"	"	
Clark, Squire	"	"	
Cowan, Matthew	"	"	
Costly, Daniel	"	"	
Dobbs, John	"	"	Absent on furlough
Erwin, Alfred	"	"	
Ferguson, James	"	"	
Fleming, Edward	"	"	
Green, Royal P	"	"	
Hurd, William	"	"	Absent on furlough
Jamison, John M	"	"	
Lofton, Ben	"	"	Absent on furlough
Lakin, Joseph	"	"	
Latham, Robert	"	"	
Means, John	"	"	
Morris, Lewis	"	"	
McCommack, John	"	"	
Means, Lewis	"	"	
Medford, Garrison	"	"	Absent without leave
Nairn, Wm	"	"	
Northam, Wm	"	"	Absent on furlough
Rouden, Wm. H	"	"	
Swan, William	"	"	
Sutton, John D	"	"	Absent on furlough
Saxton, Washington	"	"	
Thornton, Anderson	"	"	Absent without leave
Webb, Geo. W	"	"	

CAPT. DAVID CROW'S COMPANY

Of the Brigade of Mounted Militia Volunteers commanded by Brig.-Gen. Samuel Whitesides, United States Army. Mustered out of the service of the United States at the mouth of Fox river, on the Illinois, on the 27th day of May 1832; distant 250 miles from the place of enrollment.

Name and Rank.	Residence.	Enrolled	Remarks.
Captain.		1832.	
David Crow	Quincy, Ill	April 20	
First Lieutenant.			
Christopher Howard	"	"	
Second Lieutenant.			
Elijah G. Lillard	"	"	
Sergeants.			
Jno. Crawford, 1st	"	"	
George Campbell, 2d	"	"	Sick and present
John F. Battell, 3d	"	"	
James Crawford, 4th	"	"	
Corporals.			
Daniel Harty	"	"	
Coleman Talbert	"	"	
Jno. Fletcher	"	"	Furloughed
Jeremiah Stone	"	"	

Name and Rank.	Residence.	Enrolled	Remarks.
Privates.		1832.	
Beatty, Robert	Quincy, Ill.	April 20	
Campbell, Clayborn	"	"	
Campbell, Joseph	"	"	
Crow, Isaac	"	"	
Dunlap, David	"	"	
Edwards, Andrew	"	"	
Hutton, James	"	"	
Hillory, Alexander	"	"	
Hines, Wm.	"	"	
Harty, Abram	"	"	
Lang, John	"	"	Furloughed
Lewis, Jno	"	"	
McCoy, Joseph	"	"	Furloughed
McCoy, Robins	"	"	"
Points, John	"	"	
Payne, Stephen O.	"	"	
Riddle, Ebenezer	"	"	
Ruddle, John	"	"	Ret'd home from Henderson river on May 8.
Shephard, Jno	"	"	
Smith, Elisha	"	"	
Smith, Stedman	"	"	
Southward, Wm	"	"	
Williams, Benj	"	"	Furloughed; lost horse at Camp Dixon
Worrell, Atwell	"	"	

Capt. L. W. Goodan's Company

Of the Brigade of Mounted Volunteers, commanded by Gen. Samuel Whitesides. Mustered out of the service of the United States at the mouth of Fox river, Illinois, on May 28, 1832.

Name and Rank.	Residence.	Enrolled	Remarks.
Captain.		1832.	
L. W. Goodan	Springfield.	April 20	
First Lieutenant.			
John Reed	"	"	
Second Lieutenant.			
Wm. Cantrell	"	"	
Sergeants.			
Alford Wood	"	"	
Hiram Watson	"	"	
John Ridge	"	"	
Milton Humes	"	"	
Corporals.			
John Kline	"	"	
Wm. Smith	"	"	
Jairus B. Jones	"	"	Furloughed, sick, on May 19, 1832; reduced.
Geo. F. Cabenness	"	"	
Moses Brunts	"	"	Made Corporal May 19, 1832.
Privates.			
Archey, Vincon			
Archey, Michael			
Baker, John	Springfield.	April 21	
Brunfield, Moses	"	"	
Brassle, Robert	"	"	Furloughed, sick.
Brink, David M	"	"	
Bunts, Simoon			
Brown, John B			
Baker, James	Springfield.	April 21	Wagon Master from May 1.
Crow, William			
Carpenter, William	"	"	Appointed Paymaster April 30, 1832.
Calhoun, John			
Constant, Wm	Springfield.	April 21	Appointed Surgeon's Mate, 4th Regt., April 29
Chilton, Mathias	"	"	Furloughed, sick.
Devenport, Wm			
Darrow, Jesse			

WHITESIDES' BRIGADE.

Name and Rank.	Residence.	Enrolled	Remarks.
		1832.	
Dawson, Charles....			
Ditson, Simon......			
Dotson, Jesse......			
Dickison, D........	Springfield...		Joined the Spies on May 1...............
Easters, Asa.......	"	April 21	Sick................
Erby, Jacob M......	"		Appointed Surgeon of 4th Regiment April 30.
Foster, Nathaniel...			
Goode, Daniel......			
Garet, Joseph......			Joined the Spies on May 1................
Glasscock, George..			
Hurst, John........	Springfield...	April 21	
Henry, James D....	"	"	Appointed Major of the Spies on April 28, 1832
Hamilt n, Samuel...			
Iles, Elijah........			Joined the Spies on May 1................
Jones, Noah........	Springfield...	April 21	On furlough, horse muster...............
Jones, James.......			
Jones, Edward.....			Joined the Spies on May 1................
Kindle, M. C.......	Springfield...	April 21	
King, Rheubin.....			
Kirk, Jack.........	Springfield...	"	Joined my company on May 1.............
Keys, John........			Joined the Spies on May 1................
McCollister, Wm ...	Springfield...	April 21	
McKinsey, Samuel..	"	"	
Mann, Uriah.......			
Mason, Noah......			
Malugon, Samuel...			
Malugon, Zaciah...			
Morris, Achalis.....	Springfield...	April 21	Private; elected Lt. Col. of 4th Reg. April 30..
McCoy, Joseph.....	"		
Matheny, L. D.			Joined the Spies on May 1................
Neale, T. M.......			Sick; absent by leave................
Neale, Samuel O....		April 21	
Olesshart, E. P.....			Joined the Spies on May 1................
Potts, William.....			
Queenston, Richard.	Springfield...	April 21	
Robison, George....	"	"	
Rainer, Samuel.....			
Rutlage, John B....			
Richardson, Daniel.			
Rolston, Joseph....			
Richardson, Robert.			
Rusk, B. O.........	Springfield...	April 21	On extra duty from May 1...............
Radford, Reuben...			
Reed, James F.....	"		Joined the Spies on May 1................
Sims, Benjamin....	Springfield...	April 21	
Said, Jesse........			
Steel, William.....			
Sherill, Thomas....	Springfield...	April 21	Joined my company on May 18.............
Sanders, P. A......			Joined the Spies on May 1................
Stewart, John T....			
Sherell, James.....			
Thomas, Harden....		April 21	
Taylor, James......			Joined the Spies on May 1................
Welch, Jefferson....	Springfield...	April 21	
Wills, James Q.....	"	"	
Wells, William E...	"	"	

FOURTH BRIGADE.

FORTIETH REGIMENT.

Capt. Geo. B. Willis' Company

Of Mounted Volunteers belonging to the 40th Regiment, 4th Brigade, 1st Division of Illinois Militia, commanded by Col. John Strawn, called into the service by the Governor of Illinois, and mustered out of service of the United States, at Hennepin, Putnam county, on June 18th, 1832.

Name and Rank.	Residence.	Enrolled	Remarks.
Captain.	Putnam Co.	1832.	
George B. Willis	Hennepin	May 21	
First Lieutenant.			
Timothy Perkins	"	"	
Second Lieutenant.			
Samuel D. Laughlin	"	"	
Sergeants.			
James D. Laughlin	"	"	
Thomas Wafer	"	"	
Anthony Turk	"	"	
Samuel Mann	"	"	
Corporals.			
Elisha G. Powers	"	"	By leave of Capt., went with team for U. S. [June 15.
Linas B. Skeels	"	"	
Solomon Perkins	"	"	
Maron Dimic	"	"	
Privates.			
Brigham, Sylvester	"	May 21	
Blanchard, Roswell	"	" 31	
Burrow, John	"	" 21	
Benson, Lewis B	"	"	On foot
Chamberlain, O. G.	"	"	
Cole, John	"	" 24	
Corse, Christopher	"	" 31	
Carey, Abijah	"	"	On foot
Carey, Elias	"	"	On foot; 6 days off duty
Delong, Henry	"	" 21	Returned, sick, June 6th; not yet fit for duty.
Dunlary, James G	"	" 24	
Daniels, Henry	"	" 21	Six days off duty
Durley, Williamson	"	" 31	On foot [for U. S. June 15.
Doolittle, Joel	"	"	On foot; by leave of Capt. went with team
Dimic, Elijah	"	"	On foot; six days off duty
Davis, Alex	"	" 21	Horseman; 12 days off duty
Forristel James G	"	"	
Griffin, John	"	"	
Gunn, Aaron	"	"	On foot
Hart, Matthias B	"	"	

FOURTH BRIGADE.

Name and Rank.	Residence.	Enrolled	Remarks.
Harper, James	Hennepin	May 21	Left for the main army June 14
Hall, John	"	" 26	
Hoskins, William	"	"	
Ham, Wm. H.	"	" 21	On foot
Hendricks, John	"	"	No service rendered
Janess, John	"	"	On foot; taken up for stealing, and run away
Kellerman, Michael	"	" 26	
Leeper, Robert A.	"	" 21	
Leeper, Charles	"	"	Had leave to team for U. S., but did not do it.
Laughlin, Alex. M.	"	"	One day off duty
Laughlin, Thos. W.	"	"	
McCormas, David	"	"	Horseman; 6 days off duty
Mosely, Roland	"	" 31	On foot.
Moore, John	"	" 23	
Morris, William	"	" 26	
Philips, Elijah	"	" 21	Killed by Indians on Bureau June 18
Prupk, Daniel	"	" 31	On foot
Rexford, Joseph W.	"	" 21	
Ross, James G.	"	"	On foot
Roth, Solomon	"	" 31	By leave Capt., went with team for U.S. June 15
Roth, Leonard	"	" 31	On foot; 6 days off duty
Shepherd, Nelson	"	"	
Simpson, John H.	"	" 31	
Tompkins, Claud. L.	"	"	No service rendered
Taylor, Adam	"	"	
Willis, James W.	"	"	
Williamson, John	"	"	
Wilmouth, Geo. P.	Bureau Co.	" 23	Enlisted in the U. S. service
Williams, John	Hennepin	" 21	On foot; 6 days off duty
Williams, Curtis	"	"	
Warnock, Hugh	"	"	On foot
Zenor, Harsin K.	"	"	

CAPT. ROBERT BARNES' COMPANY

Of Mounted Volunteers belonging to the 40th Regiment, 4th Brigade, and 1st Division, of Illinois Militia, called by the Governor and Commander-in-Chief; was mustered into the service of the United States by Col. John Strawn, at Columbia, on May 20, 1832, and mustered out of service at Hennepin, Putnam county, Illinois, on June 18, 1832; distance 25 miles from home.

Name and Rank.	Residence.	Enrolled	Remarks.
Captain.		1832.	
Robert Barnes	Columbia	May 20	
First Lieutenant.			
William M. Neal	"	"	Lost 4 days
Second Lieutenant.			
John Weir	"	"	
Sergeants.			
James Dever	"	"	
James Hall	"	"	Lost 4 days
James N. Reeder	"	"	"
Nathan Owen	"	"	
Corporals.			
Beletha Griffith	"	"	
William Gallaher	"	"	Lost 4 days
James Harris	"	"	
Morgan Buckingh'm	"	"	Lost 4 days
Privates.			
Burt, Joseph			
Burt, William	Crow Creek	May 30	Lost 4 days
Bird, John			
Bird, Robert	Columbia	May 20	
Byms, William	"	"	Lost 4 days
Barnhart, Hiram	"	"	on foot
Barnhart, Peter	"	May 26	

Name and Rank.	Residence.	Enrolled	Remarks.
		1832.	
Babb, Benjamin	Columbia	May 20.	
Bullman, Joshua	"	May 30.	Lost 4 days
Cassel, Henry K	"	May 20.	Lost 20 days
Dawdy, Howell	"		
Davis, Milton			
Davis, William	Crow Creek	May 30.	Lost 4 days
Davis, William W	"		
Darnell, John	"	May 20.	
Earthor, George	Columbia	"	Broke his leg May 30
Edwards, Stanton	"	"	No duty
Forbes, William	"	"	Lost 4 days
Hendrick, William A	"	"	
Hendrick, John P	"	"	Lost 13 days
Hawkins, Samuel	Crow Creek	"	Lost 10 days
Hamilton, David	Columbia	"	Lost 4 days
Hiff, Robert	"	May 30.	
Johnston, John	"	June 5.	No duty
Kemp, John	"	May 20.	Lost 4 days
Keys, Elmer	"	"	
McGuire, Philip	"	"	"
Phillips, Joseph	"	"	
Russell, Lemuel	"	"	Lost 4 days
Sawyer, Jordan	"	"	
Smally, Jacob	"	May 30.	
Swan, Elisha	"	June 5.	Lost 4 days
Statler, David	"	May 20.	Said he must plough
Shaw, George H	"	"	No duty

CAPT. WILLIAM M. STEWART'S COMPANY

Of Mounted Volunteers, attached to the 40th Regiment, 4th Brigade and 1st Division of Illinois Militia commanded by Col. John Strawn; called and mustered into the service of the United States, by order of the Commander-in-Chief of the Militia of the State of Illinois, on May 21, 1832, and mustered out of the service of the United States at Hennepin, Putnam county, Illinois, on June 18, 1832.

Name and Rank.	Residence.	Enrolled	Remarks.
Captain.		1832.	
William M. Stewart	Hennepin	May 21.	
First Lieutenant.			
Mason Willson	"	"	
Second Lieutenant.			
Livingston Roberts	"	"	
Sergeants.			
William Myers	"	"	
James S. Simpson	"	"	
Jonathan F. Wilson	"	"	
Joseph S. Warnock	"	"	
Corporals.			
William Patten	"	"	
Moses G. Williams	"	"	
William Walkup	"	"	
Privates.			
Bird, William	"	"	
Bird, John	"	"	
Brock, Aquilla	"	"	Dismissed by officers; served 3 days
Couts, Benjamin	"	"	
Dugan, Robert	"	"	
Ellis, Peter	"	"	
Gunn, Daniel	"	"	
Galaher, Thomas, Sr	"	"	
Holterbrand, Isaac	"	"	
Hunt, Richard	"	"	
Haily, Washington	"	"	Dismissed by officers; served 3 days
Jones, David	"	"	
Knox, Adam	"	"	

FOURTH BRIGADE.

Name and Rank.	Residence.	Enrolled	Remarks.
		1832.	
Knox, Lewis	Hennepin	May 21	
Letts, David	"	"	
Richie, David	"	"	
Ramsey, John L	"	"	
Sturdwin, Madison	"	"	
Stewart, William	"	"	
Stewart, James T	"	"	
Stephenson, Adison	"	"	Adison Stevenson rendered only 10 days.
Thompson, David	"	"	
Thompson, Aaron	"	"	
Thomas, Franklin	"	"	
Willis, Stephen D	"	"	
Willson, Alexander	"	"	

CAPT. WM. HAWS' COMPANY

Of Mounted Volunteers, belonging to the 40th Regt., 4th Brigade and 1st Division Illinois Militia, commanded by Col. John Strawn; called into service by the Governor of Illinois, and mustered out of service at Hennepin, on the Illinois river, State of Illinois, on June 18, 1832.

Name and Rank.	Residence.	Enrolled	Remarks.
Captain.		1832.	
William Haws	Hennepin	May 2	
First Lieutenant.			
James Garvin	"	"	
Second Lieutenant.			
Wm. M. Hart	"	"	
Sergeants.			
Thomas Gunn	"	"	
George Hilterbraud	"	"	
Jacob Greenawalt	"	"	Deserted
John Hunt	"	"	
Corporals.			
John Hart	"	"	
William Kincade	"	"	
Wm. Knox	"	"	
Wm. Lathrop	"	"	
Privates.			
Allen, Hiram	"	"	
Ash, Reuben	"	"	
Ash, Joseph	"	"	
Boyle, Abner	"	"	
Dent, George	"	"	
Glenn, Thomas	"	"	
Graves, Obed	"	"	
Glenn, Samuel	"	"	
Harmon, Asael	"	"	
Hart, Wm	"	"	
Healey, Hartwell	"	"	
Isaac, Elias	"	"	
Loyd, John	"	"	
Martin, George	"	"	
Neal, Little	"	"	
Stout, Hosa	"	"	
Stacey, Julius	"	"	
Winters, Christoph'r	"	"	
Whitacre, Aaron	"	"	
Wilson, Garrison	"	"	

INDEPENDENT REGIMENTS.

COL. MOORE'S REGIMENT.

Capt. John B. Thomas' Company

Of Volunteer Mounted Gunmen of Vermilion county, Illinois, called for by the Executive of said State, and received and mustered into service by Col. Isaac R. Moore, on May 23, 1832, and remained in service until June 23, 1832, both days inclusive.

Name and Rank.	Residence.	Enrolled	Remarks.
Captain.			
John B. Thomas			
First Lieutenant.			
William Nox			
Second Lieutenant.			
Gabriel G. Rice			
Sergeants.			
James C. McGee			
Richard F. Giddens			
Mijamin Byers			
John Q. Deakin			
Corporals.			
John R. Jackson			
William O. Neal			
William Trimmel			
David Moore			
Privates.			
Atwood, William			
Buoy, Laban			
Coddington, John			
Cox, John			
Cook, Michael			
Cunningham, Wm			
Creamer, Lewis			
Chandler, William			
Conner, Stephen B			
Deer, Thomas			
Fuller, Abner			
Gill, George			
Humphreys, Enoch			
Ham, William			
Harris, James			
Jones, Crawford H			
Judy, Henry			
Jackson, Hiram			
Jackson, Elijah			
Jose, Michael H			
Lane, John			

Name and Rank.	Residence.	Enrolled	Remarks.
		1832.	
McGee, John			
McDonald, Henry			
Newell, Hugh			
Newell, David			
Newell, Wilson			
Reed, John A			
Reese, Morgan			
Shockey, Henry			
Shampaign, John B.			
Standford, Philip M.			
Smith, Jefferson			
Thomas, Joseph			
Tombs, Edwin B.			
Wright, Jesse B.			
Wilson, Henry			
Wilson, Hiram			
Wilson, John M			

We certify that Benjamin Tatam volunteered, mounted, armed and equipped and entered the service of the United States, on May 23, 1832, in Capt. Thomas' Company, but by consent of Col. Moore he was transferred and served part of the time in Capt. Ashton's Company, but rejoined this company and was mustered out of service with it; that he served the full term of 32 days; his name was omitted from this muster roll by oversight, and that he is entitled to pay and allowances with the rest of the company.

(Signed,)   JOHN B. THOMAS, Capt.
(Signed,)   ISAAC R. MOORE, Col.

Capt. Alexander Bailey's Company

Of Mounted Gunmen, belonging to Col. I. R. Moore's Regiment of Illinois Volunteers. Mustered into the service on May 23, 1832. Mustered out June 23, 1832.

Name and Rank.	Residence.	Enrolled	Remarks.
		1832.	
Captain.			
Alex. Bailey			
First Lieutenant.			
George Ware			
Second Lieutenant.			
G. S. Hubbard			
Sergeants.			
Noah Sapp			
Asa Duncan			
Isaiah M. Treat			
Ralph Martin			
Corporals.			
Robert Osbern			
John Leneeve			
Obediah Leneeve			
William Martin			
Privates.			
Andrews, A. P.			
Anglo, Jacob			
Blair, William			
Bailey, David			
Blount, William			
Beckwith, George M.			
Bowman, James			
Burbridge, Wm.			
Botts, Feeling			
Crider, Archibald			
Canady, Wm.			
Cunningham, James			
Canady, Watson			
Duncan, Alfred			
Deck, John			

Name and Rank.	Residence.	Enrolled	Remarks.
		1832.	
Ekler, Jacob..........			
Enos, Joab			
Foster, William......			
Fitch, John R........			
Gurthery, Michael...			
Gilbert, Othnial.....			
Gilbert, Sylvester...			
Hor, Warren.........			
Hall, James...........			
Hinkle, Josiah.......			
Hill, Robert..........			
Jennings, Soame.....			
Kelly, Asahel........			
Knight, David.......			
King, James R.......			
Layton, Thomas.....			
Luman, Amos........			
Loveless, Joseph R..			
More, William.......			
Miller, Abraham K..			
Oliver, Bushrod......			
Ogg, Thomas.........			
Piper, John...........			
Russell, Samuel......			
Skinner, John........			
Shobore, Isadore.....			
Skinner, James.......			
Scott, Notly C........			
Scott, John...........			
Vanvickle, Enoch...			
Watson, John R......			
White, James.........			
Willson, Robert P...			
Wiles, Sanford.......			
Young, Scott.........			
Young, John..........			

Capt. Eliakem Ashton's Company

Of Mounted Riflemen, belonging to Col. Moore's Regiment of Vermilion Volunteers of the State of Illinois. Entered service on May 23, 1832, and remained in actual service until June 23, 1832, both days inclusive.

Name and Rank.	Residence.	Enrolled	Remarks.
Captain.			
Eliakem Ashton....			
First Lieutenant.			
Wm. Mackin.........			
Privates.			
Brown, John.........			
Bryant, R. H.........			
Best, David..........			
Huntsman, Jarvas ..			
Hays, George J......			
Hays, Hiram.........			
Kester, John.........			
Moner, Christopher.			
Mann, Samuel			
McCann, Wilson B..			
Mills, Elijah.........			
Mann, William......			
Mansfield, Robert...			
Mackey, Elias.......			
Nokes, Amos.........			
Potts, John..........			
Riddle, James			
Roll, Edw............			
Shipp, Elias..........			

Capt. Morgan L. Payne's Company

Of Mounted Volunteers commanded by Major Nathaniel Buckmaster, commanding at Fort Payne, on the DuPage river, and stationed for the protection of the frontier between Ottawa and Chicago, in the county of Cook, in the State of Illinois; 135 miles from Danville, Vermilion county, State aforesaid, where recruited. Mustered out of service July 25, 1832.

Name and Rank.	Residence.	Enrolled	Remarks.
Captain.		1832.	
Morgan L. Payne	Danville	May 12	
First Lieutenants.			
Noah Ginion			Served as 1st Lt. to June 22, then resigned
John Black			Served as private to June 23, then elect'd 1st Lt
Second Lieutenant.			
Thos. McConnell			
Sergeants.			
Jonathan Pratt			Served as 1st Sergt to June 21, then as private.
Jacob Glass			Served as private to June 23, then as 1st Sergt.
Squire L. Payne			" " " " " 22, " " 2d
John Cook			
Phillomon Spicer			
Corporals.			
Greenville Groves			
John Cassel			
Joseph Spicer			
Joshua Fleming			
Privates.			
Brown, Wm			Killed by the enemy on June 16, 1832.
Bevens, James			
Cotton, Wm			
Coffee, Randolph R.			
Collins, John			
Douglass, Cyrus			
Elliott, John			
Elliott, Nathan			
Furguson, Asa			
Fisher, Wm			
Hays, Bennett			Three days on express to Fort Wilbourn.
Howell, John			
Kinny, Miram H			
Lucus, Presly			
Lucus, John			
Lucus, Reason			
Lyons, John			
Morgan, Evan S			
Morgan, John			
McBride, John	Danville	May 12	
O'Neal, Samuel			
Parkeson, Samuel			
Rutledge, Leander			
Stephens, John			
Stephens, Solomon			
Stephen, Isaac			
Springer, Levi			
Thompson, James			
Underwood, Wm			
Vankirk, Joseph			
Waters, John			
Wilson, Hardy			

Capt. James Palmer's Company

Of Mounted Volunteers, in Vermilion county, State of Illinois, called into service by order of the Executive of said State, from May 23, 1832, until June 23, 1832, both days inclusive.

Name and Rank.	Residence.	Enrolled	Remarks.
Captain.			
James Palmer			
First Lieutenant.			
John Light			
Second Lieutenant.			
Joseph Jackson			
Sergeants.			
Bluford Runyon			
Marcus Snow			
David Macumson			
Thomas Froman			
Corporals.			
Henry Streight			
Washington Lusher			
Abner M. Williams			
David Morgan			
Musicians.			
William H. Parkers'n			
Noah Delay			
Privates.			
Allen, Jared			
Atwood, Green			
Bandy, William			
Bandy, Washington			
Brown, John H			
Bensyl, John			
Banta, Solomon			
Currant, William			
Currant, Martin			
Cloe, Alexander			
Chandler, James			
Cline, Jesse			
Cravins, James C			
Dunn, Ferrel			
Delay, Henry			
Delay, Jacob			
Delay, Isaac			
Fielder, Charles			
Foley, Francis			
Fithian, William			
Fry, Jona. W			
Going, John			
Griffith, Stephen			
Gebhart, William			
Hale, Elijah B			
Henderson, Ely			
Jenkins, Malachi			
Kinkenon, William P			
Kenedy, Franklin			
Kizer, Andrew			
Lewis, David			
Love, William			
Lewis, Solomon			
Lambert, James			
Lenman, William			
Lizer, David C			
Malory, D. W. C			
Morgan, Joseph			
Macumson, Samuel			
Mendenhall, Ely			
Oiler, Abraham			
Phelps, Jonathan			
Payne, Henry B			
Prince, Francis			
Reynolds, Davis			

INDEPENDENT REGIMENTS. 133

Name and Rank.	Residence.	Enrolled	Remarks.
Rock, James			
Rutlage, Peter S.			
Simpson, George			
Thomas, John			
Wooden, Elmore			
Yount, Jonathan			

CAPT. I. M. GILLISPIE'S COMPANY

Of Volunteers of Mounted Militia, commanded by Col. I. R. Moore. Mustered into service May 23, 1832, and remained in service until June 23, 1832—both days inclusive.

Name and Rank.	Residence.	Enrolled	Remarks.
Captain.		1832.	
I. M. Gillispie		May 23	
First Lieutenant.			
Barnet Wever		"	
Second Lieutenant.			
Edwin Stanfield		"	
Sergeants.			
George Lewis		"	
James Adams		"	
Andrew Davis		"	
Corporals.			
Locklin Madden		"	
Wm. Nugent		"	
Elza Hoskins		"	
I. B. Prebble		"	
Privates.			
Bugely, Nicholas		"	
Brackall, Martin		"	
Bosely, Wm. M.		"	
Don Carlens, John		"	
Don Carlos, Archelus		"	
Don Carlos, Wm.		"	
Evans, Jonathan		"	
Foster, Samuel		"	
Freeman, James		"	
Gallion, Abram		"	
Gephart, Emanuel		"	
Howell, John		"	
Houghman, Jos. N.		"	
Lyons, John H.		"	
Millikan, Baptist		"	
Morgan, Thos.		"	
Morgan, Achelis		"	
Morgan, Levi		"	
Mayfield, Stephen		"	
Ritter, John		"	
Rowe, William		"	
Swearengen, Isaac		"	
Swank, Richard		"	
Swank, William		"	
Swank, David		"	
Swisher, Anthony		"	
Yeager, C. F.		"	
Yoke, Charles		"	

Capt. James Gregory's Company

Of Mounted Riflemen, belonging to Col. I. R. Moore's Regiment of Illinois Volunteers. Entered the service May 31, 1832, and remained in the service until June 23, 1832.

Name and Rank.	Residence.	Enrolled	Remarks.
Captain. James Gregory			
First Lieutenant. Wm. E. Williams			
Second Lieutenant. James Goodwin			
Sergeants. Jas. Cunningham			
Jas. Harnies			
Privates. Acton, James			
Bell, Elias B.			
Cook, Stephen			
Collins, James			
Conner, Luke			
Cook, Isaac			
Evans, Thomas J.			Tr. f'm Capt. Bailey's Co.; whole time, 31 days
Eccleston, Harry			
Farmer, Enoch			
Fuget, Braeston M.			
Goodwin, Thomas			
Gilbert, James			
Jackson, Alexes			
James, Jesse			
Leaman, Jacomiah J.			
Mace, Daniel			
McNeal, Benjamin			
Musgave, James			
McCoons, Thomas			
Morris, Thomas			
McCart, Edward			
McCart, John			
Staley, Jacob			
Stephenson, John			
Smith, Zion			
Sigler, George			
Watson, Charles M.			
White, David			
Wilkenson, Jacob			

The men in this company, unless otherwise stated in "Remarks," each served 24 days.

Capt. Corbin R. Hutt's Company

Of Mounted Riflemen, belonging to Col. I. R. Moore's Regiment of Illinois Volunteers. Mustered into service May 23, 1832, and remained in service until June 23, 1832, both days inclusive.

Name and Rank.	Residence.	Enrolled	Remarks.
Captain. Corbin R. Hutt			
First Lieutenant. William Jeremiah			
Second Lieutenant. John A. Green			
Sergeants. Levin Watson			
Alex. McDonnell			
Jacob Hammer			
Moses Vest			

Name and Rank.	Residence.	Enrolled	Remarks.
Privates.			
Anderson, Hiram			
Alexander, Wash't'n			
Brown, Hiram			
Brown, David			
Cole, Edward			
Cole, John			
Crusor, Robert			
Chitty, Ferguson			
Ellis, Henry Lee			
Foley, William			
Frazier, John			
Hathaway, Isaac			
Howard, Phillip			
Hammer, John			
Lowdowsky, Isaac			
Lacey, Moses			
Lacey, Willie			
McDowell, John B.			
Rheuby, John			
Scott, Fielding L.			
Smith, Luke			
Todd, Samuel			
Williams, Samuel			
Williams, William			
Wheat, John			
Yilkey, Joseph A.			

TWENTY-SEVENTH REGIMENT.

Capt. Milton M. Maugh's Company

Of the 27th Regiment of Illinois Militia, called into the service of the United States by the Governor's order dated May 15, 1832. Mustered for discharge Sept. 6, 1832, and mustered out Sept. 8, 1832.

Name and Rank.	Residence.	Enrolled		Remarks.
Captain.		1832.		
Maughs, Milton M...	....	May	19	....
First Lieutenants.				
Moses Swan	....	"		Resigned June 8...........
Wm. Johnson	....	June	9	....
Second Lieutenant.				
Mathew Johnson...	....	May	29	....
Sergeants.				
John Turney	....	May	19	Resigned July 8...........
John C. Bond	....	July	9	
Thomas Spriggins	....	May	19	
John D. Bell	....	"		
William Johnson	....	May	24	Elected 1st Lieut. June 9......
Joseph Walker	....	June	11	Discharged Aug. 1...........
Corporals.				
A. M. Wallen	....	May	19	Joined Mounted Rangers........
John G. Hulett	....	June	6	
James Jones	....	May	19	
Absolom McCorm'ck	....	"		Absent Sept. 6 without leave...
Chas. T. Saunderson	....	"		Transferred to Capt. Gear's company
Musicians.				
Abel Procter	....	"		
Greenleaf Warren	....	"		Absent without leave Sept. 6......
Privates.				
Alston, John	....	"		
Anderson, J. C.	....	"		
Avery, David	....	May	25	
Avery, William	....	"		
Binninger, Jacob	....	May	19	
Barnett, Lee L.	....	"		Discharged July 30...........
Birdsell, Renphus	....	"		
Britt, Leroy	....	"		
Blakely, J. P.	....	"		Absent without leave from June 1
Bass, George	....	"		Transferred June 9............
Brown, A.	....	May	20	Absent without leave from June 1
Brown, Julius	....	"		" " " " 10...
Brice, G. W.	....	"		
Bond, John C.	....	June	27	Appointed 1st Sergt. July 9......
Bond, Wm. B.	....	"		
Blundell, Wm	....	May	23	Sick............
Beaty, James	....	Aug.	16	
Brock, Aquilla	....	Aug.	26	
Crow, Albion T.	....	May	19	Absent with leave Sept. 6......
Culloran, T. B.	....	May	21	Attached to artillery Co. July 10.
Cook, Pleasant	....	May	19	Discharged July 13...........
Cocy, Samuel	....	May	21	" " " 10...
Digney, Barney	....	May	20	
Davis, B. G. F.	....	"		Absent without leave from July 1..
Davis, B. G.	....	"		" " " " June 1...
Davenport, James	....	"		" " " " June 1...
Dickinson, John L.	....	May	19	" with leave Sept. 6.........

INDEPENDENT REGIMENTS. 137

Name and Rank.	Residence.	Enrolled	Remarks.
		1832.	
Dillon, Levi		May 20	Absent without leave June 1
Dooling, John		May 21	
Davidson, George		May 21	Hospital Steward
Dame, J. H.		May 19	
Drummond, Rob't H.		Aug. 16	
Freth, Isaiah		May 21	
Farnsworth, Terra B		May 19	Absent with leave Sept. 6
Fore, Joseph		"	
Fanley, Jacob		"	
Fanchette, Alex		"	" without leave from June 20
Fultz, Frederick		July 5	" Sept. 6 with leave
Foreman, Moses		July 28	" from Sept. 6 with leave
Gray, Patrick		May 19	
Gruwell, John		May 24	Attached to Mounted Volunteers June 1
Gillham, Lemuel		"	Discharged July 27
Hunt, Benson		May 19	
Hendley, Esbrey		"	
Hulett, John G		"	Appointed Corporal June 6
Imns, Abraham		"	Absent without leave from June 10
Igo, Lewis		May 24	" " " "
Igo, William		"	" " " "
Igraham, John		May 25	" " " June 1
Journey, James		May 19	" " " May 20
Joslin, John		June 25	
Kelly, J		May 19	Absent without leave from June 1
Klean, Michael		June 23	" Sept. 6 with leave
King, John H		July 7	" without leave from Aug. 1
Lovell, Timothy		May 19	Transferred to Capt. Gear's Co. July 1
Lytle, William K		"	Absent Sept. 6 with leave
Lepage, Clement		"	
Lockwood, Ezekeil		"	Detached to join artillery company
Manichael, Baptiste		"	
Maughs, Henry		"	
Maughs, D. H. T		"	
Maughs, James K		June 23	
McDuff, Wm		May 19	
McClair, P		May 20	Discharged July 29
Miller, Preston N		May 19	" June 4
Maxwell, J. J		May 20	Absent without leave from May 24
McAllister, Lem. S		May 24	
McRayney, Daniel		May 20	Discharged June 11
Martin, Elkins		May 21	
Perregon, Wales		May 19	Sick
Paul, John		July 5	
Patterson, John B		May 26	Omitted in former rolls
Rice, Sylvester		May 19	Absent without leave from June 1
Rice, Thomas		May 20	
Rice, James		May 21	
Roberts, John		May 19	Discharged June 1
Rickman, Francis		"	Absent Sept. 6 with leave
Rose, Pleasant		May 20	Discharged Aug. 4
Robedeaux, Lawr'ce		May 19	
Stukey, John		May 20	
Stewart, James B		May 19	
Smith, Wm		"	Sick
Smith, Orlando		"	Discharged June 27
Smith, James		"	Absent without leave from June 26
Smith, Wm., 2d		May 20	Joined rifle company June 1
Smith, N		July 25	
Spears, Robert W		May 21	
Stoner, B		May 19	
Stephenson, Wm		May 20	Absent without leave from June 20
Saunett, Francis		"	" " " 1
Sagan, Peter		May 19	" " " July 1
Strait, John		May 20	" " " Sept. 6
Shaw, Wm		"	
Scribner, E		"	Discharged May 25
Saucer, Robt		May 26	Joined Rangers June 26
Sherman, O. P.		May 20	Absent without leave from June 1
Shaw, John		"	
Sinconr, Jacob		June 25	Absent without leave from July 24
Shirmer, Philip		May 19	Omitted in former rolls
Slayton, T		"	Absent without leave from June 1
Tharp, John		"	
Taylor, James		"	Absent Sept. 6 with leave
Turney, John		July 9	
Templeton, Robt		May 21	Absent Sept. 6 with leave
Usher, M. H		May 20	
Vansand, John		"	Discharged July 27

Name and Rank.	Residence.	Enrolled	Remarks.
		1832	
Willard, Henry		May 21	
Webb, Thos. J.		May 19	Transferred June 6 with leave
Walker, James		" "	Discharged Aug. 1
Wells, Guilford		" "	Absent without leave from June 1
Walker, Joseph		" "	Appointed Sergeant; discharged Aug. 1
Wood, Jeremiah		May 21	Absent Sept. 6 with leave
Young, Lewis		May 16	By a transfer from Mounted Rangers
Young, Hiram		May 21	Discharged June 27

CAPT. NICHOLAS DOWLING'S COMPANY

Of Artillery, 27th Regiment, Illinois Militia, called into service of the United States by the Governor's order, dated May 15, 1832, and now mustered for discharge this Sept. 6, 1832.

Name and Rank.	Residence.	Enrolled	Remarks.
		1832.	
Captains.			
I. R. B. Gardenier		May 19	By request acted as com'd't of Co. until July [14, 1832, when he resigned.
Nicholas Dowling		July 15	
First Lieutenant.			
G. W. Campbell		May 19	
Second Lieutenant.			
Charles Gratiot		May 19	
Third Lieutenant			
Leonard Goss		June 26	Detached to the staff
Sergeants.			
Nicholas Dowling		May 19	Elected Captain July 15, 1832
S. Gridley		July 15	
Z. Bell		May 19	
Daniel Argent			
George Ferguson		July 15	
Corporals.			
A. M. Delong		May 19	
N. Barber			
Michael Byrne		July 15	Lost his blanket
T. T. Davis			
Musician.			
Wm. Blair		July 15	Drew no arms nor blanket from company
Privates.			
Byrne, Michael		May 19	Appointed Corporal July 8, 1832
Byrne, Philip		" "	Sick
Brush, R. W.		June 30	
Coligan, P.			
Cullum, C. B.		July 8	
Drum, Thos.		May 19	
Davis, T. T.		" "	Appointed Corporal July 15, 1832
Ellis, P.		July 16	Drew no arms nor blanket from Co
Ferguson, George		May 19	Corporal from May 25 to July 25, when appointed Sergeant.
Farley, I. P.		" "	
Graham, Robert		" "	
Gridley, S.		" "	Corporal until July 15, 1832, when he was appointed Sergeant.
Garner, T.		" "	
Gray, M.		June 20	
Gray, B.			
Hempested, Wm.		June 30	On extra duty in ordnance department
Lockwood, Ezekial			
Mitchell, A.		July 14	
Mitchell, J.		" "	Furloughed; drew no arms nor blanket
Neville, E.		June 16	
Nutting, Josiah		July 16	Drew no arms nor blanket from company
Powell, R. B.		May 19	
Reed, Samuel		June 30	Furloughed
Roberts, I.		June 14	
Roundtree, S.		July 8	Drew no arms nor blanket from company

INDEPENDENT REGIMENTS. 139

Name and Rank.	Residence.	Enrolled	Remarks.
		1832	
Sayre, S. L......	....	May 19	....
Stuhl, F......	....	June 20	....
Smead, H......	....	May 25	Sick
Sharp, C. P......	....	May 19	Discharged June 3, 1832.
Taylor, Robert......	....		....
Towner, Wm......	....	May 27	
Vaubuskirk, J......	....	July 16	
Weather, John	....	May 19	
Wann, Daniel......	....		

CAPT. CLACK STONE'S COMPANY

Of the 27th Regiment, Illinois Militia, called into the service of the United States by the Governor's order, dated May 15, 1832. Mustered out September 6.

Name and Rank.	Residence.	Enrolled	Remarks.
Captain.		1832.	
Clack Stone........	....	May 25	
First Lieutenant.			
Heber Morris........	....	"	
Second Lieutenant.			
Samuel Jimmerson......	....	"	
Sergeants.			
George Lowry........	....	"	Quit June 15, with leave........
Jefferson Clark........	....	June 15	
Privates.			
Armstrong, John......	....	June 25	
Armstrong, David......	....	"	
Bean, Joseph........	....	"	
Bean, Charles........	....	"	Absent June 26 to July 16, on public duty....
Clark, David........	....	"	Quit June 20; discharged with leave........
Cook, Horace........	....	"	
Crane, Westley........	....	June 23	
Crane, Thomas........	....	July 13	
Fowler, Daniel........	....	May 25	Quit June 25, with leave........
Hack, Washington......	....	"	
Hack, John, Jr........	....	"	Quit August 13, with leave........
Hack, James........	....	"	
Hack, John, Sr........	....	"	
Hack, Milton........	....	"	
Hitt, Thadeus........	....	"	
Hulett, Samuel........	....	"	
Howard, Stephen P......	....	"	Killed in battle June 18........
Immerson, John B......	....	"	
Johnson, Robert B......	....	"	
Johnson, Wm., Jr......	....	"	
Kerkley, James B......	....	"	Discharged July 16........
Kilyan, Thomas........	....	"	
Knox, John........	....	July 13	
Lee, Jesse........	....	May 25	
Lawhoon, William......	....	"	Discharged June 25........
Morris, Nath'l........	....	"	
Milligan, David........	....	"	
Murdock, Fergus I......	....	"	
Milligan, Hezek........	....	"	
Murdock, John........	....	"	
Matthews, Granville......	....	"	
Nutting, Josiah........	....	"	Wounded and sent to hospital June 25........
Rittenhouse, Obed'h......	....	"	Quit June 15, with leave........
Rollings, Ezekiel........	....	July 16	" Aug. 16,
Tart, Benjamin........	....	May 25	" June 26,
Thacher, Alfred........	....	"	" June 20,
Van Vaultingburg, H......	....	"	
Vaubuskirk, Jesse......	....	"	Quit June 20, with leave........

Name and Rank.	Residence.	Enrolled	Remarks.
		1832	
Wooton, Daniel		June 19	
Wooton, Moses		May 25	
Williams, Richard			
White, Ambrose			

Capt. Charles McCoy's Company

Of Infantry, 27th Regiment of Illinois Militia, called into the service of the United States by the Governor's order, dated May 15, 1832, and was mustered for discharge this 6th day of September, 1832.

Name and Rank.	Residence.	Enrolled	Remarks.
Captain.		1832.	
Charles McCoy	JoDaviess Co.	May 27	Drew no rations for himself or servant; had a servant three months.
First Lieutenant.			
James M. Miller	"	"	Drew one month's rations only
Second Lieutenant.			
Jesse Yount		"	Drew one month's rations only
Sergeants.			
P. Thomas January		"	Discharged July 25
Dennison Billings		"	Entitled to twenty-four rations
Hezekiah Young		"	" " " "
John Tyree		"	" " " "
Corporals.			
John W. Smallwood		"	Entitled to twenty-four rations
William Barnhouse		"	" " " "
Jefferson Crawford		"	" " " "
John Brown		"	" " " "
Privates.			
Barker, Allen			Entitled to twenty-four rations
Blundrett, James		May 27	Discharged August 20
Baker, Sylvester		May 29	Drew no rations
Coffman, Abram		May 27	Entitled to twenty-four rations
Curtis, Horace		"	
Cottle, Oliver		"	
Curtis, Henry		"	
Eversoul, Chris'pher		"	Entitled to twenty-four rations
Field, William		July 1	
Gossett, Joseph		May 27	Entitled to twenty-four rations
Gillett, Benoni B		"	Drew no rations
Green, Andrew I		"	Entitled to twenty-four rations
Gilbert, Braxton		July 1	Entitled to eighteen rations
Grontjean, James		May 27	Drew no rations
Hindman, John			
Igo, Lewis		July 1	
Lillipon, Vichel		"	Entitled to eighteen rations
Langet, Francis		May 27	Entitled to twenty-four rations
Lewis, Lawson		"	
McGehee, Evan		"	
Miller, Vincent B		"	Entitled to twenty-four rations
McNair, Thomas		May 29	Drew no rations
Marlow, Rudolph		July 1	
Nicholson, John B		May 27	Discharged Aug. 20
Ogan, Irwin		"	Entitled to twenty-four rations
Phelps, George		July 1	Entitled to eighteen rations
Rand, Allen		May 27	Entitled to twenty-four rations
Reed, John		July 1	Entitled to eighteen rations
Richey, Milton		May 27	Discharged Aug. 20
Shultz, Christopher		"	Discharged Aug. 28
Stewart, Wm. M		"	Transferred to staff July 4
Stewart, John		July 1	
Town, Warren		May 27	Entitled to twenty-four rations
Tessott, Daniel		"	" " " "
Tyree, Jacob		"	" " " "

INDEPENDENT REGIMENTS.   141

Name and Rank.	Residence.	Enrolled	Remarks.
Vaughan, Peyton		July 1	
Wolcott, John		May 27	Entitled to twenty-four rations
Young, Robert R		"	"
Young, Wm. C		"	"
Yount, Benjamin M		"	"
Yount, George		"	"

CAPT. BENJAMIN J. ALDENRATH'S COMPANY

Of Infantry of the 27th Regiment of Illinois Militia, called into the service of the United States by the Governor's proclamation dated May 15, 1832, and was mustered for discharge on the 6th of September, 1832.

Name and Rank.	Residence.	Enrolled	Remarks.
Captain.		1832.	
Benj. J. Aldenrath	JoDaviess Co	May 18	
First Lieutenant.			
John C. Robinson		"	
Second Lieutenants.			
Daniel P. Price		"	Resigned June 2
James Simonds		June 10	Elected 2d Lieut. June 9
Sergeants.			
James Simonds		May 18	
Joseph Campbell		"	Absent without leave May 26
Barnett Whittimore		"	
Mynot Selleman		"	Absent without leave June 10
Samuel Moore		June 21	
George F. Smith		June 26	Absent from August, with arms, blankets, etc.
Corporals.			
Noah Thomas		May 18	Joined horse company July 1
Charles McGee		"	Absent without leave June 19
Enoch Thomas		"	
Samuel Love		"	
Privates.			
Billings, James		"	
Beasley, Ephraim		"	Quit June 19
Bilto, Charles		"	Quit May 27
Brophy, Thomas		"	Shot-bag returned
Chandler, Nathaniel		"	Quit May 27
Chaney, Osborn		"	Did no duty; return'd no arms or accoutrem's
Courts, Walter		"	Quit June 19, with leave
Carroll, Nicholaus		"	
Case, Aaron		"	
Crosby, Cyrus		July 3	
Cord, Stephen		May 24	Quit June 3; returned no gun, blanket, etc
Dickerson, George H		May 18	Quit July 1
Duncan, John		"	
Dyas, William		"	
Dyas, John		"	
Dyas, David		"	
Dooley, Linville		June 10	
Fortune, William		May 18	
Faherty, William		"	
Faherty, John		"	
Fullerton, John V		June 18	
George, Alexander		May 18	
George, Lewis		"	
George, Stephen		"	
Gentel, Perret		June 10	Drew no rations
Guthray, Thomas		"	Discharged July 23
Grafford, Lewis E		July 3	
Gocky, Gabriel		May 23	Quit June 2
Hathaway, Samuel		July 16	Joined after mustering into service
Hanniman, Thomas		May 18	
Hinman, Nelson		"	Absent without leave May 18
Hoozer, Jacob		June 18	

Name and Rank.	Residence.	Enrolled	Remarks.
		1832.	
Harrison, Daniel...	....	June 25	....
Hubbard, Thomas...	....	July 11	....
Hubbard, Goodrich...	....	"	....
Hubbard, William...	....	"	....
Hugell, Thomas...	....	May 20	Quit June 1...........................
Kenney, Patrick...	....	May 18	....
McGulpin, Samuel...	....	May 28	Quit June 7...........................
Moffitt, Benj. F...	....	May 18	Joined Horse Co. June 1; returned no arms.
McCausland, David...	....	May 19	....
McKinney, Patrick...	....	June 18	....
Minett, Toosus...	....	May 23	Quit June 1...........................
Moore, Samuel...	....	May 18	....
Phillis, John...	....	"	Quit June 10
Quinliven, Dennis...	....	"	Absent without leave................
Quinliven, Mark...	....	June 24	....
Ross, Thomas L...	....	May 18	....
Stevner, Lewis...	....	"	Quit May 28..........................
Skinner, Thomas H...	....	"	Gave certif. for 1 mo. serv.; ret'd no arms, etc.
Shannon, Daniel...	....	"	Absent without leave................
Stockton, Thomas B...	....	May 20	Disch. June 19, by order of Col. Strode......
Smith, George F...	....	May 19	....
Thomas, John...	....	May 18	Over age.............................
Thomas, Enos...	....	"	....
Williams, Wm...	....	"	....
Williams, John...	....	"	Absent without leave................
Williams, James...	....	"	....
Whalon, John...	....	"	Quit June 1..........................
Ware, Reuben S...	....	May 19	Two blankets not returned.............
Young, Joseph S...	....	June 7	Quit July 17..........................

Capt. H. H. Gear's Company

Of Infantry of the 27th Regiment, Illinois Militia, called into service of the United States by general order, dated May 15, 1832, and now mustered for discharge this 6th of September, 1832.

Name and Rank.	Residence.	Enrolled	Remarks.
		1832.	
Captain.			
H. Hezekiah Gear...	JoDaviess Co	May 19	....
First Lieutenant.			
J. W. Foster...	....	"	....
Second Lieutenant.			
Alesworth Baker...	....	"	....
Sergeants.			
Fountain Matthews...	....	....	Retained one blanket and lost one blanket...
William Alloway...	....	....	....
B. Servico...	....	June 10	Arms not retain'd, 1 rug, 2 kettles; abs'nt, sick
John K. Robinson...	....	June 14	Abs'nt, furl.; furnish'd arms, etc; abs'nt, leave
Corporals.			
Francis Sheverell...	....	May 27	....
Zelo Corey...	....	....	....
Timothy Lovell...	....	July 1	....
James Howerton...	....	May 19	....
Privates.			
Baganell, Charles...	....	June 5	Deserted July 12; carried off U.S. musket, &c.
Boxley, William...	....	May 27	Killed in battle July 1.
Bass, George...	....	July 31	....
Bias, Joseph...	....	June 1	Refuses to deliver U. S. musket.
Bryan, Leonard...	....	....	Servant to Capt. Legate, U.S.A.; disch. July 16
Bennett, G. W. B...	....	June 5	Deserted July 6; carried off U.S arms........
Bachelor, William...	....	May 19	" June 12. " & blanket
Cardinalle, Parish...	....	"	Musket returned; one blanket not returned.
Campbell, Hamilton...	....	"	One musket returned..................
Cardinalle, Eustace...	....	"	One musket and one blanket returned........

Name and Rank.	Residence.	Enrolled		Remarks.
		1832.		
Craig, Martin		May	19	Discharged June 7
Chapman, A. C		"	"	June 15
Cole, J		"		Deserted June 7
Carrigan, Charles		June	5	" June 6; carried off 2 robes, 1 musket
Dodge, John		July	17	Detailed for extra duty, Hosp. Cook, July 17.
Deslain, Thomas		June	1	
Downey, Antoine		May	19	Deserted June 12
Dement, William		June	10	
Elgin, F. C		May	19	Discharged June 7
Gray, J. H				
Guest Samuel		May	27	Deserted with blanket June 15
Gorton, William		May	19	" June 12; absent without leave June 12
Hudson, M. W		"	"	Lost one U. S. musket.[to Sept. 6; lost musk't
Hollman, Jesse		July	17	Found his own arms and equipments
Hallett, Moses		June	22	
Howell, J. W		June	5	Deserted July 6, and took off 1 U. S. musket
Hughs, Peter		May	27	" June 10, and took off his blanket
Kirkpatrick, J. F		May	19	Abs'nt without leave; joined Capt. Craig's Co.
Lestrange, Patrick		May	25	
Laport, Toulouse		May	27	Absent without leave July 16; present Sept. 6
Lepold, M		May	19	Musket and accoutrements returned
Long, A		"	"	Discharged June 7
Long, M		"	"	
Means, Jacob		"	"	Furnished own arms; rec'd 1 robe, not ret'ed
McBride, Felix		"	"	Discharged July 25
Marstin, J		July	31	
Massey, H		June	22	Detailed as an artificer
Mitchell, James		June	21	Absent without leave; never mustered
McDonald, J		June	5	Deserted June 12; took musket and blanket.
Mitchell, Augustus		June	21	Absent without leave; never mustered
Messmore, George		May	19	Discharged June 10
Nigh, Edmund		June	22	
O'Neil, John		May	19	Blanket not returned; 2 months hosp. attend.
Ontio, Peter		"	"	Absent without leave; his arms taken July 12; returned 26th; paid by Dan'l Warm, $13.25
Pelott, William		July	31	Furnished his arms and equipments
Primer, John B				
Rice, ——		June	22	Deserted July 6th
Robinson, M. C		May	19	Furnished his arms and equipments
Rhonds, Henry		May	27	
Randleman, Jacob		July	22	
Stuart, John		May	27	One musket returned; 1 blanket not returned
Scott, Samuel		June	10	Discharged August 5
Sincere, Michael		June	22	
Snider, S		May	19	Discharged June 7
Simmons, Silas G		June	5	Deserted July 12; took musket and buf. robe.
Saunderson, Chas. F		July	1	Deserted July 6; took musket and buf. robe.
Thatcher, Alfred		June	27	Furnished his own arms and equipments
Truegate, Benjamin		June	22	Discharged August 7
Truegate, Meredith				
Toulouse, J		May	27	
Tooley, Henry		May	19	Deserted June 7
Urie, Samuel		June	5	Returned musket and equipment
Urie, John				
Vaughn, Amos		May	19	
Williams, John				
Williamson, S. N		June	22	Absent without leave July 16
Webb, Thomas J		July	31	
Young, William		May	19	Discharged June 7

Capt. Samuel H. Scales' Company

Of Infantry, of the 27th Regiment of Illinois Militia, called into the service of the United States by the Governor's order dated May 15, 1832, and now mustered for discharge this 6th day of September, 1832.

Name and Rank.	Residence.	Enrolled	Remarks.
Captain. Samuel H. Scales	JoDaviess Co.	1832. June 16	
First Lieutenant. John L. Soals		"	
Second Lieutenant. George Wells		"	
Sergeants. James Smith		"	
John B. Woodson		"	Quit June 16
William Davis		"	
John Novib		"	Quit June 16
Corporals. Richard Willis		"	
Robert Hendrix		"	
Samuel Cory		"	
Emerson Chapman		"	
Privates. Brock, Elias		"	Drew no rations
Cook, Harris		"	
Charles, Elijah		"	Quit June 16
Davis, Noah		"	
Davis, John		"	
Davis, Jonathan		"	
Frost, Benjamin		July 22	
Gibson, Julius		June 16	
Hendrix, James		"	
Hale, David		"	Drew no rations
Hawkins, James L.		"	Quit June 16
House, William		"	
Lytchtenberger, Cyr.		"	
Lytchtenberger, Con		"	Quit June 15
McMath, William		"	
Miller, Geo. B.		"	
McKee, John		"	
Roberts, John		"	
Streeter, John		"	
Shook, Samuel		"	
Smitch, Isaac		"	
Streeter, Joshua		"	
Walbridge, Hiram		"	
Wood, John		"	
Wood, George		"	
Woods, William		"	
Wadhams, William		"	
Wadhams, John		"	
Woodcock, James S.		"	Quit June 16

CAPT. JONATHAN CRAIG'S COMPANY

Of Infantry of the 27th Regiment of Illinois Militia, called into the service of the United States by the Governor's order of May 15, 1832, and now mustered for discharge, this 6th day of September, 1832; enrolled for three months and twenty days.

Name and Rank.	Residence.	Enrolled	Remarks.
Captain.		1832.	
Jonathan Craig	JoDaviess Co.	May 19	
First Lieutenant.			
Thomas Kilgore		"	
Second Lieutenant.			
Robert C. Bourne		"	
Sergeants.			
John Furlong		"	
Tarlton F. Brock		"	
Joseph Claig		"	
Nathan White		"	
Corporals.			
Lewellyn Brock		"	
Hiram Morrison		"	
William Caradiff		"	
Philip Rice		"	
Privates.			
Boy, John		"	
Bruno, Peter		"	Drew a blanket; did not return it; with leave
Brock, Elisha		"	
Bowman, Benjamin		"	Quit July 6, with leave
Brady, Bernard		"	
Buster, Robert B.		"	
Biggs, William		June 27	
Bilto, Charles		July 12	
Campbell, John		May 19	
Coyle, Peter		"	
Coyle, James		"	
Dalton, William		"	Quit June 19, with leave
Dowling, Robert		July 18	
Dean, Elias		May 19	
Dugan, Patrick		June 27	
Dugan, John		"	
Fine, John		May 19	Quit July 5, with leave
Furlong, Walter		"	
Farrar, Robert		July 26	
Frost, Benjamin		May 19	Quit July 23, with leave
Foley, James		"	Quit July 4, with leave
Graham, Thomas		"	Dismissed July 6, with leave
Gilroy, Patrick		"	
Haines, Martin		"	
Kilgore, John		"	
Kirtley, J. W.		July 16	
Kelley, James		May 19	
Leary, Thomas		"	
Liddle, George		"	
Langford, William		"	
Lynch, Bernard		"	
McDermit, James		"	
Meara, Michael		"	
McCabe, James		"	
Maple, John L.		July 14	
Morrison, William		July 19	
Moore, Thomas		May 19	
Miller, Edward		"	
Murray, Keaven		June 27	
McNabb, Edward		"	
McNair, David		"	Quit July 20, with leave
O'Leary, Peter		July 6	
Parkinson, John		May 19	
Richardson, Fount'n		"	
Rice, James		"	
Roberts, James		July 14	
Rice, Henry		July 26	
Smith, Abner		May 19	
Sherrill, Adam		June 27	

146   BLACK HAWK WAR.

Name and Rank.	Residence.	Enrolled	Remarks.
		1832.	
Townsend, John		May 19	Drew blanket and did not return it
Tobin, Bartlett			
Vanbuskirk, Jesse		July 19	
Willis, Noah		July 2	

STATE OF ILLINOIS,
November 10, 1832.

I certify that James M. Strode was, on September 6 last, Colonel of the 27th Regiment of Illinois Militia, acting in said office; said company was in service under my order, and their service was necessary in the defence of the country last summer.

(Signed.)   JOHN REYNOLDS.
Commander-in-Chief Illinois Militia.

CAPT. LAMBERT P. VANSBURGH'S COMPANY

27th Regiment of Illinois Militia, called into the service of the United States by the Governor's order, dated May 15, 1832, and now mustered for discharge this 6th day of September, 1832.

Name and Rank.	Residence.	Enrolled	Remarks.
Captain.		1832.	
L. P. Vansburgh		May 18	
First Lieutenant.			
John W. Blackstone		June 20	
Second Lieutenant.			
Henry Cavener		May 18	Joined Mounted Vol. with permiss'n, June 20.
Sergeants.			
Zack Hillyard		June 20	
Thomas L. Potter		May 18	Joined Mounted Vol. with permiss'n, June 20.
John W. Blackstone		"	Elected 1st Lieut. June 20
Elias Griggs		"	Joined Mounted Vol. with permiss'n, June 20.
Alex. M. Neville		"	
Wm. Tomlinson		June 20	
Wm. Mattox		"	
Corporals.			
Thomas Reed		May 18	Joined Mounted Vol. with permiss'n, June 20.
Wm. P. Ravandaugh		"	
Edmund Mattox		June 20	
Wm. Tomlinson		May 18	Appointed Sergeant June 20
James Arwin		"	Joined Mounted Vol. with permiss'n, July 9.
Privates.			
Ashbrook, Chas. C.		"	
Ammerman, Josh.		"	Joined Mounted Vol. with permiss'n, June 20.
Austin, Hiram		July 13	Furloughed
Beard, Samuel		May 18	Absent from July 9
Ballard, John H.		"	Joined Mounted Vol. with permiss'n, June 20.
Ballard, Bartholo'ew		"	
Broody, Israel		"	Absent since June 20
Brown, William		June 20	
Broody, Washington		May 18	Absent since June 20
Crothers, Hamilton		June 20	
Cunningham, Wm.		May 18	Sick in hospital
Cunningham, John		"	
Crigan, John		"	Absent with leave July 9, sick
Clary, Patrick		"	
Craghead, John		"	Absent with leave June 20, sick
Dooly, Lindley		"	
Davenport, James		"	
Divin, David		"	
Donall, Jonathan		"	Joined Mounted Vol. with permiss'n, June 20.
East, William		"	
Fulton, W. J.		"	Absent since June 20
Fugate, Preston		"	

INDEPENDENT REGIMENTS.

Name and Rank.	Residence.	Enrolled	Remarks.
		1832.	
Funtress, Eleanzer..		June 20	
Gallager, Patrick...		May 18	Absent since June 20
Hullgate, Weston...		"	Discharged July 13.
Hoffman, Zack......		"	Discharged July 9.
Humes, Thompson..		"	
Huling, Samuel......		"	Joined Mounted Vol. with permiss'n, June 20.
Harden, Isam S......		"	
Hays, James.........		July 10	Furloughed
Ingraham, Alphs....		May 18	
Johnson, Wm........		July 6	Sick in hospital
Jourden, E..........		May 18	Joined Mounted Vol. with permiss'n, June 20.
Karnes, Patrick.....			
Knowland, Hardin..		June 20	
Larkin, James......		May 18	Absent with leave July 9, sick
Lawhorn, Willin.....		June 20	
Mattox, Wm........		May 18	Appointed Sergeant June 20.
Mattox, Edmund....		"	Appointed Corporal June 20.
Murphy, Richard...			
McKaney, Daniel....		June 29	
Obanion, George....		May 18	
Orm, Alexander.....		June 20	Absent since July 9
O'Brian, Wm........		May 18	Discharged June 20.
Palmer, John........		"	Absent since June 20, sick
Phalen, Lawrence..		June 27	
Ragan, John.........		May 18	Absent since June 20, sick
Ritter, Jacob........		"	
Robinson, Benj.....		"	
Ruggle, Edmund L.		June 20	
Stevens, George W.		May 18	Joined Mounted Vol. with permiss'n, June 20.
Smith, Wm.........		June 20	Absent since July 9
Scott, George.......		"	Sick in hospital
Sain, Philip........		July 13	Furloughed
Thompson, Willis...		May 18	Joined Mounted Vol. with permiss'n, June 20.
Tracey, Charles....		"	"
Thomas, John C....		July 2	
Williams, John.....		May 18	Absent since June 20
Wilson, Henry M...		"	
Whittle, Levi.......		"	
Walker, Samuel.....		June 26	
Wright, Hezekiah...			

ODD BATTALIONS.

ODD BATTALION COMMANDED BY MAJOR N. BUCKMASTER.

CAPT. HOLDEN SEISSION'S COMPANY

Of Mounted Volunteers, in the service of the United States, in defense of the Northern frontier of the State of Illinois, against the Sac and Fox Indians, from the county of Cook, in said State, in the year 1832. Mustered out August 15, 1832.

Name and Rank.	Residence.	Enrolled	Remarks.
Captain. Holden Seission	Cook Co.	1832. July 23	
First Lieutenant. Robert Stephens	"	"	
Second Lieutenant. William H. Bradford.	"	"	
Sergeants.			
James Sayres	"	"	
Uriah Wentworth	"	"	
John Cooper	"	"	
Abraham Franciss	"	"	
Corporals.			
Armstead Runyan	"	"	
Thomas Coons	"	"	
Edward Poor	"	"	
Cornell's C. VanHorn	"	"	
Privates.			
Barlow, William	"	"	
Cox, Joseph	"	"	
Clarke, Timothy B.	"	"	
Clarke, Barrett	"	"	
Clarke, William	"	"	
Chapman, William	"	"	
Crandell, David	"	"	
Crandell, Alva	"	"	
Darling, Enoch	"	"	
Fleming, Samuel	"	"	
Frame, Patterson	"	"	
Franciss, Thomas	"	"	
Friend, John	"	"	
Friend, Aaron	"	"	
Gougar, William	"	"	
Gougar, John	"	"	
Gougar, Nicholas	"	"	
Gougar, Daniel	"	"	
Haight, Daniel	"	"	
Henderson, Silas	"	"	

ODD BATTALIONS. 149

Name and Rank.	Residence.	Enrolled	Remarks.
		1832.	
Johnson, Alfred	Cook Co.	July 23	
Johnson, Joseph	"	"	
Johnson, James	"	"	
Lampseed, Peter	"	"	
Lemsis, Peter	"	"	
Lamfear, Selah	"	"	
More, Aaron	"	"	
Maggard, Daniel	"	"	
McDeed, John	"	"	
McDeed, James	"	"	
Mack, Daniel	"	"	
Maggard, Benjamin	"	"	
Mathews, James	"	"	
Norman, Joseph	"	"	
Pettijohn, George	"	"	
Poor, Anderson	"	"	
Rowley, Calvin	"	"	
Rodgers, William	"	"	
Rice, Rufus	"	"	
Robb, Daniel	"	"	
Scott, Wm. H	"	"	
Scott, Lucius	"	"	
Smith, David	"	"	
Stephens, Oren	"	"	
Turner, O. L.	"	"	
Van Horne, Abrah'm	"	"	
Van Horne, Simon C.	"	"	
Wares, Aaron	"	"	
Wilson, John	"	"	

I certify on honor that the company of Mounted Volunteers, under the immediate command of Capt. Holden Seission, was organized for temporary purposes on the 23d of July, 1832, by the advice and consent of Major-General Scott, for the protection of the frontier, in Cook county, State of Illinois. Which organization was recommended and approved by the said Major General Scott (in consequence of the mustering two companies out of service which constituted part of the guard for the protection of that frontier under my command); that this organization was necessary for the protection of the frontier; that said company should be in service, and that they did actually perform the service, as mentioned in said roll, up to the 13th of August, 1832, under my command as Major of an Odd Battalion, wherein said company formed a part.

Given under my hand, at Edwardsville, August 19, 1833.

(Signed.) N. BUCKMASTER,
Major Commanding.

I certify, that, at the time mentioned in the muster roll of Capt. Seission's Company of Mounted Volunteers, the above named Nathaniel Buckmaster was legally acting as Major in an Odd Battalion, including said company, and commissioned by me in that office, and, judging from the certificates of said Major Buckmaster and Capt. Seission, I have no doubt said company served as stated in said roll; and I state further, that the service of said company was necessary in the defense of the country, as stated above.

(Signed.) JOHN REYNOLDS,
Governor, and Commander-in-Chief Illinois Militia.

AUGUST 20, 1833.

CAPT. JOSEPH NAPIER'S COMPANY

Of Mounted Volunteers, in the service of the United States, in defence of the northern frontier of the State of Illinois against the Sac and Fox Indians, from the county of Cook in said State, in the year 1832. Mustered out Aug. 15, 1832.

Name and Rank.	Residence.	Enrolled	Remarks.
		1832.	
Captain. Joseph Napier	Cook Co.	July 19.	
First Lieutenant. Alanson Sweet	"	"	

BLACK HAWK WAR.

Name and Rank.	Residence.	Enrolled	Remarks.
Second Lieutenant.		1832.	
Sherman King	Cook Co.	July 19.	
Sergeants.			
S. M. Salisbury	"	"	
John Manning	"	"	
Walter Stowell	"	"	
John Napier	"	"	
Corporals.			
T. E. Parsons	"	"	
Lyman Butterfield	"	"	
J. P. Bladget	"	"	
Nelson Murray	"	"	
Privates.			
Ament, Anson	"	"	
Ament, Calvin	"	"	
Barber, William	"	"	
Clarke, Dennis	"	"	
Fox, George	"	"	
Foster, Caleb	"	"	
Fox, John	"	"	
Gault, William	"	"	
Geddiens, Josiah H.	"	"	
Hawley, Peres	"	"	
Harrison, Edmund	"	"	
Hobson, Bailey	"	"	
Langdon, Daniel	"	"	
Peck, P. F. W.	"	"	
Parsons, T.	"	"	
Paine, Uriah	"	"	
Paine, Christopher	"	"	
Stevens, John	"	"	
Stevens, John, Jr.	"	"	
Scott, Williard	"	"	
Stowell, Augustine	"	"	
Stowell, Calvin M.	"	"	
Sweet, Richard M.	"	"	
Walsteoat, Seth	"	"	
Wilson, Henry T.	"	"	
Wicoffe, Peter	"	"	

I certify on honor that the company of Mounted Volunteers under the immediate command of Capt. Joseph Napier was organized for temporary purposes on July 19, 1832, by the advice and consent of Major-General Scott, for the protection of the frontier in Cook county, State of Illinois, which organization was recommended and approved by the said Major-General Scott (in consequence of the importance of mustering two companies out of service which constituted a part of the guard for the protection of that frontier under my command); that this organization was necessary for the protection of the frontier; that said company should be in service, and that they did actually perform the service, as mentioned in said roll, up to the 13th of August, 1832, under my command as Major of an Odd Battalion wherein said company formed a part.

Given under my hand at Edwardsville, August 19, 1833.

    (Signed.)   N. BUCKMASTER,
                                               Major Commanding.

I certify that at the time mentioned in the muster roll of Capt. Joseph Napier's Company of Mounted Volunteers, the above named Nathaniel Buckmaster was legally acting as Major in an Odd Battalion including said company, and commissioned by me in that office, and judging from the certificate of Major Buckmaster and Capt. Napier, I have no doubt said company served as stated in said roll; and I further state that the service of said company was *necessary* in the defence of the country, as stated above.

    (Signed.)   JOHN REYNOLDS,
August 20, 1833.   Gov. and Com.-in-Chief Ill. Mil.

I further certify that the United States furnished no forage for the within company, and the said company was in service when I was mustered out of service on Aug. 13, 1832.

    (Signed.)   N. BUCKMASTER,
                                               Major Commanding.

ODD BATTALION OF RANGERS.

Capt. Abner Eads' Company

Of Mounted Rangers. Enrolled at Peoria, Illinois, by virtue of an order from the Commander-in-Chief of the Militia of the State of Illinois, to Brig.-Gen. Josiah Stillman. Mustered into the service of the United States April 23, 1832. Discharged June 28, 1832.

Name and Rank.	Residence.	Enrolled	Remarks.
Captain.		1832.	
Abner Eads		April 23	
First Lieutenant.			
William A. Stewart		"	
Second Lieutenant.			
John W. Caldwell		"	
Sergeants.			
Aquilla Wren		"	Promoted to Quartermaster Sergt. May 17 '32
Hiram M. Curry		"	
Edwin S. Jones		"	
John Hinkle		"	
Corporals.			
William Wright		"	
John Stringer		"	
John Hawkins		"	
Thomas Webb		"	
Privates.			
Bristol, John E		"	
Brown, Harrison		"	
Cooper, Jeremiah		"	
Clifton, John		"	
Carle, Stephen		"	
Conner, Joseph H		"	
Cox, Jefferson		"	
Cox, John		"	
Clark, Ebenezer		"	
Cleaveland, Hiram		"	
Caldwell, Alexander		"	
Doty, James		"	
Dodge, John B		"	
Eads, William		"	
Love, Elias		"	
Moffat, Alvah		"	
Moats, Jacob		"	
Moore, Sylvanus		May 8	
Miner, Harris		May 3	
Owen, John C		"	
Phillis, Joseph		April 23	
Rodick, George		"	
Ridgeway, David		"	
Root, Lucas		"	
Ross, David		"	
Ross, John		"	
Reed, Thomas B		"	
Reed, Simon		"	
Sharp, Francis		"	
Smith, Rice		"	
Talifero, Jefferson		"	
Trial, William D		"	
Thurman, Johnson T		"	
Thomas, Henry		May 1	
Wood, William L		April 23	

Capt. David W. Barnes' Company

Of Mounted Volunteer Rangers under the command of Brig.-Gen. Isaiah Stillman, acting as Major for the Battalion, according to the orders of the 19th of April, 1833, received from the Commander-in-Chie of this State, and entered into the service of the United States against the hostile band of Sac and Fox tribes of Indians, on the 21st day of April, 1832, and discharged out of service at Lewistown, Fulton county, on the 25th day of June, 1832.

Name and Rank.	Residence.	Enrolled	Remarks.
Captain.		1832	
David W. Barnes....	Fulton Co....	April 21	
First Lieutenant.			
Thos. W. Clark......	"	"	
Second Lieutenant.			
Asa Langford........	"	"	
Sergeants.			
Seth Hilton, 1st......	"	"	Sergeant 30 days after being private 35 days.
Josiah Marchant, 1st	"	"	" " balance 1st Sergt. vice Hilton
Reding, Putman.....	"	"	Wounded in battle on Sycamore C'k May 14..
David C. Murray	"	"	
Frederick Wachel ...	"	"	
Corporals.			
John Holcomb, 1st..	"	"	Paid passage home of R. Putman, w'nded; $4
Medad Comstock, 2d	"	"	
Bird W. Ellis, 3d......	"	"	Minor; killed in bat'l; disch. drawn to father
Hazel Putman, 3d ...	"	May 14	Prom. 3d Corp. May 15, vice B. W. Ellis, killed..
John W. Ward, 4th...	"	April 21	
Bugler.			
Jodisah Moore	"	"	
Privates.			
Anderson, Joseph...	"	"	Discharged at Canton May 30, 1832, sick ......
Bybee, Alfred........	"	"	
Babitt, Jacob	"	"	
Barker, William	"	May 9	
Brown, Elijah........	"	April 21	
Baughman, Samuel..	"	"	
Brink, Henry........	"	"	
Chein, Charles.......	"	"	
Cooper, Owen J.....	"	"	
Chase, Wheaton.....	"	"	
Childs, Tyrus M.....	"	"	Killed in battle May 14; disch. in favor of wife
Depriest, Charles C.	"	May 9	
Dalton, Avery........	"	May 30	
Dehart, William.....	"	April 21	Discharged May 21, 1832
Ellis, Absalom.......	"	"	
Farris, David	"	"	
Farris, Jeremiah	"	"	
Farris, Joseph B.....	"	"	Killed in battle May 14, 1832......
Hoocky, David	"	"	
Huff, John	"	"	
Hilton, Seth	"	"	
Jones, Ahriah........	"	"	
Jones, Williston.....	"	"	
Maxwell, Alex H.....	"	"	
Marchant, Josiah....	"	"	Prom.; served 1st Sergt. 30 days, vice S. Hilton
Miles, Christopher..	"	"	
Nichols, John G.....	"	June 2	
Pennington, Stephen	"	"	
Putman, Hazel	"	May 9	
Richards, Henderson	"	April 21	
Rice, Benjamin......	"	"	
Smith, Asa	"	"	
Shesin, Isaac	"	"	
Swann, Isaac	"	"	
Strickland, Isaac....	"	May 9	
Shirlock, Zachariah.	"	"	
Watchell, Henry.....	"	April 21	
Woolf, Jacob C......	"	"	
Watkins, Fountaine.	"	"	
Wilcockson, Samuel	"	"	

ODD BATTALIONS. 153

I certify on honor that this muster roll exhibits the true state of Capt. David W. Barnes' Company of Mounted Volunteer Rangers, in the Battalion commanded by Major Isaiah Stillman, for the periods herein mentioned; that the remarks set opposite the name of each officer and soldier are as nearly accurate and just, and exhibit in every particular the true state of the company, as possible.

(Signed.)   D. W. BARNES, CAPT.

Date, Lewistown, Fulton Co., Ill., Aug. 30, 1832.

Stationed as Rangers.

CAPT. ASEL F. BALL'S COMPANY

Of Mounted Volunteers, under the command of Brig.-Gen. Stillman, acting as Major for the Battalion according to the orders of the 16th of April, 1832, received from the Commander-in-Chief of this State, and entered into the service of the United States, Lewistown, Fulton county. Mustered out June 25, 1832.

Name and Rank.	Residence.	Enrolled	Remarks.
Captain.		1832.	
Asel F. Ball............	Fulton Co....	April 28	Amount of property lost in battle $35.50.......
First Lieutenant.			
William D. Baldwin.	"	May 15	
Second Lieutenant.			
David S. Baughman	"	April 28	Amount of property lost in battle $75.00.......
Sergeants.			
William Miner, 1st..	"	April 28	Amount of property lost in battle $7.25
John Walters, 2d....	"	" "	Killed in battle May 14th, 1832; amt. lost $21....
Joseph L. Sharp, 2d.	"	May 15	Appointed 2d Sergt. on 15th of May
John Heinford, 3d...	"	April 28	Amount of property lost in battle $26........
John Thompson.....	"	" "	
Corporals.			
Thomas J. Welsh....	"	May 15	
Francis Irwin.......	"	" "	
Thomas, Walters....	"	April 28	Amount of property lost in battle $9.37½......
Hugh Finley.........	"	" "	" $10.25...
Musician.			
Jonathan Cazad.....	"	May 15	
Privates.			
Arrington, Ethelbert	"	April 28	Amount of property lost in battle $30.50.......
Austin, Nathan	"	" "	" $24.87.......
Anderson, George...	"	May 15	
Brush, John........	"	" "	
Barker, William.....	"	" "	
Cary, Almon	"	" "	
Denis, Thomas......	"	" "	
Dunawin, Levering.	"	April 28	Amount of property lost in battle $12.62 ......
Ellis, James.........	"	" "	" " " $12.25 ......
Fouts, Elmsby.......	"	" "	" " " $5.25
Freeman, Moses F..	"	May 15	
Foster, James M....	"	" "	
Foster, Harvey......	"	" "	
Garner, Denyson...	"	April 28	
Howard, Zachius....	"	" "	Amount of property lost in battle $9.00 ......
Hoxton, Williamson	"	" "	" $5.50 ......
Harness, Seton......	"	May 15	
Hendricks, Price....	"	" "	
Harwick, Henry.....	"	" "	
Hill, William........	"	" "	
Langford, Thomas..	"	April 28	Property lost in battle $17, horse killed $75.00
Lanpersel, Sumn....	"	May 15	
Laswell, James......	"	" "	
Morris, Thomas.....	"	April 28	Prop. lost in battle $11.00; disch. May 25 '32....
Maxfield, Andrew H	"	" "	$36.75; 1 horse, $10.00.........
Murphy, Adam	"	May 15	
Morgan, James......	"	" "	
Scovel, Norman.....	"	April 28	Amount of property lost in battle, $25.75 .....
Walling, Ebenezer..	"	" "	" $21.12½ ....
Whipple, Sylvester..	"	" "	
Walters, John	"	" "	Amount of property lost in battle, $6.75 ......
Wilson, Charles.....	"	May 15	
Yunt, Jacob.........	"	" "	

I certify that the above return roll of all of the Mounted Volunteers under my command is a correct return, and of all the property lost in battle, and otherwise, by the said Volunteers, and who have duly certified on oath before an acting Justice of the Peace.
(Signed.) ASEL F. BALL, Capt.
Lewistown, Fulton county, June 26, 1832

I certify on honor that I have carefully examined this muster roll of the above named Battalion and find it correct.
(Signed.) THOS. W. TAYLOR,
Brig.-Major 53d Ill. Mil.,
acting Adjt. for above named Bat.
Lewistown, Fulton county, Ill., June 26, 1832.

ILLINOIS VOLUNTEERS.

I certify that John Walters volunteered and served service as a second Sergeant in a company of mounted Rangers under my command, ordered on the 16th day of April, for the protection of the Northern Frontier, in the Battalion command of Major Isaiah Stillman; that he was enrolled on the 28th day of April, 1832, and was killed in battle while in the line of duty, on the 14th day of May thereafter, having served sixteen days.
Given under my hand this 26th day of June, 1832.
(Signed.) ASEL F. BALL, Capt.
Amount of property lost in battle on the night 14th of May, $21.

STATE OF ILLINOIS, |
Schuyler County. |

Asahel F. Ball and David W. Barnes, being duly sworn, depose and saith that Jane R. Walters is the lawful wife of John W. Walters, deceased.
Sworn and subscribed before me.
(Signed.) H. FELLOWS, (Signed.)
Justice Peace
D. W. BARNES,
ASEL F. BALL.

The paymaster will pay whatever may be due me on the within contents, to Asel F. Ball, who is hereby authorized to receive and receipt for the same.
Dec. 26th, 1832.
(Signed.)
her
JANE R. + WALTERS,
mark.
Witness,
JOSIAH MOORE, { SEAL }
THOMAS U. CLARK.
(Signed.)
Relict of JOHN WALTERS, deceased.

COMPANIES IN ODD BATTALIONS.

Capt. Sain's Company

Of the Odd Battalion of Mounted Rangers, called into the service of the United States, on the requisition of Gen. Atkinson, by the Governor's proclamation, dated 30th of May, 1832. Mustered out September 4, 1832.

Name and Rank.	Residence.	Enrolled	Remarks.
Captain.		1832.	
John Sain	Fulton Co.	June 7	
First Lieutenant.			
Livings Burrington	"	"	
Second Lieutenant.			
Elijah Wilcoxson	"	"	Detached on extra duty Aug. 27
Sergeants.			
Lewis M. Ross	"	"	Detached on extra duty Aug. 27
Jerry Farris	"	"	
William Hummell	"	"	
Cyrus P. Fellows	"	"	
Corporals.			
Patrick H. Hart	"	"	
S. Harrington	"	"	Furloughed from 20th of Aug. to this date
Doctor Eccles	"	"	
James Carter	"	"	
Privates.			
Allrea, Nathan	"	"	Sick; furloughed on the 22d Aug.
Barnes, David W.	"	"	
Babbit, Jacob	"	"	Horse crippled Sept. 27.
Bartley, Joseph	"	"	Sick; furloughed on the 24th Aug.
Barker, William	"	"	
Bybee, Alfred	"	"	Furloughed; unable to march on 27th Aug.
Comstock, Medad	"	"	Detached on extra duty
Cary, Alamaran	"	"	
Cooper, Owen I.	"	"	
Chaw, Silas	"	"	
Doud, John	"	"	
Emerson, Reuben	"	"	Horse left near Winnebago swamp
France, John	"	"	
Franklin, Able	"	"	Detached on extra duty
Foster, James M.	"	"	
Farris, David	"	"	Sick on the 27th Aug.
Griffin, William	"	"	
Harris, John	"	"	
Hull, Jess	"	"	Horse lamed and left on 27th Aug.
Hull, William	"	"	
Johnson, Hiram	"	"	
Kendrick, Price	"	"	Detailed on extra duty on 20th Aug.
Long, Madison	"	"	
Long, Hanson	"	"	
Long, Lewis	"	"	
Long, William	"	"	
Langford, Thomas	"	"	Detached on extra duty the 20th Aug.
Lancaster, John	"	"	Detached on the 1st Sept. to find lost horse.
Morgan, James	"	"	
Manar, Antoin	"	"	
McKim, John H.	"	"	Detached to find lost horse on the 20th Sept.
Maxwell, Alexander	"	"	
Nichols, John	"	"	
Phelps, William	"	"	

Name and Rank.	Residence.	Enrolled	Remarks.
		1832.	
Shaw, Zachariah	Fulton Co	June 7	
Shain, Charles	"	"	
Smith, Asa	"	"	Detailed to fiued lost horse 1st Sept
Spencer, Oliver	"	"	Detached on extra duty on the 20th Aug
Ulmore, Daniel	"	"	Detailed with sick horse on the 27th Aug
Vandyke, Minard	"	"	
Wolf, David	"	"	Detailed with sick horse on the 27th Aug
Wilcoxson, Samuel	"	"	
Welch, Thomas J	"	"	Detached to find lost horse on 28th Aug
Westerfield, A. M	"	"	
Yount, Jacob	"	"	

It appears from certificates accompanying muster-roll that Jesse B. Wilcoxson volunteered as a Mounted Ranger on the 7th of June, 1832, and served as a private in the company commanded by Capt. John Sain, and that he was honorably discharged therefrom on the 4th day of September, 1832.

Capt. William McMurtry's Company

Of the Odd Battalion of Mounted Rangers, called into the service of the United States, on the requisition of Gen. Atkinson, by the Governor's proclamation, dated May 30, 1832. Mustered out September 4, 1832.

Name and Rank.	Residence.	Enrolled	Remarks.
Captain.		1832.	
William McMurtry	Knox Co	June 24	
First Lieutenant.			
George G. Lattimore	"	"	
Second Lieutenant.			
Turner R. Rountree	"	"	
Sergeants.			
Edward Martin	"	"	
Benjamin Brown	"	"	
Josiah Vaughn	"	"	
James McMurtry	"	"	
Corporals.			
Edward Fuqua	"	"	
James H. Rountree	"	"	
Thomas Maxwell, Jr	"	"	
Obediah Fuqua	"	"	
Privates.			
Adcock, Edmund	"	"	
Adkins, Jesse	"	"	
Bell, Peter	"	"	
Brown, James	"	"	
Barber, Franklin B	"	June 25	
Brown, Wilson	"	"	
Brown, Alfred	"		
Brown, George	"	Aug. 19	
Brown, Joshua	"	Aug. 20	
Bell, Henry	"	June 25	
Criswell, Jas McM	"	June 24	
Criswell, Ebnr	"		
Corban, William	"	June 25	
Coy, Erbin	"	June 24	
Davis, Solomon	"	June 25	
Fuqua, Daniel	"	June 24	
Frakes, Alexander	"	June 25	
Ferguson, James	"	"	
Fraker, John	"	"	
Gillett, Luster T	"	"	
Goff, James	"	"	
Hunt, Zachias	"	"	
Hilton, William	"	"	

ODD BATTALIONS.

Name and Rank.	Residence.	Enrolled	Remarks.
		1832.	
Hendricks, Robt. K.	Knox Co.	June 25	
Holiday, Joseph	"	Aug. 6	
Jennings, Berryman	"	June 24	
Jennings, Theodore.	"		
Jones, Reese	"	Aug. 6	
Lewis, William	"	June 25	
McKee, Thomas W.	"	June 24	
McMurtry, John	"		
McGehee, James	"	"	
Maxwell, Thomas, Sr	"		
Maxwell, James	"	"	
Miles, John	"		
McCallister, Thos C.	"	June 25	
McCallister, ——	"		
Miles, Daniel	"	Aug. 21	
Miles, Elisha	"		Sick 1st September, Henderson Block House
Norton, John	"	June 25	
Nevett, James	"		
Osbourn, Andrew	"	June 24	
Osbourn, Stephen	"		
Owen, Parnick	"	"	
Pennington, Simeon.	"		
Rountree, John D.	"		
Robinson, John P.	"	"	
Row, Joseph	"		
Rice, Jonathan	"	June 25	
Robertson, Alexan'r.	"	"	
Stillings, Josiah	"		
Vaugh, John	"	June 24	
White, Samuel S.	"	"	
Wallace, Joseph	"		
Williams, Calvin	"	June 25	
Williams, William	"	Aug. 6	

Capt. Asel F. Ball's Company

Of the Odd Battalion of Mounted Rangers, called into the service of the United States, on the requisition of Gen. Atkinson, by the Governor's proclamation dated 29th May, 1832. Mustered out Sept. 4, 1832. For 90 days.

Name and Rank.	Residence.	Enrolled	Remarks.
Captain.		1832.	
Asel F. Ball	Fulton Co.	July 27	
First Lieutenant.			
Thomas W. Clark	"	"	
Second Lieutenant.			
Asa Langford	"	"	On furlough Aug. 28 for six days
Sergeants.			
William Avery	"	"	
William Hill	"	"	On furlough Aug. 28 for six days
William Crosby	"	"	
Absalom Maxwell	"	"	
Corporals.			
Hiram Sanders	"	"	Detailed to find horse Sept. 1st
John Miller	"	"	
James R. Sharp	"	"	
Jesse Walden	"	"	
Privates.			
Anderson, Joseph	"	"	
Ashby, William	"	"	
Bradshaw, James	"	"	Furloughed Aug. 26 for six days
Brown, John	"	"	
Baldwin, William D.	"	"	
Cole, Henry	"	"	
Cozen, Jonathan	"	"	
Dorris, Josiah	"	"	

Name and Rank.	Residence.	Enrolled	Remarks.
		1832.	
Dorris, Thomas	Fulton Co	July 27	
Deprist, Charles C.	"	"	
Dixon, Hiram	"	"	Furloughed Aug. 26 for 6 days
Enos, Horace B.	"	"	
Grim, David	"	"	
Harness, Seaton	"	"	
Harrison, Samuel	"	"	
Laleiker, Frederick	"	"	
Liebfield, Lenard	"	"	
Long, Weir	"	"	
Murry, David C.	"	"	Furl'd Aug. 11; thrown by horse; sh'lder b'kn
McGehee, Allen	"	"	
Maxwell, Abner	"	"	Furloughed Aug. 5 for 6 days; supposed sick
McGehoe, Stephen	"	"	
Purtle, Peter	"	"	
Purvin, Hozy	"	"	
Richards, Henders'n	"	July 7	
Strickland, Isaac	"	"	
Shaw, John	"	"	
Sharp, Joseph L.	"	"	
Thaxton, Williamson	"	July 27	

Capt. J. W. Kenney's Company

Of an Odd Battalion, commanded by Major Bogart, called into the service of the United States on the requisition of Gen. Atkinson, by the Governor's proclamation dated May 20, 1832. Mustered out Sept. 4, 1832.

Name and Rank.	Residence.	Enrolled	Remarks.
Captain.		1832.	
John W. Kenney	R'k Island Co	May 20	
First Lieutenant.			
Joseph Danforth	"	"	
Privates.			
Davis, Thomas	"	"	
Danforth, Manly	"	"	
Danforth, Samuel	"	July 1	
Kenney, Samuel	"	May 20	
Kenney, Thomas	Adams Co	June 12	On furlough
McGee, Gentry	R'k Island Co	May 20	
McNeal, Henry	"	"	
McNeal, Neel	"	July 1	
Maskal, James	"	May 20	
Smith, Martin	"	"	
Sams, Wm. H.	"	July 1	
Thompson, Joel	"	May 20	
Thompson, Wm	"	"	
Wells, Ira	"	"	
Wells, Eri	"	"	
Wells, Asaph	"	"	
Wells, Nelson	"	"	
Wells, Hannah	"	"	
Wells, Joel, Jr.	"	"	
Wells, Joel, Sr.	"	"	
Wells, Luke, Sr.	"	"	

ODD BATTALIONS.   159

CAPT. BUTLER'S COMPANY

Of the Odd Battalion Mounted Rangers, called into the service of the United States, on the requisition of Gen. Atkinson, by the Governor's proclamation dated May 20, 1832. Mustered out September 4, 1832.

Name and Rank.	Residence.	Enrolled	Remarks.
Captain.		1832.	
Peter Butler	Warren Co...	June 11	
First Lieutenant.			
James McCalen	"	"	
Second Lieutenant.			
John Wilson	McDon'u'h Co	"	
Sergeants.			
Abraham Dover	"	"	
Asa Cook	"	"	
Erastus S. Denison	Warren Co.,	"	Sick at Yellow Banks August 30.
John Vernater	"	"	
Corporals.			
Josiah Osborn	"	"	
Lewis F. Temple	McDon'u'h Co	"	
Benjamin Tucker	Warren Co..	"	Sick at Yellow Banks September 1.
Daniel Cranshaw	Hancock Co..	"	
Privates.			
Ambrose, Ezekiel	"	"	Sick at Yellow Banks August 25.
Allen, Ezra G	Warren Co...	"	
Butler, Ira F. M	"	"	Sick at Yellow Banks August 1.
Booth, Moses	McDon'u'h Co	July 13	
Campbell, James M	"	June 11	
Clark, David	"	"	
Coffman, Jacob	"	"	
Cranshaw, Isaac	"	"	
Carter, Thomas	"	"	
Cranshaw, Paschal	Hancock Co..	June 29	
Cartwright, Danias B	Warren Co...	June 11	Sick at Yellow Banks August 20.
Caldwell, James J	"	"	
Cash, William	Hancock Co..	June 29	Detached on extra duty September 1.
Davidson, John	Warren Co..	July 2	Sick at Yellow Banks August 6.
Denison, William H	"	June 11	
Ferington, Orsemus	McDon'u'h Co	"	
Gibson, Andrew	Warren Co,.	"	
Hardisty, John	McDon'u'h Co	"	
Hays, Peter	"	"	
Hays, Nathaniel	"	"	
Hendricks, John	Warren Co...	"	
Hogus, Samuel L	"	"	
Jarves, Fields F	"	"	
Jackson, John	McDon'u'h Co	"	
Jones, Lace	"	"	
Jones, Berry	"	"	
Jones, John	"	"	
Kirkland, Zacheriah	"	"	
Lathrope, John	"	June 28	
McGuffies, James J	Hancock Co..	June 11	
McCoy, John	Warren Co...	"	
Morris, Isaac	McDon'u'h Co	"	
Osborn, Larkin	"	"	
Paxton, William S	Warren Co..	"	
Penceno, Paschal	"	"	Sick at Yellow Banks September 1, 1832.
Quinn, John	"	"	
Richey, Adam	"	"	
Richey, Thomas	"	"	Sick at Yellow Banks September 1.
Richey, John D	"	"	
Russell, John L	McDon'u'h Co	"	
Stice, Robert L	Warren Co..	"	
Smart, Josiah	"	"	Sick at Yellow Banks August 20.
Smith, Paschal H	McDon'u'h Co	"	
Smith, Charles A	Warren Co..	"	
Sacket, William	McDon'u'h Co	"	
Southward, William	"	July 2	
Stark, William	Warren Co..	June 11	
Tetherow, David	McDon'u'h Co	"	Sick at Yellow Banks August 30.

Name and Rank.	Residence.	Enrolled	Remarks.
		1832.	
Tetherow, George...	McDon'u'h Co	June 11	Sick at Yellow Banks August 30......
Tomberlin, Fount'n C	"	"	
Vertrees, Isaac......	Warren Co...	"	
Williams, Amos......	"	"	

Capt. James White's Company

Of the Odd Battalion of Mounted Rangers, called into the service of the United States on the requisition of Gen. Atkinson. Mustered out of the service of the United States September 5th, 1832.

Name and Rank.	Residence.	Enrolled	Remarks.
Captain.		1832.	
James White.........	Hancock Co...	April 30	
First Lieutenant.			
John Reynolds......	"	"	Furloughed Sept. 2, for 3 days............
Second Lieutenant.			
James Miller.........	"	"	
Sergeants.			
A. S. Foot, 1st......	"	"	
Amasah Doolittle, 2d	"	July 16	
William White, 3d..	"	April 30	
John Vance, 4th.....	"	"	
John Robinson, 5th..	"	"	
Corporals.			
Gabriel Long.........		"	
Samuel Gooch.......		"	
George Wilson		"	
Anabel Whiting.....		"	
Privates.			
Atherton, John R...		July 16	Sick at Fort Spillman on Sept. 1............
Buckanan, George..		"	
Brown, Enoch D....		"	
Burnet, William.....		"	
Barber, Samuel......		"	
Coon, David		April 30	Furloughed on Aug. 30, up to this day .....
Clark, Johnson......		July 16	
Clark, Johnson, Jr..		"	
Cheney, Richard....		"	Sick on Sept. 1; Musician...................
Carpenter, Joseph..		"	
Doolittle, Briar......		"	
Donald, Jonathan...		"	
Delong, Perry........		"	
Enslen, Squire D....		"	
Felt, Cyrus............		April 30	
Gregg, John..........		"	
Goodwin, Samuel...		July 16	
Gray, James..........		"	
Horner, John.........		"	
Harper, George W..		"	
Higgins, Wm.........		"	
Hickason, Wm.......		"	
Hickason, Elisha....		"	
Hill, Davis............		"	
Kennedy, Nathan...		"	
McNitt, Benjamin...		"	
Miller, William......		April 30	Sick Aug. 28, 1832...........................
Moffitt, James, 1st..		May 17	
Moffitt, James, 2d..		July 16	
Moffitt, John.........		"	
Middleton, George..		"	
Moore, Abraham....		July 16	
Smith, Andrew F...		April 30	Thrown from horse; shoulder dislocated.....
Spillman, Hezekiah.		July 16	
Stevens, Isaac........		"	Sick Aug. 30...................................
Tongate, Jeremiah..		"	

Name and Rank.	Residence.	Enrolled	Remarks.
		1832.	
Thompson, Daniel..		July 16	
Tanner, James......			
Vance, Samuel......		April 30	
Williams, Levi......			
White, Joseph......		July 16	
White, Alexander...		April 30	2d Sergeant.
White, Hugh........		July 16	Furloughed; detailed to guard Indian pris'rs
White, Edward.....			
Wilson, Hugh.......			
Wilson, William....		April 30	
Willes, Thomas.....		July 16	
Wallace, James.....		April 30	
Wallace, William...		July 16	

ODD COMPANIES.

COMPANIES ATTACHED TO COL. DODGE'S REGIMENT.

Capt. James Craig's Company

Of Mounted Volunteers of JoDaviess county, State of Illinois, called into service by the Governor on May 26, 1832, and by order of Gen. Atkinson, U. S. Army, attached to the command of Col. Henry Dodge, and now mustered by Lieut. Gardner, by order of Gen. Atkinson, to be discharged Sept. 14, 1832.

Name and Rank.	Residence.	Enrolled	Remarks.
Captain.		1832.	
James Craig	JoDaviess Co.	May 26	Two horses and boy
First Lieutenant.			
H. T. Camp	"	"	Rode Bush's horse
Second Lieutenants.			
Leonard Goss	"	May 20	Resigned June 26; horse lost, appraised at $60
Orn Smith	"	July 1	Served as private from June 1
Sergeants.			
Whitesides Horgess, 1	"	May 20	Deserted with gun
James B. Ketler, 1st	"	June 1	
John McDonald, 2d	"	May 20	Disch. for intemp'nce June 1; took 2 blankets
Isaac M. Reynolds, 2d	"	" 26	Rode Capt. Estes' horse
Albert Henry, 3d	"	June 1	Rode R. Shores' horse
A. M. Wallace, 4th	"	May 20	Disch. to go to Cincin. Aug. 15; took gun, etc.
James Temple, 4th	"	Aug. 15	
Corporals.			
David Morrison	"	May 26	Rode R. Shores' horse
George Sparks	"	"	Rode F. C. Kirkpatrick's horse
Benj. Sutton	"	"	Absent July 20; rode public horse
Sam'l Warren	"	"	Rode A. Kent's horse
Privates.			
Armstrong, James	"	May 20	Discharged for intemperance July 4
Avery, Azel	"	June 1	to go to Fort Clark July 13
Avery, Elias P.	"	May 26	Rode D. Avery's horse
Bernard, John	"	"	
Bush, Michael	"	"	Rode E. Brotherlen's horse
Boles, John	"	"	
Bivins, John	"	"	Transferred to hospital; 2d Surg., July 7
Bass, George	"	"	Discharged for intemperance July 4
Covel, Peter	"	June 1	July 12 stayed at Fort Winnebago
Chaney, Osborne	"	"	
Collins, William	"	June 20	Absent with leave
Crane, Thomas	"	Sept. 1	"
Charles, Elijah	"	June 16	
Dolton, William	"	" 1	
Davis, D. R.	"	Aug. 15	
Davidson, L. V.	"	May 26	
Delereon, Bazell	"	June 1	June 29 disch. to go to Selkirk's; acted as spy
Detandoberaty, M.	"	" 20	Trans. to Capt. E. Duncan's company Aug. 15

Name and Rank.	Residence.	Enrolled	Remarks.
		1832.	
Enlow, Enoch	JoDaviess Co.	July 1	Rode G. Bass' horse
Foley, James	"	June 20	" J. Furlong's horse
Flack, John	"	July 1	
Howell, Jesse	"	May 26	Disch. for disobedience of orders July 13
Howell, Wm.	"	"	Joined Jones' company in M. T. July 16
Hercleroad, G. W.	"	"	Killed by Indians at Apple River June 24
Head, N. T.	"	June 1	Rode G. White's horse
Hawkins, Jas. L.	"	" 16	
Jordan, Thomas	"	" 1	Rode Grey's horse
Kirkpatrick, F. C.	"	May 26	Rode J. Kitler's horse to July 20, then his own
Kirkpatrick, Jas. G.	"	"	Rode Lockwood's horse
Kirkpatrick, F. W.	"	"	Rode Brotherlin's horse
Kirkpatrick, Wm. M.	"	"	Captain of Spy company
Kirkpatrick, J. S.	"	"	Absent with leave; retains gun, powder horn.
Kirkpatrick, John F.	"	"	Rode Hillyard's horse
Langworthy, Edw'd.	"	July 1	Disch. Aug. 12; gone to M.T.; rode Flint's horse
Langworthy, James	"	May 26	Rode T. B. Farnsworth's horse
Lictenberger, Conr'd	"	June 16	
Moffatt, Joseph	"	" 26	56 rations due him
Moffatt, Francis	"	" 1	Discharged July 13 to go to Fort Clark
Montgomery, John	"	" 5	; rode Eades' horse
McColister, Reuben	"	" 13	: " Ketter's horse
McNair, David	"	May 26	Rode H. H. Gear's horse
Mann, Harvey	"	July 1	
Mitchell, Isaac	"	Aug. 1	Absent with leave
McKinney, Charles	"	June 1	" without leave Aug. 1
Nevil, John		" 16	
Osborn, Abraham		July 1	Rode H. H. Gear's horse
Parishon, Eustach		June 1	Disch. June 29; acted as spy; rode pub. horse
Porter, James C.		July 1	Rode Mullet's mule
Quinliven, Dennis		May 26	Rode public horse
Swan, Moses		July 1	Rode John Taylor's horse
Stevens, Sam'l F.		June 1	Disch. Jul. 29; gone to Quincy; rode pub. horse
Sancer, Robt.		"	July 21 absent without leave
Stocton, Isaac		"	Aug. 16 transferred to Capt. Duncan's Co
Stocton, William		"	
Smith, Orlando		"	Deserted June 10 with gun and 2 blankets
Sanderson, F. C.		" 6	" July 1 " blanket
Thomas, John		May 26	
Thomas, Noah		July 1	Rode Hogan's horse
Thompson, Willis		May 26	Rode A. Philco's horse
Tracy, Charles		July 1	Rode Hillyard's horse
Upton, Robert		May 26	Rode Dubois' horse
Webb, T. J.		"	Disch. July 4 for intemp'nce; rode pub. horse
White, Garey		June 1	
Woodson, John B.		" 16	
Woodcock, James S.		" 16	

John Nevil, Elijah Charles, John B. Woodson, Jas. S. Woodcock, J. L. Hawkins and Conrad Lictenberger were detached from the company under my command to act as spies in the neighborhood of Seale's Fort, on the east fork of Fever river.

Capt. Enoch Duncan's Company

Of Mounted Riflemen, maintained in the service of the United States under the command of Col. H. Dodge, by order of Brig.-Gen. H. Atkinson, U. S. Army. Mustered for discharge by Lieut. J. R. B. Gardiner, U. S. Army, Sept. 14, 1832, by order of Brig.-Gen. H. Atkinson.

Name and Rank.	Residence.	Enrolled	Remarks.
		1832.	
Captains.			
James W. Stephens'n		May 19	Elected Major June 26
Enoch Duncan		June 26	
First Lieutenants.			
James K. Hammett		May 19	Resigned June 4
Alex. Kerr		June 4	" 26
Harvey Cavanaw		Aug. 13	
James L. Kirkpatrick		June 26	Resigned Aug. 13

Name and Rank.	Residence.	Enrolled		Remarks.
		1832.		
Second Lieutenants.				
Alexander Kerr		May	19	Elected 1st Lieut. June 4
Enoch Duncan		June	4	" Captain " 26
D. S. Harris		June	26	
Sergeants.				
John Foley		May	19	Private since June 4
Fred Stahl		"		Has not done duty as Sergeant from June 4
Job Alcot		"		
John Mathews		"		
James Temple		June	4	On leave
Musicians.				
Jonathan Gallagher		June	7	On leave
S. D. Scot		May	19	"
Privates.				
Anderson, Wm. S		"		
Armstrong, Abner		"		On furlough
Atchison, Marcus		"		"
Bennett, William		"		
Bohannon, Isaiah		"		On furlough
Brophy, John		"		
Bennett, Thomas		"		
Boggess, William		"		On furlough
Burbridge, Benjamin		"		Discharged July 19
Bennett, Charles R		"		On furlough
Bain, John		"		
Blair, William		"		Absent on leave, sick
Barnet, H. C		Aug.	12	"
Cavanaw, Harvey		May	19	Elected 1st Lieut. Aug. 13
Coates, John		"		On furlough
Collins, William		"		
Cook, G. M		"		
Cooper, A		"		Discharged Aug. 12
Coates, Thomas		"		On furlough
Cormack, John		"		
Chastee, Samuel		"		On furlough
Coyle, Peter		"		
Caldwell, William		"		On furlough
Chichester, Thomas		"		Discharged July 19
Darley, William		"		Killed while on express May 19
Downs, Daniel D		"		
Duncan, Enoch		"		Elected 2d Lieut. June 4
Davis, D. R		"		Transferred to J. Craig's company
Dennison, Joseph		"		On furlough
Davidson, V. L		May	25	"
Dudley, Wm		May	19	
Dudley N		June	28	
Dixon, Fred		May	19	
Eames, Charles		"		
Eames, George		"		Killed in battle June 17
Furr, Chas		"		
Fields, Solomon		"		
Gleason, Isaac		"		
Garrison, E		"		
Gruell, John		"		
Green, Wm. B		"		On furlough
Gilbert, Hayden		"		
Ham, Mathias		"		
Harris, D. S		"		Elected 2d Lieut. June 26
Hodges, H. W		Aug.	12	
Harris, Kuler		May	19	On furlough
Hays, James		"		Discharged July 19
Hoops, George		"		
Hammond, N. I		"		Discharged July 26
Hood, Alexander		"		On furlough
Howard, Stephen P		"		Killed in battle June 17
Imus, Alfred		"		
Imus, Charles		"		
Job, Ira B		"		
Jonas, William		"		
Jourdan, James		"		
Jourdan, I. B		"		
Jourdan, William		"		
Kerns, Patrick		"		
Kirkpatrick, I. L		Aug.	16	
Kirkpatrick, Jesse I		May	19	
Koons, John		"		On furlough

ODD COMPANIES.

Name and Rank.	Residence.	Enrolled	Remarks.
		1832.	
Lukes, J		May 19	June 25 quit, by honorable discharge
Lovell, Michael		"	June 17, killed in battle
Massey, H. L		"	
Mineclear, I. B		"	
Morrison, Wm. H		"	
McNulty, John		"	On furlough
McCabe, John		"	
McDonnell, John		"	
Mann, Harvey		"	Transferred to Capt. J. Craig's Co. July 1
McNair, Alexander		"	Horse killed in battle
McBride, William		"	On furlough
McKenney, Charles		"	
Meeker, Jonathan		"	
Mulliken, John D		"	
Oliver, Solon		"	
Phillo, Addison		"	Appointed Surgeon
Putnam, H		"	
Pease, H. H		"	
Prigg, G		"	
Reed, Thomas		"	
Stocton, Isaac		Aug. 15	
Stocton, William		"	
Swan, A. C		May 19	
Stout, B. F		"	
Shull, Jesse W		"	
Smith, Malcomb		"	On furlough; wounded in battle
Smith, Vincent		"	
Shore, Richard		"	
Shipton, John		"	
Shipton, Jesse		"	
Shanance, Thos		"	
Sublett, Thos		"	
Snyder, F		"	
Snyder, S		"	
Shanley, Thomas		"	
Shannon, D		"	
Siuoker, Samuel		"	On detached service; ordnance officer
Tinan, Dennis		"	
Thomas, V. I		"	Discharged July 15
Taylor, Mason		"	
Temple, James		"	Sergeant from June 4
Thrailkill, John		"	On leave
Vance, Samuel		"	Quit June 19
Vance, William		"	
Williamson, Samuel		"	
Williams, Freeman		"	
Whitesides, Mac		"	
Whitesides, Abram		"	
Whitesides, Jno. B		"	
Whooten, Daniel		"	On furlough
Wallace, James M		"	
Wheeler, Loring		"	
Welch, Edwin		"	Sick; wounded on express
Winters, J. D		"	On leave
Young, Lewis		"	

COMPANIES UNDER BRIG.-GEN. ATKINSON.

Capt. William Gordon's Company,

A company of Mounted Volunteers of Illinois Militia, organized as a company of Spies, by order of Brig.-Gen. Atkinson, of the U. S. Army. The non-commissioned officers and privates having been taken from the lines of other companies in the service, and the officers having been appointed by Gen. Atkinson, and continued in the service as a Spy Company, during the period stated. Mustered out at Dixon's, August 14, 1832.

Name and Rank.	Residence.	Enrolled	Remarks.
Captain. William Gordon	St. Louis, Mo.	1832. June 22	
First Lieutenant. Peter Menard	Peoria, Ill.	"	
Second Lieutenant. William Morrison	Kaskaskia	"	
Sergeants.			
William Murphy	Pinckneyville	"	
Francis Swanwick	Kaskaskia	"	
William Myers	"	"	
Samuel Crawford	"	"	
Corporals.			
Medard Menar		"	
Louis Wilmot	Peoria	"	
Robert Murphy	Kaskaskia	"	
Robert Caldwell	"	"	
Privates.			
Adams, Levi	"	"	
Banson, Lewis	"	"	
Brown, John	"	"	
Champine, Lewis	"	"	
Doza, Joseph	"	"	
Hill, Lewis	"	"	
Jones, Slaughter	"	"	
Jerrard, Francis	"	"	
Kinion, James	"	"	
Kimmansu, Baptist	"	"	
Lynch, James	"	"	
Omelvany, John	"	"	
Pepper, L	"	"	
Paniguvi, Baptist	"	"	
Paschal, Francis	"	"	
Smith, Francis	"	"	
Sachappelle, Henry	"	"	
White, John	"	"	

Capt. Cyrus Mathews' Company

Of Foot Volunteers, in the service of the United States under Brig.-Gen. Atkinson. Mustered out at Fort Wilbourn August 1, 1832.

Name and Rank.	Residence.	Enrolled	Remarks.
Captain.		1832.	
Cyrus Mathews	Morgan Co	June 2	On furlough since July 23, 1832
First Lieutenant.			
William Hunter	"	"	
Second Lieutenant.			
W. R. Lindsay	"	"	Resigned June 23, 1832
Sergeants.			
William Barker	"	"	
M. Q. Dennis	"	"	
Thomas Shepherd	"	"	
W. C. Harris	"	"	
Corporals.			
A. B. Shepherd	"	"	
Enos Hobbs	"	"	
Wiley Scribner	"	"	Elected 2d Lieutenant June 23, 1832
R. S. Anderson	"	"	
Privates.			
Anderson, J. S.	"	"	
Busy, Thomas	"	"	
Bones, John	"	"	
Carson, Thomas	"	"	
Carson, James	"	"	
Crowly, C. W.	"	"	
Dickens, A. C.	"	"	
Foster, William	"	"	
Grimsley, William	"	"	
Grimsley, Fielding	"	"	Absent driving team, haul'g provis. for army
George, Francis	White Co		
Hamilton, William S.			
Holland, Berry		June 2	
Horton, William	Morgan Co	"	
Hart, Josiah	"	"	
Haymes, J. L.	"	"	
Humphrey, B.	"	"	
Huston, J. C.	"	"	
Joiner, Peter	"	"	
Kurkendall, I.	"	"	
Lutes, Daniel	"	"	
Loflin, Thomas	"	"	
Lynch, J. H.	"	"	
McGinnis, L.	"	"	
Myers, William M.	"	"	
Morris, William	"	"	
Moss, Isaac	"	"	
Ragen, L. B.	"	"	On furlough
Rodes, Joseph	"	"	
Row, G. W.	"	"	Elected 3d Corporal June 23, 1832
Row, John	"	"	
Rose, Samuel	"	"	
Reed, John A.			
Sammons, Edin	Morgan Co	June 2	
Stinson, M. L.	"	"	
Taylor, William	"	"	On furlough
Webb, William	"	"	

Capt. George McFadden's Company

Of Mounted Volunteers, in the service of the United States under Brig.-Gen. Atkinson. Mustered out of service of United States June 29, 1832.

Name and Rank.	Residence.	Enrolled	Remarks.
Captain, George McFadden	LaSalle Co.	1832. May 24	
First Lieutenant, W. F. Walker	"	"	On command
Second Lieutenant, Oliver Bangs	"	"	
Sergeants,			
H. A. Sprague	"	"	
Alex. K. Owen	"	"	On command by order of Gen. Atkinson
John Combs	"	"	
George A. Sprague	"	"	
Corporals,			
Henry Hicks	"	"	
S. Bartholomew	"	"	On command by order of Gen. Atkinson
Ezekiah Warren	"	"	On command
Samuel Warren	"	"	
Privates,			
Armstrong, Will	"	"	
Broomfield, Benj	"	"	
Beresford, John	"	"	
Beresford, James	"	"	Killed by indians June 24, 1832
Brown, James	"	"	
Brown, Charles	"	"	
Gonsoles, Peter	"	"	
Galloway, James	"	"	On furlough since May 24
Hogoboom, Richard	"	"	On command by order of Gen. Atkinson
Hogoboom, John	"	"	
Kimball, Russell	"	"	
Lewis, Will	"	"	On command by order of Gen. Atkinson
Morgan, J. W	"	"	
Morgan, Josiah	"	"	On command by order of Gen. Atkinson
Richey, Will, Sr	"	"	" " " "
Richey, Will, Jr	"	"	" " " "
Bucker, John	"	"	
Sprague, Abel	"	"	On command by order of Gen. Atkinson
Sprague, Ephriam	"	"	
Shaw, Josiah E	"	"	
Walker, George	"	"	On command by order of Gen. Atkinson
Warren, Daniel	"	"	
Workman, John	"	"	
Wilcox, John	"	"	

Capt. Samuel Smith's Company

Of Illinois Mounted Volunteers, called into the service of the United States under the command of Brig.-Gen. H. Atkinson. Mustered out June 15, 1832, by order of Brig.-Gen. Atkinson. Enrolled for 20 days.

Name and Rank.	Residence.	Enrolled	Remarks.
Captain, Samuel Smith	Greene Co.	1832. May 27	
First Lieutenant, James D. Scott	"	"	
Second Lieutenant, Jacob Waggoner	"	"	

ODD COMPANIES.

Name and Rank.	Residence.	Enrolled	Remarks.
Sergeants.			
Thomas Briggs	Greene Co	May 27	
Frederick Atchison	"	"	Absent with leave
Fielden Atchison	Morgan Co	"	
Squire Wood	Greene Co	"	On special duty as Wagon Master
Corporals.			
George Sanders	"	"	On furlough
Harrison Poindexter	"	"	
R. G. Lee	"	"	
Vincent Lee	"	"	
Privates.			
Adcock, Isam		"	
Burns, Martin	Greene Co	"	On furlough
Barnet, Benj. F	Madison Co	"	
Burton, Lemuel		"	
Baker, John	Greene Co	"	On furlough
Boggus, Preston		"	
Bonner, A. V	Madison Co	June 8	
Clark, Squire	"	May 27	
Cook, William	Greene Co	"	
Crabb, Edward	"	"	
Dun, Squire	"	"	Absent on leave
Delay, H	"	"	Appointed Surgeon May 30, 1832
Doil, Gregory	"	"	On furlough
Dansworth, Chas. W	"	"	Absent with leave
Fisher, James	"	"	On furlough
Fry, Jacob		"	Promoted Colonel May 31, 1832
Gilliland, James	"	"	On furlough
Hopper, Thomas	Greene Co	"	Absent with leave
Hill, Jonathan	"	"	On furlough
Link, Mathias S	"	"	
Link, David	"	"	
Laxton, Washington	"	"	
Lakin, Joseph		"	
Leighton, Jonathan	Morgan Co	"	Promoted Surgeon's Mate May 31, 1832
Moore, Isaac	Greene Co	"	Absent with leave
Massey, Benj. F	"	"	
Metton, David		"	
Meeker, Ambers M	St. Louis, Mo	"	
Piper, Israel	Greene Co	"	On furlough
Reddish, John	"	"	
Smith, Jeremiah	"	"	
Scott, John W	"	"	Promoted to Paymaster May 31, 1832
Story, S. S	Shelby Co	"	Disch. June 10, 1832, by order of Gen. Atkinson
Tourney, James	Greene Co	"	Horse absent
Whitesides, Levi T	"	"	
Whitesides, Wm. H	Madison Co	"	
Whitesides, John B	Greene Co	"	
Whitlock, James	"	"	
Walden, James	"	"	
Walden, Thos. R	"	"	Promoted Q. M. Sergt. May 31, 1832
Walker, Gideon	Shelby Co	"	

Capt. B. James' Company

Of Illinois Mounted Volunteers, in the service of the United States, under the command of Brig.-Gen. H. Atkinson. Mustered out of the service of the United States by order of Brig.-Gen. Atkinson, this 15th day of June, 1832. Enrolled for 20 days. Distant 250 miles from the place of enrollment.

Name and Rank.	Residence.	Enrolled	Remarks.
Captain.		1832.	
Benjamin James	Bond Co	May 27	Horse killed in the service
First Lieutenant.			
Calvert Roberts	"	"	Absent with leave
Second Lieutenant.			
W. D. Shirley	"	"	

Name and Rank.	Residence.	Enrolled	Remarks.
Sergeants.		1832.	
Sloss McAdams	Bond Co	May 27	Absent with leave; horse absent
James Downing	"	"	
John W. West	"	"	Absent with leave
James Prior	"	"	Horse absent
Corporals.			
James Walker	"	"	
Wm. Corruthers	"	"	
G. W. Conyer	"	"	
Benjamin Holbrooks	"	"	
Privates.			
Anthony, Abraham	"	"	Absent with leave
Coffey, Cleavlin S.	"	"	
Duff, G. D.	"	"	
Glen, Robert	"	"	Absent with leave
Gill, Francis	"	"	
Griffith, William	"	"	
Gillispie, Joseph R.	"	"	
Holdbrooks, Amos	"	"	
Lynch, William	"	"	
Lyles, Elbert	"	"	
Mills, Andrew P	"	"	
Mills, Daniel H	"	"	
McAdams, James	"	"	
McAdams, William	"	"	Appointed Sergeant-Major 31, 1832
Royer, Daniel	"	"	
Sellers, Benjamin E.	"	"	
Voluntine, Jackson O	"	"	
Walker, John T	"	"	Absent with leave

CAPT. STENNETT'S COMPANY

Of the Odd Battalion of the Brigade of Mounted Rangers, called into the service of the United States, on the requisition of Gen. Atkinson, by the Governor's proclamation, dated May 30, 1832. Mustered out on Sept. 4, 1832.

Name and Rank.	Residence.	Enrolled	Remarks.
Captain.		1832.	
John Stennett	Schuyler Co	June 6	
First Lieutenant.			
Daniel Mathoney		"	
Second Lieutenant.			
Joel Pennington		"	Absent on furlough from Aug. 27 to this date.
Sergeants.			
John B. Smith		"	
Samuel L. Dark		"	
Norris Hobert		"	
Philip Horney		"	
Corporals.			
Robart Martin		"	
Eli Williams		"	
James Bell		"	Absent on furlough from Aug. 27 up to date.
Isaiah Price		"	
Privates.			
Allen, William		"	Absent on furlough from Aug. 27 up to date.
Brown, William		"	
Briscow, Isaac		"	
Bristow, Mathew C.		"	
Briggs, Elias		June 26	
Brakewell, Charles		June 6	Sick on the way home
Busan, Jesse		"	
Friend, Abel		"	
Glen, Fielding T.		Aug. 1	
Golston, Benjamin		June 6	
Howard, James		"	

Name and Rank.	Residence.	Enrolled	Remarks.
		1832.	
Hartley, Eli		June 6	On furlough from Aug. 27, up to this date
Hunter, Jesse		"	
Holiday, Sandford		"	
Harrison, George H.		July 18	
Horney, Samuel	Schuyler Co	June 6	Appointed Q. M. of the Battalion on June 15.
Isaac, Allen		"	
Jones, John M		July 18	
Kennett, William	Schuyler Co	June 6	
Luster, Jesse		Aug 1	Absent on extra duty
McGeehy, William		June 6	
McKee, William	Schuyler Co	June 6	
McKee, James			
Matheny, Daniel, Jr		"	
Martin, Richard D.		"	
O'Neil, Simon P.		"	Detailed on extra duty
Osburn, Joseph		"	On furlough, arm dislocated
Pennington, Riggs			
Pennington, S. O.	Schuyler Co	Aug. 1	
Pennington, Riley	"	June 6	
Peckingham, Peter			
Penningham Wesley	Schuyler Co	Aug. 1	
Pettigrew, George M	"	June 6	
Rice, Nicholas	"	"	
Rose, Stephen	"	"	
Rose, John S	"	"	
Rigg, William T	"	"	
Smith, George	"	"	
Smith, Samuel	"	"	
Smith, Hugh	"	"	
Sallie, Oliver P.	"	"	
Stewart, Samuel	"	"	
Tallis, Joel	"	"	
VanWinkle, John	"	"	
Williams, Mervin	"	"	
White, Jeremiah	"	Aug. 1	

CAPT. M. L. COVELL'S COMPANY

Of Mounted Volunteers (Rangers), being an Odd Detachment under the direction of the Col. of McLean County, under the command of Brig.-Gen. Atkinson. Mustered out of the service of the United States at Bloomington, Illinois, on August 3, 1832, at the place of enrollment.

Name and Rank.	Residence.	Enrolled	Remarks.
		1832.	
Captain.			
M. L. Covell	Bloomington	June 3	
First Lieutenant.			
Wm. Dimmet	"	"	Absent with leave
Second Lieutenant.			
Richard Edwards	"	"	
Sergeants.			
Benjamin Depew	"	"	
John Vittito	"	"	
Stephen F. Gates	"	"	
George Wiley	"	"	
Corporals.			
Robert F. Harris	"	"	
John Toliver	"	"	Served 30 days, then employed substitute
Harrison Flesher	"	July 3	Served 30 days as substitute for John Toliver
Charles Vezay	"	June 3	
John J. McGraw	"	"	

Name and Rank.	Residence.	Enrolled	Remarks.
Privates.		1832.	
Atherton, Henry	Bloomington.	June 3	
Benson, Thomas	"	"	
Busick, Henry	"	"	
Britton, Elijah	"	"	
Britton, Nathan	"	"	
Cox, Henry	"	"	Served as substitute for George Spaur
Carlock, Reuben	"	"	
Carlock, George	"	"	
Cheney, Jonathan	"	"	
Davis, Alexander	"	"	
Downs, Lawson	"	"	
Draper, Reuben	"	"	
Foster, William	"	"	
Gaylord, Horace	"	"	
Gridley, Asahel	"	"	
Gibbs, Elias	"	"	
Glenn, John P	"	"	
Harbert, Joseph A	"	"	
Harbert, Hez. M	"	"	
Harbert, Hiram	"	"	
Harper, William	"	"	
Johnson, James	"	"	
Lane, Harrison	"	"	
Lundy, Amos	"	"	
Merryfield, Rolla	"	"	
Martin, Franklin	"	"	
Mullin, John A	"	"	
Oatman, Clement	"	"	Taken sick July 27, 1832.
Provo, Franklin N	"	"	
Patton, John	"	"	
Rook, Frederick	"	"	
Ruth, Nathan	"	"	
Spaur, George	"	"	Employed substitute for 18 days
Scott, Martin	"	"	Absent with leave.
Vincent, William	"	"	
Vandoler, Jesse	"	"	
Wyatt, L. M	"	"	Absent with leave.
Wright, James C	"	"	
Washburn, Thos. C	"	"	
Young, Briant	"	"	

CAPT. JOHN S. WILBOURN'S COMPANY

Of Illinois Infantry, in the service of the United States under command of Brig.-Gen Atkinson. Mustered out June 9, 1832.

Name and Rank.	Residence.	Enrolled	Remarks.
Captain.		1832.	
John S. Wilbourn		May 22	
First Lieutenant.			
William Chase		"	
Second Lieutenant.			
James H. Blackman		"	
Sergeants.			
P. J. O'Connor		"	
David Edgar		"	
Privates.			
Bonner, Alexand'r V		"	
Bertrand, Charles		"	
Byas, Jesse		"	
Carver, James		"	
Crosier, James		"	
Davis, Aaron		"	
Davis, John		"	
Greene, William		"	
Harper, John		"	

ODD COMPANIES. 173

Name and Rank.	Residence.	Enrolled	Remarks.
		1832.	
Hill, William.........		May 22	
Hash, Alfred.........		"	
Hays, James.........		"	
Howard, Abraham..		"	
King, Allan...........		"	
Mullan, Joseph B....		"	
Morgan, Lewis.......		"	
Manard, Antonio....		"	
Morgan, John........		"	
Moss, William.......		"	
Plasters, Lemond...		"	
Rouse, Isaac M......		"	
Smedley, John J.....		"	
Stuart, Enoch........		"	
Trent, Martin S......		"	Sick
Taylor, F. S..........		"	
Young, Achriel......		"	

Capt. Solomon Miller's Company

Of Mounted Volunteers, called into the service of the United States on a requisition o Gen. Atkinson on the Governor of the State of Illinois, and under the command of Gen. Atkinson. Mustered out at Belleville, St. Clair Co., on Aug. 2, 1832.

Name and Rank.	Residence.	Enrolled	Remarks.
Captain.		1832.	
Solomon Miller......	St. Clair Co..	April 27	
First Lieutenant.			
Jacob S. Stout.......	"	"	
Second Lieutenant.			
William H. Phillips..	"	"	
Sergeants.			
Enoch Luckey.......	"	"	
Lewis Doyle..........	"	"	
James Petitt.........	"	"	
Robert Higgins......	"	"	
Corporals.			
George Higgins.....	"	May 30	
Nathaniel Smith.....	"	April 27	
Boneham Beer	"	May 30	
Benjamin I. Smith ..	"	April 27	
Farrier.			
Thomas Ervin.......	"	"	
Saddler.			
John D. Hughes.....	"	"	
Armorer.			
Michael Randleman.	"	"	
Trumpeter.			
John W. Johnson....	"	"	
Privates.			
Beer, William........	"	"	
Carroll, William.....	"	"	
Caliehan, Vance....	"	"	
Collier, William	"	"	
Cornoyer, Narcisse.	"	"	
Dunn, John..........	"	"	
Eastwood, Daniel L.	"	"	
Franklin, John A....	"	"	
Fike, Benjamin......	"	"	
Fike, Ausby..........	"	"	
Gonville, Lawrence.	"	"	

Name and Rank.	Residence.	Enrolled	Remarks.
		1832.	
Gaskill, Samuel	St. Clair Co	May 30	
Hughes, Robert	"	April 27	
Holcomb, Joel	"	"	
Hill, William	"	"	
Hill, James	"	"	
Jarrot, Vital	"	June 5	In service of Governor
Jackson, Jarvis M	"	May 30	
Koen, John	"	April 27	
Krupp, John	"	"	
McMurtrie, George	"	"	
Maccalley, John	"	"	
O'Harro, Charles	"	"	
Phelps, Michael	"	"	
Patterson, Samuel	"	"	
Payne, George W	"	"	
Quick, Daniel P	"	"	
Quick, George C	"	"	
Reynolds, Robert	"	"	
Rogers, Samuel	"	"	
Rennies, Jesse	"	"	
Stout, William	"	"	
Stubblefield, John	"	May 30	
Short, William B	"	April 27	
Scott, James	"	"	
Taylor, Charles	"	"	
Taylor, John	"	"	
Vertrees, John	"	"	
Vannosdal, Benjam'n	"	"	
Watson, William	"	"	
Walker, Gilley	"	May 30	
Wilson, Edward	"	April 27	
Whitesides, Samuel	"	"	

NOTE.—There is a discrepancy in dates relative to the service of this company, which requires correction before it can be paid. The date of enrollment appears generally to have been April 27, 1832, whilst Gov. Reynolds' certificate says that it was called out by him under Gen. Atkinson's requisition of May 29 last.

Paymaster-General's Office, Aug. 16, 1832.

Capt. Elijah Iles' Company

Of Illinois Mounted Volunteers, in the service of the United States, under the command of Brig.-Gen. H. Atkinson. Mustered out of service June 16, 1832.

Name and Rank.	Residence.	Enrolled	Remarks.
Captain.		1832.	
Elijah Iles	Sangamon Co	May 27	
First Lieutenant.			
Jesse M. Harrison	"	"	
Second Lieutenant.			
Henry B. Roberts	Fayette Co	"	
Sergeants.			
George W. Glasscock	Sangamon Co	"	
Zachariah Millingent		"	
James A. Ward	Macon Co	"	
Benjamin Birch	Sangamon Co	"	
Corporals.			
Alexander Trent	"	"	Absent on furlough; no horse
G. W. Foster	"	"	No horse
G. W. Diamond	Fayette Co	"	
Jesse Darrow	Sangamon Co	"	Horse absent
Privates.			
Archer, Michael	"	"	
Alloy, James	Fayette Co	"	Absent, sick

ODD COMPANIES.

Name and Rank.	Residence.	Enrolled	Remarks.
		1832	
Bell, A. W............	Macon Co....	May 27	
Brents, Moses.......	Sangamon Co	"	
Brannan, John......		"	
Cole, Eldridge.......		"	
Crow, William.......		"	
Churchill, Lewis....		"	
Coventry, John......	Fayette Co...	"	
Dickinson, David....	Sangamon Co	"	
Dewees, Samuel B..	Macon Co....	"	
Esles, Asa............	Sangamon Co	"	
Earley, Jacob M.....	"	"	
Ebey, Jacob..........	"	"	
Garret, Joseph F....		"	
Ginger, Miles........	Fayette Co...	"	
Gateley, John J......	Sangamon Co	"	No horse............
Graft, John..........	JoDaviess Co	"	Absent with leave; no horse...........
Hickerson, G. W....	Fayette Co...	"	
Henry, James D.....	Sangamon Co	"	Elected Major; promoted Lieut. Col. May 31..
Harrington, John....	Fayette Co...	"	Absent with leave.................
Hanks, Joseph.......	Macon Co....	"	
Hankins, John.......	Fayette Co...	"	
Johnson, Henry.....		"	
Kirkpatrick, John...	Sangamon Co	"	
Keys, John...........	"	"	
Kirkpatrick, William	"	"	Appointed Quartermaster May 31, 1832.......
Kendall, John J......	"	"	Absent with leave; no horse...........
Lincoln, A...........	"	"	
Letcher, John.......	"	"	Deserted June 1; no horse............
Long, Thomas.......	Sangamon Co	"	
Lane, Jacob..........	Macon Co....	"	
Manly, John.........	"	"	No horse...........
McAlister, Wm.....	Sangamon Co	"	Absent with leave.............
Mason, Noah........	"	"	
McCoy, Joseph......	"	"	
Matheny, Lorenzo D	"	"	
Millugent, Samuel..	"	"	
McAlister, John.....	"	"	No horse............
McJenkins, Hugh...	Tazewell Co.	"	
Morris, Achilles.....	Sangamon Co	"	
Neale, Winston M...	"	"	
O'Neal, Samuel......	"	"	
Oliphant, F. P.......	"	"	Appointed Adjutant May 31, 1832........
Pierce, Thomas.....	"	"	
Potts, William L....	"	"	
Pickerell, William S.	"	"	
Patterson, Joseph..	Fayette Co...	"	
Paul, John...........	Tazewell Co.	"	
Querry, James.......	Macon Co....	"	Absent with leave; no horse........
Rutledge, James.....	Morgan Co...	"	Appointed Surgeon May 31, 1832......
Rutledge, John B...	Sangamon Co	"	
Reid, James F.......	"	"	
Rusk, Benjamin.....	"	"	
Saunders, Presly A.	"	"	
Stuart, John T.......	"	"	
Shirley, John........	Fayette Co...	"	Absent with leave.................
Taulbee, Isaac.......		"	
Wright, John D.....	Macon Co....	"	Absent with leave; no horse............
Welch, Jefferson....	Sangamon Co	"	No horse..............
Ward, James M.....		"	

INDEPENDENT COMPANIES.

Capt. Jacob M. Earley's Company

Of Mounted Volunteers, mustered out of the service of the United States by order of Brig.-Gen. Atkinson, U. S. Army, on White Water river of Rock river, on July 10, 1832.

Name and Rank.	Residence.	Enrolled	Remarks.
Captain.		1832.	
Jacob M. Earley	Sangamon Co	June 16	
First Lieutenant.			
G. W. Glasscock	"	"	Hunting horse with leave
Second Lieutenant.			
B. D. Rusk	"	"	
Sergeants.			
Zachariah Malugin	"	"	
Noah Mason	"	"	
Jacob Eby	"	"	Absent on furlough since June 29, 1832
W. M. Neale	"	"	Remained at Dixon's without leave
Corporals.			
R. M. Wyatt	Madison Co.	"	
M. H. Brentz	Sangamon Co	"	
William Crow	"	"	Absent horse hunting since June 29, 1832
Henry Johnson	Fayette Co.	"	
Privates.			
Bailey, David	Tazewell Co.	"	
Baker, John		June 21	
Brewer, John	Sangamon Co	"	
Climon, James	Vermilion Co.	"	Hunting horse
Darrow, Jesse	Sangamon Co	June 16	Absent with leave, horse hunting
Fanchier, G. B.	Coles Co	"	
Gilbert, R. J.		"	
Henry, James D.	Sangamon Co	"	Promoted from the ranks
Hubbard, G. S.	Vermilion Co.	"	
Harrison, George		June 21	
Harrington, John	Fayette Co.	"	
Johnston, John D.	Coles Co	June 16	Hunting horse
Lincoln, A.	Sangamon Co	"	
Loveless, J. R.		"	
Morris, Achilles	Sangamon Co	June 16	
McJenkins, Hugh	Tazewell Co.	"	Absent with leave from enrollment
Matheny, L. D.	Sangamon Co	"	
McCoy, Joseph	"	"	Absent with leave, horse hunting
McGarey, Hugh	"	"	
McGarey, Harrison	"	"	
McRoberts, Samuel	Vermilion Co.	"	
Neal, Samuel O.	Sangamon Co	"	
Paul, John	"	"	Absent with leave from date of enrollment
Pickerel, Wm. S.	"	"	Left sick at Dixon's since June 25, 1832
Potts, Wm. L.	"	"	Hunting horse
Pickerel, B. F.	"	"	
Reed, James F.	"	"	Hunting horse
Rutledge, James	Morgan Co.	June 21	
Stephenson, John L.	Sangamon Co	June 16	
Smith, Adam	"	"	Hunting horse with leave
Strawbridge, Wm.	"	June 21	
Stout, George	"	"	
Spencer, Roswell H.	R'k Island Co	"	
Stuart, John T.	Sangamon Co	June 16	
Warrick, Montgom'y	"	"	
Warrick, John C.	"	"	

Capt. Seth Pratt's Company

Of Illinois Volunteer Militia, stationed at Fort Armstrong, Rock Island, Illinois. In the service of the United States from April 21, 1832, to June 3, 1832, when mustered out.

Name and Rank.	Residence.	Enrolled	Remarks.
Captain.		1832.	
Seth Pratt...		April 21.	Commanding company...
First Lieutenant.			
John M. Crabtree...		"	For duty...
Second Lieutenant.			
Joseph Leister...		"	For duty...
Sergeants.			
Simpson Stewart...		"	
William B. Sisk...		"	
Elihu Sparks...		"	
Abraham Crabtree...		"	
Corporals.			
James Stockton...		"	
George Yates...		"	
James Kellar...		"	
James Curry...		"	
Thomas Burton...		"	Appointed Drum Major April 29, 1832...
Fifer.			
James Carr...		"	
Privates.			
Acton, Golman...		"	
Bradbury, Nathan...		"	
Brantly, Henry...		"	
Birdsell, Clark...		"	
Booth, Isaac...		"	
Brock, Daniel...		"	
Bradley, Amos...		"	
Bradshaw, John...		"	Dismissed May 12, 1832; claimed as a deserter
Bohvare, John H...		"	Sent to hospital sick May 10, 1832; furloughed.
Castlebury, Berry...		"	
Cooper, Stephen L...		"	
Davis, John...		"	
Ford, Henry...		"	
Foster, William...		"	On detached service with army May 19, 1832...
Gulliher, Isaac...		"	
Hamilton, Parnell...		"	
Hunly, Harrison...		"	
Hopper, William...		"	
Jackson, Alfred...		"	
Leighton, Jonathan...		"	Appointed Ass't Surgeon April 29, 1832...
Long, Nicholas...		"	
Low, James M...		"	
Lawrence, Iredell...		"	
Langston, Martin...		"	
Langston, Larkin B...		"	
Letcher, John...		"	On detached service with army May 19, 1832...
Melton, Henry...		"	
McConnell, Francis...		"	
McDaniel, Frederick...		"	On detached service with army May 19, 1832...
New, James...		"	
Overstreet, Wm. C...		"	
Pervine, John...		"	
Pointer, William...		"	
Russ, Jonathan...		"	
Smothers, Andrew...		"	
Schmick, Isaac...		"	
Smith, Samuel...		"	
Wells, Samuel...		"	

Capt. Alexander D. Cox's Company

Of Illinois Volunteers, in the service of the United States. Mustered out June 15, 1832, at Fort Wilbourn.

Name and Rank.	Residence.	Enrolled	Remarks.
Captain.		1832.	
Alexander D. Cox		May 28	
First Lieutenant.			
Joseph W. Duncan		" "	
Second Lieutenant.			
Thomas T. Clark		" "	
Sergeants.			
Charles Day		" "	
William F. Cox		" "	
Richard Cox		" "	
Robert Patten		" "	
Corporals.			
Harvey Graham		" "	
John M. Barnes		" "	
James McCormick		" "	
Daniel Waters		" "	
Privates.			
Atwood, William C.		" "	
Byas, James D.		" "	
Byas, Jesse		June 12	Joined my company on June 12, 1832.
Foster, William		May 28	
Hedrick, Stephen		" "	
Hutton, John		" "	
Hamilton, Frederick		" "	
Hays, John		" "	
Hays, Harrison		" "	
Hays, Jonathan		" "	
Hays, James		" "	
Massee, Elder		" "	
Snyder, Solomon R.		" "	
Tompkins, Alfred		" "	
Wright, Moses		" "	

Capt. James Walker's Company

Or Detachment of Mounted Volunteers, called into the service of the United States by the Governor of the State of Illinois, and by his order of June 19, 1832, from the date of its enrollment to the 12th of August, 1832, when mustered out. Mustered out at Fort Walker, on DuPage river.

Name and Rank.	Residence.	Enrolled	Remarks.
Captain.		1832.	
James Walker	Cook Co.	June 25	
First Lieutenant.			
Chester Smith	" "	" "	
Second Lieutenant.			
George Hollenboch	" "	" "	
Sergeants.			
William Lee	" "	" "	
Edmund Weed	" "	" "	
Chester Ingersoll	" "	" "	
Corporals.			
Elisha Fish	" "	" "	
Rueben Flagg	" "	" "	
Peter Watkins	" "	" "	

ODD COMPANIES.

Name and Rank.	Residence.	Enrolled	Remarks.
Musician.		1832.	
Edward A. Rogers	Cook Co.	June 25	
Privates.			
Ament, Edward G.	"	"	
Ament, Hiram	"	"	
Ament, Anson C.	"	"	Absent, on furlough till expiration
Clark, David K.	"	"	
Covell, Thomas R.	"	"	
Curtis, Elisha	"	"	
Fountain, Samuel	"	"	
Gilston, James	"	"	
Jones, Henry	"	"	
Smith, Ralph	"	"	
Watkins, Benj. T.	"	"	
Watkins, Peter, Jr.	"	"	
Wooley, Jeddiah	"	"	
Wooley, Thomas	"	"	
Walkeley, Henry	"	"	

Capt. William Warnick's Company

Of Mounted Volunteer Rangers, ordered out by the Governor, for the protection of the frontier of Macon county, Illinois. Mustered out of the service of the United States at Decatur, Illinois, on September 24, 1832.

Name and Rank.	Residence.	Enrolled	Remarks.
Captain.		1832.	
William Warnick	Decatur	June 4	Officers and privates found own rations, arms [and ammunition.
First Lieutenant.			
J. C. Pugh	"	"	
Second Lieutenant.			
E. Freeman	"	"	
Sergeants.			
F. G. Paine	"	"	
J. H. Johnson	"	"	
A. M. Wilson	"	"	
R. Law	"	"	
Corporals.			
J. Smith	"	"	
A. Travice	"	"	
J. Brown	"	"	
J. Miller	"	"	
Privates.			
Arnold, A.	"	"	
Alsup, Thomas	"	"	
Burrell, N.	"	"	
Brown, M.	"	"	
Butler, E.	"	"	
Church, T. G. D.	"	"	
Cunningham, H.	"	"	
Cunningham, J.	"	"	
Davis, J.	"	"	
Edwards, J.	"	"	
Farris, J.	"	"	
Hall, A.	"	"	
Howell, D.	"	"	
Hooper, W.	"	"	
Hendline, A.	"	"	
Hall, D.	"	"	
Ingram, L.	"	"	
Johnson, R.	"	"	
Jackson, L.	"	"	
Lowry, J.	"	"	

Name and Rank.	Residence.	Enrolled	Remarks.
		1832.	
Mounce, S..........	Decatur......	June 4	
McMennamy, J. H...	"		
Newcomb, D.........	"		
Owen, T............	"		
Paine, M............	"		
Paine, Mason.......	"		
Piatt, J. A..........	"		
Smith, A. W........	"		
Sinnett, S...........	"		
Stevens, J...........	"		
Slatten, Benjamin..	"		
Travis, F............	"		
Widick, S............	"		
Ward, William......	"		
Wilson, T. F.........	"		
Warnick, James.....	"		
Warnick, J..........	"		
Walker, J............	"		
Wheeler, R..........	"		

CAPT. ALEX. M. JENKINS' COMPANY

Of Illinois Volunteers, called out on the requisition of Gen. H. Atkinson, by the Governor's proclamation dated ——, 1832, and regularly mustered into the service of the United States by Lieut. J. R. Gardine, U. S. A., on July 13, 1832, and now mustered for discharge this 10th day of August, 1832, by N. W. Army Special Orders No. 45 of 1832, by Lieut. J. R. Gardine, U. S. A.

Name and Rank.	Residence.	Enrolled	Remarks.
Captain,		1832.	
Alexan'r M. Jenkins.	Jackson Co..	June 16	Horse shoes, $1; $1 due Bennett for care horse
First Lieutenant,			
James Herald.......	"	"	Horse shoes, $1........
Second Lieutenant,			
Silas Hickman......	"	"	
Sergeants,			
Milton Ladd........	"	"	
John D. Owings.....	"	"	Horse shoes, $1........
Mathias Hagler.....	"	"	Lost 1 blanket in the service, appraised at $3.
Aaron Quillman....	"	"	Horse shoes, $1........
Corporals,			
Binningson Boone..	"	"	
Daniel House.......	"	"	Horse shoes, $1........
John Logan.........	"	"	"
Jacob Schwartz.....	"	"	
Cornet.			
Wm. M. Bowring....	"	"	
Privates,			
Burkley, David.....	"	"	Lost his horse, appraised at $45 ......
Blacker, James.....		"	Absent, sick........
Blacker, David.....		"	
Casey, Henry.......	Jackson Co..	"	Horse shoes, $1........
Casey, John........	"	"	
Cram, Squire.......	"	"	
Creath, Hiram......	"	"	
Clark, John G......	"	"	Lost 1 blanket in the service, appraised at $3.
Camron, James.....	"	"	Horse shoes, $1........
Deason, James A...	"	"	
Deason, William...	"	"	
Delaplain, John.....	Randolph Co.	"	Horse shoes, $1........
Davis, Joseph......		"	Absent, sick........
Davis, Ralph.......	Jackson Co..	"	Horse shoes, $1........
Davis, Samuel......	"	"	
Etherton, James....	"	"	

Name	Residence	Enrolled	Remarks
Gardner, Robert R.	Jackson Co.	June 16, 1832	
Griffith, Geo. F.	"	"	
Hagler, Paul	"	"	Horse shoes, $1
Huff, O. M.	"	"	
Hinson, Nicholas	"	"	Horse shoes, $1
Hagler, Edmund	"	"	
Holden, John	"	"	Horse shoes, $1
Ireland, Alexander	"	"	
Logan, James	"	"	
Logan, John, 2d	"	"	Horse shoes, $1; Dr. J. Logan was app'd Surg.
Lorrels, Walker	"	"	
Lafferty, Alexander	"	"	Bridle-bit, 50c
Owings, James F.	"	"	Horse shoes, $1
Orton, William	"	"	
Richards, John	"	"	
Sorrels, James	"	"	
Shumaker, William	"	"	
Timmons, James M.	"	"	
Toague, Hezekiah	"	"	
Taylor, Richard R.	"	"	
Vote, Gilbert B.	"	"	
Vansel, George	"	"	Horse shoes, $1
Walker, Nathan D.	"	"	
Wood, Wilson D.	"	"	" Detached service

I certify that this muster roll exhibits the true state of Capt. A. M. Jenkins' Company of Illinois Militia, in the service of the United States for the period herein mentioned; that the "Remarks" set opposite the name of each officer and soldier are accurate and just, and that the recapitulation exhibits in every particular the true state of the company.

(Signed.) A. M. JENKINS,
Capt. Command'g the Co.

The company marched, by order of the Colonel, to the Wisconsin, while Gen. Atkinson, with the main army, lay at Helena, and while there tendered our service to him to pursue the Indians, but were ordered by him to return to Fort Hamilton, to guard the provisions, as we had been ordered to do by Col. Holmes.

The company have drawn, while in service, 97½ bushels of corn.

CAPT. B. B. CRAIG'S COMPANY

Of Illinois Mounted Volunteers, called into the service of the United States, on the requisition of Gen. Atkinson, by the Governor's proclamation dated May 12, 1832, and regularly mustered into the service by Lieut. J. R. B. Gardiner July 13, 1832, and was mustered for discharge this August 10, 1832, by Northwestern Army Special Order No. 45, of 1832.

Name and Rank.	Residence.	Enrolled	Remarks.
Captain.		1832	
B. B. Craig	Union Co.	June 19	Horse, etc., appraised at $79, lost in service
First Lieutenant.			
William Craig	"	"	
Second Lieutenant.			
John Newton	"	"	Horse, etc., appraised at $70, lost in service
Sergeants.			
Samuel Moland	"	"	
Solomon David	"	"	
Hezekiah Hodges	"	"	Absent on furlough
John Rendlemen	"	"	Horse, etc., appraised at $85, lost in service
Corporals.			
Joel Burker	"	"	
Adam Cauble	"	"	
Martin Ury	"	"	
Jeremiah Irvine	"	"	
Privates.			
Barringer, Aaron	"	"	Saddle, etc., appraised at $17, lost in service
Barringer, John	"	"	
Corgian, John	"	"	
Cheser, Mathew	"	"	
Ellis, Daniel	"	"	Horse, etc., appraised at $64.50, lost in service
Farmer, William	"	"	
Farmer, Thomas	"	"	

Name and Rank.	Residence.	Enrolled	Remarks.
Fisher, Moses	Union Co	1832. June 19	
Goodin, Abraham	"	"	Absent on furlough
Gavin, William G.	"	"	
Gramer, Hiram	"	"	
Gramer, William	"	"	
Hancock, Lot. W.	"	"	Saddle, etc., appraised at $10, lost in service.
Hill, Daniel P.	"	"	
Huntsucker, Jackson	"	"	
Lance, Peter	"	"	
Lance, Andrew	"	"	Horse, etc., appraised at $87, lost in service.
Langley, John	"	"	
Liveley, Moses	"	"	
Lingle, A. W.	"	"	
Murphy, John	"	"	
McCall, P. W.	"	"	Horse, etc., appraised at $67.50, lost in service
Morris, John	"	"	
McIntosh, Nimrod	"	"	
McIntosh, John A.	"	"	
Miller, Solomon	"	"	
McElyea, Thomas	"	"	
Morgan, James	"	"	
McLean, Washingt'n	"	"	
McGraw, Elijah	"	"	
Penrad, John	"	"	
Parmer, John	"	"	Horse, etc., appraised at $43, lost in service.
Quillman, John	"	"	
Rumsey, W. H.	"	"	Horse, etc., appraised at $126, lost in service.
Shepherd, Elijah	"	"	" $40, "
Salmons, Daniel	"	"	" $87, "
Staten, Preston I.	"	"	
Vincent, John	"	"	
Wright, Jesse	"	"	Horse, etc., appraised at $37, lost in service.

Capt. Wm. C. Ralls' Company,

Illinois Mounted Volunteers, mustered out of the service of the United States by order of Brig.-Gen. Atkinson, June 15, 1832.

Name and Rank.	Residence.	Enrolled	Remarks.
Captain. William C. Ralls	Schuyler Co.	1832. May 27	
First Lieutenant. Radford M. Wyatt	Monroe Co.	"	
Sergeants.			
John M. Jones	Schuyler Co.	"	
Samuel M. Pierce	Adams Co.	"	
Stephen A. St. Cyr.	St. Louis, Mo.	"	
S. G. Bond	Monroe Co.	"	
Privates.			
Briscoe, John	Schuyler Co.	"	
Brooks, Stephen	Monroe Co.	"	
Beebe, Erastes	Adams Co.	"	
Crawford, John D.	Schuyler Co.	"	
Coonrod, Jefferson	"	"	
Chapman, Johnston	"	"	
Eves, Joel	"	"	
Johnston, James W.	Shelby Co.	"	Lost his horse
Johnston, Thomas	Adams Co.	"	
Kirkland, Ezra	Schuyler Co.	"	
Lane, Ruthford	"	"	
Moore, Daniel	"	"	
Morris, William	"	"	
Melvau, Andrew	Missouri	"	
Owens, Luke	Schuyler Co.	"	
Richardson, Jacob	"	"	
Richardson, Aaron	"	"	
Trail, Xerxes F.	Monroe Co.	"	
Turner, Eben	Adams Co.	"	
Wilkerson, Jacob	Schuyler Co.	"	

CAPT. ALEXANDER WHITE'S COMPANY

Of Mounted Volunteers, called into the service of the United States by the order of the Governor of the State of Illinois, and served from May 26 to June 15, 1832.

Name and Rank.	Residence.	Enrolled	Remarks.
Captain.		1832.	
Alexander White		May 26	
First Lieutenant.			
Tolbert Shipley		"	
Sergeants.			
Ebenezer Higgins		"	
John Waggoner		"	
Ent. Perkins		"	
John O. Smith		"	
Corporals.			
Hugh Wilson		"	
William Wallace		"	
Amzi Doolittle		"	
Privates.			
Atherton, John R.		"	
Brewer, Thomas		"	
Buchannan, George		"	
Bradley, Hezekiah P.		"	
Cash, William		"	
Clark, Johnson, Sr.		"	
Clark, Johnson, Jr.		"	
Compton, Jacob		"	
Driskel, Riley		"	
Franklin, Wm. E.		"	
Forrest, John M.		"	
Goodwin, Samuel		"	
Hibbert, Davidson		"	
Higgins, William		"	
Higgerson, Elisha		"	
Hickerson, Wm. D.		"	
Kenedy, Mathase		"	
Lincoln, Abraham		"	
Maffett, John		"	
Middleton, George		"	
Marfett, James		"	
Moore, Abraham		"	
McKee, John		"	
Mutchler, Benjamin		"	
Owens, Joshua		"	
Owens, Thomas H.		"	
Perkins, Wm. G.		"	
Perkins, Andrew H.		"	
Sailors, William		"	
Spillman, Hezekiah		"	
Stephens, Isaac		"	
Turner, Andrew		"	
Thompson, Daniel		"	
Willis, Thomas		"	
White, Hugh		"	
White, Edward		"	
Wilson, James		"	
Wilson, Thomas		"	

STATE OF ILLINOIS,
Adams Co.

Alexander White, being duly sworn, states that he is the person whose name appears on this muster-roll as Captain; that Lewis Ray was a private in said company, and entered the service on May 26, 1832, and continued in the service until the company was mustered out of service, and his name was omitted from the muster-roll by accident or inadventure, and not by design.

(Signed.)   ALEXANDER WHITE.

Capt. Charles S. Dorsey's Company

Of Mounted Volunteers, called into service by the order of the Governor of Illinois, on June 8, 1832, for one month, ending on July 9.

Name and Rank.	Residence.	Enrolled	Remarks.
Captain. Charles S. Dorsey...	....	1832. June 8.	....
First Lieutenant. Thaddeus Bowman.	....	"	....
Second Lieutenant. William Burns.......	....	"	....
Sergeants. James Harvey....... John H. Reed....... Jonathan Reed...... Peter Cline	....	" " " "	....
Corporals. Peter P. Scott ...... A. W. Vanmeter .... Wm. Holland .... James McClure.....	....	" " " "	....
Privates. Bennington, Robt... Bennington, Thomas Bandy, Reuben...... Bird, Jas. .... Bennington, Joseph. Conley, Levi P...... Huddleson, Abrah'm Huddleson, Benj.... Holland, Lawson... Heath, William..... McCorkle, Rich. B... Reed, William T.... Shields, Thomas L.. Thomas, Hanson.... Wilson, William	....	" " " " " " " " " " " " " " "	....

STATE OF ILLINOIS, Nov. 20, 1832.

I certify that said Chas. L. Dorsey was the Captain commanding said company of Mounted Volunteers; that it was necessary that said company should be employed for said period, while the excitement occasioned by the affair of Major Stillman continued. Said company ranged on the portion of Tazewell county, and prevented the settlers from leaving their homes.

(Signed.) JOHN REYNOLDS,
Com.-in-Chief, Ill. Militia.

Capt. A. W. Snyder's Company

Of Mounted Volunteers. Mustered out of service on June 21, 1832, at Dixon's Ferry, Rock river, Illinois.

Name and Rank.	Residence.	Enrolled	Remarks.
Captain. Adam W. Snyder....	St. Clair Co..	1832. May 27	Horse and arms lost in battle June 16, 1832. (Not true. See note at end.)
First Lieutenant. Jas. Winstanley.....	"	"	....
Second Lieutenant. John T. Lusk	Madison Co..	"	....

ODD COMPANIES.

Name and Rank.	Residence.	Enrolled	Remarks.
Sergeants.		1832.	
Nathan Johnston	Monroe Co.	May 27	
Solomon Spurr	St. Clair Co.	"	
James Taylor		"	
Josiah R. Gillam	Madison Co.	"	
Corporals.			
H. Hartline	Monroe Co.	"	Gun lost in battle June 16, 1832
Benj. McDaniel	St. Clair Co.	"	Killed on June 16, and horse lost.
Robt. B. Pierce	Madison Co.	"	
Thos. Cook	St. Clair Co.	"	
Privates.			
Abbott, Isaac	" "	"	Horse killed June 16
Ashby, J. W.		"	
Adams, Orlen M.	Madison Co.	"	On express.
Brooks, Benjamin	St. Clair Co.	"	On command
Baker, John T.		"	
Cornelius, L.M.McTy	Monroe Co.	"	Gun lost June 16 in battle
Cleveland, Loren	Madison Co.	"	Died in service June 12, 1832.
Dikes, George P.	St. Clair Co.	"	
Gillespe, Joseph	Madison Co.	"	
Hendricks, Elijah A.	St. Clair Co.	"	Sick; absent
Herrington, Charles	Madison Co.	"	On furlough
Hamilton, Wm.	" "	"	
Hill, Pendleton	Monroe Co.	"	
Harrison, Henry	Putnam Co.	"	
Hall, John	LaSalle Co.	"	On furlough.
Jarrott, Francis	St. Clair Co.	"	
Kinney, George D.		"	
Lusk, Marcus	Madison Co.	"	
Lawrence, John		"	
Lamsett, Pier	LaSalle Co.	"	On command
Makenson, Wm. B.	St. Clair Co.	"	Killed June 16 in battle
McElroy, Jas. E.	Madison Co.	"	On command
Motley, O. C.	" "	"	
McClain, Isaac	" "	"	On furlough.
Moore, John M.	Monroe Co.	"	
McMoore, William		"	
McCalaugh, Samuel	Madison Co.	"	Delivered to civil authority June 13, 1832.
Menard, Pier	Randolph Co.	"	Absent without leave
Needles, James B.	Monroe Co.	"	
Otwell, Ceylon G.	Madison Co.	"	
Owens, Lewis	Randolph Co.	"	Absent without leave
Randle, Josias	Madison Co.	"	On furlough
Right, William	St. Clair Co.	"	
Roman, Richard	" "	"	
Randle, Richard R.	Madison Co.	"	On command
Right, John	Monroe Co.	"	
Smith, Levi	Madison Co.	"	
Scott, Charles	St. Clair Co.	"	
Stephenson, Benj.	Madison Co.	"	
Shields, George B.	" "	"	
Sample, James		"	
Scott, Benj.	St. Clair Co.	"	Killed June 16, 1832
Spencer, Russell H.	R'k Island Co.	"	
Thomas, John	St. Clair Co.	"	Promoted to Major
Thomas, W. S.	" "	"	
Teter, Solomon		"	
Teter, Philip		"	
Torence, Wm. W.	Madison Co.	"	
Whiteside, Joseph	St. Clair Co.	"	
Whitesides, Samuel	" "	"	
Woods, John	Madison Co.	"	
Welker, Joseph	St. Clair Co.	"	Gun lost June 16 in battle
Wilderman, Levi	" "	"	
Wheeler, Erastus	Madison Co.	"	On command
West, Henry H.	St. Clair Co.	"	
Whitten, B.	Pike Co.	"	On command; gun lost in battle June 16
Wells, Lucius	" "	" "	" "
Wells, John	R'k Island Co.	"	

Note as to Captain's horse: I was informed by the Major of the regiment, and various other officers and soldiers, that this statement was entirely untrue.

(Signed.)

T. P. ANDREWS,
Paymaster U. S. A.

EDWARDSVILLE, ILL.,
December 14, 1832.

Capt. Earl Pierce's Company

Of the Illinois Volunteers in the service of the United States.

Name and Rank.	Comm'ncem't of service.	Term'n of serv'e	Remarks.
Captain.	1832.	1832.	
Earl Pierce	June 18	Aug. 16	
First Lieutenant.			
Banford Morris			
Second Lieutenant.			
Loring Ames			
Sergeants.			
A. Westfall			
P. Haynes			
William Smith		Aug. 7	
Reuben Turner		Aug. 16	
Corporals.			
William Carter			
J. Black			
P. Morris		Aug. 7	
J. Hanks			
Privates.			
Bridgewater, A.			
Black, A.			
Billington, C. M.			
Benedict, D.			
Benedict, J.			
Brawelic, J. C.		Aug. 2	
Brooks, H.		Aug. 16	
Bateman, Henry			
Chapman, G. W.			
Childers, G.			
Clark, W.		Aug. 2	
Dodd, C.		Aug. —	
Dickerson, J.			
Denson, B.			
Furguson, S.			
Feet, A.			
Gillingswater, E.			
Hansucker, D.			
Hedrick, A.			
Harrison, H.			
Homes, Hol.		Aug. 16	
Harris, A.			
Howard, A.			
Jacobs, H.			
Jeffers, J. E.			
Lyell, J.			
McCarty, N.		Aug. 2	
Payne, S. O.			
Peter, J.			
Roulston, J. H.			
Roberts, J.			
Shun, J.		Aug. 2	
Shipman, Wm. M.			
Shaw, I.		June 16	
Tully, H.			
Williams, G. W.			
Whitehall, George			
Warrick, J.		Aug. 16	
Walker, J. B.			

COMPANIES IN SERVICE PREVIOUS TO 1832.

Capt. James M. Strode's Company

Of Galena Mounted Volunteers, commanded by General Henry Dodge, and serving under the command of Brig.-Gen. Henry Atkinson, of the United States Army, on the Wisconsin, from August 26, 1827, to September 16, 1827.

Name and Rank.	Residence.	Enrolled	Remarks.
Captain.		1827.	
James M. Strode	Galena, Ill.	Aug. 26.	
First Lieutenant.			
John Larrison	" "	" "	
Second Lieutenant.			
Joseph Payne	" "	" "	
Sergeants.			
Moses B. Vance	" "	" "	
Charles Gear	" "	" "	
Samuel Matthews	" "	" "	
Jas. L. Kirkpatrick	" "	" "	
Corporals.			
Charles C. Deprist	" "	" "	
John Ware	" "	" "	
John Loughary	" "	" "	
Privates.			
Alexander, Matthew	" "	" "	Serving from Aug. 26, 1827, to Sept. 2, 1827
Blake, Page	" "	" "	
Bono, John	" "	" "	
Cooper, Jeremiah	" "	" "	
Dempsey, John	" "	" "	
East, H. F. W	" "	" "	
Hall, Richard	" "	" "	
James, Benjamin	" "	" "	
Kirkpatrick, Wm. M.	" "	" "	
Kirkpatrick, John L.	" "	" "	
Kirkpatrick, Rich. H.	" "	" "	
Kirkpatrick, Fran. C.	" "	" "	
Pixley, John	" "	" "	
Phillis, Joseph	" "	" "	Serving from Aug. 26, 1827, to Sept. 2, 1827
Palmer, James	" "	" "	
Rankin, Wm. S.	" "	" "	
St. John, Willis	" "	" "	Serving from Aug. 26, 1827, to Sept. 2, 1827
Scarles, A. D.	" "	" "	
Scott, Lyman	" "	" "	
Scott, Franklin J.	" "	" "	
Scott, George	" "	" "	
Shults, John R.	" "	" "	
Shannon, Daniel	" "	" "	
Thomas, Arthur	" "	" "	
Turley, John	" "	" "	Serving from Aug. 26, 1827, to Sept. 2, 1827
Vibert, Henry	" "	" "	
Williams, David	" "	" "	

BATTALION UNDER COMMAND OF MAJOR N. BUCKMASTER.

1831.

CAPT. SOLOMON MILLER'S COMPANY

Of the Odd Battalion of Mounted Volunteers of the State of Illinois, commanded by Major Nathaniel Buckmaster, employed in the service of the United States by order of the Governor and Commander-in-Chief of the Militia of the State of Illinois, from June 2, 1831, to July 2, 1831, day of its disbandment and discharge at Rock river, 300 miles from the company's rendezvous.

Name and Rank.	Residence.	Enrolled	Remarks.
Captain.		1831.	
Solomon Miller	Belleville	June 2	
First Lieutenant.			
John Winstanley	"	"	
Second Lieutenant.			
Samuel B. Chandler	"	"	
Sergeants.			
David Angle	"	"	
Enoch Luckey	"	"	
Robert Higgins	"	"	
Stephen Brooks	"	"	
Corporals.			
David Phillips	"	"	
William Tate	"	"	
Solomon Span	"	"	
Isaac Hendrick	"	"	
Privates.			
Blackwell, John H	"	"	Appointed Q. M. Sergt. June 19, 1831
Barker, Amos T	"	"	
Brewer, Wm. M	"	"	
Clumpitt, Samuel	"	"	
Coon, Thomas	"	"	
Carr, William	"	"	
Doyle, Lewis	"	"	
Davis, James	"	"	
Demint, William	"	"	Joined the Spies June 19, 1831
Edwards, Ninian W	"	"	
France, William	"	"	
Gardner, Stephen	"	"	
Hartwell, Stephen A	"	"	Joined the Spies June 19, 1831
Holt, Jacob	"	"	
Higgins, Ichabod	"	"	
Hern, Abner	"	"	
Hill, Jonathan	"	"	
Higbee, Charles	"	"	Appointed Surgeon June 19, 1831
Krupp, John	"	"	Appointed Armorer June 19, 1831
King, Ambrose	"	"	
Lacey, Caleb	"	"	Joined the Spies June 19, 1831
Lard, Robert A	"	"	
Lemming, Thomas	"	"	Joined the Spies June 19, 1831
McDowell, Garrett	"	"	
McMurty, George	"	"	

Name and Rank.	Residence.	Enrolled	Remarks.
		1831.	
Moore, Jacob.	Belleville	June 2	
Miller, Absalom	"	"	Sick: absent on furlough
Null, Henry L	"	"	
Owen, Hopson	"	"	
Owen, Josiah	"	"	
Petitt, James	"	"	
Phillips, John	"	"	
Scott, John B	"	"	
Scott, William	"	"	
Smith, Nathaniel	"	"	
Smith, John, Sr	"	"	
Smith, John, Sr	"	"	
Smith, Daniel B	"	"	
Stooky, Aaron	"	"	
Skinner, Akeman	"	"	
Skinner, Thomas	"	"	
Sulivan, Francis	"	"	
Swaggart, Samuel	"	"	Joined the Spies June 19, 1831
Stubblefield, John	"	"	
Taylor, John	"	"	
Threefall, John	"	"	
Threefall, William	"	"	
Touchette, Francis	"	"	
Visno, Joseph	"	"	
Wood, John	"	"	
Woods, William	"	"	
Wildy, Rodolph	"	"	
Whitesides, Samuel	"	"	Joined the Spies June 19, 1831

Capt. Aaron Armstrong's Company

Of Mounted Volunteers, commanded by Major Nathaniel Buckmaster, commanding a Battalion, and stationed for the protection of the frontier between Ottawa and Chicago, at Fort Walker, in the county of Cook, in the State of Illinois, 290 miles from Edwardsville, Madison county, where recruited. Mustered out of service July 26, 1832.

Name and Rank.	Residence.	Enrolled	Remarks.
		1832.	
Captains.			
Nath'n'l Buckmaster	Madison Co.	June 2	Captain to June 20, when promoted
Aaron Armstrong	"	"	1st Lieut. until June 20, 1832, when prom. Capt.
First Lieutenant.			
Jacob Swaggart	"	"	2d Lieut. until June 20, when prom 1st Lieut.
Second Lieutenant.			
William Tindall	"	"	Orderly until June, 20, 1832, when prom. 2d Lt.
Sergeants.			
Samuel B. Gillam	"	"	
John P. Dyo	"	"	
Henry Beer	"	"	
Nicholas Felker	"	"	
Corporals.			
Martin Bridges	"	"	
Calvin Kinner	"	"	
Wm. McAninch	"	"	
George Milton	"	"	
Privates.			
Atkins, Aber			Private to June 20, when, promoted to staff
Adams, Washing'n F			
Armstrong, Wm			
Ayres, David			
Brewer, Rice			
Bensell, Chas. E			Disch'd extra duties of Ass't Quartermaster
Doney, Robert			
Day, Philip S			
Fruit, Franklin			

Name and Rank.	Residence.	Enrolled 1832.	Remarks.
Goodwin, Abner			
Gillam, John F			1st Corp. to June 20; then Armorer to Battal'n
Gillam, Isom M			2d " " promoted to staff
Gillam, Wm			Private to " " "
Hank, Daniel			
Hart, Henry			
Hart, Pleasant			
Howard, Abram			
Johns, James			
Jackson, Lon			
Johnson, Chas			Disch'd extra duty of Wagonmaster to Bat'l'n
Kennedy, George F			Priv. to June 20, when app'd Adjutant "
McFarland, William			
Murphy, Robert			
Mahwron, John			
Piper, William			
Rice, George			
Smith, Asa G			
Sampson, Peter			
Swaggart, Samuel			
Shirtloftt, John			
Thompson, William			
Taylor, Elijah			
Vincent, John			
Waddle, George			
Whittington, James			
Washburn, John A			
Wethers, Enoch B			Private to June 20, when promoted to staff
Wright, David			2d Sergt. to June 20, when prom. Q. M. to Bat.

The horses used in this service by George Milton, Pleasant Hart, John A. Washburn James Johns, Abram Howard and Henry Beer were the property of N. Buckmaster, who is to receive the wages for the same from the U. S. Government.

Capt. William Moore's Company

Of the Odd Battalion of Mounted Volunteers of Illinois, commanded by Major Nathaniel Buckmaster, employed in the service of the United States by order of the Governor and Commander-in-Chief of the Militia of Illinois, from June 2, 1831, to July 2, 1831, the day of its disbandment and discharge at Rock Island, 300 miles distant from company rendezvous.

Name and Rank.	Residence.	Enrolled 1831.	Remarks.
Captain. William Moore	Belleville	June 2	Pay due as 3d Lieut. from 2d to 18th June, and elected Capt. June 19, 1831.
First Lieutenant. Benjamin Chesney	"	"	Pay due as private from June 2; elected 1st Lieutenant June 19, 1831.
Second Lieutenant. William F. Hill	"	"	Pay due as private from June 2; elected 2d Lieutenant June 19, 1831.
Sergeants. Aaron Land	"	"	Pay due as private from June 2; elected 1st Sergeant June 19, 1831.
William Nichols	"	"	Pay due as private from June 2; elected 2d Sergeant June 19, 1831.
William Million	"	"	Pay due as private from June 2; elected 3d Sergeant June 19, 1831.
Charles S. Moore	"	"	Pay due as private from June 2
Corporals. Walcott A. Strong	"	"	Pay due as private from June 2
David Young	"	"	" " " " "
Franklin J. Scott	"	"	" " " " "
Samuel Gaskell	"	"	
Privates. Anderson, James	"	"	
Anderson, Stinson H	"	"	
Adams, William	"	"	
Brown, Hiram	"	"	

ODD COMPANIES.

Name and Rank.	Residence.	Enrolled	Remarks.
		1831.	
Brown, William G	Belleville	June 2	Appointed Paymaster-General of detachment [June 2, 1831].
Brown, Alfred	"	"	
Bradsby, Richard	"	"	Joined the Spies June 19
Briggs, Josiah	"	"	
Basey, Edmund	"	"	
Coleman, Jesse	"	"	
Crane, Lewis W	"	"	
Crocker, William	"	"	
Clemson Ell B.	"	"	Absent on furlough
Davis, Robert	"	"	
Enocks, David	"	"	
Enocks, Samuel	"	"	
Fike, John J	"	"	
Fike, A.	"	"	
Griffin, George	"	"	
Galbreath, Undrell B	"	"	
Hipes, Joseph	"	"	
Hodge, James	"	"	
Herring, Elijah	"	"	
Herring, Abner	"	"	
Jackson, John	"	"	
Jones, John J	"	"	
Kinney, Geo. D	"	"	
Lane, Thomas	"	"	
Long, Thomas	"	"	Absent on furlough
LaCroux, Rene M	"	"	
Larame, Lewis	"	"	Absent; sick
Mitchell, William D.	"	"	
Macom, Peter	"	"	
Macom, George	"	"	
McNabb, Laoui	"	"	
Mitchell, William	"	"	
Manage, Louis	"	"	
Ogle, Joseph	"	"	
Payne, Geo. W	"	"	
Pea, James	"	"	Attached to the wagons
Russell, William	"	"	
Reynolds, Thomas	"	"	
Rittenhouse, Elijah	"	"	
Russell, James	"	"	
Russell, John H	"	"	
Russell, Isaac P	"	"	
Roman, Richard	"	"	Appointed Surgeon's Mate June 19, 1831
Seymore, Grove	"	"	
Scott, Felix	"	"	
Tracewell, Edward	"	"	
Thomas, Charles	"	"	
Vernor, Zenas H	"	"	
Virgin, Hiram	"	"	
Woods, Lewis	"	"	
Woods, John W.	"	"	
Wilson, John	"	"	
Williamson, A	"	"	
Winters, Joshua	"	"	
Whiteside, Joseph	"	"	Absent on furlough

It is presumed this company was fully organized by the election of the officers and non-commissioned officers on June 19, 1831.

(Signed.)   J. BLISS,
Major, and Mustering Officer.

MEXICAN WAR.

1846-8.

—13

MEXICAN WAR.

FIRST REGIMENT.

Field and Staff of the First Regiment

Of late Col. J. J. Hardin's Illinois Foot Volunteers, commanded by Col. William Weatherford, called into the service of the United States by the President, under act of Congress approved May 13, 1846, for the term of twelve months. From the 28th day of February, 1847 (when last mustered), to the 17th day of June, 1847, when discharged.

Name and Rank.	Place of Enlistment.	Enrolled.	Remarks.
Colonels.		1846	
John J. Hardin	Alton, Ill	June 30	Killed in battle at Buena Vista, Feb. 23, 1847..
Wm. Weatherford	"	June 25	Elected at Buena Vista, Feb. 26, vice Hardin.
Lieutenant-Colonel.			
Wm. B. Warren	"	June 25	Elected from Major, at Buena Vista, Feb. 26..
Major.			
Wm. A. Richardson	"	June 26	Elected from Capt. Co. "E," at Buena V., Feb. 26
Adjutants.			
Benj. M. Prentiss	"	June 18	Appointed from 1st Lieut. Co. "A," Alton, Ill.,
Wm. H. L. Wallace	"	June 22	......[June 30; elected Capt. Co. "I," Sept. 14.
Surgeons.			
James H. White	"	June 23	Transferred at Buena Vista, in March........
C. Payton	Little R'k, Ark	June 20	....
Assistant Surgeon.			
Chris. B. Zalviskie	Alton, Ill	June 26	Transferred at Panas, Mex., in December....
A. A. Q. Ms.			
John Scanland	"	June 27	Appointed from 1st Lieut. Co. "F," Nov. 1.
William Erwin	"	June 18	................[Transferred to Co. "F," Dec. 31.
A. A. C. S.			
George S. Myers	"	June 26	....
Sergeant-Major.			
Edward A. Giller	"	June 23	....
Q. M. Sergeants.			
Thomas Smothers	"	June 25	Died at New Orleans July 27 ....
Wm. Osman	"	June 22	....
Principal Musicians.			
Austin W. Fay	"	June 22	Killed in battle at Buena Vista, Feb. 23, 1847..
Levi Bixby	"	June 19	Reduced to ranks and trans. to Co. "B," Nov. 1.
Jerome Gibson	"	June 19	....
John Aug. Stemple	"	June 18	App. at Agua Neuva, Mex., vice Fay, killed..
Levi Bixby	"	June 19	Reduced to ranks, and transferred Nov. 1....

FIRST REGIMENT. 195

Company "A."

Name and Rank.	Place of Enlistment.	Enrolled	Remarks.
Captain.		1846.	
James D. Morgan	Alton, Ill.	June 18	
First Lieutenant.			
William Y. Henry	"	"	"
Second Lieutenant.			
James Evans	"	"	"
George T. M. Davis	"	"	"	Detached serv., Aid-de-Camp to Gen. Shields
Sergeants.			
John Archer	"	"	"
Edward Everett	"	"	"	Absent, wounded; on furl'gh at San Antonio.
Ephraim B. Wood	"	"	"
John W. Burns	"	"	"	On furl'h in Q. M. Dep't, by order Gen. Taylor
Corporals.			
George Evans	"	"	"
Lewis W. Sweet	"	"	"
John P. Brook	"	"	"
Jno. T. Congers	"	"	"
Privates.			
Arnold, Abraham	"	"	"
Beck, Jacob	"	"	"	Deserted
Beck, Joseph	"	"	"
Boers, Lewis	"	"	"
Bush, Daniel B	"	"	"
Cuningh'm, Oliver H	"	"	"	On furl'h in Q. M. Dep't, by order Gen. Taylor
Cross, William N	"	"	"
Cassady, William	"	"	"
Cooper, Wendell B	"	"	"
Cooper, Benjamin	"	"	"
Collett, Leon	"	"	"
Cassill, Joseph	"	"	"
Congers, Enoch W	"	"	"
Downard, Jordan	"	"	"	Died at Saltillo March 15
Ewing, Charles L	"	"	"
Finney, William	"	"	"
Grimm, George	"	"	"
Gramper, Joseph	"	"	"
Grant, Richard	"	"	"
Gladdish, Leander J	"	"	"
Hoyt, John W	"	"	"	On furl'h in Q. M. Dep't, by order Gen. Taylor
Hoffman, Isaac	"	"	"
Humphrey, Charles	"	"	"
Hoag, Alamer	"	"	"
Houck, Thomas L. R	"	"	"
Innman, Andrew	"	"	"
Jordan, James B	"	"	"
Jordan, Wesley	"	"	"
Jordan, Harrison	"	"	"
Jordan, William J	"	"	"
Jordan, Miles	"	"	"
Johnson, Smith	"	"	"
Jenkins, Jesse H	"	"	"
Konkle, Philip	"	"	"
Knapp, Charles E	"	"	"	Died at Saltillo May 17
Lewis, Zachariah	"	"	"
Littlefield, August P	"	"	"
Lawrence, Jasper	"	"	"
Meekempson, John S	"	"	"
Mills, Elisha	"	"	"
Meir, Francis	"	"	"
Miller, William A	"	"	"
McCoy, John	"	"	"	On furl'h in Q. M. Dep't by order Gen. Taylor
McNeil, Daniel C	"	"	"
McLess, Henry	"	"	"
Owen, John F	"	"	"	Died at Saltillo, March 11.
Pounds, Benjamin A	"	"	"	Discharged for disability, at N. Orl'ns, Nov.—
Pounds, Joseph M	"	"	"
Parsons, Jeremiah	"	"	"
Pounds, Samuel	"	"	"
Piper, Albert R	"	"	"
Poake, Joseph H	"	"	"

Name and Rank.	Place of Enlistment.	Enrolled	Remarks.
		1846.	
Painter, Joseph	Alton, Ill.	June 18	
Roberts, John J	"	"	
Rupright, Martin	"	"	
Renoud, John F	"	"	
Rossell, James	"	"	
Renck, Andrew J	"	"	
Richter, Ferdinand	"	"	
Ramsey, James	"	"	
Rust, George	"	"	
Slott, Handford	"	"	
Short, James	"	"	
Smith, Marinus G	"	"	
Slouse, Michael	"	"	Absent, sick, at Presido, Rio Gr. from Oct. 16
Shepherd, Hedrick	"	"	
Shepherd, Oan	"	"	
Shear, Michael	"	"	
Sellon, William R	"	"	
Sellon, Charles J	"	"	
Tuttle, Abner J	"	"	
Vight, William S	"	"	On furl'h in Q. M. Dep't, by order Gen. Taylor
Vandenburg, John W	"	"	
Wren, Thomas	"	"	
Wade, George W. D.	"	"	
Wolfe, Frederick	"	"	
Webb, John B	"	"	
Williman, Joseph	"	"	

This company was mustered out June 17, 1847, at Camargo, Mexico.

Company "B."

Name and Rank.	Place of Enlistment.	Enrolled	Remarks.
Captain.		1846.	
M. P. Smith	Alton, Ill.	June 19	
First Lieutenant.			
Patrick Higgins	"	"	
Second Lieutenants.			
William A. Clark	"	"	
Elias B. Zabriska	"	June 25	
Sergeants.			
Authar Perry	"	June 19	
Abraham Peters	"	"	
Chauncey H. Snow	"	"	
Alfred Wrose	"	"	
Corporals.			
Patrick Mehan	"	"	
L. M. Mathews	"	"	
Geo. Mackenzie	"	"	
Geo. P. Wilmot	"	"	
Musicians.			
D. M. Burdick	"	"	
Levi Bixby	"	"	Promoted from private, by Col. Weatherford
Privates.			
Anderson, Wm. O.	"	"	
Burk, Patrick	"	"	Sick in hospital, Saltillo
Blanchard, James A.	"	"	
Burkholder, John	"	"	
Burr, Thos. J.	"	"	
Bisbee, John	"	"	
Boneby, John D.	"	"	
Conover, Peter	"	"	
Clemens, Patrick	"	"	
Crane, Henry	"	"	

FIRST REGIMENT.

Name and Rank.	Place of Enlistment.	Enrolled	Remarks.
		1846.	
Chandler, Bradley	Alton, Ill	June 19	On detached serv. in Q. M. Dept. from Aug. 8
Dilly, Junius	"	"	
Dolan, Peter	"	"	
Edson, James T	"	"	
Ells, Simeon L	"	"	
Fitch, Leroy D	"	"	
Finton, Michael	"	"	
Gavin, Thomas	"	"	Sick in hospital, Saltillo
Garregus, Edw'd D	"	"	
Gun, Hiram	"	"	
Griffin, Dennis	"	"	To be Dishon. disch. by order of Gen. Wool.
Gorman, Thomas	"	"	
Gitty, James	"	"	
Howland, John	"	"	
Hodge, William	"	"	
Huzey, Edward	"	"	
Half, Michael	"	"	
Krebbs, Geo. W	"	"	
Kirkham, Solomon	"	"	
Murry, Patrick	"	"	
Malone, John	"	"	
Mains, Philip	"	"	
Moore, Thomas S	"	"	On furlough in Q. M. Dept. from May 20
Orouke, James	"	"	
Quinn, Francis	"	"	
Pratt, Joseph H	"	"	On furlough in Q. M. Dept. from May 20
Riley, Thomas	"	"	
Richards, B. A	"	"	
Smith, John L	"	"	
Sullivan, Jeremiah	"	"	
Seary, Barney	"	"	
Tyler, O. C	"	"	
Underhill, Geo. W	"	"	On furlough in Q. M. Dept. from May 20
Wright, Edward	"	"	
White, Thomas P	"	"	Sick in hospital, Saltillo
Woolworth, S. T	"	"	
Died.			
Thomas Diley	"	"	Died at General Hospital, Saltillo, March 10

This company was discharged June 17, 1847.

Company "C."

Name and Rank.	Place of Enlistment.	Enrolled	Remarks.
		1846.	
Captain.			
Noah Fry	Alton, Ill	June 23	
First Lieutenant.			
William C. Rainey	"	"	
Second Lieutenants.			
Solomon S. Chester	"	"	On furlough from May 24
Joshua C. Winters	"	"	
Sergeants.			
John J. Sears	"	"	
Elihu Boan	"	"	
Edwin Parks	"	"	
Wm. McGovran	"	"	
Corporals.			
Rufus Cleaveland	"	"	
James H. Brock	"	"	
William C. Rainey	"	"	
Wilson Whitlock	"	"	Appointed Corporal March 18
Edward McGovran	"	"	

198   MEXICAN WAR.

Name and Rank.	Place of Enlistment.	Enrolled	Remarks.
Privates.		1846.	
Attebery, William T.	Alton, Ill	June 23	
Attebery, Stephen C	"	"	
Allen, Jas. V	"	"	
Allen, Andrew J	"	"	
Ashlock, Jas. M	"	"	Discharged on Surgeon's certificate March 23
Bowman, Calvin L.	"	"	
Bandy, James T	"	"	
Bandy, Elihu	"	"	
Bandy, Richard T.	"	"	
Blackshor, William	"	"	
Ballow, George	"	"	
Barnard, Andrew J.	"	"	
Barnett, Jno. B.	"	"	
Conway, Silas P	"	"	
Cade, James R	"	"	
Conner, George	"	"	
Clark, Hiram	"	"	
Cochran R. K. F	"	"	
Dennis, Matthew Q.	"	"	
Fisher, Elihu	"	"	
Ferguson, William B	"	"	
Fitch, George C	"	"	
Goodwin, Jno. M	"	"	
Gillam, Larkin	"	"	
Hughs, Jno. W	"	"	
Houser, Thompson	"	"	
Hudson, James	"	"	On furlough in Q. M. Dept from May 15
Kirgin, Jno. M	"	"	
Knapp, Cyrus, Jr	"	"	
Long, William A	"	"	
Leonard, Jno	"	"	
Laton, Charles	"	"	
Leonard, Jacob W	"	"	
Murry, James	"	"	
Martin, George	"	"	
Moore, Uriah	"	"	
Morrow, George W.	"	"	Discharged on Surgeon's certificate April 7.
Neece, Alfred W	"	"	
Poindexter, Lawr'ce	"	"	
Porter, William A	"	"	
Powel, Elija	"	"	
Robbins, James A	"	"	
Roe, David	"	"	
Record, James S	"	"	
Sloan, Asa	"	"	
Swinden, Jno	"	"	
Skeen, Henry W	"	"	
Stoddard, Jno. L	"	"	
Spofford, Thomas	"	"	
Stone, Craven	"	"	
Stone, Noah M	"	"	
Stephens, David	"	"	On furlough in Q. M. Dept. from May 24
Tunnel, Martin L.			
Taylor, Walter			
Watson, Hiram			
Witt, Morrill			On furlough in Q. M. Dept. from May 15

This company was mustered out June 17, 1847, at Camargo, Mexico.

COMPANY "D."

Name and Rank.	Place of Enlistment.	Enrolled	Remarks.
Captain.		1846	
John L. McConnel	Alton, Ill	June 25	
First Lieutenant.			
Samuel R. Black	"	"	
Second Lieutenants.			
James E. Dunlap	"	"	
Nathan D. Hatfield	"	"	

FIRST REGIMENT.

Name and Rank.	Place of Enlistment.	Enrolled	Remarks.
Sergeants.		1846.	
Hugh Fee	Alton, Ill	June 25	
John T. Longley	"	"	
John C. Barr	"	"	
Thomas J. Moss	"	"	
Corporals.			
John Selby	"	"	
P. L. N. Dustin	"	"	
Thomas Turley	"	"	
John Grogan	"	"	
Musician.			
Edward Hines	"	"	On furlough in Capt. Mear's Co. Mounted Volunteers, at Saltillo, May 29.
Privates.			
Adkin, George W	"	"	
Bennett, Isaac R	"	"	
Bennett, William	"	"	
Bozarth, John C	"	"	
Bozarth, A. Johnson	"	"	
Brown, George S	"	"	
Brown, Nathan	"	"	
Bryant, James	"	July 9	
Bryant, Thomas	"	June 25	
Bobbett, Wm. C	"	"	
Barr, Oliver P	"	"	
Christy, James S	"	"	
Carter, John	"	"	
Cobbs, Edward	"	"	
Clayton, Wm	"	"	
Dixon, James	"	"	
Dean, John	"	"	
Ellison, Robt	"	"	
Fuller, John	"	"	
Goodheart, John	"	"	
Huoy, George I	"	"	Extra duty (Hosp. Steward) at a post of more than 4 Co's. from July 4, order Col. Hardin.
Huoy, James S	"	"	
Hurry, David	"	"	
Howard, Henderson	"	"	
Hoppor, John	"	"	On furl. in Q.M. Dept., at Saltillo, from May 17.
Ingalls, Alphonso	"	"	
Kennett, Thomas F	"	"	
Kennett, Frank D	"	"	
Kercher, Valentine	"	"	
Kershaw, Albert	"	"	
Knight, Ezekiel	"	"	
Lewis, Wm. M	"	"	
Lossley, A. S	"	"	
Lorner, Beat	"	"	
Martin, Benj. F	"	"	
McConnel, C	"	"	
McCormick, Isham	"	"	
Neeley, James	"	"	
Ogle, John W	"	"	
O'Neil, Patrick	"	"	
Olds, Daniel	"	"	Died in Hospital at Saltillo, March 29.
Pullman, Wm. E	"	"	
Price, David	"	"	"
Puryear, John F	"	"	
Redding, Enoch	"	"	
Reeder, Levi	"	"	
Stewart, James	"	"	
Shoff, John D	"	"	
Stoker, Jacob R	"	"	
Simms, Wm. W	"	"	
Sorrels, Peter	"	"	
Sorrels, Thomas	"	"	
Servance, Preston	"	"	
Taylor, Wm	"	"	
Thornley, James	"	"	
Tefft, Willis	"	"	
Weathers, George	"	"	
Winningham, A. J	"	"	
Warner, William	"	"	
White, John	"	"	
Whitaker, Wm	"	"	

This company was mustered out June 17, 1847, at Camargo, Mexico.

Company "E."

Name and Rank.	Place of Enlistment.	Enrolled	Remarks.
Captain.		1846.	
G. W. Robertson	Alton, Ill	June 26	
First Lieutenant.			
Allen Persinger	"	"	
Second Lieutenants.			
George S. Myers	"	"	
John T. May	"	"	
Sergeants.			
George W. Calvert	"	"	
Francis R. McElroy	"	"	
Luke P. Allphin	"	"	
James Coakenour	"	"	
Corporals.			
Robt. A. Lawler	"	"	
Moses Littaker	"	"	
Reuben Allphin	"	"	
William Petefish	"	"	
Musician.			
James H. Carden	"	"	
Privates.			
Allphin, Wm. B	"	"	
Billings, Jonathan	"	"	
Black, John, Sr	"	"	Killed by the enemy near Cessalvo, Feb. 24.
Black, John, Jr	"	"	
Beach, Cyrus	"	"	
Brooks, William	"	"	
Bennett, Lemuel	"	"	
Berry, George G	"	"	
Curry, Isaac	"	"	
Curtis, George W	"	"	
Crane, Goodsell	"	"	
Clarkson, Franklin B	"	"	
Carter, Irvin F	"	"	
Davis, Moses W	"	"	
Dalton, Franklin	"	"	
Doyle, James	"	"	
File, Henry	"	"	
Garrett, John	"	"	
Gray, Hiram H	"	"	
Gray, George L	"	"	
Gillett, Leonard M	"	"	Disch. by reason of having re-vol'd to serve [dur'g war in Capt. Mear's Co.
Horney, Leonidas	"	"	
Harris, James H	"	"	
Harris, William	"	"	
Hewitt, Allen O	"	"	
Ishmael, George N	"	"	
Jones, Anderson	"	"	
Jones, Walter	"	"	Disch. on Surg.'s certif, Mar. 15, by Gen. Wool
Jacobs, Daniel	"	"	
Koch, Isaac	"	"	
Littaker, Joseph H	"	"	
Littaker, Rowland G	"	"	
Lee, John P	"	"	
Luttrell, Benjamin	"	"	
Luttrell, James H	"	"	
Lawler, Joseph T	"	"	
Lansdon, Richard	"	"	
McClelland, Daniel	"	"	
Ogden, Jonathan B	"	"	
Rose, Isaac	"	"	
Riccardson, Wm	"	"	
Richardson, W. R	"	"	
Stapleton, Wm	"	"	
Strahan, James	"	"	
Smotherman, Thos	"	"	
Smith, Charles	"	"	
St. John, Wm. H	"	"	
Stephenson, Wm	"	"	Died of wounds rec'd at Buena Vista, Mar. 25.
Thompson, John B	"	"	
Turner, Berry	"	"	

FIRST REGIMENT.

Name and Rank.	Place of Enlistment.	Enrolled	Remarks.
Thorp, Levitus M.	Alton, Ill.	1846. June 26	
Vantossell, F. M.	"	"	
Wilson, James O.	"	"	
Wilson, Thomas	"	"	

This company was discharged June 17, 1847, at Camargo, Mexico.

COMPANY "F."

Name and Rank.	Place of Enlistment.	Enrolled	Remarks.
Captain.		1846.	
Albion T. Crow	Alton, Ill.	June 27	
First Lieutenant.			
John Scanland	"	"	
Second Lieutenants.			
Robt Buzan	"	"	
Francis Ryan	"	"	
Sergeants.			
John P. McKibbin	"	"	
John Hughs	"	"	
Alonzo D. Frazer	"	"	
George Reed	"	"	
Corporals.			
John J. Ross	"	"	
Alfred M. Jarbo	"	"	
Henry Inglekink	"	"	
Henry L. Thompson	"	"	
Musician.			
Jesse Dreeser	"	"	
Privates.			
Ball, Joseph	"	"	
Birch, Luman P	"	"	
Buckman, John	"	"	
Brush, A. W	"	"	
Curry, Daniel	"	"	On furlough Buena Vista, order Gen. Wool.
Campbell, James R	"	"	
Cavanaugh, Joseph	"	"	
Donner, Levi	"	"	
Daugherty, Austin	"	"	
Evan, Evans	"	"	
Edle, John	"	"	
Furra, Samuel C	"	"	On furlough Buena Vista, order Gen. Wool.
Fuller, William	"	"	
Funk, Hezekiah	"	"	
Griffith, Samuel C	"	"	
Harper, Lafayette	"	"	
Hohl, Nicholas	"	"	
Harper, William	"	"	
Hobbs, William A	"	"	
Isbel, John K	"	"	
Kinkade, John	"	"	
Labadie, Louis	"	"	
McClure, James A	"	"	
Moss, Isaac W	"	"	
Maple, John M	"	"	
Martin, Samuel	"	"	
McBride, Archibald	"	"	
McIntosh, John	"	"	
McGinnis, James	"	"	
McLeavy, Francis	"	"	
Noble, Nelson	"	"	
Phillips, Liman D	"	"	
Pierce, Ira M	"	"	

MEXICAN WAR.

Name and Rank.	Place of Enlistment.	Enrolled	Remarks.
		1846.	
Pase, Peter	Alton, Ill	June 27	
Porterfield, Isaac M.	"	"	
Robe, William	"	"	
Ross, John	"	"	
Slater, George	"	"	
Shepherd, Roland G	"	"	
Shean, Daniel	"	"	
Schlosser, Conrad	"	"	
Taggart, William	"	"	
Taylor, Andrew J	"	"	
Upton, Michael	"	"	
Wetzel, Augustus	"	"	
Waddle, William A	"	"	

Discharged:

Name and Rank.	Place of Enlistment.	Enrolled	Remarks.			
		1846.				
Alexander, Henry	Alton, Ill	June 27	Discharged May 31, order Gen. Wool			
Brown, Job	"	"	"	"	"	"
Brown, David	"	"	"	"	"	"
Bender, Elias	"	"	"	May 28	"	"
Campbell, Thomas	"	"	"	"	"	"
Crane, Nelson R	"	"	"	"	"	"
Crum, Henry	"	"	"	"	"	"
Dignan, Dominick	"	"	"	"	"	"
Docker, Alonzo	"	"	"	"	"	"
Davison, Thomas H	"	"	"	"	"	"
Herald, Robert	"	"	"	"	"	"
Hitchcock, Thomas	"	"	"	"	"	"
Kirtley, Francis	"	"	"	"	"	"
Lockhart, William	"	"	"	"	"	"
Lacock, John M	"	"	"	"	"	"
Murray, James	"	"	"	"	"	"
Mohan, James	"	"	"	"	"	"
Peterman, Charles	"	"	"	"	"	"
Patton, Harrison	"	"	"	"	"	"
Parker, William	"	"	"	"	"	"
Rock, Francis	"	"	"	May 31	"	"
Shriver, John	"	"	"	May 28	"	"
Spencer, Ephriam	"	"	"	"	"	"
Vandergrift, Howard	"	"	"	"	"	"
Vandergrift, James	"	"	"	"	"	"
Musician.						
Gilbreath, Victor	"	"	"	"	"	"

This company was discharged on June 17, 1847 at Camarago, Mexico.

Company "G."

Name and Rank.	Place of Enlistment.	Enrolled	Remarks.
Captain.		1846.	
William J. Wyatt	Alton, Ill	June 25	
First Lieutenant.			
Jas. H. Wetherford	"	"	
Second Lieutenants.			
Isaac S. Wright	"	"	
Jas. M. Wood	"	"	
Sergeants.			
J. B. Duncan	"	"	
George W. Evans	"	"	
Dolphin F. Drew	"	"	
Jas. L. Wyatt	"	"	

FIRST REGIMENT.

Name and Rank.	Place of Enlistment.	Enrolled	Remarks.
Corporals.		1846.	
James A. Sumner	Alton, Ill.	June 25	
Abraham Grimsley	"	"	
Jas. L. Nichols	"	"	
Ananias D. Sevier	"	"	
Musician.			
Jas. Persor	"	"	
Privates.			
Ashbaugh, G. P	"	"	
Allen, G. W	"	"	
Bellows, C. S	"	"	
Brown, Elisha	"	"	
Buchanan, Jas	"	"	
Clayton, J. S	"	"	
Clayton, Elias	"	"	
Conner, J. F	"	"	
Cowden, J. W	"	"	
Carver, Thos. W	"	"	
Carver, G. W	"	"	
Coen, Jas	"	"	
Cox, Beaverly	"	"	Died at Saltillo, in hospital, March 12
Dean, W. R	"	"	
Davenport, P. E	"	"	
Detherage, Colmor	"	"	
Dodson, Benjamin	"	"	
Edwards, Thos	"	"	
Fulling, Frederick	"	"	
Fanning, A. P	"	"	
Fanning, J. M	"	"	
Foss, S. J	"	"	
Gonnels, J. D	"	"	
Henry, William	"	"	
Henry, E. R	"	"	
Hart, J. L	"	"	
Hart, Josiah	"	"	
Hill, Isaac	"	"	
Harris, Joseph	"	"	
Hague, J. W	"	"	On furl'h in Q.M. Dep't at Saltillo, from May 15
Haynes, Baxter	"	"	
Hopper, S. F	"	"	
Jones, Edward	"	"	
Joiner, Thomas	"	"	
Lorge, Adam	"	"	
Matthews, R. D	"	"	
Moore, Travice	"	"	
Miner, A. S	"	"	
McCollum, J. S	"	"	
McCormac, A. L	"	"	
McAvoy, William	"	"	
Piercy, Z. R	"	"	
Pettyjohn, Thos	"	"	
Pulliam, E. C	"	"	
Phillips, H. M	"	"	
Rogers, R. W	"	"	
Rogers, J. W	"	"	
Russel, W. L	"	"	
Russel, Jas	"	"	
Rigg, G. W	"	"	
Ruffner, Jacob	"	"	
Saunderson, S. T	"	"	
Sharp, John	"	"	
Sharp, H. H	"	"	
Swore, Abraham	"	"	
Smitherman, Jas	"	"	
Shipherd, W. A	"	"	
Vanote, William	"	"	
Ward, E. D	"	"	
Ward, Jas	"	"	
Winsor, Jesse	"	"	
White, Juo	"	"	
Witt, Enoch	"	"	
Wright, A. J	"	"	

This company was discharged June 17, 1847, at Camargo, Mexico.

Company "H."

Name and Rank.	Place of Enlistment.	Enrolled	Remarks.
Captain.		1846.	
Samuel Montgomery	Alton, Ill.	June 25.	
First Lieutenant.			
Hezekiah Evans	"	"	
Second Lieutenants.			
Thomas H. Flynn	"	"	
Thomas R. Roberts	"	"	
Sergeants.			
John C. Dinsmore	"	"	
William Lower	"	"	
Elam J. Gaither	"	"	
John M. Delapp	"	"	
Corporals.			
Ezekiel Flynn	"	"	
John Fisher	"	"	
Wm. N. Shibley	"	"	
Erastus L. Gillham	"	"	
Musician.			
Remus G. Morris	"	"	Discharged on Surg. certif. March 17, 1847
Privates.			
Allen, Joseph	"	"	
Atkinson, Elias	"	"	
Burch, William	"	"	
Burch, Tilman	"	"	
Burch, Milton	"	"	
Black, Thomas B.	"	"	
Beard, Isaac	"	"	
Beaird, Thomas	"	"	
Breeding, Wesley	"	"	
Brackett, John H.	"	"	
Cary, Dawson	"	"	
Crinion, William	"	"	
Chistison, Luther	"	"	
Carr, Calvin	"	"	
Beckman, Oliver P.	"	"	
Dawdy, Alanson	"	"	
Dunsmore, George	"	"	
Evans, Jackson	"	"	
Evans, James J	"	"	
Hulett, Joseph	"	"	
Hanback, William	"	"	
Hamilton, Jacob B.	"	"	
Hamilton, Adam	"	"	
Horrald, Alfred	"	"	
Hodge, James	"	"	
Harkins, Abram	"	"	
Jelison, Milertiap	"	"	
Kemp, James F	"	"	
Low, Edgar M.	"	"	Disch. on acc't of re-enrollment May 22, 1847
Lewis, William	"	"	
Lynn, James	"	"	
Little, Michael	"	"	
Langston, Matthew	"	"	
Lankford, William	"	"	
Martin, Caleb	"	"	
Maus, John	"	"	
Moore, John	"	"	
Morris, Jacob	"	"	
Maupin, George	"	"	
Northent, Edward	"	"	
Piko, Eli			
Peneger, William			
Pentzer, Daniel			
Reyon, Christopher			
Ros, William			
Summers, John W.			
Six, William			

FIRST REGIMENT.

Name and Rank.	Place of Enlistment.	Enrolled	Remarks.
		1846.	
Smith, Thomas			
White, Thomas			
Zimmerman, Jas. N.			
Zimmerman, Thom's			

This company was discharged on June 17, 1847, at Camargo, Mex.

Company "I."

Name and Rank.	Place of Enlistment.	Enrolled	Remarks.
Captain.		1846.	
Benjamin M. Prentiss	Alton, Ill.	June 18	
First Lieutenant.			
Edmund S. Holbrook	"	June 22	
Second Lieutenants.			
Wm. H. L. Wallace	"	"	Adjutant of Regiment from Sept. 15, 1846
John Reddick	"	"	
Sergeants.			
George S. Fisher	"	"	
John Bending	"	"	
Joseph E. Skinner	"	"	
Moses Osman	"	"	
Corporals.			
Alonzo Perkins	"	"	Absent on furl'h in Q.M. Dep't from May 30,'47
Levi Jackson	"	"	" " " " " " 31,'47
William M. McCay	"	"	Appointed from private at Saltillo Mar 23, 18—
Lindsey H. Carr	"	"	
Harley W. Clay	"	"	Died at Saltillo, Mexico, March 23, 1847
Musicians.			
Wilson L. Smith	"	"	
Salmon Z. Powers	"	"	
Privates.			
Atwood, William C.	"	"	
Bowen, Aaron, 2d	"	"	
Baker, Schuyler	"	"	
Boyd, David P.	"	"	
Black, Philip	"	"	Absent on furl'h in Q. M. Dep't, from May 28.
Bates, William W.	"	"	
Bleekely, Joseph	"	"	
Cameron, Thomas	"	"	Died at Saltillo, Mexico, April 5, 1847
Claude, Frederick E.	"	"	
Clay, Levi	"	"	
Dewitt, George N.	"	"	Absent on furl'h in Q. M. Dep't from May 28
Dickson, Wilburn F.	"	"	
Errickson, Errick	"	"	
Evans, Abraham L.	"	"	
Falston, Benjamin G	"	"	Absent, sick at Port Lavaca, Tex., from Aug.3
Gibson, William L.	"	"	Absent on furl'h in Q. M. Dep't from May 26
Goodell, Rossell E.	"	"	
Gillett, Nicholas	"	"	
Handcock, Armig'l W	"	"	
Haughterling, Chas.	"	"	Absent on furl'h in Ordn'ce Dep. from May 29
Hopper, Rowland	"	"	
Hollaker, Goll	"	"	
Hollaker, Donut	"	"	
Hoes, Peter	"	"	
Harris, Edward	"	"	
Hausman, David	"	"	
Howlet, Robert W.	"	July 9	
Kelley, William	"	June 22	Absent on furl'h in Q. M. Dep't from May 26
Kelley, Edward P.	"	"	
Lawrence, Augustus	"	"	
Lynch, John W.	"	"	
Maleure, John	"	"	

MEXICAN WAR.

Name and Rank.	Place of Enlistment.	Enrolled	Remarks.
		1846.	
Mitchell, Bradford C	Alton, Ill	June 22	
Matthews, Geo. W	"	"	
Morrell, John	"	"	
Morse, Evander	"	"	
Miller, Joseph	"	"	
Martin, Robert B	"	"	
Mattiese, Nicholas	"	"	
Mulkin, Ezra	"	"	
McCarty, Timothy	"	"	
McDonald, John T	"	"	
Napier, Dwight	"	"	
Nichol, John P	"	"	Absent on furl'h in Q. M. Dep't from May 27.
Ordway, Edson	"	"	
Pitzer, James F	"	"	
Pratt, Christopher M	"	"	
Reddick, Joseph	"	"	
Rider, Charles	"	"	
Rouse, Charles R	"	"	Absent on furl'h in Q. M. Dep't from May 30. " " 26.
Story, Joseph	"	"	
Strong, William	"	"	
Shope, Emanuel	"	"	
Skinner, William B	"	"	
Stewart, James	"	"	
Shilliker, Johannus	"	"	
Stauffer, Nicholas	"	"	
Teeters, David	"	"	
Thompson, Daniel L	"	"	
Taylor, John	"	"	
Taylor, James T	"	"	
Van Orten, James	"	"	
Woolcot, Alford	"	"	
Woodberry, Benj. F	"	"	
Williams, William	"	"	
Webb, James	"	"	
Willnor, John	"	"	

This company was discharged at Camargo, Mexico, June 17, 1847.

Company "K."

Name and Rank.	Place of Enlistment.	Enrolled	Remarks.
Captain.		1846.	
Lyman Mower	Alton, Ill	June 18	
First Lieutenant.			
Wm. Erwin	"	"	On detached service Q. M. Dept
Second Lieutenants.			
Samuel M. Parsons	"	"	On detached service with Col. Churchill, [Insp.-Gen. U. S. A.
Mathew Moran	"	"	
Sergeants.			
Joshua Herrindan	"	"	
Frederick Hallborn	"	"	
Augustus Tilford	"	"	
Dewitt C. Davis	"	"	
Corporals.			
Samuel Scott	"	"	
Chas. Banks	"	"	
Benj. VanVrankin	"	"	
Geo. D. Slack	"	"	Wounded in battle Buena Vista, Feb. 23, 1847.
Musicians.			
John Helms	"	"	
Augustus Stemple	"	"	On detached service; appointed principal Musician March 1.

FIRST REGIMENT.

Name and Rank.	Place of Enlistment.	Enrolled	Remarks.
Privates.		1846.	
Atloy, Simon	Alton, Ill	June 18	
Asant, Phillip	"	"	
Baker, David	"	"	
Bruner, Henry	"	"	
Brennan, Michle C.	"	"	
Bunker, George C.	"	"	
Battleman, Lewis	"	"	
Cline, William	"	"	
Carle, James	"	June 28	
Carlin James	"	June 18	
Devoe, Edward	"	"	
Dolson, David	"	June 28	
Durling, John H.	"	June 18	
English, Isaac	"	"	
Ellering, Harmon	"	"	Sent to San Antonio, from Presidio, Rio
Elam, Stephen	"	"	Grande, Jan. 3, 1847; sick, and not officially
Franks, Abraham	"	"	heard of since.
Fuller, Tina P.	"	"	
Fowk, Charles	"	June 28	
Gardner, Eliacune	"	June 18	
Gardner, John	"	"	
Guinnip, Lyman	"	June 28	
Groves, Jonathan	"	"	
Groves, Luther	"	"	
Hyde, Michle	"	June 18	
Handy, Austin	"	June 28	
Johnson, Nelson	"	June 18	
Lathrop, Cyrus	"	June 28	
Myers, Charles	"	June 18	
Miller, John	"	"	
Miller, Jacob	"	"	
McCarty, Michle	"	"	On furlough from May 28, 1847, in Q. M. Dept.
Olmstead, Wm. P.	"	"	
Osmand, Christian	"	"	
Phettiplace, George	"	"	
Porter, Henry	"	"	
Phinisy, Wm	"	"	On furlough from May 28, 1847, in Q. M. Dept.
Rowe, Ed. L.	"	"	
Roth, Fredrick	"	"	
Rikow, Fredrick	"	"	Wounded in battle at Buena Vista, Feb. 23
Robinson, W. H. H.	"	"	
Shrader, Frederick	"	"	
Steinhouse, Aug.	"	"	
Secomb, Harmon	"	"	
Temple, John H.	"	June 28	
Warian, John	"	"	
Wenter, Frederick	"	June 18	
Waters, Samuel	"	"	
Wells, John	"	"	On furlough from May 15, 1847, in Q. M. Dept.
Walker, James	"	"	
Wise, John	"	"	

Discharged:

		1846.	
Burroughs, Francis	Alton, Ill	June 18	[Mounted Vols. during war, May 28, 1847. Disch. by reason of joining Capt. Mear's Co.
Black, Adam	"	"	" " " " "
Upperman, George	"	"	" " " " "
Willett, Freeman	"	"	" " " " "
Weaver, Frederick	"	"	" " " " "
Carney, Franklin	"	"	Disch. by reason of having hired to Maj. Butler, Paymaster U. S. A., June 3.

This company was discharged on June 17, 1847, at Camargo, Mexico.

FIRST REGIMENT.

The Field and Staff

In the 1st Regiment of Illinois Foot Volunteers, commanded by Colonel E. W. B. Newby, called into the service of the United States by the President, under the act of Congress approved May 13, 1846, at Alton, Ill. (the place of general rendezvous), on the 8th day of June, 1847, to serve for the term of during the war with Mexico, from the date of enrollment, unless sooner discharged. From the 30th day of June, 1848, (when last paid), to the 16th day of October, 1848. The Regiment was organized by Col. Newby, at Alton, Ill., in the month of June, 1847.

Name and Rank.	Place of Enlistment.	Enrolled	Remarks.
Colonel, Edw'd W. B. Newby	Alton, Ill.	1847. June 8	Elected from Capt. in Newby's Co. "D" at Alton, Ill., June 8, 1847.
Lieutenant-Colonel, Hend'n P. Boyakins	"	"	Elected from private in Turner's Co. "C" at Alton, Ill., June 8, 1847.
Major, Israel B. Donalson	"	"	Elected from Capt. in Donalson's Co. "K" at Alton, Ill., June 8, 1847.
1st Lt. and Adjutant, William H. Snyder	"	"	1st Lieut. in Hook's Co. "E." Discharged at Alton, Oct. 14.
2d Lt. and A. A. Q. M. Rich'd N. Hamilton	"	July 16	2d Lieut. in Kenny's Co. "F"
Surgeon, Daniel Turney	Appointed by the President	" 13	
Assistant Surgeon, James D. Robinson	Appointed by the President	" 13	Absent with leave from Oct. 7 to report at N. Y.
Act. Asst. Surgeon, Thomas B. Lester	Alton, Ill.	Oct. 8	Is private in Co. "C," empl'y'd by Col. at Santa Fe Oct. 8, 1847, till Oct. 3, 1848.
Sergeant-Major, John H. White	"	Mch. 6, '48	Appointed from Sergt. in Co. "B" Mar. 6, *vice* Tappan, reduced.
Q. M. Sergeants, Charles R. Slade	"	Jun. 8, '47	Died at Santa Fe Feb. 9.
Geo. F. Bull	"	Feb. 17, '48	App'd from private Feb. 17, *vice* Slade, dec'd.
Principal Musicians, Thos. W. Pace	"	Mch. 6, '48	App'd from Co. "C," *vice* Case, reduced
John L. Kiser	"	"	" "K." *vice* Maynard, reduced

Company "A."

Name and Rank.	Place of Enlistment.	Enrolled	Remarks.
Captain, Thomas Bond	Alton, Ill.	1847. May 22	
First Lieutenants, John B. Roper	"	"	Discharged by resignation May 20, 1848.
Henry Richardson	"	"	Elected from private, *vice* Roper, resigned.

Name and Rank.	Place of Enlistment.	Enrolled	Remarks.
Second Lieutenants.		1847.	
Alex. H. Johnson	Alton, Ill	May 22	
Levi Edmunds	"	....	
Sergeants.			
William Willcocks	"	....	"
Henry A. Neely	"	....	" Sick in hospital at Alton, from Oct. 4
William White	"	....	"
Morris'n I. O'Hornett	"	....	" Appointed from Drummer, Oct. 1
Corporals.			
John L. Smith	"	....	"
Joseph Gordon	"	....	"
Wesley Myatt	"	....	"
Elijah Anderson	"	....	"
Fifer.			
Jesse Kirkham	"	....	"
Privates.			
Abbott, Charles W	"	....	"
Afflick, John M	"	....	"
Bowles, Thomas	"	....	" Sick in hospital at Alton, from Oct. 4
Bellardy, Melcher			
Bukema, Cornelius	Ottawa, Ill	Feb.,	'48 Joined, a recruit, Aug. 16
Clark, James M	Alton, Ill	May,	'47
Clark, Thomas			
Carroll, John	Ottawa, Ill	Mar.,	'48 Joined, a recruit, Aug. 16
Cox, George			
Duncan, James	Alton, Ill	May,	'47
Determann, Joseph			
Euington, James	"	....	" Sick in hospital at Alton, from Oct. 4
Epla, William	Ottawa, Ill	Mar.,	'48 Joined, a recruit, Aug. 16
Fisher, David	Alton, Ill	May,	'47
Fisk, Norman	Ottawa, Ill	Mar.,	'48 Joined, a recruit, Aug. 16
Greer, William	Alton, Ill	May,	'47
Guithouse, Chris. H			Detached as Hosp. Steward Oct. 28, 1847
Green, Charles	Ottawa, Ill	Mar.,	'48 Joined, a recruit, Aug. 16
Greenlee, Elihu	Belleville, Ill	Feb.,	'48 " " "
Hockelberg, John	Alton, Ill	May,	'47
Hammond, Charles B	"	....	"
Hill, Thomas F	"	....	"
Hughes, Arthur	"	....	"
Hutton, James	"	....	"
Hutton, Henry	"	....	"
Hale, Washington			
Hunt, Joel I	Belleville, Ill	Feb.,	'48 Joined, a recruit, Aug. 16
Hartmann, Tamerl'e	Ottawa, Ill	Mar.,	'48 " " "
Hough, Levi			
Jarvis, Alfred M	Alton, Ill	May,	'47
Johanning, Bernard			
Kopemann, Clemens			
Kennie, Sylvanus	Ottawa, Ill	Mar.,	'48 Joined, a recruit, Aug. 16
Lifert, Henry	Alton, Ill	May,	'47
Lubbers, Bernard			
Lane, Nathaniel	Ottawa, Ill	Mar.,	'48 Joined, a recruit, Aug. 16
Murray, Patrick	Alton, Ill	May,	'47
Miles, Thomas			
Myatt, Albert	Belleville, Ill	Feb.,	'48 Joined, a recruit, Aug. 16
Morgan, Comfort	Ottawa, Ill		
Nicholson, Wil'mson	Alton, Ill	May,	'47
Newton, Jabez B	"	....	"
Page, Michael			
Poll, Josiah			
Pine, Daniel	Ottawa, Ill	Mar.,	'48 Joined, a recruit, Aug. 16
Phillips, Joseph D	Belleville, Ill	Feb.,	'48 " " "
Phillips, Francis			
Ranney, William	Alton, Ill	May,	'47
Slade, Joseph A	"	....	"
Sharp, Anderson	"	....	"
Stites, Isaac	"	....	"
Shields, George T	"	....	"
Scott, William	"	....	"
Siebenburgen, H			
Sharp, Wm. H	Belleville, Ill	Feb.,	'48 Joined, a recruit, Aug. 16
Town, David	Ottawa, Ill	Mar.,	'48
Wall, Wm. A	Alton, Ill	May,	'47
Wall, James			
Warner, John	Ottawa, Ill	Feb.,	'48 Joined, a recruit, Aug. 16
Weddle, Sylvester	Belleville, Ill		

MEXICAN WAR.

Discharged:

Name and Rank.	Place of Enlistment.	Enrolled	Remarks.
		1847.	
Ballard, Henry	Alton, Ill	May 22	[heard from since; supposed deserted. Left sick at Ft. Leavenworth July 15, '47; not
Ballard, Jesse	"	"	Discharged July 24, 1847; disability
Briggs, Andrew	"	"	" July 13, 1847; "
Briggs, Arabia	"	"	" June 10, 1848; "
Dougherty, Nathan'l	"	"	" July 13, 1847; "
Gibson, William	"	"	" Apr. 10, 1848; "
Huey, James M	"	"	" June 10, 1848; "
Huey, Jefferson	"	"	Left sick July 13, 1847; supposed discharged.
Lona, Charles	"	"	Discharged July 24, 1847; disability
Martin, William	"	"	" June 10, 1848; "
Schonefeld, Bernard	"	"	" July 24, 1847; "
Toole, Theodore	"	"	" Mar. 18, 1848; "
Vogt, John P	"	"	

Died:

Sergeants.		1847.	
Story, John W	Alton, Ill	May 22	Died at Point of Rocks, Aug. 26, 1848
Hull, James M	"	"	Died at Albuquerque, N. M., April 23, 1848
Corporals.			[heard from since; supposed died.
Posey, Jabez H	"	"	Left sick at Ft. Leavenworth July 15, '47; not
Todd, Squire S	"	"	Died at Albuquerque, N. M., Feb. 24, 1848
Isaacs, Harris	"	"	" " " Feb. 27, 1848
Buck, Andrew	"	"	Died at Santa Fe, N. M., March 1, 1848
Dunlap, James H	"	"	Died at Albuquerque, N. M., April 10, 1848
Privates.			
Allen, Elias	"	"	Died at Ft. Leavenworth July 10, 1847
Ammons, Felix	"	"	Died at Santa Fe, N. M., Oct. 9, 1847
Cox, Theodore B	"	"	Left sick at Ft. Leavenworth; supposed died.
Ensley, William	"	"	Died at Santa Fe, N. M., Nov. 3, 1847
Findley, Preston	"	"	Died at Albuquerque, N. M., April 10, 1848
Gullick, John M	"	"	Died at San Miguel Aug. 11, 1848
Heeman, Henry	"	"	Died at Albuquerque, N. M., June 7, 1848
Huey, Joseph M	"	"	" " " March 8, 1848
Holley, Williamson	"	"	" " " Feb. 26, 1848
Hull, Joseph F	"	"	Died at Santa Fe, N. M., Nov. 19, 1847
Hebener, Louis	"	"	Died Aug. 18, 1847, *en route* for Santa Fe
Morton, Oliver	"	"	Died at Ft. Leavenworth June 27, 1847
Morrison, Joshua	"	"	Died at Santa Fe, N. M., Nov. 21, 1847
Matsler, John A. I	"	"	Died at Albuquerque, N. M., March 8, 1848
Outhouse, John	"	"	Died at Santa Fe, N. M., Oct. 14, 1847
Posey, Jabelee	"	"	Died at Lexington, Mo., June 24, 1847
Pierson, Isrom	"	"	Died at Santa Fe, N. M., Sept. 20, 1847
Reeves, George W	"	"	" " " Feb. 1, 1848
Shields, W. A	"	"	Died at Albuquerque, N. M., Feb. 14, 1848
Petree, George	"	"	Died at Ft. Leavenworth July 14, 1847

This company was mustered out Oct. 16, 1848, at Alton, Ill.

COMPANY "B."

Name and Rank.	Place of Enlistment.	Enrolled	Remarks.
		1847.	
Captain.			
J. M. Cunningham	Alton, Ill	May 28	
First Lieutenants.			
Benj. F. Furlong	"	"	Disch. by resign'n Mar. 6, by ord. Col. Newby
Wm. M. Eubanks	"	"	Was 1st Sergt. from enrollment until Mar. 7
Second Lieutenants.			
Robt. M. Hundley	"	"	
Dan'l B. Pulley	"	"	

FIRST REGIMENT.

Name and Rank.	Place of Enlistment.	Enrolled	Remarks.
Sergeants.		1847.	
Miles A. Dillard	Alton, Ill	May 28	Was private from enrollment till Mar. 11
Joseph W. Benson	"	....	
Larken M. Riley	"	....	"
Augustus M. Henry.	"	....	Appoin'd from private Aug. 30, 1848, *vice* Sergt. Norris, deceased.
Corporals.			
John G. Boles	"	"	Was private from enrollment till May 26, 1848.
George Q. North	"	"	
Silas M. Calvert	"	"	
Wm. D. Durham	"	....	
Musicians.			
Jesse A. McIntosh	"	....	"
Henry Sykes	"	....	
Privates.			
Ables, Sandy P	"	....	
Anderson, Jas. M	"	....	
Baker, John	"	....	
Baker, Robt.	"	....	
Bandy, Wm. P.	"	....	
Baine, Isaac	"	....	
Barber, John B	"	....	
Bradley, Mathew	"	....	
Buckner, Jas. D	"	....	
Cox, Joseph			
Clark, Benj.	Santa Fe, N.M	Jul. 13,'48	
Davis, Thos. M	Alton, Ill	M'y 28,'47	
Daniel, Reuben	"	....	
Drummond, John G.	"	....	
Drummond, William	"	....	
Duff, John	"	"	
Duff, Andrew D	"	"	
Eaton, Benjamin	"	....	
Eason, Abner			
Greene, Thomas	Santa Fe, N.M	Jul. 13,'48	
Hays, Harvey L	Alton, Ill	M'y 28,'47	
Harris, John L	"	....	
Herring, Joseph	"	M'y 30,'47	Joined by transfer from Co. "H," Nov. 1, 1847.
Huffman, John W	"	M'y 28,'47	
Jones, Edmund	"	....	"
Kelley, Robert R	"	....	
Kelley, Alex	"	....	
Lipsey, Wm. H	"	....	
Lowry, Jas. H	"	....	
Mares, Samuel	"	....	
McAnnelly, Matthew	"	....	
McCoy, Jas. M	"	"	
McKenney, Thos. J	"	"	
McNeill, Benj. F.	"	"	
Miller, Isaac	"	"	
Miller, Wm. H.	"	"	
Mitchell, John P	"	"	
Norris, John C	"	"	
Newsom, Frederick.	"	"	
Odum, Briton	"	"	
Odum, Wm. L	"	"	
Payne, Peter M			
Pierce, William	Ottawa, Ill	Feb. 3,'48	Joined, a recruit, Aug. 1
Rawlings, David	Alton, Ill	M'y 28,'47	
Rose, Alfred J			
Russell, Jas. H	Alton, Ill	M'y 28,'47	Joined by transfer from Co. "E," June 3, 1847.
Reed, James	Ottawa, Ill	Fb. 14,'48	Joined, a recruit. Aug. 1
Richardson, Fred'k	Alton, Ill	M'y 28,'47	
Sands, William	"	"	
Stacks, Benj. J.	"	"	
Shearer, Thos. W	"	....	"
Swafford, Jas	"	....	
Smith, William	"	....	
Sisney, Geo. W	"	M'y 30,'47	Joined by transfer from Co. "H," Nov. 1, 1847.
Sanders, Luke	Ottawa, Ill	Mar. 3,'48	Joined, a recruit. Aug. 1
Sells, Abram H	Alton, Ill	M'y 28,'47	
Tippy, Abram	Santa Fe, N.M	Oc. 20,'47	
Turney, Fayette	Alton, Ill	M'y 28,'47	
West, Hezekiah	"	....	
West, John	"	....	
Woods, Thomas	"	"	
Whitlock, John	"	"	
Warren, Jas. M			

MEXICAN WAR.

Name and Rank.	Place of Enlistment	Enrolled	Remarks.
		1847.	
Wiggs, Robt	Alton, Ill	May 28	
Wiley, Evan T	"	"	
Wiley, Benj. L	"	"	
Youngblood, John	"	"	

Discharged:

Name and Rank.	Place of Enlistment	Enrolled	Remarks.
		1847.	
Avery, Noah W	Alton, Ill	May 28	Disch. by reason of Surg. cert. Mar. 18, 1848
Bowyer, Horace L	"	"	" " " " " "
Cagle, Timothy	"	"	" " " " May 26, 1848
Erwin, Robt. P	"	"	" " " " Mar. 18, 1848
Garrett, Hezekiah	"	"	" " " " May 26, 1848
Lewis, Wm. W	"	"	" " " " "
Pinckum, Owen	"	"	" " " " Oct. 13, 1847

Died:

Name and Rank.	Place of Enlistment	Enrolled	Remarks.
Sergeant.		1847.	
Norris, James C	Alton, Ill	May 28	Died on march f'm Santa Fe, N.M., Aug. 30, '48.
Corporal.			
Askew, Wm. G	"	"	Died at Santa Fe, N. M., May 25, 1848
Privates.			
Daniel, Nathan	"	"	Died at Santa Fe, N. M., Feb. 15, 1848
Davis, Elihu	"	M'y 30, '47	Joined Co. "H" Nov., '47; died at Santa Fe in '48
Gaines, Joseph M	"	M'y 28, '47	Died at Louis Lopez, N.M., Dec. 14, 1847
Keel, Ira	"	"	" Santa Fe, N. M., Oct. 18, 1847
Mooneyham, Cal. I	"	"	" " " " Jan. 9, 1848
Norris, Henry C	"	"	" " " " Oct. 14, 1847
Odum, John L	"	"	" " " " May 9, 1848
Pike, John H	"	"	" Louis Lopez, N. M, Nov. 15, 1847
Ryan, William	"	"	" Alton June 3, 1847

Transferred:

Name and Rank.	Place of Enlistment	Enrolled	Remarks.
		1847.	
Carlisle, Alex. M	Alton, Ill	May 28	Trans. to Co. "H" Nov. 1; order of Col. Newby
Newman, Wm. J	"	"	" " " " " "
Wimms, Meredith	"	"	" " " " " "

This company was discharged Oct. 11, 1848, at Alton, Ill.

Company "C."

Name and Rank.	Place of Enlistment.	Enrolled	Remarks.
Captain.		1847.	
Vantrump Turner	Alton, Ill	May 21	
First Lieutenant.			
Isham N. Haynie	"	"	
Second Lieutenants.			
Levi Wright	"	"	
Benj. F. Marshall	"	"	
Sergeants.			
Jesse M. Wade	"	"	
Longin J. Wnorowski	"	"	
James S. Martin	"	"	
Joseph Wham	"	"	

FIRST REGIMENT. 213

Name and Rank.	Place of Enlistment.	Enrolled	Remarks.
Corporals.		1847.	
James N. Barr	Alton, Ill	May 21	Private from enrollment to June 9, 1848.
James Nelson	"	"	
Dwyer Tracey	"	"	
James M. B. Gaston.	"	"	Private from enrollment to Feb. 6, 1848.
Musicians.			
Cornelius N. Breese.	"	"	Private from enrollment to March 5, 1848
Wm. N. Haynie	"	"	
Privates.			
Anglin, James G	"	"	
Adams, Nathan	"	"	
Anderson, James S	"	"	
Allman, Richard S	"	"	Sick in Hospital at Alton, from Oct. 11
Ashton, George W	"	"	
Buckhout Peter	"	"	
Beasley, Augustus W	"	"	
Beasley, Wm	"	"	
Barbee, Joseph A	"	"	
Bundy, Alexander	"	"	
Bundy, Wm. K	"	"	
Bundy, Isaac	"	"	
Blackburn, Barney L	"	"	
Cox, Oliver H. P	"	"	
Cutchin, Milton	"	"	
Chasteen, James M	"	"	
Denton, James W	"	"	
Elliott, Andrew	"	"	
Elston, William	"	"	
French, Marshall	"	"	
Hill, James McD	"	"	
Jones, Dennis G	"	"	
Jones, Jasper N	"	"	
Jackson, Wm	"	"	
King, Edmund	Belleville, Ill	Feb., '48	Joined, a recruit, Aug. 14, 1848
Lester, Thomas B	Alton, Ill	May, '47	Act. Surg. with detachments of 3 and 5 Co's, [from Oct. 8, 1847, to Oct. 4, 1848.
Lester, John J	"	"	
Lewis, Wm. J	"	"	
Lature, Lewis	"	"	
Marshall, James A	"	"	
McColgan, Hamilton	"	"	
Mifford, Jacob C	"	"	
Morgan, William C	"	"	
McGuire, Joseph F	"	"	
Middleton, Geo. W	"	"	
Middleton, Pleasant.	Belleville, Ill	Mch., '48	Joined, a recruit, Aug. 14, 1848
Milliron, Ira A	Alton, Ill	May, '47	
McGregor, John	Ottawa, Ill	Feb., '48	Joined, a recruit, Aug. 14, 1848
Neel, Thomas	Alton, Ill	May, '47	
Nell, Wm. C	"	"	
Nelson, John R	"	"	
Parker, James	"	"	
Parryman, James L.	"	"	
Pettus, Thomas G	"	"	
Roach, Wm. C	"	"	
Rainey, Samuel	"	"	
Rolan, Wm. E	"	"	
Richie, George D	Ottawa, Ill	Jan., '48	Joined, a recruit, Aug. 14, 1848
Songer, Wm. F	Alton, Ill	May, '47	
Smith, Solomon	"	"	
Smith, William	"	"	
Tully, John	"	"	
Torrence, John S	"	"	
Thomas, Charles	"	"	
Tyler, Joseph B	"	June, '47	
Vaughn, John P	"	May, '47	
Wham, John McN	"	"	
Wham, Robert McM.	"	"	
Wham, Benj. A	"	"	
Winn, David A	"	"	
Walsh, Joshua D	"	"	
Wallis, Elijah	"	"	
White, John W	"	"	
Winn, John	Ottawa, Ill	Dec., '47	Joined, a recruit, Aug. 14, 1848

Died:

Name and Rank.	Place of Enlistment.	Enrolled	Remarks.
Corporal.		1847.	
James Cooper	Alton, Ill	May 21	Died at Santa Fe, N. M., Feb. 4, 1848
Privates.			
Baker, James	"	"	Died at Fort Leavenworth, July 14, 1847
Brazel, William	"	"	" " Aug. 19, 1847
Bass, William H.	"	"	" Santa Fe, N. M., Jan. 11, 1848
Collins, John W.	"	"	" *en route* to Santa Fe, N. M., July 14, 1847.
Cheely, Fountain L.	"	"	" at Santa Fe, N. M., Nov. 22, 1847
Easley, Robert	"	"	" *en route* to Santa Fe, N. M., Aug. 5, 1847
Jones, William W.	"	"	" at Santa Fe, N. M., Sept. 29, 1847
Vaughn, Uriah	"	"	" Albuquerque, N. M., April 25, 1848
White, James H.	"	"	" Santa Fe, N. M., Jan. 22, 1848
Wadkins, Joseph	"	"	" Fort Leavenworth, July 15, 1847

Discharged:

Name and Rank.	Place of Enlistment.	Enrolled	Remarks.
Corporal.		1847.	
Jesse Ray	Alton, Ill	May 21	Disch., disabil'y, Las Vegas, N. M., June 9, '48.
Privates.			
Bethard, John	"	"	Disch., disabil'y, Las Vegas, N. M., June 8, '48
Cox, James M.	"	"	" " Albuquerque,N.M.,Apr.11, '48
Jones, Alexander	"	"	" " Santa Fe, N. M., Mch. 20, '48
Minard, Lorenzo	"	"	" " Albuquerque,N.M.Apr.11, '48
Ray, Andrew	"	"	" " Las Vegas, N. M., June 8, '48
Whitlock, John M.	"	"	" expir'n serv.,Santa Fe,N.M.,Aug.14, '48
Wilson, Hartwell G.	"	"	" " Las Vegas,N.M.,Aug.18,'48
Young, Zachariah	"	"	" disabil'y, Santa Fe, N. M., June 11, '48

Transferred:

Name and Rank.	Place of Enlistment.	Enrolled	Remarks.
Musician.		1847.	
Thomas W. Pace	Alton, Ill	May 21	App. Drum Maj. Mch. 5; trans. field and staff.
Private.			
Hend'son P. Boyakin	"	"	Elected Lieut.-Colonel June 8, 1847

This company was discharged at Alton, Ill., Oct. 13, 1848.

Company "D."

Name and Rank.	Place of Enlistment.	Enrolled	Remarks.
Captains.		1847.	
Edward W. B. Newby	Alton, Ill	May 22	Elected Col. of Regiment, at Alton, June 8, '47
John C. Moses	"	"	Was 1st Sergt. from enrollment to June 9.
First Lieutenant.			
George A. Keith	"	"	
Second Lieutenants.			
James H. Easley	"	"	
Sam'l B. Alexander	"	"	
Sergeants.			
William E. Oscar	"	"	Was private from enrollment to June 9.
Thomas B. Love	"	"	
Emesley Harris	"	"	
James T. Brooks	"	"	

FIRST REGIMENT.

Name and Rank.	Place of Enlistment.	Enrolled	Remarks.
Corporals.		1847.	
Alexander Parker.	Alton, Ill....	May 22	
Thomas M. Roberts	"		
Calvin H. Wilson....	"		Was private from enrollment to December 4.
Thomas Dragoo......	"		
Musicians.			
Eli Dennis...........	"	"	
Mathew Johnson....	"		
Privates.			
Angle, Joshua.......	"	"	
Adams, Thomas D...	"		
Briscoe, William H..	"		
Bass, George W.....	"		
Burk, George J......	"		
Berry, William C....	"		
Baker, Jacob........	"		
Barker, Comfort W.	"		
Coppage, Joseph W.	"		
Clark, George W....	"		
Carter, Joseph R....	"		
Dolton, John W.....	"		
Davis, George W....	"		
Emery, John T......	"		
Forsythe, William...	"		
Fuller, Bradford....	"		
Glenn, Samuel R....	"		
Gibson, Thomas.....	"		
Grant, Hardin H....	"		
Giddings, George H.	"		
Gaston, William.....	"		
Hansell, Nathaniel..	Ottawa, Ill...	"	Joined, a recruit, August 1, 1848.
Higgins, Clark B.....	Alton, Ill....		
Hunt, William.......	"		
House, John.........	"		
Hills, Richard.......	"		
Heddleton, John....	"		
Ingles, Noah........	"		
Ishmael, William S.	"		
King, James M	"		
Kendrick, George W.	"		
Kelly, Isaac.........	"		
Lake, Myron.........	Ottawa, Ill...	Feb., '48	Joined, a recruit, August 1, 1848.
Lomax, John........	Alton, Ill....	May, '47	
McCauly, Andrew...	"		
McMeans, John.....	"		
McLane, John E....	"		
Nix, Jasper L.......	"		
Parker, Orlando M.	"		
Parker, Newborn P..	"		
Preston, Lyman....	"		
Preston, James H...	"		
Pitchford, William H	"		
Roberts, Silas H....	"		
Rainey, Abram C....	"	June, '47	
Starks, John........	"	May, '47	
Smith, James J.....	"		
Smith, John........	"		
Simons, David B....	"		
Steel, James M.....	"		Was Corporal from enrollment to Dec. 4.
Shober, John L.....	"		
Taulbee, Daniel.....	"		
Taylor, John H.....	"		
Vanwey, Charles....	"		
Wilson, Cavil K.....	"		
Woods, Joseph......	"		
Wells, James F.....	"		
Watts, John........	"		
White, Edmond R...	"		
Walker, John M....	"		
Died:			
Angel, Thomas......	Alton, Ill.....	May, '47	Died at Santa Fe, N. M., Sept. 28, 1847......
Bostick, John.......	"		" Jemez, N. M., May 28, 1848...........
Green, Augustus....	"		Died near Albuquerque, N. M., Nov. 9, 1847 ...
Huffman, Samuel....	"		" at Santa Fe, N. M., Oct. 15, 1847...
McDiggins, John....	"		" Fort Leavenworth June 27, 1847......
Nowles, John.......	"		" Santa Fe, N. M., May 17, 1848.......
Putnam, Johnson K.	"		" " " October 16, 1847......
Phillips, Joseph H..	"		" " " 18, 1847......

Discharged:

Name and Rank.	Place of Enlistment.	Enrolled	Remarks.
		1847.	
Bennett, Hiram	Alton, Ill	May 22	Disch., disabil'y, at Ft. Leavenw'th, Aug. 19, '47
Bowen, John M	" "	" "	" " at Santa Fe, May 29, 1848
Davis, Hiram	" "	" "	Drummed out of service at Santa Fe June 14, '48
Harriss, John	" "	" "	Disch., disability, at Santa Fe, March 20, 1848.
Hamilton, Horatio J.	" "	" "	" " at Las Vegas, June 8, 1848.
Langly, James R.	" "	" "	" " at Santa Fe, expiration serv., Aug. 10.
Lewis, Jacob	" "	" "	" " disabil'y, at Ft. Leavenw'th, Aug. 24, '47
Nunn, Henry	" "	" "	" " at Santa Fe, expiration serv., Aug. 10.
Phillips, James G.	" "	" "	
Raymond, Charles L.	" "	" "	" " disability, at Santa Fe, March 8, 1848..
Studdy, John J.	" "	" "	" " Ft. Leavenw'th, Aug. 24, '47
Salmon, H. P.	Ottawa, Ill	Jan. '48	" " at Santa Fe, expiration serv., Aug. 10.
Taylor, William	Alton, Ill	May, '47	" " disability, at Santa Fe, May 29, 1848...
Vansickle, Samuel B.	" "	" "	" " at Las Vegas, June 8
Waldon, Eli W.	" "	" "	" " at Santa Fe, expiration serv., Aug. 10.

This company was discharged at Alton, Illinois, October 12, 1848.

Company "E."

Name and Rank.	Residence.	Enrolled	Remarks.
		1847.	
Captains.			
G. W. Hook	Alton, Ill	May 26	
First Lieutenant.			
William H. Snyder	" "	" "	
Second Lieutenants.			
Enoch Lucky	" "	" "	
John T. Damron	Marion, Ill	" "	Died at Santa Fe, N. M., Dec. 28
Robert Beer	Belleville, Ill	" "	Sergeant from enrollment to Dec. 28
Sergeants.			
William H. Bennett	" "	" "	
William S. Flemming	" "	" "	
Thomas J. Aliff	" "	" "	
James A. Etter	" "	" "	
Corporals.			
Rand'lph C. Goddard	Marion, Ill	" "	
John A. Parker	Belleville, Ill	" "	
Augustus K. Askey	Marion, Ill	" "	
John A. J. Bragg	Belleville, Ill	" "	
Musicians.			
Benjamin F. Jones	" "	" "	
Stephen Cooper	" "	" "	
Privates.			
Boyd, William R.	" "	" "	
Bonham, James	" "	" "	
Briggs, Charles	" "	" "	
Brazewell, George A	" "	" "	
Budgly, Abijah	" "	" "	
Beattie, Francis H.	" "	" "	
Beavers, Charles W.	" "	" "	
Bullock, John W.	Marion, Ill	" "	
Burns, Elijah	" "	" "	
Badger, Chester	Ottawa, Ill	Feb., '48	Joined, a recruit, Aug. 5
Belle, George	" "	Jan. '48	" " " "
Beeler, Isaiah	" "	Feb., '48	
Collard, John C. C.	Belleville, Ill	May, '47	
Carlisle, James W	" "	" "	
Cookingham, Uri J.	" "	" "	
Carroll, Hezekiah	" "	" "	
Cobrenger, Joseph	" "	" "	
Crocker, George W.	" "	" "	
Duc, John P.	" "	" "	

FIRST REGIMENT.

Name and Rank.	Place of Enlistment.	Enrolled	Remarks.
		1847.	
Deobalt, John	Belleville, Ill	May 26	
Dietrich, Andrew	"	"	
Dingle, Jonathan	"	"	
Damron, Walt. M. C.	Marion, Ill.	"	
Drew, William	Belleville, Ill	"	
Epperson, Richard	Marion, Ill.	"	
Fitzgerald, James	Belleville, Ill	"	
Goddard, William E.	Marion, Ill.	"	
Gibbons, John	Belleville, Ill	"	
Harlow, Thomas F.	"	Feb., '48	Joined, a recruit, Aug. 5
Heath, William H.	"	May, '47	
Hendricks, Thomas J	"	"	
Hawkins, General L.	"	"	
Jones, George W.	Ottawa, Ill.	Feb., '48	Joined, a recruit, Aug. 5
Kable, Nicholas	Belleville, Ill	May, '47	
Kookler, Henry	"	"	
Kimble, John	"	"	
Koeler, Francis	Ottawa, Ill.	Mar., '48	Joined, a recruit, Aug. 5
Lacey, Franklin	Belleville, Ill	May, '47	
Lunceford, Isaac	"	"	
Longdow, Andrew	LasVegas,NM	July, '48	Joined, a recruit, July 13
Lawrence, George	Belleville, Ill	Feb., 48	" " Aug. 5
McKenzie, Elijah	LasVegas,NM	July, '48	" " July 10
Mottzfelt, John	Belleville, Ill	Feb., '48	" " Aug. 5
Majors, Huling	"	May, '47	
Peck, John Q. A	"	"	
Polson, Richard	"	"	
Rung, Jacob	"	"	
Reed, James	Marion, Ill.	"	Transferred to Co. "B" June 27, 1847
Russell, Robert R.	Belleville, Ill	"	
Springs, Samuel	Marion, Ill.	"	
Springs, Josephus	"	"	
Shefter, George T.	Belleville, Ill	"	
Stilson, Leonard	Ottawa, Ill.	Dec., '47	Joined, a recruit, Aug. 5
Stattman, Franklin	Belleville, Ill	Feb., '48	" " "
Smith, Oziel G.	"	Feb., '48	" " "
Sterrick, Charles T.	"	May, '47	
Triplett, William	"	"	
Talbott, Jesse	"	"	
Whitesides, Joseph F	"	"	
Woolley, William A.	"	"	
West, Frederick	"	"	
Wheeler, Martin	"	"	
Warton, Samuel	"	"	
Whitney, David	Ottawa, Ill.	Mar., '48	Joined, a recruit, Aug. 5
Webb, Adams	Belleville, Ill	Mar., '48	" " "
Weisenbach, George	"	Mar., '48	" " "

Died:

		1847.	
Corporals.			
Andrew J. Davis	Belleville, Ill	May 26	Died at Las Vegas, N. M., April 13
Josiah Mullen	"	"	Feb. 9
Privates.			
Allen, Thomas J.	"	"	Died at Las Vegas, N. M., Feb. 19
Brown, Franklin J.	Marion, Ill.	"	" Santa Fe, " Sept. 27
Berry, Charles B.	Belleville, Ill	"	" " " Nov. 7
Bragg, William	"	"	" Las Vegas, " Feb. 9
Crocker, Jesse W.	"	"	" Santa Fe, " Oct. 19
Campbell, Aaron J.	Marion, Ill.	"	" Fish C'k, *en route* for Santa Fe, July 20
Crabb, Thomas H.	Belleville, Ill	"	" Alton, Ill., June 11, 1847
Earl, Francis M.	"	"	" Santa Fe, N. M., Oct. 15
Gascil, Thomas	"	"	" " " Dec. 30
Lively, William	"	"	" " " Dec. 12
Maxwell, John	"	"	" " " Feb. 7
Turner, William	"	"	" Cedar Sp'gs, *en route* Santa Fe, Aug.28
Vandyde, Theodore	"	"	" Santa Fe, N. M., Jan. 12

Discharged:

Name and Rank.	Place of Enlistment.	Enrolled	Remarks.
Sergeant.		1847.	
Thomas J. Ward	Marion, Ill	May 26	App'd July 7; disch., disability, LasVegas, N.M
Privates.			
Buckner, William O.	"	"	Disch., disability, at LasVegas, N. M., April 26
Case, Coe W.	Belleville, Ill	"	" " Santa Fe. " May 27.
Hurley, Tilman	"	"	" " Las Vegas. " April 26
Layman, Jackson	"	"	" " Ft. Leavenworth, July 7.
Morray, James B.	Marion, Ill	"	
McDaniel, Abednego	"	"	" " Las Vegas, N. M., April 26
Roberts, Lewis L.	Santa Fe, N.M	Nov. 27	" exp. service. " " Aug.18,'48
Swift, John W.	Belleville, Ill	May 26	" disability, " " April 26
Stephenson, William	Marion, Ill	"	" " " "
Spaunhorst, Frederic	Belleville, Ill	"	" " " "
Vanorsdoll, Knowles	"	"	" " Ft. Leavenworth, July 7.

Deserted:

		1847.	
Christian, William	Belleville, Ill	May 26	Deserted June 16, 1847, at Alton, Ill
Farquer, John W.	"	"	" 19, " "
Lincoln, Robert	"	"	" April 13, 1848, at Jefferson B'cks, Mo

This company was mustered out on Oct. 14, 1848, at Alton, Ill.

Company "F."

Name and Rank.	Place of Enlistment.	Enrolled	Remarks.
Captain.		1847.	
Thos. B. Kinney	Alton, Ill	May 31	
First Lieutenants.			
Murray F. Tuley	"	"	Disch. by resignation, at Santa Fe, Aug. 15
Alban V. Morey	"	"	Elected f'm 1st Sergt. Aug. 19, *vice* Tuley res'd
Second Lieutenants.			
R. N. Hamilton	"	"	Detached serv., Act. A. Q. M. from July 16, '47.
James M. Hunt	"	"	Disch. by resignation, at Santa Fe, Aug. 15
John A. Knights	"	"	Elected from Sergeant Aug. 19
Sergeants.			
William Forsyth	"	"	Appointed from private Aug. 19
Geo. E. Brinsmaid	"	"	Was Corporal from enrollment to June 2, '47.
Charles C. P. Holden	"	"	Promoted from Corporal Aug. 19
Albert S. Woodford	"	"	Appointed from private Aug. 19
Corporals.			
Geo. Hewitt	"	"	
Davenport Morey	"	"	
Asa H. Cochran	"	"	
James Rote	"	"	Appointed from private Aug. 19
Fifer.			
Charles Styles	"	"	
Privates.			
Anderson, Ashley	"	"	
Brunker, Brobson W	"	"	
Bour, John M	"	"	
Burns, John	"	"	
Barnum, Nelson	"	"	
Case, Geo. W	"	"	
Danforth, Richm'd S	"	"	
Foster, James	"	"	
Gregg, William P	"	"	

FIRST REGIMENT.

Name and Rank.	Place of Enlistment.	Enrolled	Remarks.
		1847.	
Gurrad, John P	Alton, Ill	May 31	
Griffith, Amos N	"	June 14	
Gardner, Joseph	"	May 31	
Herrick, Lyman	"	.... "	
Hall, Harvey	"	.... "	
Huntington, Seth P	"	.... "	
Huntley, Daniel	"	.... "	
Halleck, Alanson	"	.... "	
Hagan, Edward	Ottawa, Ill	Jan., '48	Joined, a recruit, Aug. 1
Johnson, Iver	Alton, Ill	May, '47	
Kratzer, Frederick	"	.... "	
Lahr, Henry	"	.... "	
Lord, Rufus	Ottawa, Ill	Feb., '48	Joined, a recruit, Aug. 1
Matthews, Wm	Alton, Ill	May, '47	
Mudge, Wm	"	.... "	
Morrison, Morris H	"	.... "	
Morrison, Joshua	Ottawa, Ill	Feb., '48	Joined, a recruit, Aug. 1
McCully, David A	Alton, Ill	May, '47	
Martin, Wm	"	.... "	
McClain, Wm	"	.... "	
Michael, Theophilus	"	.... "	
Napier, Dwight	Ottawa, Ill	Jan., '48	Joined, a recruit, Aug. 1
Ramsden, James V	Alton, Ill	May, '47	(no individual disch. made.
Rodholtz, Nicholas	"	"	Left boat on pas'ge down Missouri riv., Oct. 2;
Riley, Thomas	Ottawa, Ill	Feb., '48	Joined, a recruit, Aug. 1
Stroh, Gotrich	Alton, Ill	May, '47	
Seidler, Augustus H	"	.... "	
Snight, Henry	"	.... "	
Thornton, Freeman	"	.... "	
Tappin, Alex. H	"	.... "	
Utho, Christopher F	"	.... "	
Wiley, Adam	"	.... "	
Watson, Wm. A	"	.... "	
Warren, Wm. E	"	.... "	
Warren, June	"	.... "	
Warren, James	"	.... "	
Williams, June	"	.... "	
Young, James C	"	.... "	

Discharged:

		1847.	
Sergeant.			
John D. Goodrich	Alton, Ill	May 31	Disch. by expir'n of serv. Aug. 9, '48, Santa Fe.
Drummer.			
George Cannon	"	.... "	Disch. by expir'n of serv. Aug. 9, '48, Santa Fe.
Privates.			
Brown, Erastus D	"	.... "	Disch. July 20, '47, Ft. Leavenworth; disabil'y
Backman, Peter	"	.... "	" by expir'n of serv. Aug. 11, '48, Santa Fe.
Eberhard, August	"	.... "	" Mar. 5, '48, at Santa Fe; disability
Emory, Stephen	"	.... "	" by expir'n of serv. Aug. 9, '48, Santa Fe.
Huginin, James R	"	.... "	" " " 11 "
Hipwell, John W	"	.... "	" " " 9 "
Kensling, Jacob	"	.... "	
Loring, Lorenzo D	"	.... "	" Feb. 9, '48, at Santa Fe; disability
Martin, Orange C	"	.... "	" Mar. 19, '48, " " "
Morteller, George	"	.... "	" Mar. 20, '48, " " "
Morgan, James D	"	.... "	" by expir'n of serv. Aug. 9, '48, Santa Fe.
Maynard, Lorenzo D	"	.... "	" " " Aug. 11, '48 "
McCormack, Chas. J	"	.... "	
Page, Phineas	"	.... "	Left sick at Las Vegas; supposed discharged
Rolph, John S	"	.... "	Disch. by expir'n of serv. Aug. 9, '48, Santa Fe.
Reinhard, Valentine	"	.... "	
Shepard, Julius C	"	.... "	" " " " "
Shaw, Julius C	"	.... "	
Seacon, Thomas	"	.... "	" July 5, '48, at Santa Fe; disability
Strebel, John W	"	.... "	" Mar. 6, '48, " " "
Vantassel, Levi R	"	.... "	" by expir'n of serv. Aug. 9, '48, Santa Fe.
Wilson, James	"	.... "	" Oct. 10, '47, at Santa Fe; disability
Whitbeck, Seymour	"	.... "	" July 15, '47, " " "

Died:

Name and Rank.	Place of Enlistment.	Enrolled	Remarks.
		1847.	
Allen, James H	Alton, Ill	May 31	Died at Sabinal, N. M., Dec. 10 1847
Black, Wm. H	"	June 14	" Santa Fe, Oct. 9, 1847.
Croft, Robert	"	May 31	" Ft. Leavenworth, 1847.
Daniels, Wm	"	"	" en route to Santa Fe, Aug. 19, 1847
Godfrey, James H	"	"	" at Santa Fe, Jan. 29, 1848.
Hattendorf, Hendr'k	"	"	Drowned in the Miss. river, June 11, 1847.
Pratt, Spencer	"	"	Died at Santa Fe, Sept. 19, 1847.
Pool, Edgar	"	"	" " Sept. 30, 1847.
Styles, Jeremiah	"	"	" " Nov. 3, 1847.
Wheat, John W	"	"	" " Sept. 29, 1847.

Deserted:

Name and Rank.	Place of Enlistment.	Enrolled	Remarks.
Sergeant.		1847.	
Luther G. Hager	Alton, Ill	May 31	Deserted at Alton, June 12, 1847
Privates.			
Freeman, Alexander			Deserted at Alton, June 17, 1847
Martin, Daniel			Deserted en route to Santa Fe, July 26, 1847

This company was mustered out Oct. 18, 1848, at Alton, Ill.

Company "G."

Name and Rank.	Place of Enlistment.	Enrolled	Remarks.
Captain.		1847.	
Henry J. Reed	Alton, Ill	June 1	
First Lieutenant.			
Relly Madeson	"	"	
Second Lieutenants.			
James Tebay	"	"	
Simon Lundry	"	"	
Sergeants.			
Clement L. Lakins	"	"	Appointed Sergt. Aug. 9, vice Mosten
Ceap. H. Washburn	"	"	
Hiram M. Morse	"	"	Promoted from Corporal Aug. 9
Henry Berklin	"	"	" " "
Corporals.			
Mason B. Kelly	"	"	Appointed from private Aug. 9
William A. Clements	"	"	
George Rinehart	SantaFe,N.M.	Nov. 26	" " " " 14
Mitchel T. Brewster	Alton, Ill	June 1	" " " " 9
Fifer.			
Jackson Reed	"	"	
Privates.			
Anderson, William	"	"	
Barnard, George	"	"	
Baker, Perry	"	"	
Braun, Noble J	"	"	
Carter, Benjamin F	"	"	
Cavanaugh, Luke	"	"	
Craig, Samuel	"	"	
Corbin, William	"	"	
Corbin, Elias	Ottawa, Ill	Jan., '48	Joined, a recruit, Aug. 1, 1848
Davis, Gordon	Alton, Ill	June, '47	Left sick at Ft. Leavenworth May 22
Denmick, Harmon	"	"	
Davenport, John	"	"	
Dobbs, Thomas	"	"	

FIRST REGIMENT.

Name and Rank.	Place of Enlistment.	Enrolled	Remarks.
		1847.	
Evey, Joseph	Alton, Ill	June 1	
Ellixson, Lars	"	"	
Ferguson, John	"	"	
Graham, William	"	"	
Gibson, John F	"	"	
Gibson, George	Ottawa, Ill	Feb., '48	Joined, a recruit, Aug. 1, 1848
Gibson, Theodore	"	"	
Hoxie, Joshua	Alton, Ill	June, '47	
Hayes, James	"	"	
Haight, Josiah	"	"	
Hays, Seeley, Jr	"	"	
Hardin, Elihu	"	"	
Hopper, Dudley	"	"	
Henry, Francis	SantaFe,N.M.	Nov. '47	
Helton, Oliver P	Alton, Ill	June, '47	
Love, Warren	"	"	
McHale, Michael	"	"	
Maxey, Peter	"	"	
Moore, Joseph	"	"	
Martin, Robert N	"	"	
Overacre, Franklin	"	"	
Pheps, Orvill	"	"	
Pratt, Thomas A	"	"	
Seaman, Francis	"	"	
Stone, William	"	"	
Scott, William	"	"	
Tripp, John	"	"	
Thompson, John	"	"	
Tresner, John	"	"	
VanKleeck, Wm. H	SantaFe,N.M.	Nov. '47	
Ward, Harvey B	Alton, Ill	June, '47	
Weeks, Thomas	"	"	
Woodruff, Joseph	Ottawa, Ill	Jan., '48	Joined, a recruit, Aug. 1
Watkins, James	Alton, Ill	June, '47	
Yeigh, John	"	"	

Died:

		1847.	
Corporal.			
Joab Kelly	Alton, Ill	June 1	Died at Santa Fe March 16, 1848
Privates.			
Blackman, David S	"	"	Died at Santa Fe Oct. 1, 1847
Carr, James	"	"	" " Oct. 11, 1847
Cochran, Cornelius	"	"	" " Oct. 27, 1847
Clark, Lewis M	"	"	" " May 1, 1848
Davis, Orson	"	"	" " May 22, 1848
Moore, Peter	"	"	" " April 26, 1848
Martin, Charles	"	"	" " Nov. 18, 1847
McCarty, Michael	"	"	" " Nov. 28, 1847
Watson, James	"	"	" " March 22, 1848
Tresnor, Harvey	"	"	Died on march from Ft. Leavenw'h to S. Fe.

Discharged:

		1847.	
Sergeants.			
John Mosten	Alton, Ill	June 1	Disch. at Santa Fe on expir'n of serv., Aug. 9.
Oscar F. Barnes	"	"	
Corporal.			
John Mosley	"	"	Disch. at Santa Fe on expir'n of serv., Aug. 9.
Drummer.			
Henry Crain	"	"	Disch. at Santa Fe on expir'n of serv., Aug. 9.
Privates.			
Austin, Samuel	"	"	Disch. at Santa Fe on expir'n of serv., Aug. 9.
Anderson, John	"	"	
Barnes, Oliver C	"	"	Disch. on Surg. cert. of disability Mch. 7, '48.
Brennon, John	"	"	
Betvey, Joseph, Jr	"	"	" at Santa Fe, expir'n of service, Aug. 6.
Fisher, John W	"	"	" on Surg. cert. of disability Mch. 7, '48.
Foy, Michael	"	"	" in disgrace at Santa Fe, June 14, '48
Flick, David	"	"	" at Santa Fe, expir'n of service, Aug. 9.
Harris, Joseph	"	"	" on Surg. cert. of disability July 7, '48

222　　　　　　　　　　　　　MEXICAN WAR.

Name and Rank.	Place of Enlistment.	Enrolled	Remarks.
		1847.	
Lawrence, Daniel N.	Alton, Ill.	June 1	Disch. at Santa Fe, expir'n of serv., Aug. 9.
Littrick, John	"	"	" " " " " "
Lee, John	"	"	" " " " " "
McHenry, Thomas	"	"	" " " " " "
Rood, Daniel L.	"	"	" " " " " " Aug. 14, '48
Smith, William	"	"	" " " " " " 9, '48
Stafford, Jacob E.	"	"	in disgrace Oct. 16, 1847
Tucker, Henry	"	"	at Santa Fe, expir'n of serv., Aug. 9, '48
Thompson, William	"	"	" " " " " "
Wilson, James	"	"	" " " " " "

Deserted:

		1847.	
Atkins, John N.	Alton, Ill.	June 1	Deserted at Alton June 18, 1848.
Adams, Charles	"	"	on march to Santa Fe July 25, 1847.
Bennett, Tolytus	"	"	at Ft. Leavenworth July 9, 1847
Rogerson, Charles	"	"	"
Stilson, Lyman	"	"	" July 18, 1847.
Springstead, Alberon	"	"	"
Washburn, Daniel	"	"	at Alton, Ill., June 19, 1847.

This company was mustered out Oct. 17, 1848, at Alton, Ill.

Company "H."

Name and Rank.	Place of Enlistment.	Enrolled	Remarks.
Captain.		1847.	
James Hampton	Alton, Ill.	May 29	
First Lieutenant.			
James J. Provost	"	"	
Second Lieutenants.			
John A. Logan	"	"	
James Willis	"	"	
Sergeants.			
Lindorff Osborne	"	"	
Geo. W. Peninger	"	"	Private from enrollment to Oct. 1, 1847.
John W. Grammar	"	"	" July 10, 1847.
Samuel Carlisle	"	"	
Corporals.			
Wm. Hagler	"	"	Private to April 1, 1848.
Jordan L. Randall	"	"	
Wm. Brown	"	"	Private to Oct 4, 1847
Wm. Hampton	"	"	
Musicians.			
James Y. Wilkins	"	"	Private to July 15, 1847
Jonas Mangold	"	"	
Privates.			
Alvord, Leroy	Ottawa, Ill.	Feb. '48	Joined, a recruit, Aug. 5
Burks, James	Alton, Ill.	May, '49	
Bond, Stephen	"	"	
Brandon, Hugh G.	"	"	
Bramlet, John D.	"	"	
Beaver, Eli	"	"	
Broomfield, James	"	"	
Bishop, Thomas	"	"	
Black, George W.	"	"	
Buckles, John J.	"	"	

FIRST REGIMENT.

Name and Rank.	Place of Enlistment.	Enrolled	Remarks.
Becker, Henry	Ottawa, Ill.	Feb., '48	Joined, a recruit, Aug. 5
Brown, Peter	"	"	" " "
Brunse, Henry	"	"	" " "
Conrad, Geo.	"	"	" " "
Carlisle, Alex. M.	Alton, Ill.	May, '47	
Carr, John	"	"	
Childers, Geo.	"	"	
Cuteral, John G.	"	"	
Cable, Michael	"	"	
Christy, David	"	"	
Campbell, John	"	"	
Cotner, Jacob	"	"	
Clark, John	"	"	
Doer, Francis	Ottawa, Ill.	Feb., '48	Joined, a recruit, Aug. 5
Diedreck, Christain	"	"	" " "
DeGroat, Wm.	Alton, Ill.	May, '47	
Dunn, James	"	"	
Dunn, Absalom	"	"	
Davis, James M.	"	"	
Dunn, Wm. F.	"	"	
Ehll, Joseph	Ottawa, Ill.	Feb., '48	Joined, a recruit, Aug. 5
Fox, Andrew J.	Alton, Ill.	May, '47	
Glen, John E.	"	"	
Grable, John M.	"	"	
Grable, Israel	"	"	
Grable, Eli	"	"	Sick in Hospital at Alton from Oct. 8
Goodman, Josiah	"	"	
Gordon, James P.	"	"	
Herald, John H.	"	"	
Hicks, Harrison	"	"	
Hall, James H.	"	"	
Lightner, James	"	"	
Mings, James	"	"	
Mings, William	"	"	
Miller, Ezekiel	"	"	
McAnelly, Charles	"	"	
Moor, William	"	"	
Miller, James	Ottawa, Ill.	Feb., '48	Joined, a recruit, Aug. 5
Newman, Wm. J.	Alton, Ill.	May, '47	
Owens, William	"	"	
Odle, Isaac	"	"	
Pike, Seth	Ottawa, Ill.	Jan., '48	Joined, a recruit, Aug. 5
Ramsey, Wm. T.	Santa Fe, N.M.	Nov. '47	
Scarlet, John	Alton, Ill.	May, '47	
Sorrels, John	"	"	
Spindler, Frederick	Ottawa, Ill.	Feb., '48	Joined, a recruit, Aug. 5
Strawn, Wm	"	"	" " "
Thompson, John L.	"	"	" " "
Titsel, Wm.	"	"	" " "
Taylor, Charles	"	Mch., '48	" " "
Wimms, Meredith	Alton, Ill.	May, '47	
Walker, Napoleon B.	"	"	
Williamson, John	"	"	
West, Andrew	"	"	
Wagner, Louis	"	"	
Willis, Carroll	"	"	

Died:

		1847.	
Sergeant.			
John W. Pemberton	Alton, Ill.	May 29	Died at Santa Fe, N. M., Oct. 31, 1847
Privates.			
Carr, Wm. A.	"	"	Died at Santa Fe, N. M., Oct. 6, 1847
Eakin, James M.	"	"	" Las Vegas, N. M., April 9, 1848
Ferguson, John D.	"	"	" Santa Fe, N. M., Jan. 11, 1848
Gill, Hardimon	"	"	" " " Oct. 18, 1847
Herron, Samuel M.	"	"	" " " Nov. 5, 1847
Hall, David	"	"	" " " Jan. 8, 1848
Jones, Wm.	"	"	" Ft. Leavenworth, Mo., July 20, 1847
Keiger, Thomas D.	"	"	" Santa Fe, N. M., Nov. 4, 1847
McCarty, Daniel	"	"	" Ft. Leavenworth, Mo., July 5, 1847
Morrow, Thomas W.	"	"	" " " 9, "
McCord, Richard W.	"	"	" Santa Fe, N. M., Nov. 6, 1847
Morrow, John B.	"	"	" Las Vegas, N. M., Feb. 9, 1848
Pearson, Thomas	"	"	" " " Mch. 11, 1848
Penrod, Jacob	"	"	" Ft. Leavenworth, Mo., July 19, 1847
Sitter, Simon P.	"	"	" Santa Fe, N. M., Dec. 17, 1847

MEXICAN WAR.

Discharged:

Name and Rank.	Place of Enlistment.	Enrolled	Remarks.
Musician.		1847.	
Emanuel Penrod	Alton, Ill.	May 29	Disch., Surg. cert. disabil'y, Ft. Leavenworth
Privates.			
Bramlet, Ambrose	"	"	Disch., Surg. cert. disabil'y. Ft. Leavenworth
Carr, James	"	"	April 26, '48, Las Vegas, disability
Greene, Thomas S.	"	"	" " " "
Gates, Wm	"	"	" " " "
Hampton, Robt. P.	"	"	June 10, " " "
Hampton, Wade	"	"	" " " "
Jones, Benj. F	"	"	Surg. cert. disabil'y. Ft. Leavenworth
Keiger, Jacob B	"	"	April 20, '48, Las Vegas, disability
McAnnelly, John	"	"	June 10, " " "
Robinson, John W	"	"	April 26, " " " "
Turk, Joseph	"	"	

Transferred:

Name and Rank.	Place of Enlistment.	Enrolled	Remarks.
		1847.	
Davis, Elihu W	Alton, Ill.	May 29	Transferred to Co. "B," Oct. 30, 1847
Herron, Joseph	"	"	" " " "
Sanders, Luke R	"	"	

Deserted:

Name and Rank.	Place of Enlistment.	Enrolled	Remarks.
		1847.	
Sipe, Tilman	Alton, Ill.	May 29	Deserted July 22, 1847, at Ft. Leavenworth

This company was discharged at Alton, Ill., October 16, 1848.

COMPANY "I."

Name and Rank.	Place of Enlistment.	Enrolled	Remarks.
Captains.		1847.	
Franklin Niles	Alton, Ill.	June 2	Died at 110 Creek, near Ft. Leav'th, July 24, '47
John H. Adams	"	"	1st Lieut. from enrollment till July 28, 1847
First Lieutenant.			
Aaron D. Treadway	"	"	2d Lieut. from enrollment till July 28, 1847
Second Lieutenants.			
Thos. McDowell	"	"	2d Lieut. from enrollment till July 28, 1847
Jacob Brott	"	"	Private
Sergeants.			
Alexander Craig	"	"	
William H. Starr	"	"	Appointed from private May 1, 1848
Sylvester W. Bell	"	"	
Dan'l W. Henderson	"	"	
Corporals.			
Wm. Harrison	"	"	
Lemuel Southard	"	"	
John Mise	"	"	
David R. Sparks	"	"	
Drummer.			
James Conner	"	"	

FIRST REGIMENT.

Name and Rank.	Place of Enlistment.	Enrolled	Remarks.
Privates.			
Arnold, Lerry	Ottawa, Ill.	Feb., '48	Joined, a recruit, Aug. 15
Caulk, Joshua C	Alton, Ill.	June, '47	
Caldwell, Wm. C	"	"	
Cowell, Benj. F	"	"	
Carter, Daniel	"	"	
Delaney, John	"	"	
Dougherty, John	"	"	
Davis, John	"	"	
Davis, Alfred M	"	"	
Dixon, Ambrose	"	"	
Dush, Geo. S	"	"	
Eldridge, John	"	"	
Evans, Wm. B	"	"	
Elwerthy, Walter	"	"	
Fletcher, Paulis E	"	"	
Foster, George J	"	"	
Gaskill, John Q. A	"	"	
Hodgins, Henry	Ottawa, Ill.	Mch., '48	Joined, a recruit, Aug. 15
Herrington, Harris'n	Alton, Ill.	June, '47	
Hodgman, Amos	"	"	
Humphries, Charles.	"	"	
Hartman, Louis	"	"	
Haxwell, Ludrick	"	"	
Huntermark, Henry.	"	"	
Herrin, Gorden	"	"	
Hocking, Ashberry	"	"	
Herrin, John	"	"	
Hamby, Jacob	"	"	
Hocking, Giles W	"	"	
Herrin, Henry	"	"	
Jett, Benj. F	"	"	
Johnson, Samuel	"	"	
Keho, Joseph	"	"	
Laport, Alonso	Ottawa, Ill.	Mch., '48	Joined, a recruit, Aug. 15
Lamoin, Eleaser	"	"	
Lewis, Richard C	Alton, Ill.	June, '47	
Lawrence, James	"	"	
Loveless, John	"	"	
Little, Wm. A	"	"	
Little, Edward	"	"	Reduced from 2d Sergt. April 27
Marlow, Abraham	"	"	
Merry, Wm. H	"	"	
Pool, Hughy	"	"	
Potter, Theron	Ottawa, Ill.	Mch., '48	Joined, a recruit, Aug. 15
Robbins, Oliver	Alton, Ill.	June, '47	
Sweet, Peleg	Ottawa, Ill.	Mch., '48	Joined, a recruit, Aug. 15
Smith, James H	Alton, Ill.	June, '47	
Seybolds, James	"	"	
Scroggins, Wm	"	"	
Scott, Joseph	"	"	
Sweeney, Nelson D.	"	"	
Turner, James W	"	"	
Wahlen, Frederick	"	"	
Walker, Newton	"	"	
Washburn, Elijah	"	"	
Walker, Andrew	Ottawa, Ill.	Mch., '48	Joined, a recruit, Aug. 15
Wheeler, Wm. E	Belleville, Ill.		

Died:

		1847.	
Blevins, Elihu	Alton, Ill.	June 2	Died at Savannah, N. M., Nov. 19, 1847
Cook, John	"	"	" Santa Fe, N. M., Nov. 27, 1847
Cowell, Thomas D	"	"	" San Antonio, N. M., Dec. 15, 1847
Cave, John	"	"	" Santa Fe, N. M., Jan. 19, 1848
Enstein, Balsom	"	"	" Oct. 26, 1847
Evans, Ellis	"	"	" Alton, Ill., June 19, 1847
Fetterling, Casper	"	"	" Albuquerque, N. M., Nov. 6, 1847
Grant, Daniel	"	"	" Secora, N. M., Jan. 6, 1848
Jewitt, John	"	"	Died on march to Santa Fe Sept. 17, 1847
McBroom, John	"	"	Died at Santa Fe, N. M., Dec. 12, 1847
Miller, James C	"	"	" " Feb. 12, 1848
Ossel, John	"	"	" " March 3, 1848
Purviance, Samuel	"	"	Died near Secora, N. M., Dec. 1, 1847
Scroggins, Jackson	"	"	Died at Santa Fe, N. M., Feb. 7, 1848
Vinson, James	"	"	" " Sept. 24, 1847

—15

MEXICAN WAR.

Discharged:

Name and Rank.	Place of Enlistment.	Enrolled	Remarks.
Fifer.		1847.	
Robert Weeks	Alton, Ill.	June 2	Disch., Las Vegas, N.M., June 10, '48; disability
Privates.			
Brown, James	"	"	Disch., Albuquerque, N.M., Apr. 12, '48; disabil.
Cox, Peter H.	"	"	Las Vegas, N.M., June 10, '48; disability
Grant, Dreury H.	"	"	Santa Fe, N.M., Aug. 5, '48; term expir'd
Henderson, Benj. J.	"	June 12	Oct. 12, '48; disability...
Knight, William	"	June 2	Ft. Leavenw'th, July 12, '47; disability.
Lager, Gabriel	"	"	Santa Fe, N. M., Aug. 15, '48; term exp'd
Miller, Jordan	"	"	Las Vegas, N.M., Aug. 19, '48; term exp'd
Perrin, John	"	"	Santa Fe, N.M., Aug. 15, '48; term exp'd
Pinckard, Amos G.	"	"	Oct. 12, '47; disability..
Weathers, Enoch B.	"	"	Council Grove, July 29, '47; disability..
White, James A.	"	"	with disgrace at Santa Fe Feb. 12, '47.

Deserted:

Name and Rank.	Place of Enlistment.	Enrolled	Remarks.
		1847.	
Bankson, Stephen	Alton, Ill.	June 12	Deserted at Ft. Leavenworth July 5, 1847
Gibson, Aaron B.	"	June 2	"
McCoy, Thomas	"	"	Alton, Ill., June 3, 1847
Stewart, Riley	"	"	Ft. Leavenworth July 5, 1847
Thornbrough, Wm.	"	"	"

This company was discharged at Alton, Ill., Oct. 17, 1848.

Company "K."

Name and Rank.	Place of Enlistment.	Enrolled	Remarks.
Captains.		1847.	
Israel B. Donalson	Alton, Ill.	May 22	Elected Major of Reg't at Alton June 8. 1847..
William Kinman	"	"	2d Lieut. from enrollment to June 8, 1847
First Lieutenant.			
Manoah T. Bostick	"	"	
Second Lieutenants.			
Robert E. Hicks	"	"	Suspended 4 months Feb. 1, 1848, sen. G. C.-M.
Constantine Hicks	"	"	" 3 " 6 " Resi'd Aug. 11
Sergeants.			
David K. Hobbs	"	"	
Andrew Main	"	"	
Austin W. Matthews	"	"	Appointed from private May 1, 1848
Uriah Thomas	"	"	Promoted from Corporal Sept. 1, 1848
Corporals.			
Daniel Gray	"	"	
Joseph W. Ingalls	"	"	Appointed from private May 1, 1848
George W. Freeman	"	"	" " "
Jarvis P. Rudd	"	"	" " " Sept. 1, 1848
Musicians.			
William Kiser	"	"	
John Moore	"	"	
Privates.			
Arnett, John	"	"	
Atkins, James H.	"	"	
Barthelow, Jasper	Ottawa, Ill.	Jan., '48	Joined, a recruit, July 31
Broadwater, Henry	"	Feb., '48	" " "
Barber, George	"	"	" " " 1848
Beard, Edward	"	Jan., '48	" " "
Beck, Christopher	"	Jan., '48	" " "

FIRST REGIMENT.

Name and Rank.	Place of Enlistment.	Enrolled	Remarks.
		1847.	
Brown, Archibald A.	Alton, Ill.	May 22	
Bobbett, William B.	"	"	
Blair, Alfred I.	"	"	
Bell, Jackson	"	"	
Bristow, Lawrence C.	"	"	
Baldwin, David P.	"	"	
Bulson, Frederick M.	"	"	
Bissell, Alfred	"	"	
Babcock, Robert F.	"	"	
Crum, Ephraim	"	"	
Cooper, John	"	"	
Davis, Calvin	"	"	
Durall, Alney	"	"	
Durall, Duran	"	"	
Fuks, George W.	Ottawa, Ill.	Mar., '48	Joined, a recruit, July 31
Filbert, Sebastian	"	Feb., '48	"
Gray, Burton T.	Alton, Ill.	May, '47	
Hart, Nathaniel P.	"	"	
Hawker, John	"	"	
Heavener, John C.	"	"	
Heavener, Christoph	"	"	
Henry, George	"	"	
Hedrick, Anderson	"	"	
Jennings, Jackson	"	"	
Jordan, Thomas I.	"	"	
Kneeland, John W.	"	"	
Kendall, Hiram G.	"	"	
Kinney, Joseph W.	"	"	
Lewis, James W.	"	"	
Lippincott, Josiah	"	"	
Looper, James	"	"	
Leonard, Joseph A.	Ottawa, Ill.	Jan., '48	Joined, a recruit, July 31
Main, Philip	Alton, Ill.	May, '47	
Mastin, Benjamin L.	"	"	
Main, Nicholas	"	"	
Meredith, Daniel W.	"	"	
Madison, Franklin	"	"	
Mace, John	"	"	
Main, William	"	"	
McDade, Joseph	"	"	
McDade, Reuben	"	"	
Neely, Andrew J.	"	"	
Neely, John	"	"	
Peterson, Robert	"	"	
Parks, Lemuel	"	"	
Seybold, Jacob	"	"	
Seavers, John G.	"	"	
Smart, Zachariah L.	"	"	
Spencer, Charles A.	"	"	
Spencer, Hiram G. W.	"	"	
Schanck, Samuel	"	"	
Underwood, John L.	"	"	
Wade, Benjamin F.	"	"	
Welch, McDaniel	"	"	
Yorke, Henry P.	"	"	
Yorke, Hezekiel D.	Santa Fe, N.M.	Feb., '48	

Died:

Privates.		1847.	
Brents, William H.	Alton, Ill.	May 22	Died at Santa Fe, N. M., Oct. 3, 1847
Burland, John	"	"	Killed, affray on m'ch, R'k Corral, N.M.,Aug.,'48
Crawford, Josiah	"	"	Died en route Santa Fe to Chihuahua, Nov.4,'47
Hobbs, William M.	"	"	" " to Aug. 31, 1847
Hughes, Hardin	"	"	" at Santa Fe, N. M., Oct. 24, 1848
Howland, Nounan	"	"	" en route San. Fe to Chihuahua, Nov.15,'47
Smith, Ransom	"	"	" at Santa Fe, N. M., Feb. 12, 1848
Seeley, Gersham	"	"	" en route to Santa Fe, Sept. 4, 1847
String, Thomas D.	"	"	" at Santa Fe, N. M., Oct. 15, 1847
Waller, Aaron J.	"	"	" en route Santa Fe to Chihuahua, Dec.8,'47
Williams, Elijah W.	"	"	" at Santa Fe, N. M., Feb. 11, 1848

MEXICAN WAR.

Discharged:

Name and Rank.	Place of Enlistment.	Enrolled	Remarks.
Sergeants.		1847	
Samuel N. Hoyt	Alton, Ill.	May 22	Disch. at Santa Fe, exp. of service, Aug. 11,'48
Richard Lucas	"	"	" " " May 5, 1848, disability
Corporals.			
Samuel P. Mace	"	"	Disch. at Santa Fe, Feb. 19, 1848, disability
Anson Rudd	"	"	" " " April 29, "
Privates.			
Allen, Alfred	"	"	Disch. at Las Vegas June 8, 1848, disability
Chandler, William	"	"	" Santa Fe, March 7, " "
Cavender, James	"	"	" " " " "
Lester, John	"	"	" " May 5, " "
Nye, Seth S.	"	"	" Alton, Ill., June 21, 1847, "
Powell, Elijah L.	"	"	" Santa Fe, May 5, 1848, "
Seaver, William B.	"	"	" " " " "
Shin, John H.	"		
Smith, Hiram	"	"	Left sick at Ft. Leavenworth, July 15, 1847

Transferred:

Musician.		1847.	
John L. Kiser	Alton, Ill.	May 22	Appointed Fifer Mar. 5,'48; transferred to staff

This company was discharged from service Oct. 13, 1848, at Alton, Ill.

SECOND REGIMENT.

THE FIELD AND STAFF

Of the 2d Regiment of Illinois Foot Volunteers, commanded by Col. Wm. H. Bissell, called into the service of the United States by the President, under the act of Congress, approved May 13, 1846, for the term of twelve months, from the 28th day of February, when last mustered, to the 18th day of June, 1847, when discharged.

Name and Rank.	Place of Enlistment.	Enrolled	Remarks.
		1846.	
Colonel. Wm. H. Bissell	Alton, Ill	June 17	Elected from Captain, at Alton, June 30
Lieut.-Colonel. Jas. L. D. Morrison	"	June 16	Elected from Captain (in Raith's Co.) July 11; [on furl. till expir'n of serv.; ill health.
Major. Xerxes F. Trail	"	June 24	Elected f'm Captain (in Miller's Co.) at Alton, [July 1.
1st Lieut. and Adj't. August. G. Whiteside	"	"	Appointed (1st Lieut. in Miller's Co.) July 1; [wounded in bat. at B. Vista, Feb. 23, '47.
1st Lieut. and A. A. Geo. W. Prickett	"	June 16	Appointed by Col. Bissell, Feb. 28
Surgeon. Edward B. Price	"		Appointed by the President July 7
Sergeant-Major. Christian H. Ketler	"	June 16	App'd f'm 1st Sergt. Co. "H" Jan. 1; wounded [in bat. at B. Vista Feb. 23, '47.
Q. M. Sergeant. Nelson S. Moore	"	June 24	App'd f'm Sergt. Co. "I"; disch. on account of [wounds at bat. of B. Vista, Feb. 23, '47.
Principal Musicians. John Hopkins	"	June 20	From Company "A"
Reub'n M. Pendexter	"	June 17	" "E"
Corp'l and A. C. S. Wm. Fuedlander	"	June 17	

COMPANY "A."

Name and Rank.	Place of Enlistment.	Enrolled	Remarks.
		1846.	
Captain. Elzey C. Coffey	Alton, Ill	June 20	
First Lieutenant. Harvy Nevill	"	"	
Second Lieutenants. William B. Rountree	"	"	(killed.
Jackson Dennis	"	"	Promoted from Sergt. Feb. 28, *vice* Rountree.
Sergeants. Geo. W. Hotchkiss	"	"	Furloughed from May 15
James W. Farmer	"	"	Wounded in bat Feb. 23; cert. for full pension
Hugh B. McElhanan	"	"	
Richard M. Clayton	"	"	

Name and Rank.	Place of Enlistment.	Enrolled	Remarks.
Corporals.		1846.	
James T. Christian	Alton, Ill	June 20	
Thomas M. Reed	"	"	Wounded in battle Feb. 23
Joseph Kinyon	"	"	Left sick at Rio Grande from Oct. 26
Thomas Atchison	"	"	
Musicians.			
John Hopkins	"	"	
Robert W. Fulton	"	"	
Privates.			
Atchison, George W.	"	"	
Auldridge, James	"	"	
Brazel, Robert	"	"	
Burnet, John	"	"	Wounded in battle Feb. 23
Bird, William	"	"	
Bird, Thomas	"	"	" " "
Brown, John W.	"	"	
Brown, Jacob	"	"	
Cox, Adison	"	"	
Cooper, Gilbert	"	"	Wounded in battle Feb. 23; leg amputated
Clark, Alfred	"	"	
Castleberry, Mark	"	"	
Chapman, Edw'd R.	"	"	
Chick, Edley A.	"	"	
Coleman, Nathan T.	"	"	
Cheek, Robert R.	"	"	
Cheek, James A.	"	"	
Davis, James H. H.	"	"	
Dempsey, William	"	"	Wounded in battle Feb. 23
Dickerson, Willis	"	"	Detached as Hosp. Attend't in San Antonio
Folson, Thos. D. M.	"	"	
Farmer, John	"	"	
Friend, Isaac	"	"	
Faulkner, Gilbert	"	"	
Gore, Gideon S.	"	"	
Green, William L.	"	"	
Hodges, James D.	"	"	
Hensley, John M.	"	"	
Hagans, William H.	"	"	Lost musket in bat'l, retreating, flag to carry
Hutchings, Wes. W.	"	"	
Hall, Jesse	"	"	
Johnson, Archer B.	"	"	
Johnson, Joseph W.	"	"	
Jolliff, James E.	"	"	
Jenkins, Louis S.	"	"	
Lee, Abner G.	"	"	
Lee, James T.	"	"	
Lee, Ephriam W.	"	"	
Morris, Joseph	"	"	
Morton, James R.	"	"	
Mitchell, William F.	"	"	
Mansker, John G.	"	"	Lost musket by being wounded Feb. 23
Myers, Dedrick R.	"	"	
Newman, John	"	"	
Pate, Joseph	"	"	Wounded in battle Feb. 23
Raney, Geo. W.	"	"	
Rountree, John M.	"	"	
Redferne, James	"	"	
Robins, John	"	"	Wounded in battle Feb. 23
Ragland, Richard B.	"	"	
Raney, William	"	"	
Stoker, William	"	"	
Sronce, Stephen	"	"	
Slade, Andrew J.	"	"	Wounded in battle Feb. 23
Thomas, George L.	"	"	
Williams, Alexander	"	"	
Wheeler, Allen B.	"	"	
White, Willis	"	"	Wounded in battle Feb. 23
West, Thompson C.	"	"	
Williams, Matth'w B.	"	"	

Discharged:

Name and Rank.	Place of Enlistment.	Enrolled	Remarks.
Privates.		1846.	
Boatright, Alex.	Alton, Ill.	June 20	Discharged at Camp Buena Vista May 30.
Flanagan, John B.	"	"	"
Starkwell, Albert C.	"	"	"
Underwood, Wm. T.	"	"	"

Died:

Name and Rank.	Place of Enlistment.	Enrolled	Remarks.
Privates.		1846.	
Casnor, Jonas	Alton, Ill.	June 20	Died at Parros Dec. 25, 1846.
Penter, George W.	"	"	" Saltillo March 23, 1847.
Stilley, Hezekiah.	"	"	" Buena Vista April 19, 1847.

This company was discharged at Camargo, Mexico, June 18, 1847.

Company "B."

Name and Rank.	Place of Enlistment.	Enrolled	Remarks.
Captain.		1846.	
Anderson P. Cordo.	Alton, Ill.	June 26	
First Lieutenant.			
John W. Rigby	"	June 30	
Second Lieutenants.			
Wm. W. Tate	"	"	
James M. Gaunt	"	"	
Sergeants.			
Watho F. Hargus	"	"	
Abraham S. Latta	"	"	Detached service, Hospital Steward, Sept. 29.
Calvin Brown	"	"	
John Delaney	"	"	
Corporals.			
John L. Barber	"	"	
Robt. E. Hall	"	"	
James Cuppin	"	"	
James H. Gorrell	"	"	Absent, sick at Laracco, from Aug. 11.
Musician.			
Andrew I. Ring	"	"	
Privates.			
Abbott, John	"	"	
Anglin, Wm. C.	"	"	Taken prisoner at battle of Buena Vista.
Bartleson, Edwin	"	"	
Bartleson, Augustus	"	"	
Baccus, Abner	"	"	
Boren, Welbourn	"	"	
Barnett, John	"	"	
Burkhardt, Henry	"	"	
Crippin, William	"	"	
Cole, Robert	"	"	
Cole, Jiles M.	"	"	
Curry, John	"	"	Taken prisoner at battle of Buena Vista.
Davis, Marion M.	"	"	
Doebeaker, Henry.	"	"	
Evans, Joseph	"	"	Taken prisoner at battle of Buena Vista.
Echols, Miller	"	"	
Emerick, Daniel	"	"	
Goodall, Charles	"	"	Wounded at battle of Buena Vista.
Goodwin, John	"	"	
Harnback, Joseph B	"	"	
Hughes, William	"	"	
Hale, James M.	"	"	

Name and Rank.	Place of Enlistment.	Enrolled	Remarks.
		1846.	
Johnson, Reason I..	Alton, Ill....	June 30	
Johnson, William ..	"	"	
Ladd, Elisha........	"	"	
London, James L...	"	"	
London, Thomas E.	"	"	
Lefler, Pleasant....	"	"	
McGee, Patrick H...	"	"	
Metcalf, James H...	"	"	
Phillips, Enos A....	"	"	
Purdy, George......	"	"	
Parker, Framuel....	"	"	
Russell, John B....	"	"	
Russell, Pinkney...	"	"	
Russell, John......	"	"	
Renfrow, David.....	"	"	
Story, Jonathan....	"	"	
Smith, Columbus C.	"	"	
Scott, Calvin L.....	"	"	Absent, sick at Laracco, from Aug. 11.........
Summerville, Jack'n	"	"	
Shepherd, Elijah....	"	"	Absent, sick at Laracco, from Aug. 11.........
Stephens, Cyrus....	"	"	
Thorp, James.......	"	"	Taken prisoner at Buena Vista...............
Tiner, Andrew J....	"	"	
Tiner, William E...	"	"	
Tiner, Isham L.....	"	"	
Thompson, Thomas.	"	"	
Vaugh, Reuben.....	"	"	
White, John........	"	"	
Whittaker, William.	"	"	Absent, sick at Laracco, from Aug. 11.........
Young, H. A........	"	"	

Died :

Privates.		1846.	
Bankston, Alfred....	Alton, Ill.....	June 30	Died at Saltillo March 21.................
Jones, Thomas......	"	"	" 4........................
Kelso, Enoch........	"	"	Laracco, time not known...........

Discharged :

Private.		1846.	
Kitchell, John.......	Alton, Ill.....	June 30	Discharged on Surgeon's certif. March 20....

This company was discharged from service at Camargo, Mex., June 18, 1847.

Company "C."

Name and Rank.	Place of Enlistment.	Enrolled	Remarks.
Captain.		1846.	
James W. Baker.....	Alton, Ill.....	June 12	Wounded at Buena Vista; absent on furlough
First Lieutenant.			
Turner R. DeButts ..	"	"	
Second Lieutenants.			
John Brown.........	"	"	Wounded in battle of Buena Vista, Feb. 23...
James Smith........	"	"	
Sergeants.			
North West.........	"	"	
Charles Chaney.....	"	"	
Emanuel Webber....	"	"	
Martin T. Smith.....	"	"	

SECOND REGIMENT. 233

Name and Rank.	Place of Enlistment.	Enrolled	Remarks.
Corporals.		1846.	
Edward Twaddle	Alton, Ill	June 12	
John Robinson	"	"	
William Austin	"	"	
James Shelby	"	"	
Privates.			
Bings, John	"	"	
Black, Hugh	"	"	
Brown, Cornelius W.	"	"	
Bivins, Clayton	"	"	
Bryant, John M	"	"	Wounded in battle of Buena Vista, Feb. 23.
Bivins, James C	"	"	
Clarage, Francis A	"	"	Wounded in battle of Buena Vista, Feb. 23.
Crabb, John W	"	"	On furlough in Q. M. Departm't, from May 16.
Dimond, John P	"	"	
Deffenbacker, Jacob	"	"	
Easley, William	"	"	Wounded in battle of Buena Vista, Feb. 23.
Foyles, James	"	"	Wounded, and on furl., in Q. M. Dep't May 8.
Fletcher, George	"	"	Wounded in battle of Buena Vista, Feb. 23.
Grace, James T	"	"	
Groves, Jacob	"	"	
Griffith, William	"	"	
Griffith, Joseph	"	"	
Graham, John	"	"	On furlough in Com'sary Dep't from May 17.
Hayse, John	"	"	
Harness, Joseph	"	"	On furlough in Q. M. Departm'nt from May 16
Johnson, Edward H	"	"	
James, Stephen	"	"	On furlough in Q. M. Departm'nt from May 16
McMichael, Obed	"	"	Taken prisoner at Buena Vista, Feb. 23.
Mulligan, James	"	"	On furlough from May 15
McGrau, James A	"	"	
Mansure, Charles	"	"	
Montgomery, Thos	"	"	Wounded in battle of Buena Vista, Feb. 23.
McCann, David	"	"	
Nolland, Jasper N	"	"	
Nolland, John M	"	"	Wounded in battle of Buena Vista, Feb. 23.
Nettelton, James M	"	"	
Parker, James	"	"	
Ricketts, David M	"	"	Wounded in battle of Buena Vista, Feb. 23.
Ryon, John J	"	"	
Stuart, John W	"	"	
Smith, Henry C	"	"	Wounded in battle of Buena Vista, Feb. 23.
Smith, Isaac P	"	"	
Stamps, George W	"	"	
Stratham, Charles H	"	"	
Sidel, Jacob	"	"	
Therman, Jesse T	"	"	Taken prisoner at Buena Vista, Feb. 23.
Torum, Samuel	"	"	
VanCamp, Charles	"	"	On furl'h Q. M. Dep't; wounded, Buena Vista.
Whippill, Laurist'n W	"	"	
Whitmore, Samuel	"	"	On furlough in Q. M. Dep't from May 8.

Discharged:

Privates.		1846.	
Burk, Robert	Alton, Ill	June 12	[Mounted Vols. May 29; wounded. Disch. by reason of joining Capt. Meyer's Co.
Coil, Peter	"	"	"
Kelly, Patrick	"	"	"
Lanon, Patrick	"	"	"
Loomis, Ralph I	"	"	"
Luther, Francis	"	"	empl't in Ordn'nce Dep't
Maxwell, George R	"	"	at Monterey; wounded at Buena Vista

Died:

		1846.	
Fenk, Nicholas	Alton, Ill	June 12	Wounded, Buena Vista, Feb. 23; died April 25

This company was discharged at Camargo, Mexico, June 18, 1847.

MEXICAN WAR.

Company "D."

Name and Rank.	Place of Enlistment.	Enrolled	Remarks.
Captain.		1846.	
Erastus Wheeler	Alton, Ill.	June 16	
First Lieutenant.			
Geo. W. Prickett	"	"	Acting Q. M. for the Regiment from Feb. 28.
Second Lieutenants.			
Joel Foster	"	"	
Wm. B. Reynolds	"	"	
Sergeants.			
Geo. T. Cochran	"	"	
Chas. W. Ward	"	"	
Wm. Peel	"	"	
Wm. E. Wheeler	"	"	
Corporals.			
Constantine Smith	"	"	
Elisha Axley	"	"	Absent, sick at San Antonio, from Oct. 14.
Wm. Calvert	"	"	
Jas. A. Henderson	"	"	
Musician.			
Joseph Shoemaker	"	"	
Privates.			
Aker, Stephan	"	"	
Bell, Wiley H	"	"	
Barnrighter, Conrad	"	"	
Blake, Chas. W	"	"	
Bartels, Engelhart	"	"	
Biggerstaff, John W.	"	"	
Brown, John	"	"	
Borks, Richard	"	"	
Campbell, Dennis	"	"	
Creed, Colby	"	"	
Douglas, Alexander	"	"	
Davis, Enneis C	"	"	
Duff, Hiram D	"	"	
Davis, Joseph	"	"	
Devine, Charles	"	June 30	
Emmerson, James H	"	June 16	
Fulfer, James	"	June 13	
Gregory, Lisles	"	June 30	
Goodwin, John	"		
Goodwin, Richard	"	June 16	
Glaser, Ludwick	"	"	Absent, sick at San Antonio, from Oct. 14.
Gayler, Joseph E	"	"	
Hays, Andrew	"	"	
Hare, Jephtha	"	"	Absent on furl. f'm May 8; emp. in Q. M. Dep.
Hoop, Philip	"	"	
Jackman, Asborne C	"	"	
Jackson, Andrew	"	June 30	
Kinder, George	"	June 16	
Keppy, Christopher	"	"	
Lancaster, James	"	"	
Lowdner, Wolf	"	"	
Lewis, Thomas	"	"	
Mings, Crinh	"	June 30	
Murphy, John D	"	June 16	
Murphy, Bonham	"	"	
Muir, Jefferson	"	"	
Massey, Richard	"	"	
Malry, Richard G	"	"	
McCoy, James S	"	"	
Paynter, Robert	"	June 30	
Preg, Andrew	"	June 16	
Paine, Moses R	"	"	
Parker, Wilson	"	"	
Pierce, Mortimer R	"	"	
Robinson, Jesse	"	"	
Ramsey, Gardner	"	"	
Robinson, James	"	"	
Ramson, Wm. F	"	"	
Swain, Andrew, Jr.	"	"	
Sobber, Charles	"	"	

Name and Rank.	Place of Enlistment.	Enrolled	Remarks.
		1846.	
Squires, James	Alton, Ill.	June 16	
Saunders, Marion	"	....	
Sachse, Lewis	"	....	
Taylor, James H.	"	....	Absent on furl. f'm May 9; emp. in Q. M. Dep.
Tarkinton, Thos. J.	"	....	
Thomas, Leander	"	....	
Updyke, Holcombe	"	....	
VanCamp, Aaron	"	....	Disch. March 24, on Surg. certif.; disability.
VanShaffer, Elworth	"	....	Absent on furl. f'm May 9; emp. in Q. M. Dep.
Warren, Hardy	"	....	
Wingleman, Edward	"	....	

This company was discharged June 18, 1847, at Camargo, Mexico.

Company "E."

Name and Rank.	Place of Enlistment.	Enrolled	Remarks.
Captain.		1846.	
Peter Lott	Alton, Ill.	June 20	Ass't C. S. from July 17 to Sept. 14; then Capt.
First Lieutenant.			
John A. Prickett	"	June 17	Absent on furl., wounds rec'd in bat'l Feb. 23.
Second Lieutenants.			
James Catron	"	....	Disch. at Buena Vista May 22; re-enlistment.
Aston Madeira	"	....	Formerly Sergeant
Sergeants.			
John Roberts	"	June 17	
William Kelley	"	June 20	
John S. Selden	"	June 17	
Corporals.			
Joseph Quigley	"	....	
Hardy R. Carroll	"	....	
Isaac E. Hardy	"	....	
Privates.			
Botkin, John B.	"	....	
Burns, Myron S.	"	....	
Carpenter, David M.	"	....	
Clark, Samuel	"	....	
Clark, Thomas	"	June 20	
Cruise, Patrick	"	....	
Duncan, John R.	"	June 17	
Drury, Edward A.	"	....	
Dought, Isaac H.	"	....	
Davidson, John	"	June 20	
Dwyer, John	"	....	
Elwell, Joseph S.	"	....	
Field, Aaron	"	....	Absent on furlough in Q. M. Dept. from May 8
Falkner, William	"	....	
Falkner, James	"	....	
Garrison, John	"	....	
Hutchinson, Pierson	"	....	
Hill, George M.	"	....	
Hatch, Edwin	"	....	
Hunter, Charles	"	....	Absent on furlough in Q. M. Dept. from May 8
Hoffmaster, Chris.	"	....	
Hackney, James	"	....	
Hill, Ephraim P.	"	....	
Jenkins, Ezekiel	"	....	Absent on furlough in Q. M. Dept. from May 8
Joice, William B.	"	....	
King, Josephus	"	....	
Kellor, John F.	"	....	
Kennedy, William	"	....	
Lovelace, Perry	"	June 17	Absent on furlough in Q. M. Dept. from May 8
Lewis, James	"	....	
Marsh, Caleb N.	"	....	
McGovern, James	"	....	

Name and Rank.	Place of Enlistment.	Enrolled	Remarks.
		1846.	
O'Conner, James	Alton, Ill	June 20	
Prickett, Thomas J.	"	June 17	
Quick, John	"	"	
Roberts, George	"	"	
Roder, John B.	"	"	
Riley, Michael	"	June 20	
Rogers, Andrew F.	"	June 17	
Sprague, William	"	"	Reduced from Corporal from Oct. 2
Stewart, Charles	"	"	
Stanley, John R.	"	"	
Twaddle, William A.	"	"	
Wright, James H.	"	"	
Wiswell, Benj. F.	"	"	
Wright, William R.	"	"	
West, Horace B.	"	"	
Waldron, Elias	"	"	
Wagner, Rufus M.	"	"	
Warnick, Fred'k E.	"	"	

Discharged:

		1846.	
Sergeant.			
Robert McFarland	Alton, Ill	June 17	Disch. at Buena Vista May 23; re-enlistment.
Privates.			
Bramble, Thomas			Disch. at Buena Vista May 23; re-enlistment.
Brinker, Clark			" " " " "
Graves, Jason			" " " " "
Griffin, John W.			" " " " "
Nettleton, James			" " " " "

Died:

		1846.	
Field, Edwin	Alton, Ill	June 17	Died at Saltillo Mar. 12, of wounds received
Fisher, William	"	"	" " " " 5, " " "
Robinson, John	"	"	" " " " 1. " " "
Ryan, James	"	June 20	Murdered near Saltillo March 26

This company was discharged at Camargo, Mexico, on June 18, 1847.

Company "F."

Name and Rank.	Place of Enlistment.	Enrolled	Remarks.
		1846.	
Captain.			
John S. Hacker	Alton, Ill	June 25	
First Lieutenant.			
Sidney S. Condon	"	"	
Second Lieutenants.			
Alphonso Grammar	"	"	
Joseph Martin	"	"	Elected from Corp. Jan. 26, *vice* Selby, dec'd.
Sergeants.			
John C. Hunsaker	"	"	
Alex. J. Nimmo	"	"	
Abram Hargrave	"	"	
John Grammar	"	"	
Corporals.			
Adam Creese	"	"	
Wright C. Pender	"	"	
Henderson Brown	"	"	
Abram Cover	"	"	

SECOND REGIMENT.

Name and Rank.	Place of Enlistment.	Enrolled	Remarks.
Musicians.		1846.	
Jacob Greer	Alton, Ill	June 25	
George H. Hemley	"	"	
Privates.			
Brown, Talbot	"	"	
Bevins, John	"	"	
Brown, John	"	"	
Barringer, Charles	"	"	
Burgess, John Z	"	"	
Cripps, Peter	"	"	
Casper, Peter H	"	"	
Coffman, Elijah	"	"	
Davie, Scipio A. B	"	"	
Davie, John	"	"	
Dougherty, Daniel	"	"	
Fisher, Simeon	"	"	
Findley, Charles A	"	"	On detached service in Q. M. Dept. Dec. 30
Fike, James	"	"	
Gray, Jesse	"	"	
Geargus, Franklin	"	"	
Grammar, James	"	"	
Haugh, Henry	"	"	
Hamby, Wm. N	"	"	
Henry, William	"	"	
Hess, Samuel	"	"	
Hayward, Benj. F	"	"	
Hacker, Henry C	"	"	Hospital Steward from July 25 to Oct. 5, and [from Dec. 17 to Jan. 20.
Jones, Fielding A	"	"	
Jones, Silas	"	"	
Kerr, John	"	"	
King, Frederick	"	"	
Lingle, Adam	"	"	
Lewis, Philip	"	"	
Lingle, John	"	"	
Lingle, Henry	"	"	
Lyerley, Daniel W	"	"	
Lemons, Andrew J	"	"	
Lingle, Daniel	"	"	
Langley, Chesterfi'ld	"	"	
Mances, John	"	"	
McCoy, Harrison	"	"	
Maneese, Jefferson	"	"	
Miller, William	"	"	
Milliken, John H	"	"	
Moland, John	"	"	
Martin, Samuel	"	"	
McIntosh, Wash'n L	"	"	
McGinnis, John	"	"	
Phelan, James M	"	"	
Parker, Samuel	"	"	
Resink, Garrett	"	"	
Regan, John W	"	"	
Sprey, Franklin	"	"	
Simons, Amalphus W	"	"	
Springs, Jas. A	"	"	
Thornton, Azel	"	"	
Thomas, LeRoy	"	"	
Toler, Jas. I	"	"	
Thurman, Thos. F	"	"	
Vick, Reuben	"	"	
Walker, James	"	"	

Discharged:

Private.		1846.	
Pless, Martin	Alton, Ill	June 25	Discharged at Saltillo, Mch. 21, on Surg. cert.

Died:

Privates.		1846.	
Anderson, Felix G	Alton, Ill	June 25	Died in Hospital at Saltillo April 9
Davie, Alexander	"	"	" at San Antonio, Texas; date not known.
Ledgerwood, Joseph	"	"	" in Hospital at Saltillo March 21

This company was discharged on June 18, 1847, at Camargo, Mex.

Company "G."

Name and Rank.	Place of Enlistment.	Enrolled	Remarks.
Captain.		1846.	
Joseph K. Lemon	Alton, Ill.	June 17	
First Lieutenant.			
Jacob C. Hinkley	"	"	
Second Lieutenants.			
Gilb'rt P. McFarland	"	"	
Andrew J. Miller	"	"	Elected from private, Dec. 17
Sergeants.			
William Wastfield	"	"	
John Fincher	"	"	
James L. Roman	"	"	
Joseph Penn	"	"	
Corporals.			
William S. Peck	"	"	
Jas. L. Garretson	"	"	
Jas. G. Abbott	"	"	
John Gaston	"	"	
Musician.			
James H. Beach	"	"	
Privates.			
Benson, Wm. V.	"	"	
Brown, Mathew W.	"	"	
Burnett, Thomas J.	"	"	
Bragg, Solomon	"	"	
Bragg, Thomas	"	"	
Blair, Peter W.	"	"	
Boone, Daniel	"	July 1	
Clark, John	"	June 17	Absent, sick, at San Antonio, from Oct. 14
Evans, John D.	"	"	
Forquer, Eli	"	"	
Fishter, Joseph	"	"	
Friedlander, Wm.	"	"	On detach. serv., Acting A. C. S., from Sept. 4
Green, Mahlon A.	"	"	
Gelwicks, Daniel W.	"	"	
Glenn, Alexander	"	"	
Gallagher, Arthur I.	"	"	On extra duty, Hosp. Steward, from June
Gaskill, Clayton	"	"	
Goree, John C.	"	"	
Holbert, David W.	"	"	
Hammond, Willis M.	"	"	
Hill, Thomas	"	"	
Hornett, John M. O.	"	"	
Hall, Robert	"	"	
James, Langsworth	"	"	
Kertz, Gen. LaFay'e	"	"	
Kennedy, John J.	"	"	
Long, Thomas	"	"	
Lockhart, Gideon	"	"	
Loe, George F.	"	"	
McKenzie, Calvin	"	"	
McLain, Allen	"	"	Wounded in battle of Buena Vista, Feb. 23
Miller, Robert C.	"	"	
Million, Wm. K.	"	"	
McNail, Pierson W.	"	"	
Murray, William	"	"	
McKenzie, Elijah	"	"	
McKinney, Marcus E.	"	"	
Martin, Henry	"	July 1	
Nelson, John S.	"	June 17	
Owing, Washington	"	"	
Parks, Joseph M.	"	"	
Reaves, Samuel	"	"	
Randleman, Joel	"	"	
Stuart, Charles H.	"	"	
Steele, Andrew J.	"	"	
Shall, James	"	"	
Sterling, Henry C.	"	"	
Thomas, Samuel K.	"	"	
Teters, David W.	"	"	

SECOND REGIMENT.

Name and Rank.	Place of Enlistment.	Enrolled	Remarks.
		1847.	
Tunstall, James M.	Alton, Ill.	June 17	
Wood, Alfred H.	"	"	
Wiley, Joseph	"	"	Wounded in battle of Buena Vista, Feb. 23.
Walker, James	"	July 1	

Discharged:

		1846.	
Melton, Aaron B.	Alton, Ill.	June 17	Disch. at B. Vista; emp. in Q. M. D't f'm May 8
Melton, Guilford M.	"	"	Disch. at B. Vista; joined Capt. Myers' Co.

Died:

		1846.	
Cheek, Allen	Alton, Ill.	June 17	Died at Buena Vista April 21.
Lewis, John	"	"	Saltillo May 3.

This company was discharged on June 18, 1847, at Camargo, Mex.

Company "H."

Name and Rank.	Place of Enlistment.	Enrolled	Remarks.
Captain.		1846.	
Julius Raith	Alton, Ill.	June 16	
First Lieutenant.			
Nathaniel Niles	"	"	Discharged at Buena Vista May 31, 1847.
Second Lieutenants.			
Adolph Engelmann	"	"	Absent on furl. f'm May 23 till expir'n of serv.
Louis Stock	"	"	
Sergeants.			
Charles A. Fritz	"	"	
Robert Morrison	"	"	Absent on furl. f'm May 31 till expir'n of serv.
Fridolin Schetterer	"	"	
Corporals.			
Adol. Schlotterback	"	"	
Charles Gooding	"	"	
Adam Ewing	"	"	
H. W. Waldmann	"	"	
Musicians.			
Gabriel W. Cox	"	"	
Jacob Kuebli	"	"	
Privates.			
Alexander, Tucker	"	"	
Becker, John Ph.	"	"	
Becker, Urban	"	"	
Berry, John	"	"	
Berdoux, Charles	"	"	
Buyotte, Louis	"	"	
Bridges, Charles	"	"	
Busch, Herman	"	"	
Brownfield, William	"	"	
Burg, Valetin	"	"	
Clark, John	"	"	
Clemen, Charles	"	"	
Doer, Jacob	"	"	
Edwards, F. O.	"	"	
Eastes, George	"	"	
Erhard, William	"	"	

240 MEXICAN WAR.

Name and Rank.	Place of Enlistment.	Enrolled	Remarks.
		1846.	
Elimger, Augustus	Alton, Ill	June 16	
Funk, Valetin	"	"	
Frank, Jacob	"	"	
Francis, James	"	"	
Feldmeier, William	"	"	
Gerhard, John	"	"	
Gerstenshloeger, J.	"	"	
Gollinger, John	"	"	
Hantz, Joseph	"	"	
King, William	"	"	
Knight, John	"	"	
Kirk, F. M.	"	"	
Lambert, Caspar	"	"	
Ledergerher, Joseph	"	"	
Mauerer, Nic.	"	"	
Meyer, John G.	"	"	
McDonald, Daniel	"	"	Absent on furl. f'm May 31 till expir'n of serv.
Rice, George	"	"	
Roberts, Charles	"	"	
Ronneberg, Fritz	"	"	
Reeves, William	"	"	
Scheel, Maxmilian	"	"	Absent on furl. f'm May 23 till expir'n of serv.
Schenerer, John	"	"	
Schnebelin, Barth	"	"	
Sauerwein, Michael	"	"	
Schloesinger, Henry	"	"	
Talbert, James	"	"	
Trautwein, Chas. H.	"	"	
Trautwein, Ph. John	"	"	
Traenkle, Conrad	"	"	
Todd, Jackson	"	"	
Upmann, Hermann	"	July 1	
Voelker, George	"	June 16	
Wedekind, E. O.	"	"	
Wilver, David	"	"	
West, James	"	"	
Wolf, John	"	"	
Weiseborn, John C.	"	"	

Discharged:

		1846.	
Third Sergeant.			
Charles Sominoky	Alton, Ill	June 16	Discharged at Buena Vista May 31, 1847
Privates.			
Baker, Daniel	"	"	Discharged at Buena Vista May 31, 1847
Deuker, John	"	"	" " " " "
Kruse, William	"	"	" " " " "
Kurkman, Noble	"	"	" " " " "
Newell, J. H.	"	"	" on Surg. cert. disabil. Mch. 25, '47.
Queuby, Abraham	"	"	" " " " "
Wolf, Philip	"	"	" " " " "

Died:

		1846.	
Kuehfus, John	Alton, Ill	June 16	Killed bet. Saltillo and Camp Bu. Vista Ap. 15
Seutzinger, John	"	"	Died in hospital at Saltillo May 7, 1847

This company was discharged at Camargo, Mexico, June 18, 1847.

SECOND REGIMENT. 241

Company "I."

Name and Rank.	Place of Enlistment.	Enrolled	Remarks.
Captain. Morrison Miller	Alton, Ill	1846 June 24	
First Lieutenant. August. G. Whiteside	"	"	Detached service, Adj't of Regt., order Col Bissell, from July 1
Second Lieutenants. John L. Wilson	"	"	
James H. Waddle	"	"	
Sergeants. James C. B. Reed	"	"	Absent on furl'h from May 23 till exp. service
Thomas W. Morgan	"	"	Appointed from private March 1
William S. Agnew	"	"	Appointed from Corporal, March 15
Jacob Frick	"	"	
Corporals. Isaac Tolin	"	"	
John Agnew	"	"	Appointed from private March 1
Jackson M. Lockert	"	"	" " " " 15
Samuel McMurtry	"	"	" " " " 1; wounded in battle of Feb. 23.
Musicians. John Cook	"	"	Appointed from private
Henry Iman	"	"	
Privates. Agnew, Francis	"	"	
Applegate, Aaron H	"	"	Wounded in battle of Feb. 23
Bruns, Frederic	"	"	
Clark, Felix	"	"	
Clark, Edward	"	"	
Curey, George	"	"	
Divers, Ananias	"	"	
Everett, Edward	"	"	
Fisher, William	"	"	
Finger, Theodore	"	"	Hospital attendant at San Antonio from Oct. 6
Hiltman, Lewis	"	"	Wounded in battle of Feb. 23
Hewett, Jacob	"	"	
Hinkler, Charles	"	"	Wounded in battle of Feb. 23
Hardin, James L	"	"	
Hill, Samuel G	"	"	
Harker, Thomas	"	"	
Hobbs, William	"	"	
Iman, Samuel	"	"	
Irmaker, Henry	"	"	
Johnson, William	"	"	
Klinkhard, Joseph	"	"	
King, William	"	"	
Kell, Solomon	"	"	Wounded in battle of Feb. 23
Lacey, William	"	"	
Lilly, James H	"	"	
McMurtry, Joseph	"	"	
Morrison, William	"	"	
Mummert, Michael	"	"	Wounded in battle of Feb. 23
Mohr, John Jacob	"	"	
Moore, Lewis W	"	"	
Moore, I. Milton	"	"	
Moore, Nelson S	"	"	Reduced from Sergt. Mar. 15; transf'd to staff
Murray, Carter	"	"	
O'Brien, John	"	"	
Pilliard, Jacob	"	"	
Sennott, James	"	"	
Sexton, Daniel	"	"	
Stong, John L	"	"	
Smith, Nicholas	"	"	
Thackeray, William	"	"	
Thompson, James	"	"	
Talbott, Elijah	"	"	
Tope, George W	"	"	
Wilson, Edward	"	"	
Warnock, Joseph	"	"	
Werbein, Voluntine	"	"	Wounded in battle of Feb. 23

—16

Name and Rank.	Place of Enlistment.	Enrolled	Remarks.
Wallice, George	Alton, Ill.	1846 June 24	
Ward, Philip	"	"	
Helm, William	"	"	Reduced from Corporal March 1 " " Sergeant
Long, John	"	"	

Discharged:

Name and Rank.	Place of Enlistment.	Enrolled	Remarks.
Dains, William	Alton, Ill.	1846 June 24	Disch., Buena Vista, May 30; wounded Feb. 23
Runyan, Courtland	"	"	" " "
White, John M.	"	"	

Died:

Name and Rank.	Place of Enlistment.	Enrolled	Remarks.
Leerning, George	Alton, Ill	1846 June 24	Died May 8. at Camp Buena Vista
Squires, Hiram	"	"	" of wounds rec'd at Buena Vista, Feb. 23.
Wilcox, James M.	"	"	" at Parros; time not known

This company was mustered out at Camargo, Mexico, June 18, 1847.

Company "K."

Name and Rank.	Place of Enlistment.	Enrolled	Remarks.
Captain.		1846.	
Chas. L. Starbuck	Alton, Ill.	June 26	
First Lieutenant.			
Nath'l B. Dilhorn	"	"	
Second Lieutenants.			
Niccodemus West	"	"	Wounded in battle of Feb. 23.
John D. Rees	"	"	
Sergeants.			
Davidson C. Moore	"	"	
Richard H. Williams	"	"	
Jerome B. West	"	"	
Guilford H. Haggard	"	"	
Corporals.			
John A. Fanin	"	"	
John P. Ford	"	"	
John D. Bourland	"	"	
Elias G. Chappell	"	"	
Privates.			
Armstrong, Robt. W.	"	"	
Anderson, Wm. P.	"	"	
Brown, Isaac M.	"	"	
Brown, Wm. G.	"	"	
Bridges, Wm. W.	"	"	
Campbell, Geo. W.	"	"	Detached service; Ward Master in Camp Hospital from Jan. 27.
Carmack, Samuel	"	"	
Crawford, Marshall	"	"	
Crawford, Hampton	"	"	
Dalley, Hiram	"	"	
Dry, John M.	"	"	
Dry, Edmund	"	"	
Fannin, Wm. P.	"	"	
Foster, Wm. A.	"	"	
Hawkins, Marcus C.	"	"	
Hoge, Marion D.	"	"	Wounded in battle of Feb. 23.

SECOND REGIMENT.

Name and Rank.	Place of Enlistment.	Enrolled	Remarks.
		1846.	
Hamilton, Alex. A	Alton, Ill.	June 26	
Humphreys, Ferd.G.	"	"	
Hammock, Lewis	"	"	
Johnson, Wm. L.	"	"	
Kelley, Uriah D.	"	"	Wounded in battle of Feb. 23.
Lynch, Adam W.	"	"	
Lynch, David G.	"	"	
Lee, George E.	"	"	
Malone, Edwin	"	"	
Marlow, William	"	"	
Marlow, Richard	"	"	
Montague, Cave	"	"	
Montague, Geo. T.	"	"	
Neil, Wm.	"	"	
Pyatt, John W.	"	"	
Pritchett, Levi	"	"	
Pettit, John D.	"	"	On furlough from May 28; carpenter in Engineer's Dept.
Pettit, Geo. F.	"	"	
Peague, Joshua	"	"	
Robinson, Larkin L.	"	"	
Robinson, John	"	"	Wounded in battle of Feb. 23.
Ramsay, Nathan	"	"	
Ragland, John B.	"	"	Absent sick at camp near Savacca, from Aug. 11; supposed to be dead.
Spong, David	"	"	
Stewart, James	"	"	
Terry, Hansel	"	"	
Taylor, Wm. B.	"	"	
West, Van R	"	"	
Welts, Giles	"	"	
Wilks, Richard	"	"	

Died:

		1846.	
Delinger, Wm. H.	Alton, Ill.	June 26	Died at Saltillo, Mex., May 13
Higgarson, John P.	"	"	" Buena Vista, Mex., May 16
Terry, Carter	"	"	" Saltillo, Mex., March 11

Discharged:

		1846.	
Ramsey, Eli	Alton, Ill.	June 26	Re-enlisted at Buena Vista, Mex., May 28, [and discharged.
Stewart, Robt. W.	"	"	

This company was discharged at Camargo, Mex., June 18, 1847.

SECOND REGIMENT.

THE FIELD AND STAFF

Of the 2d Regiment of Illinois Foot Volunteers, commanded by Colonel James Collins, called into the service of the United States by the President, under the act of Congress approved May 13, 1846, at Alton, Ill. (the place of general rendezvous), organized on the 3d day of August, 1847, to serve for the term of during the war with Mexico. From the 30th day of April, 1848, (when last paid), to the 25th day of July, when discharged. The Regiment was organized by Col. James Collins, at Alton, Ill., in the month of August, 1847.

Name and Rank.	Place of Enlistment.	Enrolled	Remarks.
Colonel.		1847.	
James Collins.......	Galena	June 22	Elected Col. f'm Capt. Co. F., Aug. 3, '47; discharged at New Orleans July 8, '48.
Lieutenant-Colonel.			
Stephen G. Hicks...	Nashville	July 10	Present, commanding the Regiment........ ..
Major.			
Thos. S. Livingston.	....	....	Must'd as Major on day of elect'n, Aug. 3, '47.
Adjutants.			
Henry S. Fitch......	Whitehall	....	App'd Adjt. Aug. 3, '47; elect. Capt. of Co. "D"
Jas. H. Sampson	Galena	June 21	App'd Adjt. Feb. 29, '48.............[Feb. 29, '48.
A. A. C. S. and A. A. Q. M.			on acct. of prolonged absence f'm reg't.
Elisha Lewis........	Belvidere	June 4	App'd Aug. 3, '48; deprived of app't Feb. 16, '48,
Lewis A. Norton....	St. Charles...	July 1	App'd Feb. 16, '48; must'd out in Co. "I." ......
Surgeon.			
John L. Miller.......	Appointed by the President	....	Present ....
Assistant Surgeons.			
Nathan H. Ash......	Appointed by the President	....	Disch. at Jalapa, Mex., Dec. 22, '47; disability
Franc's B. Thompson	Appointed by the President	....	Date of commission, Mar. 29, '48; present.....

NON-COMMISSIONED STAFF.

Sergeant-Majors.		1847.	
Erasmus D. House..	Whitehall	May 12	Appointed from Sergt. in Co. "D" Jan. 17, '48.
James B. Hinde.....	Mt. Vernon...	June 3	Appointed Aug. 3, '47; elected 1st Lieut. Co. "A," Jan. 17, '48.
Q. M. Sergeants.			
Thos. G. Coffy......	Galena	June 22	Appointed from Sergt. in Co. "F," Dec. 23, '47.
Wm. G. Taylor......	Waterloo.....	....	Appointed Aug. 3, '47; died at Jalapa, Mex., Dec. 22, '47.
Principal Musicians.			
Ferdinand Pallaris..		....	Appointed and mustered Aug. 3, '47...........
Harrison Ramsey...	Galena	June 21	Appointed Aug. 3, '47..............................

SECOND REGIMENT. 245

Company "A."

Name and Rank.	Place of Enlistment	Enrolled	Remarks.
		1847.	
Captains.			
James Bowman	Alton, Ill	June 3	Died at Jalapa, Mex., Dec. 28, 1847
Levin H. Powell	"	"	Must'd in as private; app'd 1st Sergt. Oct. 23; elected Capt. Jan. 17.
First Lieutenants.			
Eli Anderson	"	....	" Died at Very, Mex., Sept. 11, 1847; yellow fever
James B. Hinde	"	....	" Must'd in as private; app'd Sergt.-Maj. Aug. 3
Willis B. Holder	"	....	" Died at Jalapa, Mex., Jan. 2, 1848
Second Lieutenants.			
Hezekiah B. Newby	"	....	" Died at Nat. Bridge, Mex., Sept. 16; yell. fever
Jabers J. Anderson	"	....	" Must'd in as Sergt.; elec'd 2d Lieut. Mar. 23, '48
Alonzo H. Cox	"	....	" " " private; " " Sept. 24 ..
Jacob B. Keller	"	....	" Must'd in as private; elec'd Lieut. Sept. 24, '47; resigned March 23, '48.
Sergeants.			
Jonathan Wells	"	....	" Must'd in as private; app'd 1st Sergt. Jan. 17 '48
Gilford D. Connolly	"	....	" " " corpor'l; " Sergt. Feb. 7, '48
John P. Newell	"	....	" " " private; " " Jan. 17, '48
Jonathan S. Cook	"	....	" " " corpor'l; " " Mar. 24, '48
Corporals.			
Edward Bond	"	....	" Must'd as private; app'd corporal Mar. 24, 1848
Robert R. Ingram	"	....	" " " " " Feb. 7, 1848
Elias M. Holmes	"	....	" " " " " Mar. 24, 1848
William Bullock	"	....	" " " " " Jan. 17, 1848
Drummer.			
John W. Hartley	"	....	
Fifer.			
Thomas Casey	"	....	"
Privates.			
Ames, John			
Anderson, Robert C			
Brown, Calvin			
Cassidy, William			
Cummins, James			
Childers, Richard			
Clark, Martin	Chicago, Ill	Feb.,	'48
Crey, Thomas D	St.Charl's, Ill	Mar.,	'48
Elce, Julian			
Green, John B	Alton, Ill	June,	'47
Godfrey, Caleb	St.Charl's, Ill	Mar.,	'48
Gaston, Newton A	Alton, Ill	June	'47
Hillhouse, Robert S			
Johnson, Lewis	Chicago, Ill	Mar.,	'48
Kimball, Henderson	Alton, Ill	June,	'47
Kaltenbach, Peter	"		
Kinman, Andrew J			
Kennady, Damon C	Chicago, Ill	April,	'48
McCormick, Josiah	Alton, Ill	June,	'47
McCulloch, Preston	"	....	
McCassilin, William			
Mullen, Thomas	Chicago, Ill	Feb.,	'48
Messechar, Aaron	"	"	
McRorgh, Martin	"	"	
McDonald, James	"	"	
Orton, Job A	"	"	
Osborn, James L	Alton, Ill	June,	'47
Root, Welcome			
Rose, John	St.Charl's, Ill	Mar.,	'48
Stephens, Andrew	"	"	
Soule, Alonso	"	"	
Safford, Oliver			
Stull, Lawrence	Alton, Ill	June,	'47
Sanders, Jacob			
Thornton, William A	Chicago, Ill	Feb.,	'48
Vance, Thomas J	Alton, Ill	June,	'47
Wilson, Isaac	"	....	
Watts, John D	"	....	
Weymon, Thomas			
Weldon, Benett M			
Wood, Sherman D	St.Charl's, Ill	Mar.,	'48
Wentworth, Henry	"		

MEXICAN WAR.

Died:

Name and Rank.	Place of Enlistment.	Enrolled	Remarks.
Sergeants.		1847.	
James Mathewson..	Alton, Ill.....	June 3	Died Oct. 28, '47, at V. Cruz hospital...........
Benjamin F. Bogan..	"	.... "	" Jan. 11, '47, at Reg. Hosp., Jalapa, Mex..
Corporals.			
William C. Cook.....	"	.... "	Died Dec. 2, '47, at Reg. Hosp., Jalapa, Mex..
Jonathan Reilley....	"	.... "	" Sept. 14, '47, at Gen. Hosp., New Orleans
Privates.			
Bodine, John			Died Nov. 13, '47, at Gen. Hosp., New Orleans
Ballard, Mathew ...			" Nov. 22, '47, " " V. Cruz ......
Bruce, Hiram.......			" May 17, '47, at Puebla, Mex..
Cummings, William.			" Dec. 18, '47, at Reg. Hosp., Jalapa, Mex..
Crooms, John			" Feb. 1, '48, " " "
Carter, Dillard B...			" Jan. 15, '48, " " "
Clarke, William			" Dec. 14, '47, " " "
Dawson, Isaac			" Jan. 2, '48, " " "
Dorrell, Joseph.....			" Sept. 10, '47, at Gen. Hosp., V. Cruz.....
Dornell, Geo. W.....			" Aug. 17, '47, at Reg. Hosp., Jalapa .....
Griffith, James F...			" Dec. 16, '47, " " "
Goodrich, Robert ...			" Aug. 28, '47, at Gen. Hosp., New Orleans.
Gilbert, John			" May 4, '48, " " Pueblo ......
Jenkins, John A.....			" Sept. 17, '47 " " V. Cruz.....
Knox, William......			" April 21, '48, at Puebla, Mex...........
Keller, John			" Jan. 11, '48, at Gen. Hosp., Jalapa.......
Inglett, John			" Dec. 16, '47, " " "
Leonard, Hiram			" Dec. 28, '47, " " "
Long, Thomas M....			" Nov. 24, '47, " " V. Cruz.......
Lawson, Henry.....			" Dec. 1, '47, " " New Orleans..
Light, Reuben......			" Dec. 2, '47, " " Jalapa.......
Marlow, Zedick.....			" Dec. 1, '47, " " "
Maynor, William R.	Alton, Ill.....	June 3	" June 30, '48, at Carrollton, La...........
McConnell, James...	"	.... "	" Sept. 12, '47, at Camp Bergara, Mex.....
Moss, William N ...	"	.... "	" Aug. 16, '47, at Alton, Ill...............
McLaughlin, John...	"	.... "	" April 2, '48, at Gen. Hosp., Puebla ....
Piper, Henry	"	.... "	" Dec. 5, '47, at Reg. Hosp., Jalapa.......
Pierce, William.....	"	.... "	" Oct. 12, '47, at Gen. Hosp., V. Cruz......
Redman, John	"	.... "	" Dec. 29, '47, at Reg. Hosp., Jalapa.......
Reynolds, William R.	"	.... "	" Mar. 5, '48, " " "
Stewart, William....	"	.... "	" Jan. 23, '48, " " "
Stull, John H.......	"	.... "	" Sept. 5, '47, at Camp Bergara ....
Taylor, Wright.....	"	.... "	" May 6, '48, at New Orleans.............
Worley, William G..	"	.... "	" Sept. 10, '47, at Gen. Hosp., V. Cruz.....
Weston, Charles	Bergara, Mex.	Aug. '47	" Sept. 2, '47, at Camp Bergara ....
White, Thomas A...	Alton, Ill.....	June 3	" Feb. 1, '48, at Reg. Hosp., Jalapa........
Wallace, Daniel	"	.... "	" Feb. 15, '48, " " "

Discharged:

Sergeant.		1847.	
Jeremiah Morgan...	Alton, Ill.....	June 3	Disch. by certificate of disability Feb. 6, 1848..
Privates.			
Baker, William	"	.... "	Disch. by certificate of disability Sept. 27, '47.
Brooks, William C...	Bergara, Mex.	Aug. 31	" " " Feb. 6, '48..
Brown, Clinton......	Alton, Ill.....	June 3	" " " Oct. 10, '47..
Ballard, Robert......	"	.... "	Sent to N. Orleans to be disch. from Jalapa..
Forward, Oliver	"	.... "	Disch. by certificate of disability Feb. 1, '48..
Green, George W....	"	.... "	" " " Mar. 27, '48.
Hovey, Simeon A ...	"	.... "	" " " Dec. 2, '47..
Leach, Arthur	"	.... "	" " " Jan. 12, '48.
Osborn, Robert......	"	.... "	Sent to N. Orleans to be disch. at Jalapa, Mex.
Vickory, John	"	.... "	Disch. by certificate of disability Jan. 12, '48.

Deserted:

		1847.	
Porter, Charles......	Alton, Ill.....	June 3	Deserted July 6, 1847, at Alton, Ill.............

This company was discharged at Alton, Ill., on July 21, 1848.

COMPANY "B."

Name and Rank.	Place of Enlistment.	Enrolled	Remarks.
Captain.		1847.	
Calmes L. Wright	Alton, Ill.	June 21	
First Lieutenant.			
Bushrod B. Howard.	"	"	
Second Lieutenants.			
James H. Sampson	"	"	Appointed Adjutant 2d Ill. Vol., 1848.
Wm. A. Poillon	"	"	
Sergeants.			
James McFadden	"	"	
George Nolan	"	"	
Wm. H. Noble	"	"	
Jackson Parks	"	"	
Corporals.			
Thomas Sheridan	"	"	
Samuel Woodhouse	"	"	
Franklin Ward	"	"	Private to March 22, 1848, then Corporal
Thomes R. Waring	"	"	" May 28, " "
Fifer.			
Cornelius Mellinger	"	"	Private to May 1, 1848, then Fifer
Drummer.			
Oliver P. Welker	"	"	Private to Aug. 1, 1847, then Drummer
Privates.			
Adams, John	"	"	
Alexander, Samuel	"	"	
Author, Robert	"	"	
Baggs, John T	"	"	
Beckwith, Ezra	"	"	
Casey, Patrick	"	"	
Casey, Francis	"	"	
Carnahan, Thomas	"	"	
Carr, Wm. L	"	"	
Childs, Charles	"	"	
Connor, John	"	"	
Cobb, Amasa	"	"	
Depue, Simon	"	"	
Ely, Morris M	"	"	
Flanagan, Warwick	"	"	
Fisher, Thomas	"	"	
Funston, John	"	"	Left sick in Hospital at Vera Cruz, Feb. 6, '48.
Fitzgerald, John	"	"	
Hall, John	"	"	
Higby, Wilder	"	"	
Herrell, James	"	"	
Hare, Henry	"	"	
Jackson, Andrew	"	"	
Kupser, John	"	"	
Kuykendall, Benj	"	"	
Long, James	"	"	Left sick in Hospital at Vera Cruz, Feb. 6, '48.
Mathews, Philip	"	"	
Miller, Christopher	"	"	
McKinney, Robert C.	"	June 30	
McKinney, John	"	June 21	Left sick in Hospital at Vera Cruz, Feb. 6, '48.
McGinnis, Keran	"	"	
McMillan, John	"	"	
Morris, Bluford S	"	"	
Noble, Albert L	"	"	
O'Leary, James	"	"	
Posey, David C	"	"	
Prickett, James R	"	"	
Price, Thomas	"	"	Absent, sick, from Feb. 11, 1848.
Robt, Orwin T	"	"	
Rogers, Coleman F	"	"	
Robertson, James	"	"	
Rossiter, Wm. H	"	"	[Mounted Men, Feb. 1, 1848.
Sample, Thomas	Tampico, Mex	July 8	Joined by transfer from Capt. West's Co.
Sasfield, John	Puebla, Mex.	April, '48	Joined by enlist. at Puebla, Mex., April 18, '48.

MEXICAN WAR.

Name and Rank.	Place of Enlistment.	Enrolled	Remarks.
		1847.	
Shaw, Robert I......	Alton, Ill....	June 21	
Shattuck, Munroe...	"	"	
Simms, Jeremiah....	"	"	
Sisler, John..........	"	"	Absent, sick, from Aug. 23, 1847
Spires, Fergus M....	"	"	
Sumner, Alfred......	"	"	
Taylor, James E.....	"	"	
Tate, Samuel........	"	"	Drummer to Aug. 1, 1847, then private
Thomas, John W....	"	"	
Tong, Theodore F...	"	"	
Wade, James A......	"	"	
Wolfinger, Thomas..	"	"	
Zuller, John	"	Mch., '48	Joined by enlist. at Puebla, Mex., Mch. 1, '48.

Died:

		1847.	
Corporals.			
McAllister, John C..	Alton, Ill....	June 21	Died at Tampico, Mex., Sept. 27, 1847
Rhodes, Jacob.......	"	"	" Jalapa, " May 28, 1848
Privates.			
Alvoid, Wm. B......	"	"	Died at Tampico, Mex., Dec. 20, 1847
Barnett, George W..	"	"	" New Orleans, La., June 7, 1848
Benhardt, John J....	"	"	" Tampico, Mex., Dec. 2, 1847
Crankshaw, Peter J.	"	"	" on the Gulf of Mexico, June 25, 1848
Donley, Wm.........	"	"	" at Jalapa, Mex., May 29, 1848
Enos, Horace B.....	"	"	" Tampico, Mex., Dec. 23, 1847
Ellis, Francis M.....	"	"	" " Jan. 23, 1848
Faherty, Patrick	"	"	" " Nov. 28, 1847
Hawkins, Stephen ..	"	"	" " Sept. 24, 1847
High, David.........	"	"	Vera Cruz, Mex., April 2, 1848
Leonard, Wm.......	"	"	Puebla, Mex., Mch. 18, '48; poisoned.
Loyd, John	"	"	Tampico, Mex., Oct. 3, 1847
McGuire, George....	"	"	" " " 25, "
Ramsey, Andrew....	"	"	Puebla, " May 16, 1848
Sumner, Jerome B..	"	"	Tampico. " Oct. 24, 1847
Stobaugh, Isaac.....	"	"	" " Nov. 6, "

Discharged:

		1847.	
Corporal.			
John S. Miller........	Alton, Ill....	June 21	Discharged Mch. 22, 1848; disability
Privates.			
John Applebury.....	"	"	Discharged Mch. 3, 1848; disability
Keyes, Joseph L....	"	"	" Mch. 19, " "
McGregor, Archibald	"	"	" Jan. 19, " "
Murphy, James......	"	"	" Mch. 22, " "
Olmstead, John B...	"	"	" Jan. 19, " "

Transferred:

		1847.	
Fifer.			
Ramsey, Harrison ..	Alton, Ill....	June 21	Trans. to Staff 2d Regt. as principal Musician, Aug. 10, 1847.
Privates.			
Kelley, Wm.........	"	"	Trans. to Capt. West's Co., Feb. 1, 1848
Quinche, Fred. L....	"	"	Appointed Hosp. Steward March 23, 1848

This company was mustered out July 20, 1848.

SECOND REGIMENT.

Company "C."

Name and Rank.	Place of Enlistment.	Enrolled	Remarks.
Captain.		1847.	
Harvey Lee	Alton, Ill	July 5	
First Lieutenant.			
Henry W. Good	"	"	
Second Lieutenants.			
William J. Hankins	"	"	
Jesse W. Curlee	"	"	Sergeant to April 1. 1848; then elected 2d Lt.
Richard M. Hankins	"	"	Died at Puebla, Mex., March 28, 1848.
Sergeants.			
Samuel Fortney	"	"	Sergt. to April 1, 1848; then app'nted 1st Sergt
Thos J. Gillenwaters	"	"	Private to Mar. 2, '48; then Corp'l; then Sergt.
Hugh D. Kelly	"	"	" Nov. 1, '47; Corp. to Mar. 2, '48; Sergt
Levi McBride	"	"	" May 2, 1848; then appointed Serg'nt
Corporals.			
James L. Ledbetter	"	"	Private to Feb. 16, 1848; then appointed Corp'l
William Owens	"	"	
Jonathan H. Tucker	"	"	Private to May 28, 1848; then appointed Corp'l
Camm McBride	"	"	
Privates.			
Ashley, William	"	"	
Bryant, William	"	"	
Brown, William	"	"	
Carr, Charles	"	"	
Coy, Stephen	"	"	
Clark, Tillman	"	"	
Candle, John	"	"	
Doleplain, John	"	"	
Davis, William F	"	"	
Dickman, George H	"	"	Reduced from Sergeant May 28, 1848
Davidson, William H	"	"	
Dorman, Benjamin	"	"	
Dunham, Henry	"	"	Left sick in Gen. Hosp., Vera Cruz, Feb. 6, '48
Elliott, John, Jr	"	"	
Elder, Duma B	"	"	
Elam, William D	"	"	
Funk, Jeremiah R	"	"	
Ginger, John P	"	"	
Gerrick, Christian	"	"	
Gillenwaters, Jas. S	"	"	
Gillespie, Matthew	"	"	
Green, Patrick	"	"	
Gerbot, Frederick	"	"	
Hynkins, Samuel F	"	"	
Harris, Joseph	"	"	
Lane, Joseph	"	"	Left sick in hospital, Vera Cruz, Feb. 6, 1848
Ledbetter, H'nders'n	"	"	
Lecrone, Mathias	"	"	
Loy, James B	"	"	
Loy, George W	"	"	Corporal to Sept. 1, 1847; then resigned
Lee, Andrew J	"	"	
Ludwick, Henry	"	"	
Martin, James	Shelbyv'le, Ill	Jan., '48	
Maxfield, Hiram	Alton, Ill	July, '47	Sergeant to Feb. 16, 1848; then resigned
Miller, Hampton	"	"	Transferred to ranks from Musician
Mills, Jesse A	"	"	
McConkey, George	"	"	
Martin, Eli	"	"	
Perkins, David	"	"	
Parks, William	"	"	
Porter, James	"	"	
Radcliff, Simon	"	"	Corporal to Oct. 31; then reduced
Redfield, Benjamin	"	"	
Rafferty, James	"	"	
Rhodes, Henry	"	"	
Shindle, George S	"	"	
Sears, George	"	"	
Shaw, Andrew	"	"	
Stolle, Ewing	"	"	

MEXICAN WAR.

Name and Rank.	Place of Enlistment.	Enrolled		Remarks.
Smith, Thomas	Shelbyv'le, Ill	Jan.,	'48	
Tucker, James	Alton, Ill	July,	'47	
Thomps, Thomas H.	"	....	"	Priv. to Apr. 1, '48; then Sergt.; reduced May 28
Victor, Davis	"	....	"	
Wicke, Cyrus F.	"	....	"	Absent without leave; supposed in Q.M. Dep.
Wright, William	"	....	"	

Died:

		1847.		
Sergeant. Isaac M. Willis	Alton, Ill	July	5	Died in Hosp., Puebla, Mex., March 1, 1848
Corporal. Joseph C. Sawyer	"	....	"	Died in Hosp., Tampico, Mex., Dec. 8, 1848
Privates.				
Ames, James	"	....	"	Died in Hosp., Tampico, Mex., Sept. 25, 1847
Browning, James M.	"	....	"	" Puebla, " Mar. 12, 1848
Brazil, Robert	"	....	"	" Tampico, " Nov. 15, 1847
Buradge, John	"	....	"	" " " Oct. 28, 1847
Crawford, Martin	"	....	"	" " " Sept. 26, 1847
Clark, Francis A.	"	....	"	" " " Oct. 29, 1847
Davis, Samuel I.	"	....	"	" Puebla, " April 8, 1848
Dougherty, Alex. B.	Shelbyv'le, Ill	Jan.,	'48	Died at sea (Gulf of Mexico), June 28, 1848
Dutton, Abram H.	"	Feb.,	'48	" at Alton, Ill., July 17, 1848
Frankum, William	Alton, Ill	July,	'47	Died in Hosp., Puebla, Mex., Mar. 31, 1848
Laremore, William	"	....	"	" Tampico, " Sept. 25, 1847
Moore, Doris	"	....	"	" " " Oct. 26, "
McMullin, William	"	....	"	" " " Dec. 25, "
Morgan, James	"	....	"	" " " Oct. 29, "
Mills, Jesse	"	....	"	Died at Alton, July 9, 1847
Parks, Samuel A.	"	....	"	Died in Hosp., Puebla, Mex., April 30, 1848
Parks, Andrew C.	"	....	"	" " " May 26, 1848
Pomroy, John	"	....	"	" Tampico, " Oct. 24, 1847
Tanner, Andrew	Shelbyv'le, Ill	Dec.	29	" Jalapa, Mex., June 9, 1848

Discharged:

		1847.		
Privates.				
Baker, John I.	Ewington, Ill.	May	28	Disch., Surg. certif., at Tampico, M., Jan. 27, '48
Collier, James T.	Alton, Ill	July	5	" " " "
Cronie, Emanuel	"	....	"	" " " Sept. 28, '47
Edwards, John	"	....	"	" " " "
Edwards, Adam	"	....	"	" " " "
Greer, James T.	"	....	"	" " " "
Lewis, James	"	....	"	" " " Jan. 27, '48
Philips, Henry	"	....	"	" " " Sept. 28, '47
Reynolds, Dosin T.	"	....	"	" " " "

This company was discharged at Alton, Ill., July 20, 1848.

SECOND REGIMENT. 251

Company "D."

Name and Rank.	Place of Enlistment.	Enrolled	Remarks.
		1847.	
Captains.			
John Bristow	Alton, Ill	June 21	Resigned, to take effect March 11, '48.
Henry S. Fitch	"	"	Elected from 1st Lieut. to March 11, '48.
First Lieutenant.			
John H. Hart	"	"	Elected from 2d Lieut. March 11, '48.
Second Lieutenants.			
John Wyatt	"	"	Resigned, taking effect Feb. 5, '48.
Hampton Hunter	"	"	Elected from the ranks, Feb. 5, '48.
Lorenzo E. Carter	"	"	Elected from 4th Sergt., March 11, *vice* Hart, promoted.
Sergeants.			
Ashley L. Sleetman	"	"	Appointed from 3d Sergt., June 18, '48.
Henry P. Garrison	"	"	Appointed from the ranks, Feb. 17, '48.
William Bamber	"	"	Appointed from the ranks, June 18, '48.
Corporals.			
James Bell	"	"	
Samuel Thompson	"	"	Appointed from the ranks, June 13, '48.
Nathaniel Walker	"	"	
Cyrus Little	"	"	Appointed from the ranks, June 13, '48.
Drummer.			
Edward B. Walker	"	July 6	
Fifer.			
Clinton A. Wood	"	June 21	
Privates.			
Bell, John	"	June 2	
Barrett, Jonathan	"	July 6	Appointed Hospital Steward, March 14, '48.
Barr, James	"	June 21	
Brown, Jehu	"		
Carroll, Isaiah	"		
Crawford, Lewis	"		
Conden, Jacob F	"	July 6	
Davis, John	"	June 21	
Flatt, Dennis	"		
Frank, Abraham F	"		
Flagg, William	"	July 6	
Grizzle, James	"	June 21	Reduced from 4th Corporal, June 13, '48.
Gale, William H	"		
Hankins, Andrew J	"		
Harrington, William	"		Reduced from 2d Corporal, June 13, '48.
Harrington, Thomas	"		
Harrow, Robert	"		
Miller, Milton	"		
Miller, Joseph A	"		
McClure, William	"	June 28	
McFarland, James	"	Aug. 6	
Nelson, John	"	June 21	
Richards, Thomas	"	July 6	
Roberts, Henry H	"	June 21	
Stahls, John	"		
Scott, Oscar	"		
Scott, Robert B	"		
Simmons, Edward	"		
Sutton, Joseph	"		
Silkwood, Obediah	"		
Smith, James	"		
Slaton, Jesse	"	July 6	
Thompson, Peter	"	June 21	
Taylor, William	"		
Wheeler, Fielding	"		
Wilder, Elias	"		

Died :

		1847.	
Sergeants.			
John B. King	Alton, Ill	June 21	Died at Cerro Gordo, Mex., June 17, '48.
George Kain	"	"	Alton, Ill., July 17, '48.

MEXICAN WAR.

Name and Rank.	Place of Enlistment.	Enrolled		Remarks.
Privates.		1847.		
Byram, Ephriam....	Alton, Ill.....	June	21	Died on boat *en route* to Mexico, Aug. 17, '47.
Brownlee, David....	"	"	"	at Jalapa, Mex., Jan. 3, '48.
Bader, Frederick....	"	"	"	April 7, '48.
Cannon, Andrew....	"	"	"	Dec. 29, '47.
Carter, Joseph......	"	"	"	Vera Cruz, Mex., Dec. 23, '47.
Crawford, James....	"	"	"	Jalapa, Mex., April 12, '48.
Denny, Bolivar......	"	"	"	Dec. 8, '47
Dixon, Charles......	"	"	"	Vera Cruz, Mex., Jan. 25, '48.
Day, Henry..........	"	"	"	Napoluca, Mex., June 4, '48.
Edwards, William...	"	"	"	Alton, Ill., July 16, '48.
Edwards, Henry L..	"	"	"	Jalapa, Mex., Feb. 5, '48.
Griffith, Daniel.....	"	"	"	Nov. 28, '47.
Hammond, James...	"	"	"	Perote, Mex., April 23, '48.
Henry, Patrick......	"	"	"	En Cerro, Mex., June 12, '48.
Johnson, John D....	"	"	"	Jalapa, Mex., Jan. 2, '48.
Kasinger, William..	"	"	"	San Juan, Mex., Oct. 28, '47.
Kirgan, Arthur......	"	"	"	Jalapa, Mex., Jan. 18, '48.
Lee, Michael........	"	"	"	Nov. 28, '47
Phillips, Samuel....	"	"	"	Vera Cruz, Mex., Dec. 28, '47.
Shinautt, Stephen...	"	"	"	Jalapa, Mex., Dec. 20, '47.
Thompson, Thomas.	"	Aug.	8	Vera Cruz, Mex., Feb. 7, '48.
Wisely, James.......	"	June	25	Oct. 23, '47.

Discharged:

Privates.		1847.		
Brown, Charles......	Alton, Ill.....	June	21	Disch. at N. Orleans, Aug. 23, '47; disability..
Barton, Andrew J...	"	"	"	Jalapa, Mex., Jan. 8, '48 "
Bryant, Elijah.......	"	"	"	Feb. 6, '48 "
Bowen, Asa..........	"	"	"	N. Orleans, date unk'n "
Bowen, David.......	"	"	"	" "
Guthrie, Daniel.....	"	"	"		
Colelonzhh, Joseph.	"	"	"	Jalapa, Mex., Jan. 18. '48 "
Harvill, Lewis.......	"	"	"	Feb. 21, '48 "
Hunnicent, John....	"	"	"	N. Orleans, date unkn'n "
Johnson, Moses.....	"	"	"	" " "
Johnson, Andrew...	"	"	"	" " "
Logan, John F......	"	"	"	" " "
McIlvaine, William.	"	"	"	" " "
Powell, Young......	"	"	"	" " "
Quinten, Samuel K..	"	"	"	Jalapa, Mex., Jan. 18, '48 "
Rountree, John D...	"	"	"	" " "
Sisk, William B.....	"	"	"	" " "

Transferred:

Second Sergeant.		1847.		
House, Erasmus D..	Alton, Ill.....	July	6	Appointed Sergt.-Major, Feb. 11, '48...........

Deserted:

Privates.		1847.		
Conden, Christian...	Alton, Ill.....	July	6	Deserted at Cape Girardeau, Mo., Aug. 16, '47.
Gibson, William S...	"	"	"	Alton, Ill., Aug. 7, '47.............
Stevens, John.......	"	"	"	" "

This company was discharged at Alton, Ill., July 20, 1848.

SECOND REGIMENT. 253

Company "E."

Name and Rank.	Place of Enlistment.	Enrolled	Remarks.
Captain.		1847.	
William Shepard....	Belvidere, Ill.	June 4	
First Lieutenants.			
Thomas Oates......	"	"	Died at San Juan, Mexico, Oct. 2, 1847..........
Lyman Andrews....	"	"	Elect'd (from 2d Lt.) Oct., '47; resig'd Mar. 11, '48
Thomas D. Timoney.	"	"	App'd Dec. 24, '47; elec'd Mar., '47; died Apr. '48.
Sylv'us M. Geotchius	"	"	Sergt. Mar. 22, '48; elec'd 1st Lt. Apr. 25, '48
Second Lieutenants.			
William Haywood...	"	"	Supp'd resig'd; left at Jalapa, sick, Mar. 14, '48
Elisha Lewis.........	"	"	
Sergeants.			
John Pook..........	"	"	Appointed from Corporal March 12, 1848......
John Joel...........	"	"	" " " private February 7, 1848......
Moses Doyle........	"	"	" " " April 30, 1848........
Corporals.			
Leroy Benson	"	"	Appointed from private December, 1848......
William Bush.......	"	"	" " " April 30, 1848......
George S. Whitman.	"	"	" " "
John Lower.........	"	"	
Privates.			
Bowman, Ira	"	"	
Burton, Burwell....	"	"	
Cox, Robert L......	"	"	
Dewey, George S....	St. Charles, Ill	Mar., '48	
Dennis, George.....	Belvidere, Ill.	June, '47	
Durkin, Frederick...	"	"	
Harrison, John C....	"	"	
Hanlon, John.......	"	"	
Irish, John F.......	"	"	
Judy, Andrew......	"	July '47	
Jones, Thomas C....	Chicago, Ill..	April, '48	
Kellogg, Lockwood.	"	Feb., '48	
Kingsley, DeWitt C.	Belvidere, Ill.	June, '47	
Keenan, John.......	"	"	
Kasters, Theodore..	"	"	
Lynch, William.....	"	"	
Miller, Reuben.....	"	"	
Mier, John.........	"	"	
Murphy, Peter......	"	"	
Mullery, John......	"	"	
Moore, William.....	"	"	
Rose, William L....	"	"	
Pearsall, Philetus...	"	"	
Smith, Frank.......	Chicago, Ill..	Feb., '48	
Shearer, Alvin.....	Belvidere, Ill.	June, '47	
Shepard, David N...	"	"	
Schwatkin, John....	"	"	
Thomas, John P.....	"	"	
Worrell, John.......	Chicago, Ill..	Feb., '47	

Died:

		1847.	
Sergeants.			
Matthew Smith......	Belvidere, Ill.	June 4	Died at Jalapa, Mex., Dec. 21, 1847...........
Nathan Taylor.......	"	"	" Feb. 6, 1848............
Corporals.			
Oliver B. Whitmore.	"	"	Died at National Bridge Nov. 5, 1847..........
Alexander Rice......	"	"	" Jalapa, Mex., Dec. 29, 1847..........
Henry A. Granger...	"	"	" Jan. 19, 1848............
Musicians.			
Roman P. Holcomb.	"	"	Died at Jalapa, Mex., Dec. 21, 1847 ....
Frederick Van Dyke.	"	July 11	" Dec. 12, 1847............

MEXICAN WAR.

Name and Rank.	Residence.	Enrolled	Remarks.
Privates.		1847.	
Astrop, John	Belvidere, Ill.	June 4	Died at Jalapa. Mex., Jan. 25, 1848
Allen, Conolly S	"	"	" " Dec. 29, 1847
Allen, Simon	"	"	" " Feb. 14, 1848
Applehoff, Adolphus	"	"	" " Nov. 27, 1847
Beecham, George	"	"	" " Dec. 26, 1847
Brown, Charles	Chicago, Ill.	Feb., '48	" New Orleans, La., July 4, 1848
Bronan, Michael	Belvidere, Ill.	June, '47	" Puebla, Mex., May 5, 1848
Cunniman, Freder'k.	"	"	" " May 28, 1848
Doyle, Daniel	"	"	" Jalapa, Mex., Jan. 9, 1848
Fuller, James E	"	"	" Vera Cruz, Mex., Dec. 4, 1847
Harran, John	"	"	" " Nov. 11, 1847
Hawes, Solomon	"	"	" Jalapa, Mex., Dec. 13, 1847
Hyde, William	"	"	" Vera Cruz, Mex., Nov. 15, 1847
Kraaganger, Wm	Alton, Ill.	Aug., '47	" Puebla, May 19, '48; murd'd by Mexic's
Kodling, William K.	Belvidere, Ill.	June, '47	" Vera Crux, Mex., Nov. 22, 1847
Johnson, Thomas	"	"	" Puebla, Mex., April 15, 1848
Lewis, James H	"	"	" Jalapa, Mex., Jan. 7, 1848
Manson, John M	"	"	" New Orleans, La., Nov. 8, 1847
Mills, John J	"	"	" Jalapa, Mex., Dec. 17, 1847
Miller, Samuel H	"	"	" " Dec. 23, 1847
Myers, Abraham	"	"	" " Dec. 25, 1847
Oswald, William H.	"	"	" Puebla, Mex., May 19, 1848
Phelps, Alanson H.	"	"	" Jalapa, Mex., Jan. 13, 1848
Phelps, Elisha	Alton, Ill.	Aug., '47	" Puebla, Mex., May 10, 1848
Rollins, Charles	Belvidere, Ill.	June, '47	" National Bridge, Mex., Nov. 10, 1847
Robinson, George	Chicago, Ill.	Mar., '48	" St. Louis, Mo., July 14, 1848; drowned
Reams, John	Belvidere, Ill.	June, '47	" Jalapa, Mex., Nov. 10, 1847
Sullivan, David E	"	"	" " Dec. 22, 1847
Schwatkin, Gerard H	"	"	\. " Jan. 3, 1848
Swift, Warren	"	"	" " Dec. 25, 1847
Sponable, William	"	"	" " Dec. 30, 1847
Ward, John C	"	"	" " Dec. 12, 1847
Whitback, Jasper	"	"	" " May 19, 1848
Young, Joseph A	"	July, '47	" Vera Cruz. Mex., Oct. 29, 1847

Deserted:

		1847.	
Burlingame, Rhodes	Belvidere	June 4	Deserted at New Orleans Aug. 24, 1847
Dunsing, Henry	"	"	
Koter, Ditherik	"	July 5	" " Aug. 21, 1847
Sutton, Ebbert	"	June 4	" " Jan. 15, 1848

Discharged:

Sergeants.		1847.	
James L. Kennedy	Belvidere, Ill.	June 4	Disch. at New Orleans, La., June, 1848
Matthew McWorter	"	"	" Vera Cruz, Mex., Jan. 3, 1848
Privates.			
Duvall, Augustus	"	"	Left at V. Cruz Hosp. Sept., '47; supp'd disch.
Giese, Henry	"	"	Disch. at Jalapa, Mex., Jan. 11, 1848
Gilmore, James W.	"	"	" "
Loop, Murray	"	"	" " Dec. 19, 1847
Loop, Edgar S	"	"	" New Orleans, La., June, 1848
Russell, Francis A	"	"	" Jalapa, Mex., Feb. 21, 1848
Rogers, John	"	"	" " Jan. 11, 1848
Sherwood, Jackson A	"	"	" New Orleans, La., June, 1848
Towner, Hiram G	"	June 27	"
Ward, Alfred	"	June 4	" " March 15, 1848
Wheeler, John L	"	"	" Jalapa Mex., Jan. 11, 1848
Wyde, George	"	July 7	" New Orleans, La., June, 1847

Missing:

		1847.	
John Coleman	Belvidere	June 4	Lost on march from Puebla to Vera Cruz June, '48; supposed captured.

This company was discharged on July 24, 1848, at Alton, Illinois.

SECOND REGIMENT. 255

Company "F."

Name and Rank.	Place of Enlistment.	Enrolled	Remarks.
Captains.		1847.	
James Collins	Galena, Ill.	June 22	Elected Col. of regiment, Aug. 3, 1847
David C. Berry	"	....	Elected Capt. (from 1st Lieut.) Aug. 3, 1847
First Lieutenant.			[died at San Juan, Mex, Sept. 2, 1847.
John Boaney	"	....	Elected 1st Lieut. (from 2d Lieut.) Aug. 3, 1847;
Frank Wheeler	"	....	" Sept. 25, '47.
Second Lieutenants.			[resigned, April 23, 1848.
Spencer H. Hill	"	....	Elected 2d Lieut. (from priv.) *vice* Van Hook.
Thos. J. Andrews	"	....	" " " Aug. 3, 1847
Lorenzo D. VanHook	"	....	" " " Sergt., Sept. 25, 1847; resigned April 23, 1848.
Sergeants.			
John Alexander	"	....	
Abraham Leir	"	....	Appointed from Corporal, Oct. 5, 1847
Henry Conroy	"	....	" " private, Dec. 28, 1847
Thos. A. Sanders	"	....	
Corporals.			
Festus Gideon	"	....	
John A. Mullen	"	....	
John F. A. Eckard	"	....	
Ira Stevens	"	....	
Musicians.			
Miller Blair	"	....	
Samuel W. Earnest	"	....	
Privates.			
Bauder, Andrew	Chicago, Ill.	Feb., '48	
Boss, James R	"	....	
Berry, Henry	Galena, Ill.	June, '47	
Barker, George	"	....	
Butterfield, Chas. P.	"	....	
Bradley, Wm. H	"	....	
Boswell, Geo. W	"	....	
Bixler, Noah W	"	....	
Currant, Alpheus	"	....	
Drury, John	"	....	
Dodson, James B	"	....	
Gregory, William	"	....	
Henry, Theodore	"	....	
Hannon, Patrick	"	....	
Hopkins, Vernon J.	Chicago, Ill.	Feb., '48	
Holcomb, Oscar M.	Aurora, Ill.	"	
Hedges, William A	Chicago, Ill.	"	
Johnson, James M	"	....	
Jones, Washington	Galena, Ill.	June, '47	
Lasure, John B	"	....	
Leakley, Thomas	"	....	Left sick at Jalapa; supposed discharged
McGuire, Henry	Chicago, Ill.	Feb., '48	
McLane, Thomas A.	Galena, Ill.	June, '47	Left sick at Jalapa; supposed discharged
Melton, James	"	....	
Mackay, Andrew	Chicago, Ill.	Feb., '48	
May, John	Galena, Ill.	June, '47	
Mitchell, John	"	....	
Nelson, James A	Chicago, Ill	Feb., '48	
Price, David	Galena, Ill.	July, '47	
Pipkins, Jesse	"	....	
Procter, James	"	....	
Reynolds, John	Chicago, Ill.	Feb., '48	
Robinson, James	Galena, Ill.	June, '47	
Reese, Evan	"	....	
Simpson, William D.	"	....	
Smith, Martin	"	....	
Smith, Terrence	"	....	
Shulder, Henry	"	....	

Died:

Name and Rank.	Place of Enlistment.	Enrolled	Remarks.
Sergeants.		1847.	
J. M. Lichtenberger	Galena, Ill.	June 22	Died at Alton, Ill., Aug., 1847.
Henry Whysall	"	"	" San Juan, Mex., Oct. 2, 1847.
Corporal.			
James M. Norris	"	"	Died at Jalapa, Mex., Dec. 24, 1847.
Privates.			
Biggs, Henry	"	"	Died at Jalapa, Mex., June 12, 1848.
Brower, John T.	"	"	" New Orleans, La., June, 1848.
Brundige, Hiram	Alton, Ill.	Aug. 1	" Vera Cruz, Mex., Jan. 3, 1848.
Davis, Lewis	Galena, Ill.	June 22	" " Oct. 25, 1847.
Forbes, William	"	"	" Jalapa, Mex., March 23, 1848.
Gentry, Thomas H.	"	"	" New Orleans, La., Nov. 19, 1847.
Gregory, Joel	"	"	" Perote, Mex., 1848.
Hull, Joseph	"	"	" Jalapa, Mex., Dec. 30, 1847
Helmick, Gerand	"	"	" Vera Cruz, Mex., Oct. 24, 1847.
Henly, William	"	"	Died on Gulf of Mexico June 27, 1848.
Jasper, Francis	"	"	Died at Vera Cruz Sept. 30, 1847.
Long, John	"	"	" Jalapa, Mex., Dec. 16, 1847.
Pogue, William R.	"	"	" " " 8, 1847.
Robinson, Henry W.	"	"	" " " 1, 1847.
Robinson, Henry	"	"	" " " 29, 1847.
Russell, Stephen	"	"	" " March 30, 1848.
Randall, Harrison P.	"	"	" New Orleans, La., Nov. 11, 1847.
Seaman, Peter F.	"	"	" Vera Cruz, Mex., Oct. 5, 1847.
Shaw, James	"	"	" Jalapa, Mex., 1848.
Simpson, Robt. K.	"	"	" Puebla, " May 13, 1848.
Swayne, John W.	"	"	" Perote, " April 17, 1848.
Shultz, William	"	"	" Jalapa, " Dec. 19, 1847.
Sanders, David	"	"	" Alton, Ill., July 29, 1847
Stoner, Jacob	"	"	" Jalapa, Mex., Feb. 24, 1848.
Simpson, Thomas	"	"	" New Orleans, La., Dec. 24, 1847.
Tindall, George S.	"	"	" Jalapa, Mex., Dec. 18, 1847.
Tindall, John	"	"	" " Nov. 30, 1847.
Truett, Samuel	Alton, Ill.	Aug. 1	" " Dec. 17, 1847.

Deserted:

Name and Rank.	Place of Enlistment.	Enrolled	Remarks.
		1847.	
Collins, John	Galena, Ill.	June 22	Deserted at Alton, Ill., July 10, 1847.
Otis, Ralph	"	"	" " " "
Wood, John W.	"	"	" " " "

Discharged:

Name and Rank.	Place of Enlistment.	Enrolled	Remarks.
Privates.		1847.	
Brown, Samuel	Galena, Ill.	June 22	Disch. at New Orleans, June, '47; disability.
Coleman, Paul E.	"	"	" Jalapa, Mex., Dec. 22, '47 "
Cottle, Orville	"	"	" Vera Cruz, Mex., Jan. 25, '48 "
Duffey, Hugh	"	"	" New Orleans, June, '48 "
Beauchard, Edw. D.	"	"	" Jalapa, Mex., Jan. 7, '48 "
Gibbons, John	"	"	" New Orleans, June, '48 "
Gloder, David	"	"	" " June 8, '48 "
Gaffney, Thomas	"	"	" Vera Cruz, Mex., Dec. 26, '47 "
Harcourt, Gustavus	"	"	" New Orleans, July 8, '48 "
James, Richard H.	"	"	" " June, '48 "
McQuay, John	"	"	" Vera Cruz, Mex., Jan. 15, '48 "
Stiles, Nathan	"	"	" Jalapa, Mex., Jan. 7, '48 "
Shultz, John G.	"	"	" " " "
Vaughn, John	"	"	" " " "
Wilson, Edward	"	"	" New Orleans.

Transferred:

Name and Rank.	Place of Enlistment.	Enrolled	Remarks.
Sergeant.		1847.	
Thomas G. Coffy	Galena, Ill.	June 22	Appointed Q. M. Sergeant Dec. 31, 1847.

SECOND REGIMENT.   257

Missing :

Name and Rank.	Place of Enlistment.	Enrolled	Remarks.
Corporal. Wm. H. Antis	Galena, Ill	1847. June 22	Supposed captured by guerillas Nov. 8, 1847.

This company was discharged at Alton, Illinois, July 20, 1848.

Company "G."

Name and Rank.	Place of Enlistment.	Enrolled	Remarks.
Captain. John M. Moore	Alton, Ill	1847. July 7	
First Lieutenant. Edward O'Melveney	"	"	
Second Lieutenants. Wm. C. Starkey	"	"	
Austin James	"	"	
Thomas James	"	"	
Sergeants. James Close	"	"	
Lewis I. Eyman	"	"	
Solomon Varnum	"	"	
William Hillburn	"	"	
Corporals. Benjamin Atwell	"	"	Appointed from private May 1, 1848.
Peter Dowling	"	"	
John Hillburn	"	"	
Elijah Adams	"	"	
Musicians. Augustus Holley	"	"	
Conrad Kimell	"	"	
Privates. Abernathy, James	"	"	
Alred, Samuel	"	"	Left sick in Hospital at Vera Cruz: supposed to be discharged.
Axley, James R	Waterloo, Ill.	June 19	
Burk, Andrew	Alton, Ill.	July 7	
Brant, Jacob	"	"	
Butcher, Solomon G	"	"	
Clarke, Samuel C	"	"	
Clark, Millington	"	"	
Crowley, John	"	"	
Criley, Isaac	"	"	
Criley, Harman	"	"	
Chester, Samuel C	"	"	
Clover, James M	"	"	
Coleman, John	"	"	
Denton, Liberty	"	"	
Dolson, John	"	"	
Ellis, Wm	"	"	
Frazer, Maxwell	"	"	
Glass, Michael	"	"	
Hartley, Wm	"	"	
Hinton, John	"	"	
Husband, Wm	"	"	
Hyson, Henry	"	"	
Haber, George	"	"	
Henley, Washington	"	"	
Jackson, Andrew	"	"	
Land, Moses	"	"	
Lybarger, Henry	"	"	
Lasouse, James	"	"	
Lakin, John	"	"	
Lively, George	"	"	

—17

Name and Rank.	Place of Enlistment.	Enrolled	Remarks.
McCannah, John	Alton, Ill.	1847. July 7	
McCullock, Wm. G.	"	"	
Murphy, Patrick	"	"	
Mann, Joseph	"	"	
Oman, Martin	"	"	
Peterman, Philip	"	"	
Perry, John	"	"	
Rogers, Wm	"	"	
Reed, Wm	"	"	
Small, Wm	"	"	
Simpkins, Hawkins	"	"	
Swank, John	"	"	
Smith, Wm. J.	"	"	
Swear, Charles	"	"	
Willman, Jackson	"	"	
Wilcox, Abraham	"	"	
Wallace, Charles	Puebla, Mex.	April, '48	

Died:

Sergeant. Thomas Spencer	Waterloo, Ill.	1847. July 15	Died in Hospital at Tampico, Mex., Nov. 4, '47
Privates. Adams, Edward	"	"	Died in Hospital at Tampico, Mex., Nov., 1847
Blunt, Britain	"	"	" " " Nov. 4, '47
Bishop, George	"	"	" " " Nov. 10, '47
Blackstone, George	"	"	" Puebla, " Apr. 22, '48
Bishop, Evans	"	"	" Jalapa, date unknown
Burgett, Charles	"	"	" New Orleans, May 16, '48
Brugel, Nicholas	"	"	" Tampico, Mex., Sep. 25, '47
Burch, Gustavus	"	"	" Puebla, " April 24, '48
Dicken, John	"	"	" Tampico, " Jan. 10, '48
Foshee, Benjamin	"	"	" " " Jan. 11, '48
Holbrook, John A.	"	"	" Encerro, " June 9, '48
Locum, Wm	"	"	" Tampico, " Nov. 1, '47
Nixon, James N.	"	"	" " " Nov. 25, '47
Rydenbork, Pasmore	"	"	" Puebla, " May 1, '48
Tope, Andrew J.	"	"	" Tampico, " Sep. 21, '47
Taylor, Wm	"	"	" Jalapa, Dec. 22, '47; prom'd Aug. 3, '47
Welch, John G.	"	"	" in hospital at Tampico, Mex., Oct. 18, '47
Wetzel, Henry	"	"	" " " Feb. 11, '48

Discharged:

Musician. John H. Dixon	Waterloo, Ill.	1847. July 15	Disch. at Vera Cruz, Feb. 7, 1848; disability
Privates. Beabers, Thomas	"	"	Disch. at Tampico, Sept. 14, 1847; disability
Brewer, Henry	"	"	" " " 28, " "
Biggs, Asa	"	"	" " " 18, " "
Bennett, Franklin	"	"	" " Jan. 20, 1848; " "
Dickerman, Manas'h	"	"	" " " 20, " "
McKinley, Hugh F.	"	"	" " Sept. 14, 1847; " "
Morgan, Solomon	"	"	" " " 28, " "
Spots, Leonard	"	"	" " " 28, " "
Witmer, John	"	"	Vera Cruz, Feb. 7, 1848; " "

Transferred:

Sergeant. Wm. King	Waterloo, Ill.	1847. July 15	Transferred by order of Col. Gates
Private. Edward Tilley	"	"	Transferred by order of Col. Gates
Corporal. Joseph Wilcox	"	"	Discharged at Puebla, Mex., April 24, 1848

Deserted:

Name and Rank.	Place of Enlistment.	Enrolled	Remarks.
Privates.		1817.	
Heath, Daniel L	Waterloo, Ill.	July 15	Deserted at Alton, Aug. 13, 1847
Youngman, Jacob	"	" "	date unknown

This company was discharged at Alton, Ill., July 21, 1848.

Company "H."

Name and Rank.	Place of Enlistment.	Enrolled	Remarks.
Captain.		1817.	
James Burns	Nashville, Ill.	July 10	
First Lieutenant.			
Malachi Jenkins	"	"	Died on Gulf of Mexico June 26, 1848
Second Lieutenants.			
George W. Walker	"	"	Resigned at Jalapa, Mexico, Dec. 17, 1847
James R. Lynch	"	"	Died at Vera Cruz, Mex., Sept. 12, 1847
Isaac B. Jack	"	"	2d Sergt. Sept. 24,'47; prom. 2d Lt. Feb. 28,'48
Marquis L. Burns	"	"	Elected Sergt. at San Juan, Mex., Sept. 23,'47
Sergeants.			
David A. Patterson	"	"	Appointed from private Jan. 22, 1848
Robert St. Livingston	"	"	Appointed from private Feb. 21, 1848
Thomas W. Anders'n	"	"	
John Robinson	Jalapa, Mex.	Nov. 24	Appointed from private Jan. 17, 1848
Corporals.			
John C. Burns	Nashville, Ill.	July 10	
David W. Lowe	"	"	Appointed from private Jan. 1, 1848
Richard P. Carter	"	"	
James B. Logan	"	"	
Musician.			
Matthew M. Curtis	"	"	
Privates.			
Anderson, Richard	"	"	
Aldridge, Peter	"	"	
Cook, William	"	"	
Carter, Emanuel C	"	"	
Crabtree, James	"	"	
Drew, Newton	"	"	
Darter, Nicholas H	"	"	
Franklin, David	"	"	
Forbes, David	"	"	
Gillen, Owen	"	"	
Hawkins, Benjamin	"	"	
Hitt, John B	"	"	
Hitt, Thomas J	"	"	
Jones, Leander	"	"	
Jordan, Robert B	"	"	
Losson, John	"	"	
Livesay, Alfred	"	"	
Mills, Jesse	"	"	
Mathews, William	"	"	
Moore, Samuel	"	"	
Morgan, Reuben M	"	"	
Norris, Alfred	"	"	
Newcombe, Levi	"	"	
Pitchford, George W	"	"	
Pitchford, William C	"	"	
Parker, Ellison W	"	"	

MEXICAN WAR.

Name and Rank.	Place of Enlistment.	Enrolled	Remarks.
		1847.	
Pate, Lewis	Nashville, Ill.	July 10	
Rogers, Sylvester	"	"	
Rogers, Horatio	"	"	
Shelton, Cuthbert H.	"	"	
Smithers, Elisha	"	"	
Summers, William	"	"	
Taylor, John C.	"	"	
Vanwinekle, Robert	"	"	
Walker, John	"	"	
Walker, Thomas	"	"	
Waldron, George	"	"	
Weaver, James	"	"	

Died:

		1847.	
Sergeants.			
Anderson, James	Nashville, Ill.	July 10	Died at Jalapa, Mex., Dec. 3, 1847
Sanders, Thomas B.	"	"	" Vera Cruz, Mex., Sept. 7, 1847
Privates.			
Carr, Ephriam W.	"	"	Died on Gulf of Mexico, Aug. 28, 1847
Christain, Charles	"	"	" at Vera Cruz, Mex., Oct. 15, 1847
Campbell, Alexander	"	"	" " Sept. 15, "
Field, John	"	"	Killed in action at San Juan, Mex., Sept. 18,'47
Franklin, John F.	"	"	Died at Jalapa, Mex., Dec. 22, 1847
Gore, Thomas	"	"	" " 15, "
Gibson, Josiah	"	"	Died on Gulf of Mexico, Aug. 29, 1847
Hale, Enoch	"	"	" at Jalapa, Mex., Feb. 5, 1848
Livesay, John C.	"	"	" " " May 11, "
Miller, Cyrus	"	"	" at San Juan, Oct. 30, 1847
Miller, Pleasant	"	"	" at Puebla, Mex., April 5, 1848
Owen, William F.	"	"	" " " June 2, "
Pate, Simeon	"	"	" at Camp Encorro, Mex., June 14, 1848
Stoker, Isaac	"	"	" at Alton, Ill., Aug. 3, 1847
Smith, George	"	"	" at San Juan, Mex., Sept. 28, 1848
Summers, Major G.	"	"	" at Jalapa, " Jan. 19, "
Summers, John A.	"	"	" " " 23, "
Thurman, David W.	"	"	" " " Feb. 18, "
Walker, Ezekiah	"	"	" at Vera Cruz, " Sept. 10, 1847
Williams, John	"	"	" " " Nov. 9, "
Wright, James	"	"	" at Jalapa, " Jan. 26, 1848

Deserted:

		1847.	
Manseker, Thos. W. G.	Nashville, Ill.	July 10	Deserted from Hosp., New Orleans, Jan. 15,'48
Morrison, Manly F.	"	"	" at St. Louis, Mo., Aug. 13, 1847

Discharged:

		1847.	
Privates.			
Cameron, James D.	Nashville, Ill.	July 10	Disch., New Orleans, June 8, 1848, disability
Craft, John A.	"	"	" Jalapa, Mex., Feb. 4, " "
Edrington, James P.	"	"	" " " " "
Fitzgerald, James	"	"	" New Orleans, Mar. 9, 1848 "
Gaskill, Thomas J.	"	"	" " " Dec. 29, 1847 "
Hutchings, Richard	"	"	" Vera Cruz, Mex., Jan. 2, 1848, "
Harris, Caleb	"	"	" New Orleans, Mar. 13, " "
Harris, Gustavus	"	"	" " " " "
Ingram, Robert	"	"	" " " " "
Jones, John	"	"	
Lossom, Thomas	"	"	" Jalapa, Mex., Feb. 4, 1848, "
Livesay, Carter H.	"	"	
Martin, John D.	"	"	" New Orleans, Mar. 13, 1848, "
Rice, John	"	"	" Vera Cruz, Mex., Jan. 2, 1848, "
Serance, Peter	"	"	" " " Dec. 29, 1847, "
Thurman, James M.	"	"	" Jalapa, " " "
Underwood, John	"	"	" " " June, 1848, "
Walker, John	"	"	" " " " "

Transferred:

Name and Rank.	Place of Enlistment.	Enrolled	Remarks.
Private. Stephen G. Hicks....	Nashville, Ill.	1847. July 10	Elected Lieut.-Col. of Regiment, Aug. 3, 1847.

This company was discharged at Alton, Ill., on July 22, 1848.

Company "I."

Name and Rank.	Place of Enlistment.	Enrolled	Remarks.
Captains. Edward E. Harvey.. Sewell W. Smith.....	St. Charles, Ill "	1847. July 1 "	Died at Puebla, Mex., March 19, 1848.......... Elected from private March 22, 1848............
First Lieutenant. Lewis A. Norton.....	"	"	A. A. C. S. and A. A. Q. M........................
Second Lieutenants. Hugh Fullerton...... William G. Conklin..	" "	" "	
Sergeants. Nelson, Warner...... Chas. E. Merrifield.. Phillue Efner........ John Spencer........	" " " "	" " " "	 Appointed Sergt., from Musician, Nov. 5, 1847 Elec'd Corp'l, fr'm priv.; elec'd Sergt. Feb.6,'48 Appointed Sergeant Feb. 14, 1848...............
Corporals. John A. Patten...... Timothy Ryan....... Henry Foot.......... George A. Thompson	" " " "	" " " "	 Elected, from private, Feb. 7, 1848............. " " 6, 1848............ " " Nov. 5, 1847............
Musicians. William H. Lawson. Spaulding Lewis....	" "	" "	
Privates. Anderson, Joseph R. Benjamin, Artemus L Blowney, Henry..... Boose, George....... Brewer, Jacob....... Bennett, Thomas.... Brough, David...... Button, Enos........ Coreman, Aop....... Chase, Freedom..... Crap, John.......... Dunfield, Perry...... Ellis, John I........ Fouts, Jacob........ Finch, Stephen...... Gorton, Samuel A. I. Hicks, George....... Hoffman, Paul...... Herrick, Edward.... Hill, Asa I.......... Johnson, Edward H. Jaqusch, Charles.... Kleyburgh, Charles. Keesar, Sallas...... Leibienstien, Lesser Leligar, John....... Lock, LaFayette.... Matthews, Peter.... Moran, Matthew.... Massey, Robert D...	Chicago, Ill.. " " St. Charles, Ill " " " " " " " " " " " " Alton, Ill.... St. Charles, Ill " " Alton, Ill.... St. Charles, Ill " " " " Chicago, Ill. St. Charles, Ill " "	Feb., '48 Mch., '48 " July, '47 " " " " " " " " " " " Mch., '48 July, '47 " " " " " " " " " Feb., '48 July, '47 " "	 Must'd as Corp'l; reduc'd at own request Feb.6

Name and Rank.	Place of Enlistment.	Enrolled	Remarks.
McDonald, Patrick..	St. Charles, Ill	Mar., '48	
McGill, Thomas.....			
Norton, John.......	Puebla, Mex	May, '48	
Norris, John S.....	St. Charles, Ill	July, '47	
Newton, David.....			
Philip, Michael.....	Alton, Ill..	"	
Philips, Orran H....	St. Charles, Ill	"	
Paddy, Jacob.......		"	
Pridemore, Thomas.			
Pollard, Thomas....	Chicago, Ill..	Feb., '48	
Riley, Hugh........			
Rintew, George W..	St. Charles, Ill	July, '47	
Sargeant, Philip H..			
Stickler, Henry.....		"	
Sloss, William......		"	
Thatcher, Benj. B...		"	Originally must'd by name Benj. B. Hampton
Walker, John M.....		"	
Wilson, Joseph P...		Mar., '48	

Died:

Musician.			
Welch, James........	St. Charles, Ill	July, '47	Died at Tampico, Mex., Nov. 2, 1847........

Privates.					
Austin, Z. C........	"	Feb., '48	Died on Mississippi July 10, 1848........		
Bulson, Warren.....	"	July, '47	" at Tampico, Mex., Nov. 26, 1847..		
Brown, Charles P...	Tampico, Mex	"	" on march from Puebla June 5, 1848.....		
Courtner, William...	St. Charles, Ill	"	" on Gulf of Mexico June 28, 1848.....		
Dorchester, Fred'k.	"	"	" at Tampico, Mex., Sept. 27, 1847.....		
Frebert, George.....	"	"	" " " Oct. 2, 1847		
Friend, Asa M.......	"	"	" Puebla, " March 14, 1848.........		
Freeman, William...	"	"	" Tampico, " Nov. 10, 1847		
Furgeson, Stephen..	"	"	" " " Oct. 25, 1847		
Henries, Henrie.....	"	"	" " " Oct. 6, 1847		
Lewis, Isaac........	"	"	" " " Oct. 29, 1847		
McDonald, Samuel..	"	"	" Vera Cruz, " Feb. 28, 1848.		
Mooney, David......	"	"	" Tampico, " Dec. 3, 1847		
Moore, Nicholas....	"	"	" " " Sept. 11, 1847...		
Marshall, Henry....	"	"	" " " Oct. 6, 1847		
Mead, John.........	"	"	" " " Nov. 7, 1847		
McColum, Malcolm..	"	"	" Vera Cruz, " Feb. 13, 1848..		
Price, James........	"	"	" Puebla, " May 18, 1848.		
Portord, Stephen B.	"	"	" Tampico, " Sept. 28, 1847..		
Phelps, John........	"	"	" " " Sept., 1847...		
Phillips, Jedediah...	"	"	" " " Dec. 20, 1847.		
Romine, Alfred......	"	"	" Puebla, " April 13, 1848		
Serber, Thomas.....	"	"	" Tampico, " Dec. 19, 1847....		
Schoomaker, John D	"	"	" " " Sept. 23, 1847..		
Smith, Henry........	"	"	" near Rio Frio, " March 3, 1848; killed.		
Tubbs, David.......	"	"	" at Tampico, " Oct. 6, 1847...		
Thompson, James...	"	"	" " " Dec., 1847.....		
Wilger, Frederick...	"	"	" Puebla, " May 11, 1848....		

Deserted:

Sergeant.		1847.	
Reed Haywood......	St. Charles, Ill	July 1	Deserted at Alton, Ill., Aug. 10, 1847........

Privates.			
Barnim, George W..	"	"	Deserted at Carrollton, La., Aug. 23, 1847....
Dortort, Stephen....	"	"	" " " " ......
Eglehough, Alfred...		"	
Henry, Thomas......	"	"	" Alton, Ill., Aug. 9, 1847........
Johnson, Sween.....		"	
Koose, John C.......	"	"	" Carrollton, La., Aug. 23, 1847....
Loet, Niles..........	"	"	" Alton, Ill., Aug. 9, 1847
Munster, Augustus..		"	
Mahar, John.........	"	"	" " " "
McLain, Robert......	"	"	" " " Aug. 4, 1847........
Patrick, Willey C....	"	"	Drummed out, sentence Court Mar. Aug. 2, '47.
Pervis, Elisha.......	"	"	Deserted at Alton, Ill., Aug. 4, 1847.........

SECOND REGIMENT.

Name and Rank.	Place of Enlistment.	Enrolled	Remarks.
		1847.	
Thompson, Thos. H.		July 1	Deserted at Alton, Ill., Aug. 4, 1847
Wood, Samuel R.		" "	" " " " 17, 1847
Zahuki, Fornan		" "	" " " " " "
Zahar, Jacob		" "	" " " " " "

Discharged:

Name and Rank.	Place of Enlistment.	Enrolled	Remarks.
Sergeants.		1847.	
Garfield, Benjamin F		July 1	Disch. at Vera Cruz., Mar. 22, '48; disability
Berry, Smith M		" "	Tampico, Mex., Jan. 19, '48; disability
Corporal.			
Paddleford, Sam'l D.		" "	Discharged
Privates.			
Carlisle, Wm. H. S.		" "	Disch. at Tampico, Mex., Oct. 14, '47; disability
Christie, Thomas		" "	" " " " " "
Ganga, James		" "	" " " Jan. 19, '48 "
Kleyberg, George		" "	" " Vera Cruz, Mex., Feb. 7, '48 "
McNelon, Alexander		" "	" " Tampico " Jan. 29, '48 "
Roberts, George D.	Alton, Ill	Aug. 7	" " " " " "

This company was discharged at Alton, Ill., July 24, 1848.

Company "K."

Name and Rank.	Place of Enlistment.	Enrolled	Remarks.
Captains.		1847.	
John Ewing	Benton, Ill.	July 18	Died at Tampico, Mex., Oct. 3, '49, in quarters
Pierce, James R.	" "	" "	Elect. Capt. Oct.7; died Mch. 28, '48, at Puebla
Mooneyham, Thos. J	" "	" "	" " April 4, 1848, from 1st Lieut.
First Lieutenant.			
Mooneyham, Daniel	" "	" "	Elected 1st Lieut. April 4, 1848, from 2d Lieut.
Second Lieutenants.			
William P. Maddox	" "	" "	Died in Puebla, Mex., Mch. 28, 1848
William Bates	" "	" "	Elected 2d Lieut. April 4, 1848, from private
John H. Mulkey	" "	" "	" " " " " " from Sergt
Sergeants.			
William Rogers	" "	" "	
James S. Rotramel	" "	" "	Appointed 2d Sergt. April 4, 1848, from private
William Foster	" "	" "	" " 3d " Oct. 8, 1847, " "
Zachariah Young	" "	" "	" " 4th " April 4, 1848, " "
Corporals.			
Dixon Glover	" "	" "	Appointed 1st Corp'l Mch. 24, 1848
William D. Coin	" "	" "	
Brunson Daniel	" "	" "	
Musicians.			
Elijah Rotramel	" "	" "	
William G. Winn	" "	" "	
Privates.			
Browning, Joseph	" "	" "	
Burket, James	" "	" "	
Burleson, James R.	" "	" "	
Bramlet, Benjamin	" "	" "	
Briley, Green W	" "	" "	
Collins, James	" "	" "	
Connuff, Edward	Chicago, Ill.	April, '48	
Dawson, Francis	St. Charles, Ill	" "	

MEXICAN WAR.

Name and Rank.	Place of Enlistment.	Enrolled	Remarks.
Donnis, James H.	Benton, Ill.	July, '47	
Elkins, Andrew P.	"	"	
Elkins, Gasaway	"	"	
Hamilton, Andr'w R.	"	"	
Hopper, Geo. W.	"	"	
Isaac, John W.	"	"	Discharged June 15, 1848, for disability
Johnson, Nathaniel	"	"	
Kidwell, Johnson	"	"	
Lewis, Jeremiah T.F.	"	"	
Martin, Oliver C.	"	"	
Maddox, Moses I.	"	"	
Maddox, Henry	"	"	
Melvin, John	"	"	
McAmy, William W.	"	"	
Odle, Martin	"	"	
Petty, William A.	Tampico, Mex	Aug. 28	
Phillips, John H.	Benton, Ill.	July 18	
Pitchford, William	"	"	
Parker, Noah	"	"	
Pease, Anson	St. Charles, Ill	Mar., '48	
Reed, John	Chicago, Ill.		
Roberts, Clark W.	"	April, '48	
Ryan, Timothy	"	Feb., '48	Died at Alton, July 17, 1848, while making roll
Rotramel, Walter I.	Benton, Ill.	July, '47	
Rodburn, John	"	"	
Roberson, Geo. W.	"	"	
Swafford, Emanuel I.	"	"	
Shihorn, William	"	"	
Stricklin, Wm. H.	"	"	
Shook, Hiram	Chicago, Ill.	Feb., '48	
Williams, Benj. H.	Benton, Ill.	July, '47	
Wilkinson, James	"	"	

Discharged:

		1847.	
Privates.			
Burlison, Jonath'n H.	Benton, Ill.	July 18	Disch. at Tampico, Jan. 19, '48; disability
Cleeveland, And'w J.	"	"	Sick at Tampico Feb. 1, '48; supposed disch.
Duff, Daniel	"	"	Disch. at Vera Cruz, March 4, '48; disability
Flint, James	"	"	Tampico, Jan. 19, '48; "
Isaac, George	"	"	Vera Cruz, March 7, '47; "
Lane, Jacob	"	"	Tampico, Oct. 2, '47; "
Price, Wesley	"	"	New Orleans, June 13, '48; "
Rice, John T.	"	"	Vera Cruz, May 18, '48; "
Ronche, John	"	"	Jeff. Barracks; reduced to ranks
Summers, Elisha	"	"	Vera Cruz, Mch. 4, 48; disability
Swafford, William A.	"	"	Tampico, Jan. 19, '48; "
Towns, Robert T.	"	"	

Died:

		1847.	
Sergeant.			
Cornelius Martin	Benton, Ill.	July 18	Died at Puebla, Mex., March 30, 1848
Corporals.			
Lemuel Rancher	"	"	Died at Puebla, Mex., March 18, 1848
Wm. D. McKeoun	"	"	" Alton, Ill., July 14, "
Cautrell Bluford	"	"	" Puebla, Mex., March 14, "
Privates.			
Avery, John	"	"	Died at Tampico, Mex., Oct. 21, 1847
Baker, Reuben	"	"	" " " 20, "
Crawford, George R.	"	"	" " " March 14, "
Crawford, John	"	"	" " " Sept. 29, "
Candle, John W.	"	"	" " " Oct. 10, "
Crossner, George H.	"	"	" Puebla, " April 13, 1848
Clem, Jesse R.	"	"	" Tampico, " Oct. 6, "
Crawford, Joel S.	"	"	" " " Sept. 9, "
Corder, Andrew	"	"	" " " " 27, 1847
Clampit, Jonathan H.	"	"	" " " " 30, "
Eubanks, John	"	"	" " " Nov. 23, "
Estiss, Thompson P.	"	"	" " " Oct. 4, "
Foster, George E.	"	"	" " " " 15, "
Flint, William	"	"	" " " Nov. 13, "
Goff, John	"	"	" " " Oct. 28, "

SECOND REGIMENT.

Name and Rank.	Place of Enlistment.	Enrolled	Remarks.
		1847.	
Giles, John I	Benton, Ill	July 18	Died at Camp Encerro, Mex., June 11, 1848
Maddox, Noah	"	"	Puebla, Mex., May 21, 1848
Morse, Nathaniel	"	"	Camp Encerro, Mex., June 9, 1848
Martin, James	"	"	Jalapa, Mex., June 9, 1848
Mooneyham, Heze'h	"	"	Tampico, Mex., Nov. 29, 1847
Phillips, Wesley	"	"	" " Oct. 20, "
Patton, Thomas I	"	"	" " Dec. 21, "
Rice, James	"	"	" " Sept. 25, "
Rawlings, Nathan	"	"	" " Nov. 19, "
Sweaton, Richard R.	"	"	" " Sept. 6, "
Swafford, John L	"	"	" " Oct. 17, "
Thomas, Joseph B	"	"	" " Nov. 3, "
Walter, James H. O.	"	"	" " Oct. 28, "
Ward, Willis	"	"	" " Aug. 28, "
Wall, Frederick	"	"	" " Nov. 11, "

This company was discharged at Alton, Ill., July 21, 1848,

THIRD REGIMENT.

THE FIELD AND STAFF

Of the Third Regiment of the Brigade of Illinois Volunteers Militia commanded by Col. Ferris Forman, ordered into service of the United States by the President. From the 30th day of April to the 25th day of May, 1847, when discharged.

Name and Rank.	Place of Enlistment.	Enrolled	Remarks.
Colonel. F. Forman		1846. June 21	
Lieutenant-Colonel. W. W. Willey		June 21	
Major. S. D. Marshall		July 4	
Adjt. and 2d Lieut. C. Everett, Jr		July 8	App. Sergt-Major July 9, '46; elected 2d Lt. and app Adjt. Sept. 2, 1846.
Adjt. and 1st Lieut. J. T. B. Stapp		June 21	Resigned, Sept. 1, 1846
A. Q. M. and Capt. Nath'l Parker			App. Asst. Q. M. July 19, 1846; mustered out of service May 22, 1847.
Surgeons. J. Mahan		Aug. 29	Detached to take charge of hospital; app. by [President.
J. O'Niel		June 23	Left sick at N. Orleans, Aug. 6; died Aug. 13, '46
Assistant Surgeon. D. Turney		Aug. 26	Relieved by order of Gen. Patterson; app. by President.
Actg. Asst. Surg. J. Burch		July 2	Relieved by Asst. Surg. Turney Aug 26, 1846
A. C. S. and Capt. J. S. Bradford		Sept. 17 1847.	Absent by leave Gen. Scott since April 1, '47; app. by President.
S. Hackleton		April 8 1846.	Appointed by President
J. M. Campbell		Aug. 26	Relieved by Capt. J. S. Bradford Sept 17, 1846; app. by President.
Sergeant-Major. Henry Hamilton		July 1	Mustered out of service May 25, 1847
Q. M. Sergeant. J. Willbanks		June 22	App. July 9, 1846; mustered out May 21, 1847.
Principal Musicians Jas. Lamburth		July 2	Tran. to Co. "K;" reduced to private Dec. 9,1846.
Thos. Mapes		July 4	" Co. "C;" " " Dec. 31, 1846.
W. W. Caton		June 29	App. Dec. 9, 1846; mustered out May 21, 1847
A. Wiley		June 27	" " 31, " " " "

THIRD REGIMENT. 267

Company "A."

Name and Rank.	Place of Enlistment.	Enrolled	Remarks.
Captains.		1846.	
F. Forman		June 21	Elected Col. July 8
Philip Stout	"	"	2d Lieut. to July 3
First Lieutenants.			
James T. B. Stapp		"	Resigned Sept. 1, 1846
James W. Boothe		"	Elected 2d Lt. June 27, '46; 1st Lt. Sept. 1, '46
Second Lieutenants.			
Richard Hawkins		"	Resigned Sept. 2, 1846
Cyrus Hall		"	Elected 2d Lieut. Sept. 2, 1846
Charles Everett, Jr		July 8	App'd Sergt.-Maj. July 9; Adjt. Sept. 2, 1846
Sergeants.			
Raford B. Reeves		June 21	Corp'l from Jan. 1 to Feb. 12; then 1st Sergt
James W. Welch		"	
William Terry		"	Appointed Sergeant Sept. 2, 1846
Lansing B. Mezner		"	Detached as Interpreter; private to Sept. 2, '46
Corporals.			
Jacob Kifer		"	
William Beal		"	Pay due as Corporal from Feb. 12
Benjamin F. Rees		"	
Josiah Williams		"	Wounded slightly at Cerro Gordo
Musician.			
Andrew Browning		"	
Privates.			
Arny, James		"	
Bowles, Robert		"	
Briton, Isah		"	
Beal, James		"	
Barringer, Julius		"	
Buniard, James		"	
Chandler, Samuel		"	
Cluxton, Henry J		"	Sick at Matamoras since Dec. 14, 1846
Conner, Sherwood L		"	
Condra, Herod		"	
Cronk, American		"	
Cubbertson, James		"	Sick at Matamoras since Dec. 14, 1846
Croy, Robin		"	" " " "
Clark, James H		"	
Forbis, William B		"	
Garland, Benjamin		"	
George, John		"	
Haley, George W		"	Wounded slightly at Cerro Gordo
Hinston, Hardy		"	
Hamilton, Henry		"	Appointed Sergeant-Major
Ishmael, James M. C		"	
Karney, Arnindith		"	
Leadbetter, Joseph		"	
Larimore, Samuel		"	
Miller, Jacob		"	
Meek, Wm		"	
Nowlin, Pleasant		"	
Nowlin, James		"	
Nowlin, William		"	
Nifong, Joseph		"	
Pennington, Josiah		"	
Prater, Holloway		"	
Roseberry, James		"	
Sears, John		"	
Sears, Joseph		"	
Shears, William B		"	
Stokes, Bird		"	
Stigall, Peter		"	
Tucker, Robert		"	
Thompson, John C		"	Detached in charge of wounded at Jalapa
Whitfield, Elan B		"	
Watwood, Addison		"	Left in hospital at Jalapa; wounded by ac'd't
Wiley, George		"	

Discharged:

Name and Rank.	Place of Enlistment.	Enrolled	Remarks.
Sergeant. John McNicker		1846. June 21	Discharged, disability, Aug. 13, 1846
Privates.			
Aldrich, Jackson		"	Discharged, disability, Nov. 3, 1846
Baley, A. G		"	" " " "
Baley, John		"	" " " "
Daniels, Robert		"	" " " Aug. 13, 1846
Forbis, Eli H		"	" " " Sept. 3, 1846
Griffith, William O.		"	" " " "
Hartman, Benjamin		"	" " " "
Jackson, Able		"	" " " March 31, 1847
Netherby, Andrew J.		"	" " " Nov. 3, 1846
Richards, James		"	" " " Aug. 13, 1846
Shipley, Russell		"	" " " Sept. 3, 1846
Stamps, Lewis		"	" " " Feb. 21, 1847
Smith, Alexander		"	" " " Sept. 3, 1846
Williams, Thomas C		"	" " " Oct. 28, 1846
Woolsey, John		"	" " " Aug. 13, 1846
Whitfield, Charles		"	" " " Sept. 3, 1846

Died:

Name and Rank.	Place of Enlistment.	Enrolled	Remarks.
Corporal. Thomas I. Baley		1846. June 21	Died at Camp Matamoras Dec. 26, 1846
Privates.			
Bone, Marion		"	Died at Camp Tampico, Feb. 23, 1847
Ballinger, Leander		"	" " " Camargo, Oct. 29, 1846
Donton, John C		"	" " " Nov. 3, 1846
Hays, Zachariah		"	" " " Matamoras, Nov. 6, 1846
Inman, Robert K.		"	" " " Dec 24, 1846
Inman, Joseph O.		"	" " " Camargo, Oct. 18, 1846
Johnson, George W.		"	" " " Point Isabel, Tex., Mar. 3, 1847
Loveless, James		"	" " " Camargo, Nov. 5, 1846
Pissen, Nicholas W.		"	" " " Matamoras, Mex., Nov. 6, 1846
Price, William		"	" " " Camargo, Nov. 13, 1846
Roseberry, William		"	" " " Matamoras, Oct. 8, 1846
Smith, David		"	" " " Patterson, Tex., Sept. 3, 1846
West, William		"	" " " Bureta, Mex., Sept. 14, 1846
White, James		"	" " " Camargo, Nov. 21, 1846

This company was discharged at New Orleans on May 23, 1847.

COMPANY "B."

Name and Rank.	Place of Enlistment.	Enrolled	Remarks.
Captain. James Freeman		1846. June 21	Resigned
First Lieutenants.			
Eli Hooper		"	Resigned
W. L. McNeil		"	Commanding company since Nov. 1, 1846
Second Lieutenant. David Evey		"	Was 2d Lieutenant
Sergeants.			
John Casey		"	
Lemuel A. Rankins		"	
Benjamin F. Chew		"	
Orville Robertson		"	

THIRD REGIMENT.

Name and Rank.	Place of Enlistment.	Enrolled	Remarks.
Corporals.		1846.	
William Price		June 27	
L. F. Doyle		"	
Sabin C. Stanwood		"	
Joseph G. Harris		"	
Musician.			
Samuel Bolyjack		"	
Privates.			
Bankson, Arthur C.		"	
Brown, James		"	
Beck, Benton		"	
Barns, John C.		"	Sick at Matamoras since Dec. 14, 1846
Chatham, Franklin		"	
Chatham, James		"	
Cook, John		"	Sick at Matamoras since Dec. 14, 1846
Clair, Jones C.		"	
Cooch, Martin		"	
Dixon, Lawson H.		"	
Delap, Grandville W.		"	
Griffith, William J.		"	
Gordon, Benjamin		"	
Gorden, Abraham		"	
Hooper, Cla'borne R.		"	
Hooper, Joseph F.		"	
Henderson, Quant'n.		"	Sick at Matamoras
Lang, Elon M. C.		"	
Massey, Hezekiah		"	
Massey, Burrel J.		"	
Matney, Leonard		"	
Matney, Walter		"	
Matney, Samuel K.		"	
McKenzie, George		"	
Mosley, John		"	
Norman, Solomon H.		"	
Phelps, Josiah		"	Sick at Matamoras Dec. 14, 1846
Phelps, Henderson		"	
Row, John R.		"	
Renfrow, William B.		"	
Ring, Stephen		"	
Riley, Josiah O.		"	
Rogers, James F.		"	Sick at Matamoras
Smith, William		"	
Smith, Hardin		"	
Story, James		"	
Truitt, David		"	
Templeton, Geo. W.		"	
Tetbrich, William		"	
Turner, Martin L.		"	
Walton, Benjamin		"	
Wade, James		"	
Wheat, Levi		"	
Warren, Laborn		"	

Discharged:

		1846.	
Sergeant.			
Nathaniel Corley		June 27	Disch. Nov. 30, 1846, at Matamoras, Mex.
Corporal.			
Enoch R. Vanwinkle		"	Disch. Nov. 2, 1846, at Matamoras, Mex.
Musician.			
James Jones		"	Disch. Nov. 2, 1846, at Matamoras, Mex.
Privates.			
Armstrong, Joseph		"	Disch. Nov. 2, 1846, at Matamoras, Mex.
Banning, Adolph. A.		"	" " " " "
Banning, Clark		"	" " " " "
Beck, Benjamin J.		"	" " " " "
Branden, James P.		"	" Aug. 13, 1846, at Brazos Is., Texas
Barker, Aaron M.		"	"
Classon, Frederic		"	" Sept. 18, '46, at Up. Camp Pat'rs'n, Mex.
Conner, Elijah W.		"	" Nov. 3, 1846, at Matamoras, Mex.
Corben, John L.		"	" Nov. 2, 1846, " "
Daniels, John		"	" Mar. 3, 1847, " "
Fanning, Wash'n P.		"	" Sept. 18, '46, at Up. Camp Pat'rs'n, Mex.

Name and Rank.	Place of Enlistment.	Enrolled	Remarks.
		1846.	
Furlow, Nelson		June 27	Disch. Aug. 13, 1846, at Brazos Is., Texas
Jackson, William H.		"	Mar. 3, 1847, at Matamoras, Mex.
Killam, William		"	Sept. 18, '46, at Up. Camp Pat'rs'n, Mex.
Milliken, Jesse		"	Sept. 6, '46, at Lower Camp Pat'rs'n, Tex.
Pierce, Solomon		"	Nov. 3, 1846, at Matamoras, Mex.
Reed, Jesse J.		"	Nov. 2, 1846, " "
Scribner, Lewis		"	
Seales, Burrel		"	Sept. 6, '46, at Lower Camp Pat'rs'n, Tex.
Stafford, Thomas R.		"	Sept. 18, '46, at Up. Camp Pat'rs'n, Mex.
Vanwinkle, David C.		"	Nov. 2, 1846, at Matamoras, Mex.
Webb, Berry T.		"	Mar. 3, 1847, " "

Died:

Name and Rank.	Place of Enlistment.	Enrolled	Remarks.
Corporal.		1846.	
Michager Holbrook		June 27	Died at Camp Patterson, Tex., Sept. 6, '46.
Privates.			
Curry, James S.		"	Died at camp near Camargo, Mex., Nov. 12, '46
Dixon, Alexander W.		"	" " Sept. 15, '46
Goodwin, James		"	" Matamoras, Mex., Oct. 2, '46
Henderson, Andr. J.		"	" Camp Patterson, Mex., Sept. 18, '46
Jayne, John		"	" camp near Camargo, Mex., Nov. 5, '46
Moore, Washington		"	" " Oct. 28, '46
Myers, John		"	" Matamoras, Mex., Nov. 4, '46
Williams, Calvin		"	" camp near Camargo, Mex., Nov. 3, '46

Deserted:

Name and Rank.	Place of Enlistment.	Enrolled	Remarks.
Private.		1846.	
Spencer Smith		June 27	Deserted July 7, 1846, previous to muster

This company was discharged at New Orleans, La., May 23, 1847.

Company "C."

Name and Rank.	Place of Enlistment.	Enrolled	Remarks.
Captain.		1846.	
James C. McAdams		June 26	Died, Jan. 4, 1847, at Matamoras, Mex.
First Lieutenant.			
Thomas Rose		"	In command of company since Dec. 1, 1846
Second Lieutenants.			
John Burk		"	
John Corlew		"	
Sergeants.			
Jas. M. Wilford		"	Promoted 1st Sergt. Jan. 31, 1847
Miles Morris		"	
Jep. J. McDavid		"	
Corporals.			
Wm. Stephenson		"	
Benj. Blockberger		"	Appointed Corporal, March 23, 1847
Chas. H. Rutledge		"	
Musicians.			
Joseph Mapes		"	Left sick at Matamoras since Dec. 14, 1846
Jas. F. Witherspoon		"	

Name and Rank.	Place of Enlistment.	Enrolled	Remarks.
Privates.		1846.	
Acres, Claborn		June 26	
Anderson, Jas. B		"	
Boyd, Wm. R		"	
Bodkin, John		"	
Bennett, John Q. A		"	
Bennett, Nelson		"	
Card, Benson		"	
Corlew, Ransom		"	
Craig, John		"	
Cardwell, Lafayette		"	
Davis, Robert W		"	
Edwards, Wm. A		"	
Edwards, Mark W		"	
Frost, Johnson A		"	
Fullar, John		"	
Finney, Jackson		"	
Garner, James B		"	
Graf, Daniel		"	
Gunter, Thomas		"	Left sick at Matamoras since Dec. 20, 1846
Grubbs, Higgason B		"	Reduced to ranks from Corp'l, Mar. 23, 1847
Harman, Stephen		"	
Harman, Achilles		"	
Isaacks, Wilborn		"	
Ishmel, Benj. R		"	
Kingston, William		"	
Koonts, John		"	
Lerla, Jacob		"	
Loomis, John T		"	
Lyngle, John M		"	
McWilliams, Thos		"	
McPhail, Joseph		"	
McPhail, James		"	
McPhail, Samuel		"	
Mapes, Thomas		"	
Penter, Joseph		"	
Pruett, John		"	
Pruett, Major		"	
Rose, George W		"	
Starr, Abraham B		"	
Smith, Wiley B		"	
Scott, James M		"	
Turrentine, John		"	
Thomas, Alanson B		"	
Varner, Wm. H		"	
Wright, Joseph G		"	
Wright, Thomas F		"	
Williams, James S		"	
Wright, Jarrett		"	
Wilson, Joseph C		"	Left sick at Matamoras Dec. 14, 1846

Discharged:

Name and Rank.	Place of Enlistment.	Enrolled	Remarks.
Sergeants.		1846.	
Jas. B. McDavid		June 26	Disch. on Surgeon's certificate March 3, 1847.
James M. Quellman		"	" " " Jan. 23, 1847
Privates.			
Bishop, Isaac J		"	Disch. on Surgeon's certificate, date unkn'wn
Colyar, Wm. D		"	" " " Jan. 23, 1847
Cress, Martin A		"	" " " Aug. 31, 1846
Foglemen, Joel N		"	" " " date unkn'wn
Grubbs, Edwin B		"	" " " "
King, Samuel F		"	" " " "
Lewey, Isaac		"	" " " March 3, 1847
McCaslin, Wm. B		"	" " " Aug. 13, 1846
Norman, Thos. A		"	" " " date unkn'wn
Peacock, Eli		"	" " " Aug. 31, 1846
Seymour, William		"	" " " April 23, 1847
Walker, James		"	" " " March 3, 1847

MEXICAN WAR.

Died:

Name and Rank.	Place of Enlistment.	Enrolled	Remarks.
1st Sergeant. Robt. Williamson		1846. June 26	Died Oct. 26, 1846, at Camargo
Corporal. Elijah Isaacs		"	Died March 8, 1847, at Point Isabel
Privates.			
Barnett, William H.		"	Died Oct. 13, 1846, at Matamoras
Burringer, Moses		"	" Oct. 22, 1846, "
Burk, Wm. C.		"	" Dec. 26, 1846, "
Briants, George		"	" Dec. 27, 1846, "
Card, Levi		"	" May, '47, at Jalapa, wo'nds rec'd C. Gordo
Colman, John J.		"	" Oct. 21, 1846, at Matamoras
Gaston, John C.		"	" Jan. 8, 1847, "
Hill, Henry		"	" Dec. 27, 1846, "
Halford, Wm. S.		"	" Sept. 8, 1846, at Camp Patterson
Knight, Ezra P.		"	" Jan. 8, 1847, at Matamoras
Lazenby, Razin G.		"	" Nov. 25, —, at Camargo
Lynch, Charles W.		"	" Oct. 9, 1846, at Matamoras
Pearson, Alex. W.		"	" Sept. 12, 1846, at Camp Patterson
Roper, Franklin		"	" Oct. 26, 1846, at Camargo
Williams, John A.		"	" Sept. 24, 1846, at Matamoras

This company was discharged at New Orleans, May 21, 1847.

Company "D."

Name and Rank.	Place of Enlistment.	Enrolled	Remarks.
Captain. W. W. Bishop		1847. June 27	
First Lieutenant. John J. Adams		"	
Second Lieutenants.			
E. C. Jones		"	Died at St. Louis, Mo., March 4, 1847
H. C. Dunbar		"	
Sergeants.			
Burns Harlan		"	Left at Vera Cruz, in hospital, wounded, [May 7, 1847.
Darius Wiley		"	
LeRoy Wiley		"	
James H. Bayley		"	
Corporals.			
James C. Robinson		"	Appointed Oct. 31, 1846, *vice* Sublett, reduced.
John Chandler		"	" " " " McCollister, "
S. W. Ewing		"	" Mch. 7, " " McDaniel, disch.
P. P. Miller		"	
Musicians.			
Arick Sutherland		"	
Austin Wiley		"	Transferred to regular Staff Oct. 31, 1846
Privates.			
Brann, George		"	
Barney, David		"	
Benedict, Tera		"	
Cox, Ulysses D.		"	
Cox, James		"	
Cartwell, George W.		"	
Dyer, James		"	
Dowling, Thomas		"	
Downs, Samuel B.		"	
Firls, Jonathan		"	Left sick at Matamoras, Mex., Dec. 14, 1846
Grant, Jesse K.		"	
Griffin, Alexander		"	

Name		1846.	Notes
Good, Joseph		June 27	
Harmon, Samuel H.		"	
Hoge, Westley		"	
Hays, Tyne		"	Left sick at Matamoras, Mex., Dec. 14, 1846
Hains, John		"	
Henry, William		"	
Ivins, John L.		"	
Kelly, Thomas		"	
Luark, John		"	
Lowthan, Henry W.		"	
Logan, William		"	
Miller, George W.		"	
Miller, Samuel		"	
Marion, Francis		"	
Morgan, James		"	
Moore, Alexander		"	Left sick at Matamoras, Mex., Dec. 14, 1846
Mitchell, Thomas		"	
McKelvy, Patrick		"	
McCollester, Samuel		"	Left sick at Matamoras, Mex., Dec. 14, 1846
Parker, Nathaniel		"	Appointed A. Q. M. July 19, 1846
Romines, George		"	
Rimmer, Nathaniel		"	
Thompson, Fred. G.		"	
Turner, Thomas		"	
Sublett, Jackson		"	Left sick at Matamoras, Mex., Dec. 14, 1846
White, Hiram		"	
White, James		"	
White, Johnson		"	
White, George		"	Left sick at Matamoras, Mex., Dec. 14, 1846
White, William		"	
Winters, James P.		"	
Weston, Isaiah		"	Re-enlisted, May 11, at Vera Cruz
Wiley, James		"	
Wiley, Reason		"	

Discharged:

Sergeants.		1846.	
S. B. Logan		June 27	Discharged Oct. 13, 1846, disability
Alfred Jones		"	" 8, " "
Corporals.			
Andrew Jeans		"	Discharged Sept. 3, 1846, disability
George Wells		"	" Oct. 13, " "
Joseph Piper		"	" Dec. 6, " "
George McDaniel		"	" Mch. 6, 1847, "
Privates.			
Ashmore, Wm. C.		"	Discharged Oct. 28, 1846, disability
Abbott, John		"	" " 22, " "
Bragg, Alex		"	
Bryant, Lewis		"	" Sept. 3, " "
Clements, Thomas		"	
Carter, Joseph		"	" Oct. 22, " "
Francher, Thomas		"	" Sept. 3, " "
Foster, J. C.		"	" Oct. 8, " "
Grant, Adam		"	" " 28, " "
Harmon, Wm. C.		"	" Sept. 3, " "
Hart, Moses		"	" Oct. 8, " "
Hunt, George		"	" Nov. 17, " "
Lawrence, Robert		"	" Oct. 13, " "
McCollister, Wm. C.		"	" Nov. 17, " "
Owings, James P.		"	" Oct. 13, " "
Pinnell, Henry H.		"	" Sept. 3, " "
Parish, John R.		"	" Nov. 17, " "
Poulten, John D.		"	" Oct. 22, " "
Sublett, William		"	" " 8, " "
Wilson, Marcus		"	" " 22, " "

—18

MEXICAN WAR.

Died:

Name and Rank.	Place of Enlistment.	Enrolled	Remarks.
Privates.		1846.	
Cornwell, Bennett		June 27	Died at Matamoras, Jan. 13, 1847
Drummond, William		"	" Sept. 27, 1846
Eastin, Harmon		"	" New Orleans, Aug. 2, "
Fetty, C. D.		"	" Matamoras, Sept. 27, "
Frost, Harvey D.		"	" Tampico, Feb. 28, 1847
Hart, Thomas		"	" Matamoras, Sept. 27, 1846
Jarvis, Marion		"	" Point Isabel, Mch. 3, 1847
Winkler, Joseph L.		"	" Matamoras, Sept. 24, 1846

This company was discharged at New Orleans, May 21, 1847.
The company was at the seige of Vera Cruz, and at the battle of Cerro Gordo on April 18.

Company "E."

Name and Rank.	Place of Enlistment.	Enrolled	Remarks.
Captain.		1846.	
Benjamin E. Sellers		June 21	
First Lieutenants.			
James M. Hubbard		"	Resigned, to take effect Nov. 15, 1846
Samuel G. McAdams		"	
Second Lieutenant.			
Isaac Redfearn		"	
Sergeants.			
John A. Washburn		"	Promoted from 2d Sergeant May 1, 1847
Theophilus Short		"	" " private April 4, 1847
Felix McGower		"	
Richard Roberts		"	" " 1st Corporal May 1, 1847
Corporals.			
Lemuel L. Washburn		"	
Larkin Jackson		"	
George Allen		"	Promoted from private April 4, 1847
William Ray		"	" " May 1, 1847
Privates.			
Alexander, John		"	Left in hospital at Matamoras, Dec. 14, 1846
Alderman, William		"	
Adams, James J.		"	Reduced from 3d Sergeant April 4, 1847
Brown, Calvin		"	
Boothe, Robert C.		"	
Cruthis, Henry		"	
Cruthis, James C.		"	
Diamond, Harvey W.		"	
Etzler, George P.		"	
Elmore, Hardin		"	
Forbes, William		"	
Gilbert, Andrew W.		"	
Gilmore, James H.		"	
Hilliard, Charles		"	
Harris, James A.		"	Left in hospital at Tampico, March 1, 1847
Higginbotham, N. D.		"	
Kuykendall, James		"	Left in hospital at Matamoras, Dec. 14, 1846
Ledbetter, Job		"	
McCracken, John P.		"	Left in hospital at Matamoras, Dec. 14, 1846
McCracken, Nathan C.		"	
McCollum, Alexand'r		"	
Padfield, John		"	
Ray, Henry D.		"	
Royer, Daniel		"	
Snodgrass, Kilburn M		"	
Spratt, John		"	
Smith, Lowell		"	
Smith, John M.		"	

THIRD REGIMENT.

Name and Rank.	Place of Enlistment.	Enrolled	Remarks.
		1846	
Simmons, Charles T.		June 21	Left in hospital at Matamoras, Dec. 14, 1846.
Sugg, Josiah F.		"	Same, and reduced to ranks April 4, 1847.
Thorp, Calvin H.		"	
Wade, John T.		"	
White, Stephen		"	
Williford, Robert		"	
Webster, Francis		"	
White, Robert O.		"	

Discharged:

		1846	
Musician.			
Joseph Isaacs		June 21	Discharged, disability, Aug. 31, 1846
Privates.			
Alexander, Henry B.		"	Discharged, disability, Aug. 20, 1846
Ames, Frederic		"	" " Oct. 20, "
Blankenship, James		"	" " Aug. 25, "
Douglas, James A.		"	" " Oct. 20, "
Douglas, John M.		"	" " Aug. 26, "
Ewing, Thomas A.		"	" " Oct. 5, "
Evans, Wilson		"	" " Nov. 3, "
Gray, Samuel		"	" " Aug. 14, "
Gilmore, John M.		"	" " Oct. 20, "
Hignight, James		"	" " Aug. 26, "
Hunter, William M.		"	" " Aug. 20, "
Holland, John		"	" " Aug. 20, "
Jay, Joseph A.		"	" " Oct. 5, "
Larrison, Thomas T.		"	" " Aug. 26, "
Lyttaker, Peter		"	" " Aug. 26, "
Netherly, Nathan H.		"	" " Nov. 3, "
Noland, Enoch M.		"	" " Oct. 31, "
Patterson, John		"	" " Aug. 14, "
Phipps, David		"	" " Aug. 31, "
Reed, Isaac N.		"	" " Aug. 11, "
Reed, George A.		"	" " Aug. 26, "
Steele, Andrew J.		"	" " Aug. 14, "
Sherrod, Joel H.		"	" " Nov. 16, "
Thacker, Henry C.		"	" " Oct. 20, "
Willis, Nathan B.		"	" " Oct. 10, "

Died:

		1846.	
First Sergeant.			
William S. Allen		June 21	Died at Jalapa, May 1,'47, wounds at Cer. Gor.
Privates.			
Arnold, Robert		"	Died in hospital, Matamoras, Oct. 12, 1846
Ewing, Samuel J.		"	Died at Camp Patterson, Mex., Sept. 13, 1846
Grigg, Joseph W.		"	" near Tampico, Feb. 25, 1847
Jett, Thomas J.		"	" Camargo, Oct. 26, 1846
Jarvis, Henry W.		"	" hospital, Matamoras, March 2, 1847
Larrison, James		"	" Camargo, Oct. 9, 1846
Lucas, William		"	" Matamoras, Sept. 28, 1846
Mackay, John C.		"	" " Oct. 29, 1846
Madray, William		"	" " Dec. 27, 1846
Patterson, Robert		"	" Camargo, Nov. 6, 1846
Seybert, William		"	" Matamoras, Dec. 24, 1846
Wood, William		"	" Camp Patterson, Sept. 19, 1846

Deserted:

		1846.	
Privates.			
Alexander, Rufus B.		June 21	Deserted at Baton Rouge, La., July 29, 1846
Little, John		"	Leave of absence till July 16, 1846, not heard of since.

This company was discharged at New Orleans May 21, 1847.

Company "F."

Name and Rank.	Place of Enlistment.	Enrolled	Remarks.
Captain,		1846,	
John A. Campbell		July 1	
First Lieutenants.			
Jacob Love		"	Died Oct. 5, 1846, at Camargo, Mex.
Ephraim Merritt		"	Resigned Nov. 28, 1846, at Matamoras, Mex.
Samuel Hooper		"	Elec'd 2d Lieut. from Sergt. Oct. 1, 1846; promoted to 1st Lt. Nov. 28, 1846.
Second Lieutenant.			
Samuel J. R. Wilson		"	Resigned Aug. 28, '46, at Camp Patterson, Tex.
Sergeants.			
Austin Organ		"	
William Merritt		"	
James Turner		"	
Warren E. McMackin		"	
Corporals.			
Daniel Simpson		"	
John W. Wallace		"	
William B. Wilson		"	
Joseph J. R. Turney		"	
Musician.			
Jeffers'n W. Barnhill		"	
Privates.			
Armstrong, Wm. R.		"	Sick at Matamoras since Dec. 14, 1846
Barnhill, Rigdon S.		"	
Crews, Nathan		"	
Cox, James E.		"	
Cook, Hiram H.		"	
Cook, Howlett H.		"	
Cook, William M.		"	
Clevenger, Benj. W.		"	
Dorris, John G.		"	
Day, David H.		"	
Ellis, Sterlin C. B.		"	Wounded at battle of Cerro Gordo Apl. 18, '47
Edwards, John Y. C.		"	
Ewing, John		"	
Funkhouser, Benj		"	
Fitzgerred, Samuel		"	
Frazier, William J.		"	Sick at Matamoras Dec. 14, 1846
Gray, William		"	
Gray, Ellis S.		"	
Harris, Sion		"	
Ham, William D.		"	
Hartin, William F.		"	
Hulshcraft, John		"	
Johnson, Riley V.		"	
Johnson, Silas		"	Sick at Matamoras since Dec. 14, 1846
Kimmel, William		"	" " Sept. 24, 1846
Lard, Bluford		"	
Lacy, James		"	Sick at Matamoras since Dec. 14, 1846
Matthews, Wm. T.		"	
Morris, Willis		"	
Murphy, Davis		"	
McCullough, Jas. W.		"	
McCollum, David		"	
McCollum, Samuel		"	
Owen, David		"	
Phelps, Hosea C.		"	
Phelps, William C.		"	
Reed, James		"	
Reed, William, 2d		"	
Rusher, Jeremiah		"	
Rusher, Henry C.		"	
Simpson, William C		"	
Simpson, Andrew J.		"	
Simpson, William		"	
Shannon, Rowl'nd H.		"	
Sloan, Jefferson		"	
Taylor, Ninian R.		"	
Taylor, James H.		"	
Tims, John		"	
White, John		"	
West, Alfred		"	

Died:

Name and Rank.	Place of Enlistment.	Enrolled	Remarks.
Privates.		1846.	
Copeland, Joseph		July 1	Died Dec. 9, '46, at hospital, Matamoras
Frazur, John R		"	" Dec. 7, '46.
Lockhart, Wm. J		"	" Aug. 14, '47, at Brazos Island, Texas
Maybry, Wm. H		"	" Aug. 10, '46, on ship cross'g Gulf of Mex.
Merritt, Benjamin		"	Shot at battle of Cerro Gordo April 18, '47
Rister, Abraham		"	Died Sept. 24, '46, in hospital, Matamoras
Reed, William, 1st		"	" Oct. 2, '46, at Camargo, Mex.

Discharged:

Name and Rank.	Place of Enlistment.	Enrolled	Remarks.
Sergeant.		1846.	
Isaac S. Warmouth		July 1	Disch. on Surg. cert. of disability, Jan. 10, '47
Second Corporal.			
James H. Farley		"	Disch. on Surg. cert. of disability, Aug. 14, '46
Privates.			
Black, William		"	Disch. on Surg. cert. of disability, Nov. 5, '46
Beech, Benjamin		"	" " " " Nov. 28, '46
Cox, David		"	" " " " Oct. 26, '46
Campbell, Moses M		"	" " " " Aug. 31, '46
Clevenger, Dan'l H		"	" " " " Mar. 31, '47
Fitch, Henry		"	" " " " Nov. 28, '46
Harris, James M		"	" " " " Sept. 2, '46
Harris, Thomas J		"	
Holmes, John B		"	" " " " Sept. 3, '46
Linder, Abraham		"	" " " " Mar. 3, '47
McCrary, James		"	" " " " Oct. 20, '46
Matthews, Geo. W		"	" " " " Sept. 3, '46
Palmer, Jacob		"	" " " " Mar. 3, '47
Reed, Henry		"	" " " " Nov. 28, '46
Robinson, Tyra		"	" " " " Aug. 31, '46
Trotter, Shirley		"	" " " " Sept. 3, '46

This company was discharged at New Orleans, La., on May 21, 1847.

Company "G."

Name and Rank.	Place of Enlistment.	Enrolled	Remarks.
Captain.		1846.	
W. K. Lawler		June 29	
First Lieutenants.			
Samuel S. M. Proctor		"	
Alexander W. Pool		"	Resigned Oct. 20, 1846
Second Lieutenants.			
William Stricklin		"	Resigned Oct. 1, 1846
James S. Rearden		"	
Sergeants.			
Timothy Ingram		"	Promoted 1st Sergt. from Corporal Jan. 1, '47
Patrick Scully		"	
Alfred Karnes		"	Promoted from Corporal Jan. 13, 1847
John Howard		"	
Corporals.			
Robert A. Boyd		"	Appointed Corporal Jan. 1, 1847
George M. Weed		"	" " " Jan. 13, 1847
Edward Jones		"	
Isaac M. Sketoe		"	
Musician.			
James Creed		"	

MEXICAN WAR.

Name and Rank.	Place of Enlistment.	Enrolled	Remarks.
Privates.			
Addison, Sir Sidney		June 29	
Baker, David P		"	
Barnett, David C		"	
Bennett, Joseph C		"	
Brazier, Riley		"	
Carpenter, William		"	
Choisser, Attalias		"	
Choisser, Edmund		"	
Crenshaw, Abraham		"	
Cummings, Jacob		"	
Davenport, William		"	
Davis, John B. M		"	
Donovon, James		"	
Duncan, Stephen		"	
Evans, William G		"	
Fugate, John M		"	
Gaston, Wesley W		"	
Grayson, Jesse F		"	
Harmons, George		"	
Hardin, Joseph		"	
Hill, James		"	
Holt, William		"	
Hubbs, James		"	
Hudgins, James		"	
Ingram, John W		"	
Jones, John W		"	
Lewis, Charles		"	
Lowrey, Charles		"	
Lynch, Logan		"	
Mann, John		"	
McChiskey, Hiram		"	
Moore, Ransom		"	
Page, William W		"	
Parker, John		"	
Porter, Robert W		"	
Price, Berry		"	
Reynolds, Thomas		"	
Scarborough, John		"	
Sisk, Albert		"	
Sisk, Benjamin		"	
Sitles, Henry		"	
Skelton, William J		"	
Smith, John		"	
Smith, William T		"	
Sneed, Eldridge		"	
Stiff, Nathaniel		"	
Stricklin, Lewis		"	
Wamack, Sheph'd F		"	
Warren, Chas. M. C		"	
Weddle, Andrew		"	
Weddle, William		"	
Weaver, Stokeley		"	

Discharged :

Name and Rank.	Place of Enlistment.	Enrolled	Remarks.
First Sergeant.		1846.	
Hanson Q. Roberts		June 29	Disch. Sept. 18, '46, Camp Patterson, disabil'y
Corporal.			
Americus Henrick		"	Disch. Aug. 17, '46, Brazos Santiago, disabil'y
Privates.			
Bond, William		"	Disch. Sept. 6, '46, Camp Patterson, disabil'y
Bennett, Thomas Y		"	" Oct. 28, '46, Matamoras, "
Bramlet, Alfred J		"	" Nov. 27, '46, " "
Creed, Robert		"	" Nov. 2, '46, " "
Daws, Edmund		"	" Aug. 30, '46, Camp Patterson, "
Emory, Jacob		"	" Nov. 29, '46, Matamoras, "
Griggs, Hubbard A		"	" Aug. 17, '46, Brazos Santiago, "
Hamilton, James		"	" " " "
Karnes, David B		"	" Aug. 31, '46, " "
Moody, John		"	" Nov. 27, '46, Matamoras, "
Proctor, Giles		"	" Aug. 30, '46, Camp Patterson, "
Paisley, Joseph P		"	" Aug. 31, '46, " "
Reid, Johnson		"	" Nov. 2, '46, Matamoras, "
Slavens, A. Calvin		"	" Nov. 29, '46, " "

THIRD REGIMENT.

Name and Rank.	Place of Enlistment.	Enrolled	Remarks.
		1846.	
Stricklin, J. Garner		June 29	Disch. Sept. 6, '46, Camp Patterson, disabil'y
Taylor, Henry		" "	Aug. 17, '46, Brazos Santiago, "
Vinson, Stokely		" "	" " " "
Williams, William G.		" "	" " " "
Williams, John		" "	Aug. 30, '46, Camp Patterson, "

Died:

Sergeant.			
Safford B. Eddy			Died at Victoria Jan. 13, 1847
Privates.			
Baugher, John J			Died at Camp Patterson Aug. 30, 1846
Cain, James M			" Matamoras Dec. 20, 1846
McCauslin, John			" Vera Cruz April 12, 1847
Oxberry, James			" Camp Patterson Sept. 1, 1846
Powell, John			" Matamoras Oct. 24, 1846

This company was discharged at New Orleans, La., May 21, 1847.

Company "H."

Name and Rank.	Place of Enlistment.	Enrolled	Remarks.
Captain.		1846.	
S. G. Hicks		June 4	
First Lieutenants.			
Lewis F. Casey		"	Resigned Nov. 1, 1846, at Matamoras, Mex.
William A. Thomas		"	Promoted from 2d to 1st Lieut. Nov. 1, 1846
Second Lieutenant.			
Thos. S. Levington		"	
Sergeants.			
John Bagwell		"	
Garaway Elkins		"	
Jacob Casey		"	Appointed Sergt. Oct. 18, 1846
Marcus D. Bruce		"	" " July 8, 1846
Corporals.			
Jos. F. Thomisson		"	Appointed Corporal —— 15, 1846
John Q. A. Bay		"	" " April 30, 1847
William Sumnors		"	" " Jan. 26, 1847
John McConnell		"	" " Jan. 21, 1847
Privates.			
Atchison, Thomas I.		"	
Bean, Peter		"	
Brown, James R.		"	
Ballard, Thomas H.		"	
Blalock, Eli		"	
Brady, John		"	
Bullock, Samuel		"	
Butler, John		"	
Bateman, James C.		"	
Buckout, Benjamin		"	
Beal, Loring R.		"	
Caldwell, James		"	
Donohoo, James		"	
Dorris, William H.		"	
Fly, Jesse I.		"	
Fields, Abraham W.		"	Left sick at hospital, Tampico, Mex.
Gray, Nicholas		"	Disch. Mar. 3, '47, on Surg. cert. of disability.
Garrison, Jeffers'n I.		"	
Galbreath, James M.		"	

Name and Rank.	Place of Enlistment.	Enrolled	Remarks.
		1846.	
Hull, James		June 4	
Harlow, Thomas		"	
Hawkins, John		"	
Hawkins, Jesse		"	
Hales, Marcus		"	
Hicks, William		"	
Hales, Albert		"	
Hatfield, Johnson		"	
Knox, George		"	
Kelly, James		"	
Lynch, John B.		"	
Lisenby, John R.		"	
Lutz, James W.		"	
Murphy, James		"	
Milborn, John		"	
Moor, Alexander		"	
McCarver, James		"	
McFarland, Pleasant		"	
McGuire, Andrew		"	
McAtee, Edward		"	Appointed Hospital Steward —— 18, 1847
Overby, James C.		"	
Patterson, Benjamin		"	
Poston, John M.		"	
Scott, James		"	
Wilkinson, H. H.		"	
Wilbanks, Quincy A.		"	Left sick in hospital, Matamoras, Mex
Westcoat, James		"	
Warren, David		"	

Discharged:

Name and Rank.	Place of Enlistment.	Enrolled	Remarks.
Sergeant,		1846.	
William B. Braden		June 4	Disch. on Surg. cert. of disability Oct. 18, 1846
Privates,			
Atchison, Joseph T.		"	Disch. on Surg. cert. of disability Nov. 9, 1846
Arant, Samuel W.		"	" " " " Aug. 12, 1846
Foster, William		"	" " " " Nov. 30, 1846
Hill, Alexander M.		"	" " " " Sept. 1, 1846
Harvey, Elijah B.		"	" " " " Oct. 26, 1846
Ivy, Benjamin		"	" " " " Oct. 18, 1846
Crisel, William I.		"	" " " " Sept. 1, 1846
Moss, Lucillus C.		"	
McClendon, Wm. R.		"	" " " " Oct. 18, 1846
Owens, Sampson R.		"	" " " " Dec. 1, 1846
Newby, John E.		"	" " " " Oct. 9, 1846
Rankin, Robert B.		"	" " " " Dec. 1, 1846
Sterns, Charles W.		"	" " " " Jan. 21, 1846
Summors, James E.		"	" " " " Oct. 18, 1846
Stephenson, Wm. I.		"	" " " " Aug. 15, 1846
Smith, Daniel		"	" " " " " "
Thurman, Patrick T.		"	
Teeters, James		"	" " " " Sept. 1, 1846
Veasey, Benjamin		"	" " " " Oct. 9, 1846
Wallace, John A.		"	" " " " Aug. 15, 1846
Williamson, Vine't P.		"	" " " " Sept. 1, 1846
Wilkey, Harrison		"	" " " " " "
Yearwood, John		"	
Williams, John		"	

Died:

Name and Rank.	Place of Enlistment.	Enrolled	Remarks.
Corporals,		1846.	
James Bruce		June 4	Died Jan. 16, '47, *en route* to Tampico, Mex.
James Wimberly		"	" April 30; killed near Jalapa, Mex
Privates,			
Breeze, Jonathan H.		"	Died Dec. 7, '46, at gen. hosp., Matamoras
Harlow, Moses		"	" Oct. 26 at Matamoras, Mex., gen. hosp
Harvy, Joseph		"	" May 13; fell overboard on way to N. Orl's
Newby, James C.		"	" Aug. 13, 1846, at Brazos Santiago, Tex.

This company was discharged May 21, 1847, at New Orleans, La.

Company "I."

Name and Rank.	Place of Enlistment.	Enrolled	Remarks.
Captain.		1846.	
Jonathan P. Harvey.		June 6	
First Lieutenants.			
Charles Coker		"	Resigned, to take effect Oct. 1, 1846.
Enos A. Lasater		"	Elected from private, Oct. 1, 1846
Second Lieutenants.			
Warden C. Coons		"	Resigned, to take effect Nov. 15, 1846
John J. Ritchie		"	
Sergeants.			
Charles Atchison		"	Appointed 1st Sergt., from private, June 6, '47
Hiram W. Hall		"	
Moses Hutson		"	
James Hughes		"	Appointed Sergt., from private, Nov. 9, 1846
Corporals.			
Joseph Koger		"	Appointed from private Dec. 4, 1846
William G. Burnett.		"	
John B. Smith		"	Appointed from private Oct. 12, 1846
Edward Trammel		"	" " " Nov. 17, "
Musician.			
Thomas Braden		"	
Privates.			
Askey, Jackson		"	
Barnes, Thomas		"	
Brill, Solomon S		"	
Boster, Jacob		"	
Burnett, George		"	
Clark, William		"	
Cross, John C		"	
Crisell, George W		"	
Coons, John		"	
Durham, John W		"	
Denny, Joseph H		"	
Davis, Alfred		"	Reduced to ranks, from 1st Sergt., Jan. 6, '47.
Estes, William		"	
Flannikin, David O		"	
Ford, Abram		"	
Farmer, William		"	
Gibson, James W		"	
Galliher, James F		"	
Hays, William		"	
Heard, Wm. B		"	
Johnson, Jesse		"	
Lane, James		"	
Maulding, John		"	On furlough, at Jalapa, May 6, 1847
Mayberry, Wm. H		"	
Mayberry, James H		"	
Mayberry, Jacob		"	
McDaniel, Andrew J.		"	
Shasteen, John K		"	
Shell, Calvin		"	
Stanfield, Thomas		"	
Starnater, William		"	
Trammel, Elijah		"	
Trammel, Philip		"	
Wheeler, Abner P		"	Reduced to ranks, from Sergt., Nov. 9, 1846
Webb, John		"	

Deserted:

Name and Rank.	Place of Enlistment.	Enrolled	Remarks.
Private.		1846.	
William L. Morris		June 6	Deserted at Alton, Ill., July 8, 1846

MEXICAN WAR.

Discharged:

Name and Rank.	Place of Enlistment.	Enrolled	Remarks.
Corporals.		1846.	
Jasper Ghormley		June 6	Discharged Nov. 17, 1846; disability
Wm. L. Stevens		" "	" Dec. 1, " "
Musician.			
William Gross		" "	Discharged Oct. 18, 1846; disability
Privates.			
Allen, Dudley R		" "	Discharged Aug. 17, 1846; disability
Adaire, Philip		" "	" Oct. 17, " "
Biggerstaff, Joshua		" "	" Sept. 8, " "
Boyd, Lyle		" "	" Oct. 17, " "
Boyer, Anderson		" "	" Nov. 17, " "
Cape, Hiram		" "	" Oct. 18, " "
Clark, John, Sr		" "	" Nov. 26, " "
Coker, Leonard		" "	" for disability; date unknown
Cannada, William		" "	" Nov. 17, 1846; disability
Davis, Thomas P		" "	" Nov. 26, " "
Frazer, John		" "	" Oct. 18, " "
Fields, James		" "	" for disability; date unknown
Flanniken, James W		" "	" Oct. 17, 1846; disability
Gibson, Daniel		" "	
Ghormly, Michael		" "	
Hamilton, Parsons L		" "	" Nov. 17, " "
Hayes, John		" "	" Oct. 17, " "
Hardester, James		" "	" Aug. 31, " "
Lane, James, Sr		" "	" for disability; date unknown
Morris, Hiram		" "	" Nov. 25, 1846; disability
Mundy, Elias		" "	" Oct. 17, " "
Proctor, Saml. H. F.		" "	" Sept. 8, " "
Sloane, Andrew		" "	" Oct. 18, " "
Smiddy, Jeremiah		" "	" Nov. 25, " "
Stelle, David		" "	" Nov. 17, " "
Williams, William		" "	" for disability; date unknown
Williams, Wm. K		" "	" Aug. 31, 1846; disability
Willis, Eli S		" "	

Died:

Name and Rank.	Place of Enlistment.	Enrolled	Remarks.
Corporal.		1846.	
David Hutson		June 26	Died at Matamoras, Mex., Sept. 28, 1846
Privates.			
Adams, John R		" "	Died at Matamoras, Mex., Oct. 4, 1846
Berry, William P		" "	" " " Nov. 30, "
Cholee, John		" "	" Rio Grande, " Nov. 12, "
Cook, John		" "	" Camp Patterson, Sept. 3, "
Cheek, Aseur S		" "	" Matamoras, Mex., Oct. 2, "
Clark, John, Jr		" "	" Camargo, " Oct. 28, "
Epperson, James		" "	" Matamoras, " Sept. 29, "
Flannekin, Ewing G		" "	" Matamoras, " Dec. 20, "
Hood, Dempsey		" "	" Brazos Santiago, Mex., Aug. 18, 1846
McGuire, Wm. C		" "	" Camp Patterson, Sept. 6, 1846
McBroom, John S		" "	" Matamoras, Mex., Dec. 3, "
Wright, Elijah		" "	" Camargo, " Dec. 3, "

This company was discharged at New Orleans, May 21, 1847.

THIRD REGIMENT.

Company "K."

Name and Rank.	Place of Enlistment.	Enrolled	Remarks.
Captain. Theodore McGinnis.		1846 July 2.	Commanding company.
First Lieutenant. George Walker.		"	
Second Lieutenant. Green B. Field.		"	
Third Lieutenant. James McDonald.		"	
Sergeants.			
Stephen D. Kennard		"	
William S. Hodge		"	
George F. James		"	On furlough, Vera Cruz, Mexico.
Abraham Gothings		"	
Corporals.			
John F. Johnson		"	
John C. Compton		"	
Elijah E. Trevilion		"	
Huberry G. Glass		"	
Privates.			
Alcock, Edmund		"	
Bolan, Dennis		"	On furlough, Vera Cruz, Mexico.
Belford, Patterson		"	
Boze, Ambrose		"	
Boze, James		"	
Bowman, John A		"	
Craig, Nathaniel		"	
Church, William E		"	
Cranson, Daniel		"	
Cary, Benjamin R		"	
Carr, John		"	
Dyke, David A		"	
Degan, John		"	
Egan, James F		"	On furlough, at Jalapa, Mexico.
Fath, John D		"	
Gray, Thomas S		"	
Green, Isaac		"	
Henry, Willis		"	
Holt, Robert C		"	
Jackson, John T		"	Sick at Matamoras, Mexico.
King, James		"	
Lamburth, James T		"	
Lewis, Joseph		"	
Murphy, Peter		"	
McDaniel, Jacob		"	
McCosland, William		"	
McGary, John		"	
McGuire, James		"	
McElhanny, Moses		"	
McLaughlin, Charles		"	
Pfeninger, John R		"	
Shoemaker, Moses		"	
Sherdon, Daniel		"	
Tomy, Patrick		"	
Wells, John		"	

Deserted:

Privates.		1846	
Foy, Peter		July 2.	Deserted, Alton, July 7, before must'd in serv.
Shaw, William		"	15.

Died:

Privates.	1846	
Belford, John	July 2.	Died on Gulf, near Brazos Sant'go, Aug. 12, '46
Boze, Calvin	" "	" at Camargo, Oct. 16, 1846
Grim, Martin	" "	" " Oct. 13, 1846
Lemons, Alfred B.	" "	" Matamoras, Sept. 22, 1846
Young, Benjamin F.	" "	" Camargo, Nov. 5, 1846

Discharged:

Sergeants.	1846	
James C. Hancock	July 2.	Disch. at Camp Patterson, Tex., Aug. 3, 1846
Joseph Brannon	" "	" " " " " 30, "

Corporals.		
William P. Grace	" "	Disch. at Camp Patterson, Tex., Aug. 31, 1846
George Williamson	" "	" " " " "

Privates.		
Bazore, Esau	" "	Disch. at Matamoras, Mex., Oct. 20, 1846
Breedlove, James E.	" "	" " " " "
Carrico, Thomas	" "	" " " " "
Corey, Granville	" "	" Camp Patterson, Tex., Aug. 31, 1846
Ennis, Thomas	" "	" " " " 28, "
Glass, John R	" "	" " " " 31, "
Hancock, William F.	" "	" Matamoras, Mex., Oct. 20, 1846
Hodge, George D.	" "	" " " " "
Keef, Benjamin F.	" "	" " " " "
Lamar, John P.	" "	" " " " "
Lewis, Thomas C.	" "	" " " " "
Moody, Samuel H.	" "	" Brazos Santiago, Aug. 16, 1846
Modglin, James M.	" "	" Camargo, Mex., Nov. 18, 1846
Marsh, Josephus	" "	" Matamoras, " Oct. 20, "
McDonald, John	" "	" Camargo, " Nov. 15, "
Paisley, Andrew J.	" "	" Matamoras, " Oct. 20, "
Rubel, Nathan	" "	" Camp Patterson, Tex., Sept. 6, 1846
Simpson, Jesse	" "	" " " " Aug. 21, 1846
Thompson, Rufus L.	" "	" Brazos Santiago, Aug. 16, 1846
Welch, Patrick	" "	" Fort Polk, March 3, 1847

Musician.		
William Robinson	" "	Disch. at Camp Patterson, Tex., Aug. 17, 1846

This company was discharged at New Orleans May 23, 1847.

FOURTH REGIMENT.

The Field and Staff

Of the 4th Regiment of Illinois Volunteers, 3d Brigade of Volunteer Division commanded by Colonel Edward D. Baker, called into the service of the United States by the President. From the 30th day of April, 1847, to the 20th day of May, 1847.

Name and Rank.	Place of Enlistment.	Enrolled	Remarks.
Colonel. Edward D. Baker		1846. June 6	
Lieut.-Colonel. John Moore		June 13	Elected from 1st Lieut. in Co. "B," July 4, 1846
Major. Thomas L. Harris		June 16	Elected from Capt. of Co. "F," July 4, 1846
Adjutant. William B. Fondey		June 6	Second Lieutenant
Surgeon. Wm. M. P. Quinn			Regular Government appointee
A. C. S. and Capt. Joel Seth Post			Regular Government appointee
A. Q. M. and Capt. James A. Barrett		June 6	Appointed from private in Co. "A," Sept. 7,'46.
Sergeant-Major. James H. Merryman		"	Appointed from private in Co. "A," July 19,'46.
Q. M. Sergeant. Richard F. Barrett		"	Appointed from private in Co. "A," April 23,'47
Gilbert E. Winter		June 17	Appoin'd; reduc'd; reappoin'd; again reduc'd
Levi Hite		June 12	App'd Dec. 22,'46; reduced Feb. 6,'47
Principal Musicians. Samuel Barnes		Aug. 10	
Charles Brown		"	Furl'h May 6,'47, to May 31,'47; to enlist for war

Company "A."

Name and Rank.	Place of Enlistment.	Enrolled	Remarks.
Captain. Horatio E. Roberts		1846. June 6	
First Lieutenant. William T. Barrett		"	Absent without leave from April 6, 1847
Second Lieutenants. John S. Bradford		"	Resigned Sept. 16, 1846
William B. Fondey		"	Adjutant from July 6, 1846

MEXICAN WAR.

Name and Rank.	Place of Enlistment.	Enrolled	Remarks.
Sergeants.		1846.	
Walter Davis		June 6	
David Logan		"	
Dudley Wickersham		"	
Argyle W. Farr		"	
Corporals.			
Thomas Hessey		"	
Shelton Ransdall		"	
Edward Connor		"	
Lawson Thomas		"	
Musician.			
William C. B. Lewis		July 5	
Privates.			
Addison, Grandison		June 6	
Ballard, Chris. A.		"	
Balantine, John J.		"	
Barrett, James A.		"	Appointed Ass't Q. M. Sept. 7, 1846
Brown, William W.		"	
Butler, Joshua		"	
Buel, Abel M.		July 24	Left sick in Hospital at Jalapa, May 6, 1847
Cabaniss, Zebulon P.		June 6	Absent on furl. f'm Feb. 1, '47, till exp'n of term
Capoot, John		"	
Chapman, John		"	
Crowl, Upton		"	
Darnell, Harvey		"	
Ferrel, William C		"	
Foster, John E.		"	
Funk, George W.		"	
Frink, John S		July 3	
Gideon, Alfred L.		June 6	
Garrett, Ezra L		July 11	
Haines, Fletcher		June 6	
Harworth, George		"	
House, Erasmus D.		"	
James, George		"	
Keeling, Singleton		"	
Marsh, Joseph		"	
Millington, Aug. O.		"	
Murray, Mathew		"	
Peters, Peter C		"	
Ransdall, James B.		"	
Rape, Henry		"	
Ryan, Jackson		"	
Spotswood, Jas. H.		"	On furlough from April 3 to June 6, 1847
Smith, Joseph H.		July 29	" May 11 to July 29, 1847
Wickersham, W. H.		June 6	
Wilkinson, Reuben		"	
Wilcox, Ephriam		"	
Watson, Charles F.		"	
Watts, Levi P		"	
Whitehurst, Thomas		"	
Weber, George R.		"	Sent home with sick in charge, Aug. 30, 1846
Yeakle, Joseph		"	

Discharged:

		1846.	
Sergeant.			
William W. Pease		June 6	Disch. on Surg. cert. of disability, Oct. 29, '46.
Corporals.			
Joseph B. Pirkins		"	Disch. on Surg. cert. of disability
Samuel O. White		"	
Musician.			
Joseph H. Fultz		"	Disch. on Surg. cert. of disability, Feb. 28, '47.
Privates.			
Alguire, Nicholas		"	Disch. Oct. 4, '46, at Matamoras
Butler, John C.		"	" Aug. —, '46, at Camp. Patterson
Cole, Samuel		"	" Oct. 4, 1846.
Depuey, John		"	" on Surgeon's certificate of disability
Dowdell, Silas		"	
Davis, Isaac		"	
Goodell, William R.		"	Disch. Oct. 9, 1846, at Matamoras
Gorley, Levi		"	" on Surg. cert. of disability, Mar. 3, 1847.

FOURTH REGIMENT.

Name and Rank.	Place of Enlistment.	Enrolled	Remarks.
		1846.	
Hall, George W		June 6	Disch ——, 1846, at Camp Patterson
McDonald, Benj. F		" "	Oct. 29, 1846, at Matamoras
Mathews, Marion F		" "	on Surgeon's certificate of disability
Ransdall, Presley		" "	
Ridgely, Vincent		" "	Disch. on Surgeon's certificate of disability
Sechorn, Alex. J		" "	Aug. 29, 1846
Whitlock, George C		" "	
Waugh, James A		" "	
Westbrook, Henry		" "	
Wise, Jacob		" "	Disch. on Surgeon's certificate of disability

Transferred:

		1846.	
Privates.			
Barrett, Richard F		June 6	Appointed Q. M. Sergt., April 23, 1847
Merriman, James H		" "	July 19, 1846

Died:

		1846.	
Privates.			
Conolly, James		June 6	Died at Matamoras, Sept. 27, 1846
Hokey, Daniel		" "	Oct. 2, 1846
Hardin, William		" "	Camargo, Oct. 31, 1846
Moore, Henry J		" "	Matamoras, Sept. 17, 1846
McCabe, James		" "	Vera Cruz, in hospital, May 4, 1847
Newman, Joseph		" "	Killed by the enemy at battle of Cerro Gordo.
Stipp, Joseph		" "	Died at Matamoras, Oct. 2, 1846

This company was discharged May 28, 1847, at New Orleans.

COMPANY "B."

Name and Rank.	Place of Enlistment.	Enrolled	Remarks.
		1846.	
Captain.			
Garrett Elkin	"	June 13	Resignation accepted Oct. 20, 1846
First Lieutenant.			
Andrew J. Wallace		June 26	Died
Second Lieutenants.			
James M. Withers		June 13	Resignation accepted Oct. 20, 1846
William L. Duncan		" "	Assumed command Oct. 6, 1846
Sergeants.			
B. M. Wyatt		" "	
John D. Lander		" "	Wounded, Cerro Gordo, Mex., April 18, 1847
E. S. Dukshier		" "	
Seaborn Gilmore		June 26	
Corporals.			
Samuel Ogden		June 13	
John G. Crammer		" "	
E. W. Nanty		June 26	
A. J. Mason		June 13	Appointed Feb. 15, 1847, from private
Privates.			
Baldwin, William F		" "	
Brumfield, William		" "	
Baker, Mason		" "	
Burnett, William		June 26	

Name and Rank.	Place of Enlistment.	Enrolled	Remarks.
		1846.	
Brown, Isaac		June 13	In hosp., Matamoras, Dec. 12, '46; sup. disch...
Depew, James		"	Wounded, Cerro Gordo, Mex., April 18, 1847..
Dodson, Ichabod		"	
Elliott, Edward		June 26	
Good, John		June 13	
Glimpse, Joseph		"	
Gwinn, William		June 26	
Graham, Joseph		"	
Graham, Levi		"	
Guy, R. B. R		"	
Harbard, William		June 13	
Harris, J. C		June 26	
Harris, A. J		"	
Hall, John		"	
Hampton, Felix T		"	
Jones, John		June 13	
Johnston, Thomas P		"	
Jenkins, James M		"	Left in Hosp. as nurse, at Jalapa, April 20, 1847
Lash, William		"	
Lamer, William		"	
McIntyre, R. N		"	
McCarroll, Justus		"	
Mitchell, Wilson		June 26	
Newton, Anderson		June 13	In hosp., Matamoras, Dec. 12, '46; sup. disch..
Owen, Thomas J. V		"	Detailed as Hospital Steward July 6, 1846...
Palmer, Allen		"	
Rule, Alexander		June 26	
Series, Julius H		June 13	
Stout, James		"	
Stockton, Jackson C		June 26	Rejected July 18, 1846, lame ankle...
Seaman, Sylvanus		"	
Smock, Fulcard		"	
Tennis, John F		"	
Vanhorn, William M		June 13	
Walker, John		"	Wounded, Cerro Gordo, Mex., April 18, 1847...
Walker, J. E		"	
Williams, David		"	
Withers, Peter		"	

Discharged:

Sergeant.		1846.	
James E. Park		June 13	Disch. by certificate of disability Sept. 24, '46.
Corporals.			
Nicholas Savage		"	Disch. by certificate of disability Sept. 24, 46.
Thomas H. Haines		"	" " " " "
Musicians.			
Charles E. Fling		"	Disch. by certificate of disability Sept. 24, '46.
Samuel Hall		June 26	" " " " Oct. 13, '46..
Privates.			
Crumbaugh, John I		June 13	Disch. by certificate of disability, Oct. 27, '46..
Davis, William S		"	" " " " Oct. 3, '46...
Daponte, Durant		"	
Eskew, Jas. W (name, John H. Eskew)		"	Disch. by certificate of disability Aug. 28, 46..
Gwinn, Alexander		"	" " " " Mar. 3, '47..
Hall, Alfred		June 26	" " " " Oct. 3, '46..
Hall, Felix		"	Discharged by Col. Baker for disability
Johnson, John S. W		June 13	Disch. by certificate of disability Sept.
Lash, Henry		"	" " " " Dec. 3, '46..
Little, William I		"	" " " " Oct. 27, '46..
Mahon, David		"	" " " " Oct. 3, '46 .
Moor, Thomas		June 26	" " " " Sept. 24, '46.
Miller, James M		June 13	" " " " Dec. 3, '46..
Poindexter, Clinton		"	" " " " Oct. 27, '46..
Palmer, Leroy G		"	" " " " Mar. 3, '47..
Reamer, E. C		"	" July 23, '46, by Col. Baker
Toppas, William A		"	" by certificate of disability Dec. 3, '46 ..
Warnuck, Massam'lo		June 26	" by Col. Baker, July 14, '46, disability ..

Died:

Name and Rank.	Place of Enlistment.	Enrolled	Remarks.
Corporals.		1846.	
George Perry		June 13	Died Nov. 3, 1846
John Misner		" "	" Nov. 18, 1846; appointed Corp'l Oct. 19, '46.
Privates.			
Hodge, Andrew J		" "	Died Sept. 9, 1846
Ruth, George		" "	" in Hosp., Matamoras, Feb. 12, 1847
Wallace, Marion		June 26	" Tampico, Feb. 10, 1847
Young, E. B		June 13	" Nov. 30, 1846

Deserted:

Name and Rank.	Place of Enlistment.	Enrolled	Remarks.
Privates.		1846.	
James Pearson		July 3	Deserted from Jefferson Barracks July 4, '46.
Joseph Bozarth		" "	" " " " " "
Stanley S. Foss		" "	" " " " " "

This company was discharged at New Orleans May 26, 1847.

Company "C."

Name and Rank.	Place of Enlistment.	Enrolled	Remarks.
Captain.		1846.	
J. C. Pugh		June 13	
First Lieutenant.			
R. J. Oglesby		" "	
Second Lieutenants.			
A. Foreman		" "	
John P. Post		" "	
Sergeants.			
Stephen Osborn		" "	
Samuel K. Herrell		" "	
Benjamin F. Oglesby		" "	
James Rea		" "	
Corporals.			
John B. Travis		" "	Hospital attendant in Jalapa, Mexico.
William I. Usrey		" "	
John B. Case		" "	
Privates.			
Atwood, John		" "	Wounded in battle at Cerro Gordo, Apr. 18, '47;
Ause, Charles		July 20	in hospital at Jalapa, Mex.
Barnwell, R. G		June 13	
Butler, Jesse		" "	
Bailor, David		" "	
Bradshaw, Madison		" "	
Braden, George M		" "	
Church, George W		" "	
Chapman, Wm. W		" "	
Chambers, Laban		" "	Wounded in right arm Apr. 18, '47, battle of C. Gordo; arm amput'd, hosp. in Jalapa, Mex.
Carver, George		" "	Wounded severely, battle of C. Gordo, Apr. 18, 1847; in hospital at Jalapa, Mex.
Dean, William		" "	
Dial, Davis		" "	
Freeman, James		Aug. 27	
Greenfield, Ambrose		June 13	

Name and Rank.	Place of Enlistment.	Enrolled	Remarks.
		1846.	
Huffman, David		June 13	
Horner, Israel		"	
Henry, Moses M		"	
Henry, William D. B.		"	
Lourie, James A		"	
Lord, Henry			
Lord, Thomas		June 13	
Lee, Alsa B.		July 3	
Martin, Benjamin		June 13	
Martin, Josiah		"	
McDaniel, William		"	
Mair, Christian		"	
Rice, Etherage		"	
Shepperd, Abram		"	
Sprague, Jason		"	
See, William E.		"	
Spangler, Daniel		"	
Turner, James R		"	
Turner, James		"	
Travis, Finis E.		"	
Ward, Lewis		"	
Warnick, Robert		"	
White, John W		"	

Transferred:

		1846.	
Post, Joel Seth		June 13	Commiss'd June 26, 1846, and transf'd to Field and Staff; appoint'd by President A. C. of S.

Discharged:

		1846.	
Sergeants.			
George W. Galbreath		June 13	Disch., Surg's certif. of disability, Aug. 27, '46
John B. Brown		"	" " " " " "
Lawrence S. Helm		"	" " " " Oct. 6, '46
Privates.			
Bosworth, Miles		"	Disch., Surg's certif. of disability, Oct. 6, '46
Botkin, Amos		"	" " " " " "
Greenfield, James		"	" " " " Oct. 18, '46
Hollingsworth, J. H.		"	" " " " Aug. 27, '46
Hawks, William		"	
Ledbetter, James		"	Disch., Surg's certif. of disability, Oct. 6, '46
Malson, George I.		"	" " " " Oct. 18, '46
Martin, Harvey		"	" " " " Oct. 6, '46
Nesbett, William		"	" " " " "
Stevens, Donis		"	" " " " "
Stewart, Robert		"	" " " " "
Travis, John D.		"	" " " " "
Wheeler, William R.		"	" " " " "
Wells, Bazel E.		"	" " " " "

Died:

		1846.	
Corporals.			
Bennett, L. Martin		June 13	Died at Camp Patterson, Aug. 31, 1846
Nelson, George W		"	" in hosp., Jalapa, Apr. 29, '47; wound rec'd in battle of Cerro Gordo, Apr. 18, '47
Privates.			
Bebee, Pomeroy T.		"	Died in hospital at Matamoras, Oct. 20, 1846
Dillon, Charles W.		"	" Camp Patterson, Mex., Sept. 1, 1846
Dickey, John M		"	" " " " 18, 1846
Davidson, William P.		"	" in hospital, Matamoras, Oct. 10, 1846
Howell, David		"	" " " " 1, 1846
Malson, James C		"	" C. Gordo, Apr. 22, wound rec'd Apr. 18, '47
Reece, Samuel		"	Died in hospital at Matamoras, Oct. 3, 1846
Robinson, William P		"	" " " " 12, 1846
Shepperd, James A		"	" " " " Sept. 27, 1846

FOURTH REGIMENT.

Name and Rank.	Place of Enlistment.	Enrolled	Remarks.
		1846.	
Saunders, John		June 13	Died in hospital at Matamoras, Sept. 22, 1846.
Souther, Temple		"	Camp Patterson, Mex., Sept. 19, 1846.
Wheeler, William		"	in hospital at Matamoras, Oct. 1, 1846.
White, Bazel B		"	" Sept. 26, 1846.

This company was discharged at New Orleans, May 25, 1847.

Company "D."

Name and Rank.	Place of Enlistment.	Enrolled	Remarks.
Captain.		1846.	
Achilles Morris		June 9	Died at Tampico, Mex., Feb. 15, 1847.
Second Lieutenants.			
Alfred C. Campbell		"	Assumed command of company Feb. 15, 1847.
John D. Foster		"	
Sergeants.			
Henry M. Spotswood		"	On furl'h from May 1, 1847, in Q. M. Dep't.
David Meigs		"	
John Davis		"	
Jonathan Morris		"	
Corporals.			
William Campbell		"	
Thomas Higgins		"	
Chris. C. Holyer		"	
Hugh Paul		"	
Privates.			
Alsbury, Edward R		"	
Brannon, Josiah		"	
Bloyd, James B		"	
Cast, Archibald		"	Detailed as wardmaster in hospital, Jalapa.
Cutter, William		"	
Dunlap, James T		"	Left at Matamoras, sick, Dec. 17, 1846.
Daly, John		"	
Darnielle, John C		"	
Dodd, John C		"	
Dillman, David		"	
Duncan, Jerome		"	
Edwards, David		"	
Emmett, Robert S		"	
Foster, Peyton		"	
Foster, William		"	
Henwood, William		"	
Henwood, Henry		"	
Hillyard, James P		"	
Howey, William		"	
Huckleberry, John		"	
Huffmaster, Edward		"	
Huffmaster, William		"	
Hoskins, John S		July 29	
Jones, T. B		"	
Kent, Alexander		June 9	
King, John W		"	On furlough in Q. M. Dept. from Jan. 6, 1847, [till June 9, 1847.
Morris, Hamilton		"	
Morris, Randall G		"	
Meigs, Severell		"	
Odell, John		"	Left sick in Matamoras Sept. 15, 1846.
Phelps, Joshua		"	
Rhodes, William G		"	
Shoemaker, Thos. C.		"	
Short, James F		"	
Shelton, John		"	
Smith, Alonzo H		July 19	
Skinner, John H		"	

MEXICAN WAR.

Name and Rank.	Place of Enlistment.	Enrolled	Remarks.
Tinker, William		1846. June 9	
Thompson, Saml. M.		"	Left in hospital, Matamoras, Dec. 14, 1846.
Terpin, James		"	
Williams, John R.		"	
Wilcox, Daniel		"	
Workman, Benjamin		"	

Discharged:

Sergeants.		1846.	
Ashley Walker		June 9	Discharged, disability, Oct. 8, 1846.
Chris. R. Pierce		" "	" " Nov. 17, 1846
Privates.			
Bridges, Joseph		" "	Discharged by order Col. Baker, July 23, 1846.
Campbell, Levi		" "	" " disability, Oct. 5, 1846.
Cross, Riley		" "	" " " "
Cross, Daniel		" "	" " " " Oct. 8, 1846.
Drennan, Samuel		" "	" " by order of Col. Baker, July 23, '46
Dodd, Newton		" "	" " disability, Aug. 29, 1846.
Finger, Jefferson		" "	" " " " Oct. 8, 1846.
Henwood, Berryman		" "	" " " " " "
Lindsay, David		" "	" " " " " "
Morris, Asa L.		" "	" " " " Oct. 5, 1846.
McCrillis, Lafayette.		" "	" " " " Oct. 13, 1846.
Morris, James		" "	" " " " Feb. 28, 1847.
Ponix, William		" "	" " " " Aug. 29, 1846.
Pierce, Samuel		" "	" " " "
Robbins, Wilson		" "	" " " " March 7, 1847.
Sullivan, Benjamin		" "	" " " " Feb. 28, 1847.
Sexton, Calvay		" "	" " " " Nov. 17, 1846.
Short, Rowan I.		" "	" " " "
Sampson, William		" "	" " " " Oct. 5, 1846.
Snyder, Logan C.		" "	" " " " " "
Terpin, William		" "	" " " "
Vermillion, William		" "	" " " "
Walker, Joel H.		" "	" " " " Nov. 1, 1846.

Died :

Privates.		1846.	
Allison, John		June 9	Died at Camargo, Mex., Oct. 28, 1846.
Hellyard, John		" "	" " " " Oct. 26, 1846.
Harralson, James		" "	" " Matamoras, Mex., Dec. 20, 1846.
Jones, James		" "	" " Camargo, Mex., Nov. 16, 1846.
Morris, Jacob		" "	" " " " Oct. 22, 1846.
Morris, Milton		" "	" " " " Nov. 1, 1846.
McKee, Samuel		" "	Killed, by accident, April 16, 1847.
Nation, Wm. F.		" "	Died at Camargo, Mex., Oct. 18, 1846.
Reed, Henry B.		" "	" " " " Oct. 28, 1846.
Shelton, Morris		" "	Killed by Mexicans April 17, 1847.

Deserted:

		1846.	
Peyton Foster, Jr.		June 9	Deserted on march to Jefferson Barracks, sick
Wm. Heridith		" "	" " from Jefferson Barracks July 22, 1846

This company was discharged at New Orleans on May 26, 1847.

COMPANY "E."

Name and Rank.	Place of Enlistment.	Enrolled	Remarks.
Captain.		1846.	
Daniel Newcomb		June 12	
Second Lieutenants.			
Benjamin Howard		"	
Charles Maltby		"	
Sergeants.			
William Lowry		"	Left sick in hospital, at Jalapa, May 7, 1847
G. E. Bennett		"	
John Vinson		July 3	
Absalom Hamilton		June 12	
Corporals.			
Isaiah Davenport		"	
William Allsop		"	
William Kinney		"	Hospital attendant at Jalapa, May 7, 1847
William Davis		July 6	
Musician.			
John Mason		"	
Privates.			
Benson, Charles H		June 12	Left sick at Matamoras Hospital, Oct. 9, 1846
Brown, Samuel J		"	" Jalapa Hospital, May 7, 1847
Boyer, George M		"	
Bobo, Phario		"	
Clifton, William		"	
Cappenberger, Jos.		"	
Chack, Adam		"	
Chapman, James F		July 2	Left sick at Matamoras, Oct. 9, 1846
Cornell, Samuel		July 6	
Davis, Remas		June 12	
Farris, Benjamin H		"	Left sick at Matamoras, Dec. 14, 1846
Glenn, Samuel P		"	
Guinn, Darby		July 2	[turned as priv. Feb. 6, 1847. Sergt. until Dec. 6, '46; app't'd Q. M. Sergt; re-
Hite, Levi		"	
Hill, Egbert O		June 12	Left sick at Matamoras, Oct. 9, 1846
Hutchins, Thomas		"	
Harp, William		"	
Henry, James		July 2	
Innman, James		"	Left sick at Matamoras, Dec. 14, 1846
Logan, James A		June 12	
McDeed, John		"	
Martin, James		"	
Martin, Benjamin		"	
Purdy, William		July 2	
Purdy, John H		"	
Price, John		July 6	
Pennyman, James		July 2	
Russell, Lowe Z		June 12	
Stratten, Joseph		"	
Star, Conrad		"	
Scroggins, Anders'n		July 2	
Sawyer, Solick		July 3	
Sawyer, Snowden		July 6	
Skidmore, Rueben		"	
Smith, James		June 12	Left sick at Matamoras, Dec. 14, 1846
Thornby, Leroy		"	" Jalapa, May 7, 1847
Tenery, Thomas		July 2	
Vanate, Isaac		June 12	
Welch, Richard D		"	
Wright, William W		"	
Whillis, Isaac W		"	

MEXICAN WAR.

Discharged:

Name and Rank.	Place of Enlistment.	Enrolled	Remarks.
1st Sergeant.		1846.	
John Hutchins		June 12	Discharged on Surgeon's certif., Aug. 22, 1846
Privates.			
Brock, Elias		"	Discharged on Surgeon's certif., Oct. 13, 1846
Brock, Andrew		"	" " " "
Dawson, James B		"	" " " "
Emland, Alfred		"	" " " " Oct. 18, 1846
Halsey, Solomon		"	" " " " Oct. 13, 1846
Harp, Thomas		"	" " " "
Hammitt, Joseph		"	" " " " May 8, 1847
King, Daniel		"	" " " " Oct. 13, 1846
Linton, James	July 6	"	" " " "
McCuddy, Isaac	June 12	"	" " " " Nov. 10, 1846
Pomroy, Franklin		"	" " " " Oct. 13, 1846
Richards, Evan		"	" " " "
Williams, Jared		"	" " " " Aug. 22, 1846

Died:

Name and Rank.	Place of Enlistment.	Enrolled	Remarks.
Privates.		1846.	
Blankenship, Jess		June 12	Died at Camp Matamoras, Oct. 5, 1846
Beebe, David		"	" " Camargo, Nov. 14, 1846
Butler, William		"	" " Matamoras, Dec. 23, 1846
Belford, Owen		"	" " Tampico, Feb. 14, 1847
Clifton, Job		"	" " Matamoras, Dec. 18, 1846
Kinney, Ambrose		"	" " Camargo, Nov. 11, 1846
Johnson, Theophilus		"	" " " Nov. 8, 1846
Jackson, Joshua E		"	" " Cerro Gordo, April 21, 1847
Murphy, Richard		"	" " Rio del Plan
McPherson, Jesse L		"	" " Patterson, Aug. 25, 1846
Payne, Calvin		"	" " " Sept. 10, 1846
Richards, Isaac N		"	" " " " 8, 1846
Wallace, William		"	" " Camargo, Nov. 3, 1846

This company was discharged at New Orleans, May 28, 1847.

Company "F."

Name and Rank.	Place of Enlistment.	Enrolled	Remarks.
Captain.		1846.	
Asa D. Wright		June 16	
First Lieutenant.			
Robert C. Scott		"	Elected 1st Lieut. July 8, 1846, from Sergt
Second Lieutenant.			
Sheldon J. Johnson		"	Died May 13 of wounds received at Jalapa April 18, 1847.
Sergeants.			
Franceway Day		"	
William P. Berry		"	
James P. Walker		"	
Cornelius Rourke		"	Left in hosp. at Jalapa; wounded April 18, '47.
Corporals.			
C. B. Altig		"	
Thomas Watkins		"	
Robert N. Jones		"	
Napoleon B. Greer		"	Appointed Corporal from private Feb. 10, 1847

FOURTH REGIMENT.

Name and Rank.	Place of Enlistment.	Enrolled	Remarks.
Privates.		1846.	
Bishop, Robert		June 16	On furlough April 6, 1847; time not known....
Bond, Bannister		"	
Bell, A. G.		"	Detailed in hosp. as nurse, Jalapa, Apr. 18, '47
Bond, Green		"	
Brown, Jesse		"	
Clary, Daniel		"	
Close, William		"	
Day, Philip S		"	
Danton, Geo. W.		"	
Elmon, Elijah		"	
Guernsay, Amos		"	
Garber, John		"	
Goldsby, Richard W.		"	
Goodman, Christian		"	
Hutcherson, William		"	Detailed in hosp. as nurse, Jalapa, Apr. 18, '47
Haughton, Aaron		"	
Johnson, A. K.		"	Left in hospital at Jalapa, sick, May 6, 1847 ...
Jones, John		"	
King, Walter W		"	
Lukins, Jesse		"	
Moore, Robert		"	
Morris, Philmon		"	
Miller, Royal		"	
Nance, George W.		"	
Patterson, James H.		"	
Rhodes, Nathan		"	
Ritchie, Thomas		"	
Smith, John B.		"	Left in hosp., sick, at Tampico, Mch. 11, 1847 ..
Slaton, Daniel		"	
Senter, William		"	
Tebbs, Samuel		"	
Troxell, James		"	*Left in hosp. at Matamoras, Dec. 14, '46; sick
Wood, McLeu		"	
Wilt, Richard		"	
Wiseman, Enoch		"	
Wiseman, Lewis		"	
Wright, Thomas L		"	

* Reported on the Regimental Returns for April, 1847, discharged 3d March, 1847, at Matamoras, on Surgeon's certificate of disability.

Discharged :

Name and Rank.	Place of Enlistment.	Enrolled	Remarks.
Privates.		1846.	
Boss, James W		June 16	Discharged on Surg. certificate, Aug. 29, 1846.
Bond, John		"	" " " Oct. 18, 1846..
Clark, David		"	" " " Aug. 29, 1846.
Clary, Thomas		"	" " " Oct. 8, 1846..
Clary, Robert C		"	" " " "
Cox, Randolph		"	" " " Nov., 1846 ...
Ely, Samuel G. W.		"	" " " Oct. 8, 1846..
Estill, Isaac		"	" " " Mch. 7, 1847..
Green, Ivans		"	" " " Aug. 29, 1846.
Gum, Charles		"	ord. of Col. Baker, before service
Hohimer, Elias		"	" " " July 29, 1846...
Raybourn, Robert A.		"	on Surg. certificate, Oct. 20, 1846..
Smith, O. H. P		"	" " " Oct. 8, 1846 ..
Stone, William A.		"	" " " Dec. 14, 1846.
Smedley, Richard H.		"	" " " Aug. 29, 1846.
Watkins, James		"	" " " Oct. 8, 1846 ..

Died:

Name and Rank.	Place of Enlistment.	Enrolled	Remarks.
Sergeants.		1846.	
Potter, Robert		June 16	Died at sea, Aug. 5, 1846 ....
Short, David B.		"	Died at Camargo, Nov. 27, 1846 ....
Corporal.			
Hadwick, Michael		"	Died at Matamoras, Jan. —, 1847.........
Musician.			
Gum, Robert C.		"	Died at Camargo, Oct. 5, 1846 ....

296 MEXICAN WAR.

Name and Rank.	Place of Enlistment.	Enrolled	Remarks.
Privates.		1846.	
Atcherson, Lewis C.		June 16	Died at Camargo, Oct. 31, 1846.
Combs, William S.		" "	" " Nov. 11, 1846.
Durbin, Aaron		" "	" " Oct. 11, 1846.
Goldsby, Elias		" "	" Matamoras, Sept. 21, 1846.
Hamilton, Peter		" "	" " Dec. 5, 1846.
Hornback, Alvin		" "	Killed in action, April 18, 1817
King, Joseph M.		" "	Died at Matamoras, Oct. 20, 1846.
Miller, John C.		" "	" " Dec. 4, 1846.
Nance, Henry		" "	" " Jan. —, 1847.
Nance, Willis T.		" "	" Camargo, Oct. 22, 1846.
Simpson, Jonat'n H.		" "	Died Aug. 6, 1846.
Thomas, Owen		" "	Died at Camargo, Oct. 19, 1846.
Trust, Anderson C.		" "	" " Nov. 6, 1846
Wiseman, Benjamin		" "	" " Oct. 28, 1846
Yeokum, James N.		" "	" " Oct. 18, 1846.
Yeokum, Geo. N.		" "	Died April 23, 1847, of wounds received in action of April 18, 1847.

Deserted :

Sergeant.		1846.	
William C. Phillips			Received furlough from July 18 to Sept. 7, '46; has not since re-joined his company.

This company was discharged at New Orleans, May 26, 1847.

Company "G."

Name and Rank.	Place of Enlistment	Enrolled	Remarks.
Captain.		1846.	
Edward Jones	Springfield, Ill	June 17	
First Lieutenant.			
Leonard A. Knott	" "	" "	Died at sea, May 22, '47, *en route* to N. Orleans
Second Lieutenant.			
Wm. A. Tinney	" "	" "	
Sergeants.			
Samuel Rhodes	" "	" "	
John N. Gill	" "	" "	
George Burton	" "	" "	Promoted from Corporal, March 1, 1847.
Corporals.			
Henry I. Heath	" "	" "	
John G. Hammer	" "	" "	
Jesse A. Nason	" "	" "	
John Chandler	Jeff. Barracks Mo.	July 22	Appointed from private, March 1, 1847.
Privates.			
Allen, Buzill	Springfield, Ill	June 17	
Booth, William	" "	" "	Left sick in hospital at Matamoras, Dec. 6, '46.
Briggs, Thomas	" "	" "	
Bradstreet, Dudley	" "	" "	
Billsboro, Henry	Jeff. Barracks	July 23	
Becker, Wm. E.	Springfield, Ill	June 17	
Brown, Wm. H.	" "	" "	
Cox, Ezekiel	" "	" "	
Cullen, A. Dillingh'm	" "	" "	
Drury, John	" "	" "	
Dixon, Rensalaer H.	" "	" "	
Fugitt, George W.	Jeff. Barracks	July 22	
Farren, Samuel	Springfield, Ill	June 17	
Flippin, William	Jeff. Barracks	July 22	

Name and Rank.	Place of Enlistment.	Enrolled	Remarks.
		1846	
Frayer, DeWitt C....	Springfield, Ill	June 17	
Hornbecker, John S.	"	"	Left sick in hospital at Matamoras, Dec. 6, '46.
Hall, Robert.........	"	"	
Hawks, John.........	"	"	
Johnson, Crawford.	Jeff. Barracks	July 22	
Koogin, Daniel......	Springfield, Ill	June 17	Left at Matamoras Dec. 6, '46, to go to Tampico
Kelso, David........	"	"	
Leonard, Zeba.......	"	"	
Miller, Christopher.	"	"	
Mountz, Milton......	"	"	
Mullen, Samuel......	"	"	
Merethew, Jonathan	"	"	
Morris, George W...	"	"	
Montgomery, Wm...	"	"	
McMullen, Wm......	"	"	
McKassen, Thomas.	"	"	
Nicholls, Samuel....	"	"	
Norris, John........	"	"	
Page, Samuel T.....	"	"	
Preddy, Selden.....	"	"	
Preddy, Charles.....	"	"	
Rhoads, John.......	"	"	
Rhoads, Franklin L.	"	"	
Ricketts, James.....	"	"	
Rogers, David.......	"	"	Left sick in hospital at Tampico, March, 1847.
Scott, Peter P.......	"	"	
Sullivan, Robert....	"	"	
Sampson, John......	"	"	
Shepherd, Thomas..	"	"	
Thomason, Thomas.	Jeff. Barracks	July 23	
Taney, Marcus D....	Springfield, Ill	June 17	
Town, Hoza P......	"	"	
Walden, Abraham...	"	"	
Weise, Landolen....	"	"	
Winters, Gilbert E..	"	"	Was appointed Qr. Mr. Sergt. July 8, '46; was reduced to private Dec. 22, '46; was re-appointed Qr. Mr. Sergt. Feb. 6, '47, and was again reduced to private April 23, '47.

Died:

Musician.		1846.	
Joseph Turner.......	Springfield, Ill	June 17	Died in hospital at Matamoras, Nov. —, 1846..
Privates.			
Bennett, Sylvester..	"	"	Died in hospital at Matamoras, Dec. 8, 1846..
Hammond, James...	"	"	" " " Nov. 15, 1846..
Thorp, Joseph.......	"	"	" at Jalapa, April 28, 1847, of wounds received in battle of Cerro Gordo.

Transferred:

1st Sergeant.		1846.	
William Campbell...	Springfield, Ill	June 17	To N. C. Staff, July 19, 1846..................

Honorably discharged:

Sergeants.		1846.	
John W. Page.......	Springfield, Ill	June 17	Disch. on Surg. cert. of disability, Mar. 1, '47.
Richard S. Updycke	"	"	" " " May 2, '47.
Privates.			
Dale, Jeremiah......	"	"	Disch. Nov., '46, from gen. hosp., Matamoras
McCracken, John...	"	"	" on Surg. cert. of disability, Aug., 1846..
Martin, Robert.....	"	"	" " " " "
Snyder, Isaac.......	"	"	
Slaughter, Wm.....	"	"	" Nov., '46, from gen. hosp., Matamoras
Smith, John........	"	"	" on Surg. cert. of disability, Dec. 1, '46.
Searcy, Opian O.....	"	"	" May 8, '47, from gen. hosp., Vera Cruz.
Woodrow, Stephen..	"	"	Disch. on Surg. cert. of disability, Aug. 1846..

Deserted:

Name and Rank.	Place of Enlistment.	Enrolled	Remarks.
Corporal. William M. Moore	Springfield, Ill	1846. June 17	Deserted at Tampico, March 6, 1847
Privates. Dunn, John		"	Deserted at New Orleans, July 30, 1846
Wilson, Charles		"	Deserted f'm Jefferson Barracks, July 24, '46.

This company was discharged on May 26, 1847, at New Orleans.

Company "H."

Name and Rank.	Place of Enlistment.	Enrolled	Remarks.
Captain. John S. McConkey		1846. June 20	
Second Lieutenants. J. W. S. Alexander		"	
Albert F. Shaw		"	
Sergeants. Daniel G. Barr		"	
Keefer Laufman		"	Appointed Sergt. March 1, 1847, from private.
Joseph B. McCown		"	
Jira J. Blackman		"	Left sick at Tampico, March 6, 1847
Corporals. Samuel Adams		"	Appointed Corporal Mar. 1, 1847, from private.
Woodruf Rowland		"	
A. J. Shrader		June 21	
Musicians. Johna V. Brown		"	
G. W. Longnecker		June 20	
Privates. Brown, Solomon W.		"	
Ball, Noah C.		"	
Ball, William		"	
Cary, Horace		"	
Cunningham, James		"	
Cunningham, Geo.		"	
Clark, Josiah W.		"	
Downs, Noble		"	
Daughhetoe, Joel C.		"	
Ewing, Isaac N.		"	
Evans, Henry B.		"	
Givins, Joseph R.		"	
Givins, William		"	
Gorthwait, Wm. S.		"	
Hill, Wesley		"	
Hogue, William		"	
Hogue, John		"	
King, John P.		"	
Kelsoe, Noah		"	
McConkey, G. W.		"	
McConkey, Leander		"	
Miller, James M.		"	
Mitchell, Samuel		"	
McDavitt, Jas. R.		June 21	
Parish, David C.		June 20	
Pinson, Aaron		"	
Ryon, John W.		"	Left sick at Matamoras, Dec. 14, 1846
Righmier, James		"	
Stephenson, William		"	Left sick at Matamoras, Dec. 14, 1846

FOURTH REGIMENT.

Name and Rank.	Residence.	Enrolled	Remarks.
		1846.	
Shoffer, Alexander		June 20	
Smith, James M		June 21	Reduced from Corporal, May 6, 1847.
Welton, John		June 20	
Wright, Bird			

Died:

Privates.		1846.	
Daughhete, J. W		June 20	Died at Matamoras, Oct. 9, 1846.
Smith, Himelion		" "	" Camp Patterson, Sept. 5, 1846.
Smith, Wm. Y		" "	" Matamoras, Oct. 24 1846.
Smith, Joseph		" "	" " Dec. 5, 1846.
Wright, H. M		" "	" " Oct. 11, 1846.

Discharged:

Sergeants.		1846.	
J. W. McMillan		June 20	Disch. on surg's certif. of disabil., Oct. 13, '46
J. Y. Utter		" "	" " " " " " Mar. 1, '47
Corporals.			
J. H. Sanford		" "	Disch. on surg's certif. of disabil., Oct. 7, '46
D. J. Connely		" "	" " " " " " Aug. 31, '46
Privates.			
Buntain, Wm		" "	Disch. on surg's certif. of disabil., Oct. 7, '46
Black, Samuel		" "	" " " " " " Oct. 21, '46
Blevins, Thomas		June 21	" " " " " " Nov. 2, '46
Broad, David		July 2	" " " " " " Nov. 2, '46
Brown, T. B		June 20	" " " " " " Nov. 2, '46
Culberson, O. E. D		" "	" " " " " " Oct. 7, '46
Cox, Benard		" "	" " " " " " Oct. 8, '46
Cusick, Vance		" "	" " " " " " Oct. 22, '46
Culver, Reuben		" "	" " " " " " Nov. 4, '46
Duncan, W. S		" "	" " " " " " Nov. 2, '46
Eaton, R. H		" "	" " " " " " Oct. 13, '46
Givins, Wm. M		" "	" " " " " " Oct. 7, '46
House, Samuel		" "	" " " " " " Oct. 22, '46
Hunsinger, Benj		" "	" " " " " " Oct. 22, '46
Lawry, J. F		" "	" " " " " " Oct. 7, '46
Leathers, Wm		" "	" " " " " " Oct. 8, '46
Lightfoot, J. G		" "	" " " " " " Nov. 2, '46
Link, David		" "	" " " " " " Oct. 18, '46
Metcalf, G. W		" "	" " " " " " Mar. 31, '47
Milburn, Wm. M		" "	" " " " " " Oct. 21, '46
Morgan, Michael		" "	" " " " " " Oct. 18, '46
Metcalf, S. R		June 21	" " " " " " Oct. 8, '46
Pease, S. W		June 20	" " " " " " Oct. 18, '46
Pease, D. W		" "	" " " " " " Oct. 18, '46
Reed, B. F		" "	" " " " " " Oct. 22, '46
Rowland, John		" "	" " " " " " Oct. 5, '46
Stephenson, Geo. W		" "	" " " " " " Feb. 1, '47
Tucker, F. B		" "	" " " " " " Dec. 8, '46
Turner, George		" "	" " " " " " Mar. 31, '47
Welch, Benjamin		" "	" " " " " " Oct. 21, '46
Wayne, B. F		" "	" " " " " " Aug. 31, '46
Young, W. F		" "	" " " " " " Aug. 31, '46
Wright, J. G		" "	" " " " " " Oct. 13, '46

Deserted:

		1846.	
Andrew Puison		June 20	Deserted at New Orleans, Aug. 4, 1846.
H. H. James		" "	

This company was discharged on May 26, 1847, at New Orleans.

Company "I."

Name and Rank.	Place of Enlistment.	Enrolled	Remarks.
Captain.		1846.	
John C. Hurt........	....	June 14	....
First Lieutenant.			
Geo. M. Cowardin...	....	"	Killed in battle at Cerro Gordo, April 18, 1847.
Second Lieutenants.			
Jacob P. Shaum.....	....	"	Resigned..
David A. Brown	....	"	Private to June 27, 1846, then took rank as 2d gr. Lieutenant.
Sergeants.			
John M. Handchey...	....	"	
Chris. C. Mason	....	"	Appointed Sergeant from private, Oct. 21, '46.
John Allison.........	....	"	Appointed Sergeant, April 29, 1847.............
Corporals.			
Wm. J. Dudney.....	....	"	Appointed Corporal from private, Oct. 21, '46.
Wm. Donavan.......	....	"	
Hiram A. Bristol ...	....	"	Appointed Corporal from private, Oct. 21, '46.
W. J. Allison.........	....	"	Appointed Corporal, April 29, 1847.............
Privates.			
Ashing, Thomas.....	....	"	
Braugher, Fred......	....	"	
Brown, Leroy T.....	....	"	
Barnes, Joseph......	....	"	Left sick in hosp. at Matamoras, Dec. 13, 1846.
Brown, Elmore S....	....	"	
Brundage, Sol.......	....	"	
Barney, M. W.......	....	July 18	
Bentley, John.......	....	"	
Chapin, Merrick....	....	June 14	
Downing, John E...	....	"	
Davis, Cyrus........	....	"	
Davenport, John ...	....	"	
Fanning, Chas......	....	July 18	
Glenn, Jas	....	June 14	
Gibson, John W. H..	....	"	
Greenwood, John ..	....	"	
Hutchinson, Eli H...	....	"	
McGarvey, Francis..	....	"	
Melton, Austin P...	....	"	
Myers, Leo. W	....	"	
Milton, Perry.......	....	"	
Mason, Thomas	....	"	
Randolph, Jas.......	....	"	
Salmonds, Wm	....	"	
Sands, Robt.........	....	July 18	
Todd, Jas. I. D......	....	June 14	Left wounded in hosp. at Jalapa, May 7, 1847.
Trumbull, Cryl.....	....	"	
Wiley, Henry.......	....	"	

Discharged:

Name and Rank.	Place of Enlistment.	Enrolled	Remarks.
Sergeants.		1846.	
Willis Phillips......	....	June 14	Disch. on Surgeon's certificate Aug. 26, 1846..
William H. Young...	....	"	" " " " Aug. 26, 1846..
John Cowardin.....	....	"	" " " " Oct. 18, 1846..
Jas. McGraw........	....	"	Promoted 3d Sergt. from private, Sept. 15, '46, disch. on Surg's certif. Mar. 17, 1847........
Corporals.			
Wm. Loughery.....	....	"	Disch. on Surgeon's certificate, Oct. 13, 1846..
Adolphus Vonforull.	....	"	" " " " " "..
James R. Phillips ...	....	"	" " " " " "..
Privates.			
Collins, Thomas.....	....	"	Disch. on Surgeon's certificate, Aug. 26, 1846..
Clark, Peter	....	"	" " " " Oct. 13, 1846..
Douglass, James....	....	"	" " " " " "..
Davis, Robert.......	....	"	" " " " Nov. 2, 1846..
Gregory, L. M......	....	"	" " " " Oct. 13, 1846..
Glenn, G. D.........	....	"	" " " " " "..

Name and Rank.	Place of Enlistment.	Enrolled	Remarks.
		1846.	
Lee, Franklin		June 14	Disch. on Surgeon's certificate, Aug. 26, 1846.
Lucas, F. A.		" "	" " " " Oct. 13, 1846.
Ray, John G.		" "	" " " " " "
Robinson, George W.		" "	" " " " " "
Stapleton, James		" "	" " " " " "
Sullins, Wm.		" "	" " " " Aug. 26, 1846.
Turner, Emanuel		" "	" " " " Nov. 3, 1846.
White, William		" "	" " " " Mar. 2, 1846.

Died:

Name and Rank.	Place of Enlistment.	Enrolled	Remarks.
Sergeant.		1846.	
Uriah Davenport		June 14	Died of wounds rec'd in action, Cerro Gordo, April 18, 1847.
Corporal.			
Nathaniel H. Milton		" "	Killed in action at Cerro Gordo, April 18, 1847.
Privates.			
Beason, William		" "	Died Sept. 15, 1846, on the Rio Grande.
Bowman, John		" "	" Nov. 15, 1846, at Camargo.
Brown, John E.		" "	" March 15, 1847, at Matamoras.
Cavenaugh, John		" "	Drowned in Mississippi, July 3, 1846.
Donavan, Joseph		" "	Died Sept. 15, 1846, on the Rio Grande.
Devault, Abram		" "	" Nov. 7, 1846, at Camargo.
McGarvey, Alex'dria		" "	" July 11, 1846.
Mundy, Henry		" "	" Sept. 29, 1846, on the Rio Grande.
McGarvey, Henry		" "	" Feb. 6. 1847.
Rudder, Thomas		" "	Supposed to be killed by Mexicans.
Rees, Chas		" "	Died Sept. 30, 1846, on the Rio Grande.

Wounded:

Name and Rank.	Place of Enlistment.	Enrolled	Remarks.
1st Sergeant.		1846.	
John M. Handchey		June 14	Wounded in action, Cerro Gordo, April 18, '47
Privates.			
Todd, James I. D.		" "	Wounded in action, Cerro Gordo, April 18, '47
Fanning, Chas.		" "	" " " " " "

Deserted:

Name and Rank.	Place of Enlistment.	Enrolled	Remarks.
		1846.	
Downing, Robert		June 14	Deserted July 9, 1846, Jefferson Barracks.
Wilkinson, Andrew		" "	" " 20, " " "

This company was discharged on May 25, 1847, at New Orleans.

Company "K."

Name and Rank.	Place of Enlistment.	Enrolled	Remarks.
Captain.		1846.	
Lewis W. Ross		July 4	
First Lieutenants.			
George W. Stipp		July 4	Resigned Aug. 30, 1846, at Camp Patterson.
Leonard F. Ross		July 18	Elected 1st Lieutenant from private Sept 4, '46

MEXICAN WAR.

Name and Rank.	Place of Enlistment.	Enrolled		Remarks.
Second Lieutenant.		1846.		
Joseph L. Sharp		July	4	Resigned company at New Orleans May 23, '47
Bre't 2d Lieutenants.				
John B. McDowell		July	4	Resigned Aug. 30, 1846, at Camp Patterson....
Robert Johnson		"	"	" Dec. 20, 1846, " Matamoras...
Sergeants.				
Marvin Scudder, Jr		July	4	
Samuel D Reynolds		"	"	
Milton C. Dewey		"	"	
James B. Anderson		"	"	
Corporals.				
Tracy Stroud		July	4	
James W. Anderson		"	"	
Edward Brannon		July	18	
Simeon Cannon		July	4	
Privates.				
Ackerson, Garrett		July	4	
Andrews, Harman		"	"	
Bennington, George		"	"	
Bristow, Isaac M		"	"	
Clark, David		"	"	
Crittenden, Uriah		"	"	
Crawford, James		"	"	
Collins, David		"	"	
Carter, Simeon		"	"	
Coon, Ross		"	"	
Cannon, John		"	"	
Dalley, Charles		"	"	
Ellis, John		"	"	
Ellis, Jacob		"	"	
Engle, William H		"	"	
Foote, Zachariah		"	"	
Freebourne, P. T		"	"	
Fitzpatrick, Michael		"	"	
Gregory, Jesse		July	20	
Hoover, Richard		"	"	
Hammon, Joshua B		July	4	
King, Horace B		"	"	
Kimball, Myran		"	"	
Lyon, Eli		"	"	
Land, John		"	"	
Morton, Richard W		"	"	
Mayall, Joseph		"	"	
Millslagle, Elias		"	"	['47, and left at Hosp. at Jalapa, Mex.
Morris, William		"	"	Wounded in battle of Cerro Gordo April 18,
Myers, Jonas H		"	"	Detailed in Hosp. at Jalapa, Mex. April 18, '47.
Murphy, William		July	20	
Patton, Hugh		July	4	
Powell, Andrew M		"	"	
Reid, John H		"	"	
Rigdon, Stephen		"	"	
Ross, Pike C		"	"	
Shields, David		"	"	
Steele, John N		"	"	Detailed in Hosp., Jalapa, Mex., April 15, 1847
Smith, James H		"	"	
Smith, Davis		July	20	
Stephenson, Thomas		July	4	
Taylor, Julius I		"	"	

Discharged:

First Sergeant,		1846		
Robert Carter		July	4	Disch. on Surg. cert. of disability, Nov. 9, '46 ..
First Corporal.				
Thomas H. Head		July	4	Disch. on Surg. cert. of disability, Nov. 25, '46
Privates.				
Bevord, John		July	4	Disch. on Surg. cert. of disability, Dec. 20, '46 .
Beadles, William		"	"	" " " " Mar. 7, '47...
Dobson, Joseph		"	"	" " " " Feb. 8, '47...
Dobbins, John F. P		"	"	" " " " Nov. 9, '46..
Deiter, John		"	"	" " " " Aug. 24, '46..
Deiter, Joel		"	"	" " " " Aug. 24, '46..

FOURTH REGIMENT.

Name and Rank.	Place of Enlistment.	Enrolled	Remarks.
		1846.	
Kelley, Ephram		July 20	Disch. on Serg. cert. of disability, Sept. 18, '46
Mason, William C		July 18	" " " Aug. 30, '46
McNeil, Malcolm		July 4	" " " Oct. 8, '46
McKee, Patrick		" "	" " " by order of Col. Baker July 17, '46
Monroe, Thomas		July 20	" " " Surg. cert. of disability, Feb. 8, '47
Painter, William C		July 4	" " " Nov. 9, '46
Pigg, John		July 20	" " " Sept. 28, '46
Turner, Orren		July 4	" " " Oct. 8, '46
Wilson, Samuel B		" "	" " " Oct. 4, '46

Died:

Third Sergeant. Stephen D. Webb		July 4	Died Oct. 24, '46, at hospital, Matamoras
Second Corporal. James Dunsmore		July 4	" Oct. 1, '46, " "
Privates. Carter, John S. S		July 4	" Oct. 27, '46, " Camargo
Yan, Alonzo A		" "	" Sept. 10, '46, at Camp Patterson

Deserted:

Privates. Ashworth, Chris		July 4	Deserted July 9, Jefferson Barracks, Mo
Barker, James		" "	" July 23, " "
Hamilton, J. R		" "	" " " "
Langford, Asa		" "	Leave of absence 10 days; did not rejoin Co

This company was discharged May 26, 1847, at New Orleans.

INDEPENDENT COMPANIES

Of Illinois Mounted Volunteers, called into the service of the United States by the President, under the act of Congress, approved May 13, 1846, to serve for the term of during the war with Mexico, from the date of enrollment, unless sooner discharged.

Capt. A. Dunlap's Company,

Called into the United States service and mustered in at Alton, Ill., on May 21, 1847. The company was organized by Capt. Dunlap, at Rushville, Ill., in the month of May, 1847.

Name and Rank.	Place of Enlistment.	Enrolled	Remarks.
Captain.		1847.	
Adams Dunlap	Alton, Ill	May 21	
First Lieutenant.			
Samuel Lambert	"	"	
Second Lieutenants.			
Simon Doyle	"	"	
Calvin Jackson	"	"	
Sergeants.			
Samuel W. Boring	"	"	
James B. Wright	"	"	
George O. Backman	"	"	Was private from enrollment to July 9, 1847.
Rich. W. Stephenson	"	"	Appointed from private May 16, 1848.
Corporals.			
Victor C. Putman	"	"	
William Ritchey	"	"	
Newton D. Witt	"	"	
John W. Snider	"	"	Was private from enrollment to Feb. 16, 1848.
Bugler.			
Theodore Smith	"	"	
Charles Hynes	"	"	
Farrier and Bl'ks'ith.			
David Duff	"	"	
Privates.			
Angle, John	"	"	
Allen, Mark	Nauvoo, Ill	Mar. '48	Joined, a recruit, in Mex., May 26, 1848.
Brown, Robert	Vermont, Ill	Feb. '48	" " " " "
Brown, Alexander	"	"	
Bowen, James F	Alton, Ill	May '47	
Bricklee, Henry	"	"	
Berry, Daniel T	"	"	
Beals, Sam'l O	"	"	
Boyd, David	"	"	
Boyd, Robert	"	"	
Chipman, Seth	"	"	
Chapman, William W	"	"	

INDEPENDENT COMPANIES. 305

Name and Rank.	Place of Enlistment.	Enrolled	Remarks.
		1-47.	
Cumings, Alfred	Alton, Ill.	May 21	
Cuningham, Caleb	"	"	
Chipman, Philip	"	"	
Crain, Henry	"	"	
Carden, Washi'gt'nA.	"	"	
Curtis, Jesse	Rushville, Ill.	Feb. '48	Joined, a recruit, in Mex., May 26, 1848
Corbridge, Thomas	Vermont, Ill.	"	" " " " "
Carter, Rutherford	"	"	" " " " "
Carnes, John T	Warsaw, Ill.	Mar. '48	" " " " "
Duhamell, Benj. F	Vermont, Ill.	Feb. '48	" " " " "
Densmore, James C.	Pittsfield, Ill.	April '48	" " " " "
Dirickson, Joseph M.	Alton, Ill.	May '47	
Erwin, George W	"	"	
Easley, William	"	"	
Easley, Thomas M	"	"	
Elliott, William	"	"	
Fisher, Jacob	Rushville, Ill.	Jan. '48	Joined, a recruit, in Mex., May 26, 1848
Geiger, Davidson M.	Nauvoo, Ill.	Mar. '48	" " " " "
Gillett, Charles W	"	"	
Gilbreth, Samuel	Alton, Ill.	May '47	
Green, William	"	"	
Gitchell, Calvin L.	"	"	
Green, David	"	"	
Gordon, Franklin	"	"	
Gibson, Isaac W	"	"	
Haverkluft, C. H. C.	"	"	
Holloway, William	"	"	
Hatfield, Abraham	"	"	
Hymer, George	"	"	
Hoyt, Albert	"	"	
Hurry, David	Rushville Ill.	Jan. '48	Joined, a recruit, in Mex., May 26, 1848
Hopkins, Lemuel B.	Vermont, Ill.	Feb. '48	" " " " "
Hopkins, David R.	"	"	" " " " "
Hanson, William B	Warsaw, Ill.	Mar. '48	" " " " "
Jump, James D	Rushville, Ill.	May '48	
Jones, James B	Alton, Ill.	May '47	
Jones, Levi	"	"	
Kelly, Patrick	"	"	
Lambert, Henry	"	"	
Lamaster, Erwin	"	"	
Lincoln, Jefferson	Rushville, Ill	Jan. '48	Joined, a recruit, in Mex., May 26, 1848
Mullane, Carroll	"	"	" " " " "
Mauck, Abram R	"	"	" " " " "
McGee, Elijah	"	"	
Myres, Jacob L	Vermont, Ill.	Feb. '48	" " " " "
Maynard, Robert H.	Winch'ter, Ill.	April '48	" " " " "
Mars, John L	"	"	
Martin, George W	Alton, Ill.	May '47	
McKinney, John	"	"	
McNeely, John	"	"	
McMasters, William	"	"	
Murran, James	"	"	
Patterson, CharlesR.	"	"	
Parrott, Josiah	"	"	
Puler, Jefferson	"	"	
Presson, William	"	"	
Peirce, George	"	"	
Parker, Oscar J	Vermont, Ill.	Feb. '48	Joined, a recruit, in Mexico, May 26, 1848
Roberts, Dewitt C.	Winch'ter, Ill.	April '48	" " " " "
Redmon, William	Matamor's, M.	July '47	" " " July 9, 1847
Rhodes, Hinman	Alton, Ill.	May '47	
Scott, George R	"	"	
Scott, William B	"	"	
Spencer, Elijah	"	"	
Smith, William E	"	"	
Smith, Robert	"	"	
Sidwell, James C	Vermont, Ill.	Feb. '47	Joined, a recruit, in Mexico, May 26, 1848
Seemon, Cornelius	Matamor's, M.	July '47	" " " July 9, 1847
Stetson, Clinton	Nauvoo, Ill.	Mar. '48	" " " May 26, 1848
Turnbull, Thomas	Rushville, Ill.	Jan. '48	" " " " "
Todd, Simeon S	"	"	" " " " "
Tucker, William	Vermont, Ill.	Feb. '48	" " " " "
Troy, Jerome S	Pittsfield, Ill.	April '48	" " " " "
Thompson, James	Alton, Ill.	May '47	
Thompson, James D.	"	"	
Throughman, John	"	"	
Vance, John	"	"	
Vancourt, Benj. P	Warsaw, Ill.	Mar. '48	Joined, a recruit, in Mexico, May 26, 1848
Winsor, Clark	Nauvoo, Ill.		

—20

MEXICAN WAR.

Name and Rank.	Place of Enlistment.	Enrolled	Remarks.
Weatherbee, Wm. B.	Carthage, Ill.	Mar., '48	Joined, a recruit, in Mexico, May 26, 1848......
Whitehurst, Willis G.	Winch'ter, Ill.	April, '48	" " " " " ....
Ward, Alfred........	Alton, Ill.....	May, '47	
Whitlock, George C.	"	....	
Wright, Isaac S. W..	"	....	
Ward, Luke G.......	Matamor's, M.	July, '47	Joined, a recruit, in Mexico, July 9, 1847......

Died:

		1847.	
Sergeant. Thomas Tyre........	Alton, Ill.....	May 21	Died at Matamoras, Mex., July 10, 1847........
Corporal. Anthony Porgolio...	"	"	Died at Matamoras, Mex., Oct. 8, 1847..........
Privates. Beales, Angustus F..	"	"	Died at Matamoras, Mex., Sept. 18, 1847 ......
Biggs, Henry	"	"	" " " Oct. 23, 1847 ....
Burton, George W...	"	"	" Point Isabel, Tex., July 18, 1848............
Castle, Henry........	"	"	" Matamoras, Mex., Oct. 28, 1847............
Clark, John	"	"	" " " Aug. 1, 1847..........
Cook, William W....	"	"	" " " Sept. 28, 1847.........
Dyson, Samuel	"	"	" " " Oct. 30, 1847..........
Edmonson, N. H. R..	"	"	" " " Oct. 18, 1847..........
Fletcher, James C...	"	"	" " " Aug. 7, 1847..........
Gipson, Benjamin F.	"	"	" " " Oct. 13, 1847..........
Gillett, Plinney P...	Warsaw, Ill..	Mar., '48	" Alton, Ill., Aug. 31, 1848 ....
Ren, Thomas	Alton, Ill.....	May, '47	" Matamoras, Mex., July 15, 1847 ....
Smith, John..........	"	"	" " " Sept. 27, 1847 ....

Deserted:

Brunt, (?) William ...	Alton, Ill.....	May '47	Deserted at Matamoras, Mex., Dec. 1, 1847....
Brooks, William......	Rushville, Ill.	July, '48	" Camargo, Mex., August —......
Hoovey, Simeon A..	Alton, Ill.....	May, '47	" Alton, Ill., June 9, 1847 ....
Smith, Thomas J....	"	....	" " June 5, 1847 ....
Wright, David	"	....	" New Orleans, La., June 25, 1847...

Discharged:

Sergeant. Marcus Serrott.......	Alton, Ill.....	May '47	Discharged on Surg. certificate, April 27, 1848.
Privates. Cross, Thomas J.....	Rushville, Ill.	Feb., '48	Left sick at San Antonio, Tex., Sept. 9 ....
Dickson, Francis....	Alton, Ill.....	May, '47	Discharged on Surg. certificate, April 27, 1848.
Lansdon, William A.	"	....	" " " Dec. 5, 1847 ..
Whitcher, Pat'rs'n V.	Warsaw, Ill..	Mar., '48	" expiration of service, Oct. 3.....

This company was discharged at Alton, Ill., on Nov. 7, 1848.

INDEPENDENT COMPANIES. 307

Capt. Wyatt B. Stapp's Company,

Called into the service of the United States and mustered in August 10, 1847, at Quincy, Ill This company was organized at Monmouth, Ill., in month of June, 1847.

Name and Rank.	Place of Enlistment.	Enrolled	Remarks.
Captain.		1847.	
Wyat B. Stapp	Quincy, Ill.	Aug. 6	
First Lieutenant.			
George C. Lanphere	"	"	
Second Lieutenants.			
George W. Palmer	"	"	Resigned Oct. 29, 1847
John H. Mitchell	"	"	
Second Second Lieut.			
John G. Fonda	Jeffers'n Bar.	Aug. 17	Elected from Sergt., June 13, 1848
Sergeants.			
John B. Holliday	Quincy, Ill.	Aug. 6	
Brice M. Henry	"	"	Appointed from private, Feb. 29, 1849
Thomas H. Davidson	"	"	Elected from private, June 13, 1848
Elias Guthrie	"	"	" " " Feb. 29, 1848
Corporals.			
Robert C. Armstrong	"	"	Elected from private, Feb. 29, 1848
Esau Brown	"	"	" " " Dec. 31, 1847
Joseph D. Mackey	"	"	
Darius Dennis	"	"	Elected from private, Feb. 29, 1848
Buglers.			
Benj. I. Tifield	"	"	
Robert M. Snapp	"	"	
Blacksmith and Farrier.			
Robert C. West	"	"	
Privates.			
Avarill, Wm.	"	"	
Brownlee, David	"	"	
Barnard, Geo. R. A.	"	"	
Berry, Isaiah	"	"	
Barnaby, Wm.	"	"	
Beebe, Edward O	"	"	
Backus, Samuel I	"	"	
Birch, Louis	Perote. Mex.	Jan., '48	
Cowan, David S.	Quincy, Ill.	Aug. 6, '47	
Carter, Job L.	"	"	
Daniel, Dickson S.	"	"	
Drain, Charles	"	"	
Dunlap, Nicholas	"	"	
Eads, James D.	"	"	
Furgus, James	"	"	
Gordon, James E.	"	"	
Grover, Alonzo	"	"	
Hatton, Richard	"	"	
Harding, Samuel	"	"	
Henderson, Samuel	"	"	
Howard, John D.	"	"	
King, Michael	"	"	
Kelly, Calvin	"	"	
Lanphere, George	"	"	
Lillard, Augustine	"	"	
Monteith, Wm. H.	"	"	
McWilliams, John T.	"	"	
Moffitt, John	"	"	
Motley, John B	"	"	
Poland, James H	"	"	
Pickenough, Absal'm	"	"	
Parmenter, James S	"	"	
Parmenter, Leinster	"	"	
Rhodes, Job	"	"	
Ruddle, John F.	"	"	
Ruddle, George H	"	"	
Reed, John	"	"	

308   MEXICAN WAR.

Name and Rank.	Place of Enlistment.	Enrolled	Remarks.
Rodriguez, Janquine	C'y of Mexico.	May 1, '48	
Stanley, Leander	Quincy, Ill.	Aug. 6, '47	
Stigall, Geo. W.	"	"	
Williams, Wm.	"	"	
Wells, Cyrus	"	"	
Watkins, Luther P.	"	"	
Worden, John I.	"	"	
Wilson, James E.	"	"	

Died:

		1847.	
Sergeant. Ishmael H. Holcomb	Quincy, Ill.	Aug. 6	Died at Perote, Mex., March 10, 1848
Corporal. Wm. D. Day	"	"	Died at Perote, Mex., April 3, 1848
Privates. Bartram, Ezra G.	"	"	Died at Perote, Mex., Dec. 26, 1847
Black, John	"	"	" " Jan. 2, 1848
Cullip, Zachariah	"	"	" " Dec. 26, 1847
Claunin, Oliver	"	"	" " Dec. 28, 1847
Fitzpatrick, Michael	"	"	Vera Cruz, Mex., Dec. 14, 1847
Hatton, William	"	"	Jalapa, Mex., Feb. 7, 1848
Morgan, Geo. W.	"	"	en route to Mexico, Sept. 15, 1847
McNeil, Geo. W.	"	"	Jalapa, Mex., Dec. 7, 1847
Miles, James A.	"	"	Perote, Mex., Feb. 5, 1848
Nicholas, Ezra H.	"	"	" " Jan. 2, 1848
Owens, Wm. C.	"	"	" " Jan. 26, 1848
Porter, Orlando	"	"	" " Jan. 7, 1848
Sissell, John	"	"	" " Jan. 16, 1848
Shields, James	"	"	Jalapa, Mex., April 23, 1848
Webb, Albert	"	"	Perote, Mex., Dec. 26, 1847
Wilson, Warren R.	"	"	" " Jan. 4, 1848
Wells, Larkin	"	"	Jalapa, Mex., Dec. 10, 1847

Deserted:

		1847.	
Private. William Kelley	Quincy, Ill.	Aug. 6	Deserted March 17, 1848

Discharged:

		1847.	
Sergeants. Samuel Douglas	Quincy, Ill.	Aug. 6	Discharged March 11, 1848
James Townsley	"	"	Disch. by certificate of disability Mar. 11, '48.
Nicholas P. Earp	"	"	" " " " Dec. 24, '47.
Corporals. Geo. L. Shippey	"	"	Disch. by certificate of disability, Jan. 3, '48.
James W. Robson	"	"	" " " " Feb. 6, '48.
Privates. Coe, Reuben M.	"	"	Discharged, date unknown
Daniel, Warner I.	"	"	March 14, 1848.
De LaBar, Joseph M	"	"	Disch. by certificate of disability Dec. 15, '47.
Foster, Geo. W.	"	"	" " " " Jan. 29, '48.
Hogue, Thomas G.	"	"	" " " " Jan. 3, '48.
Kent, Ezekiel	"	"	" " " " Dec. 15, '47.
Lanphere, Clark	"	"	" " " " Jan. 29, '48.
Mitchell, Jas. W., Jr.	"	"	" " " " Dec. 15, '47.
Pike, Samuel	"	"	" " " " Jan. 29, '48.
Wilson, Isaac	"	"	" " " " Mar. 14, '48.
Weston, Henry	"	"	Discharged, date unknown

This company was discharged at Alton, Ill., July 26, 1848.

INDEPENDENT COMPANIES. 309

LIEUT. G. C. LANPHERE'S DETACHMENT

Of Recruits belonging to Capt. W. B. Stapp's Company of Mounted Volunteers, mustered in on the date of their respective enrollment at Monmouth, Ill. This detachment was organized by Lt. G. C. Lanphere, at Monmouth, Ill.

Name and Rank.	Place of Enlistment.	Enrolled	Remarks.
Privates.		1848.	
Allison, Samuel M...	Monmouth, Ill	April 12	
Allen, William F.....	"	May 13	
Bigelow, Debois.....	"	Mar. 9	
Butler, Peter.........	"	Mar. 29	
Day, John............	"	Mar. 16	
Dunham, Christ'er N.	"	April 17	
Dargin, John.........	"	May 21	
Elder, William.......	"		
Fitzjerrell, John.....	"	Mar. 11	
Fuller, Limon P.....	"	June 1	Rejected........
Griffits, Thomas B...	"	April 5	
Hume, Charles R....	"	Feb. 26	
Huddleston, Richard	"	Mar. 6	
Holmes, George B...	"	May 13	
Hurn, George W.....	"	June 1	
Lawrence, Sol. K., Jr.	"	May 21	
Mekemson, John S..	"	Mar. 10	
Meredeth, John J...	"		
Norton, James L....	"	May 21	
Pratt, Abram, Jr....	"	Feb. 19	
Peck, James M......	"	April 1	
Pool, John..........	"	June 1	
Rumpf, Philip.......	"	May 17	
Rennard, John D...	"	June 1	
Shelton, David R...	"	Mar. 14	
Shelton, Samuel....	"		
Spencer, Franklin...	"	April 14	
Tadlock, Benjamin..	"	Feb. 20	
Tadlock, Edward I..	"	Mar. 8	
Teice, Tandy H......	"	Mar. 13	
Worthen, James.....	"	May 21	

This detachment was mustered out June 28, 1848, at Jefferson Barracks, Mo.

CAPT. MICHAEL K. LAWLER'S COMPANY,

Called into the United States service, and mustered in at Shawneetown, Ill., on August 13, 1847. This company was organized at Shawneetown, Ill., in the month of August, 1847.

Name and Rank.	Place of Enlistment.	Enrolled	Remarks.
Captain.		1847.	
Michael K. Lawler...	Shawn't'n, Ill.	Aug. 13	
First Lieutenant.			
Walter S. Clark......	"	"	
Second Lieutenants.			
Samuel L. M. Proctor	"	"	
John G. Ridgway....	"	"	
Sergeants.			
Howell Sloo.........	"	"	Was private from enrollment to Oct. 25......
Theod're L. Lockhart	"	"	" " " " Dec. 1.....
George F. White.....	"	"	" Corpl. from " Mar. 25.....
Robert M. Peeples..	"	"	" private " June 20.....
Corporals.			
Thomas J. Powell...	"	"	
Samuel H. T. Proctor	"	"	Was private from enrollment to March 25....
Lorenzo W. Stone...	"	"	" " " " May 1......
John C. Mitchell.....	"	"	" " " " June 16.....

MEXICAN WAR.

Name and Rank.	Place of Enlistment.	Enrolled	Remarks.
Buglers.		1847.	
William J. Gatewood	Shawn't'n, Ill.	Aug. 13	Was private from enrollment to Oct. 25
Sanford Cockran	"	"	" April 1
Farrier.			
Benedict Crandle	"	"	
Privates.			
Baker, William	"	"	
Becraft, John	"	"	
Berry, Charles	"	"	
Bramlet, Sanford	"	"	
Bruce, James	"	"	
Buckner, Edwin	"	"	
Burrel, Mars	"	"	
Burrel, William	"	"	
Calicoat, John	"	"	
Campbell, Chalon G.	"	"	
Catt, Levi B.	"	"	
Catt, Pilate S.	"	"	
Caughman, Charles J	"	"	
Caughman, John	"	"	
Cayton, William W.	"	"	Was Sergeant from enrollment to Jan. 1.
Chapman, Isaac	"	"	
Christian, Rufus	"	"	
Clark, Josiah	"	"	
Conyers, Isaac	"	"	
Crenshaw, Abraham	"	"	
Davis, James B.	"	"	
Eastman, Jacob L.	"	"	
Eaton, William H.	"	"	Was missing from enrollment to April 1.
Ensminger, Stephen	"	"	Hospital Steward from June 19
Gaston, Robert	"	"	
Gates, William	"	"	
Gillerson, Pat'rson H	"	"	
Groathouse, Tevis	"	"	
Greer, Payton	"	"	Died at Equality, Ill., Oct. 24, 1848.
Hair, James	"	"	
Harget, William	"	"	
Hargrave, Thomas	"	"	
Henson, Elijah	"	"	
Hill, Morris	"	"	
Hood, James	"	"	Absent, sick at Carmi, from Oct. 3.
Hood, William	"	"	
Hughes, Alexander	"	"	
Hughes, Cephas G.	"	"	Was Sergeant from enrollment to March 25.
Hughes, Champ. T.	"	"	
Hughes, George	"	"	
Jameson, John D.	"	"	Was Corporal from enrollment to Sept. 18.
Jones, Richard M.	"	"	
Kennedy, Daniel	"	"	
Leavell, Benjamin	"	"	
Lynch, John Q. A.	"	"	Sick, in Shawneetown, from Oct. 24.
McClusky, Daniel	"	"	
O'Malley, John	Tampico, Mex	Dec. 8	Joined, a recruit, at Tampico, Dec. 8.
Overbee, John	Shawn't'n, Ill.	Aug. 13	
Perry, Washington	"	"	
Pennell, Willis Y.	"	"	
Pipe, Thomas	"	"	
Rawson, Thomas	"	"	
Renwick, John G.	"	"	
Reynolds, Isaac	"	"	
Ritchey, Williamson	"	"	
Rourk, David H.	"	"	
Robison, John	"	"	
Shirley, Nimrod	"	"	
Sinks, Zachariah	"	"	
Stickney, Geo. W.	"	"	Was Corporal from enrollment to Oct. 25.
Trimble, John	"	"	
Turner, John	"	"	
Walters, William	"	"	
Watts, Lewis F.	"	"	
White, Joseph	"	"	
Wolf, Stephen	"	"	

INDEPENDENT COMPANIES. 311

Discharged:

Name and Rank.	Place of Enlistment.	Enrolled	Remarks.
		1847.	
Bozman, Phineas	Shawn't'n, Ill.	Aug. 13	Discharged Jan. 26, 1848; disability
Boyer, Wm. L.	"	"	Reports himself discharged April 1, —
Brooks, Luke	New Orleans.	Sept. 27	Ordered to N. Orleans to be disch.; fract. leg
Crissup, Thomas	Shawn't'n, Ill.	Aug. 13	Discharged Jan. 26, 1848; disability
Dorsey, Wm.	"	"	Ord. to N. Orleans to be disch. on exp'n term
Eubanks, George W.	"	"	" " " " " " for fract. leg.
Fowler, James	"	"	" " " " " " on exp'n term
Hill, Edward	"	"	Discharged Jan. 26, 1848; disability
Hudgins, Ambrose	"	"	
Linderman, Isaac	"	"	Ord. to N. Orleans to be disch. on exp'n term
McCarty, Charles	"	"	Discharged Sept. 20, 1847; disability
Miller, John W.	"	"	" Jan. 26, 1848; "
Pool, Thomas	"	"	
Pelham, John	"	"	Ord. to N. Orleans to be disch. on exp'n term
Pillow, Parker B.	"	"	
Reynolds, Thomas	"	"	Discharged Jan. 26, 1848; disability
Ritchey, Francis P.	"	"	Ord. to N. Orleans to be disch. on exp'n term
Sharp, Holmes	"	"	" " " " " "
Spivey, Lindley M.	"	"	" " " " " "
Sumpter, William	"	"	" " " " " "
Vaugh, Thomas B.	"	"	" " " " " "
Webb, Asa B.	"	"	" " " " " "
Wright, Robert	"	"	" " " " " "
Wright, Alanson G.	"	"	Discharged Jan. 26, 1848; disability

Died:

		1847.	
Sergeants.			
Elias Umsnider	Shawn't'n, Ill.	Aug. 13	Died at Tampico, Mex., Oct. 30, 1847
John Cadle	"	"	" " " June 19, —
Privates.			
Burrell, John	"	"	Died at Baton Rouge, La., Sept 21, 1847
Gaston, John	"	"	" Tancasmqui, Mex., May 26, —
Hudson, Sanford	"	"	" Alto Morn, " Dec. 10, —
Jones, Wm. H.	"	"	" Tampico, Mex., Oct. 1, 1847
Mahoney, Cornelius	"	"	" " " " Feb. 11, —
Morris, Robison B.	"	"	" Tancasmqui, Mex., May 31, —
Mulligan, Thos	Tampico, Mex	Dec. 18	" Alton, Ill., Aug. 27, 1848
O'Neil, Peter	Shawn't'n, Ill.	Aug. 13	" Tampico, Mex., Jan. 12, —
Rearden, Henry T.	"	"	" " " Oct. 15, 1847
Reeves, Jeremiah H.	"	"	" " " Oct. 16, 1847
White, Benj. F.	"	"	" " " Jan. 1, —

Deserted:

		1847.	
Harbaugh, Jeremiah	Baton Rouge.	Sept. 20.	Deserted Sept. 21, 1847

This company was discharged at Shawneetown, Ill., Oct. 26, 1848.

Capt. Josiah Littell's Company,

Called into the service of the United States at Alton, Ill., and mustered in on Sept. 18, 1847. This company was organized at Alton, Ill., in month of September, 1847.

Name and Rank.	Place of Enlistment.	Enrolled	Remarks.
Captain.		1847.	
Josiah Littell	Alton, Ill.	Aug. 28	
First Lieutenants.			
Charles P. Hazard	"	"	Died at Memphis, Tenn., Oct. 19, 1847
Thomas L. Buck	"	"	Elected from 2d Lieut. Oct. 26, 1847
Second Lieutenants.			
Josiah Caswell	"	"	Elected from 2d 2d Lieut. Oct. 26, 1847
Robert S. Green	"	"	" private Oct. 26, 1847
Sergeants.			
T. D. Linn	"	"	Appointed from private Oct. 26, 1847
James McMahon	N. Orleans, La	Oct. 26	" " " Jan. 1, 1848
John Douthit	Alton, Ill.	Aug. 28	
Corporals.			
Jeptha Muer	Alton, Ill.	"	
Thomas Bacon	"	"	Appointed Feb. 27, 1848
Jerome Taylor	"	"	
George D. P. Coonrod	"	"	Appointed April 17, 1848
Bugler.			
William Edwards	"	"	
Privates.			
Adams, David	"	"	
Abbott, Howard W.	City of Mexico	Feb., '48	
Benson, William	Alton, Ill.	Aug., '47	
Blanchard, James W	"	"	
Boyd, George M.	"	"	
Buck, Andrew P.	"	"	
Bush, Robert	"	"	
Chester, Solomon S.	"	"	
Cummings, Jesse	"	"	
Condon, John	"	"	
Carroll, Hardy R	"	"	Reduced from Sergeant Jan. 1, 1848
Denton, Thomas I.	"	"	
Darkham, Jonathan	City of Mexico	Jan., '48	
Elwell, Ellis	Alton, Ill.	Aug., '47	
Easter, Joseph R. W	"	"	
Fountain, Pleasant	"	"	
Finney, Clinton	"	"	
Gowen, George A	"	"	
Givinn, John	"	"	
Griffith, Jefferson	"	"	Resigned from 2d Corporal Oct. 26, 1847
Gray, William	"	"	
Hackney, Joseph B.	"	"	
Higham, John L.	"	"	
Howarton, William L	"	"	
Harris, Rufus	"	"	
Hill, Wyatt R.	"	"	
Hoover, Samuel	"	"	
Holley, James H.	"	"	
Jones, Joshua	"	"	
Kueffell, Francis	City of Mexi'o	Feb., '48	
Lancaster, James	Alton, Ill.	Aug., '47	
McGraham, Henry	"	"	
McWain, William	"	"	
Moore, John	"	"	
Moore, Samuel W.	"	"	
Miller, William E.	"	"	
Mott, Sherwood	"	"	
Murphy, James C.	"	"	
Noels, William	"	"	
Nettleton, James H.	"	"	
Parrish, Isaac	"	"	
Parrish, Samuel	"	"	
Powles, John	"	"	
Phelan, James	"	"	
Rice, Hugh	"	"	
Sprunce, William	"	"	

INDEPENDENT COMPANIES.

Name and Rank.	Place of Enlistment.	Enrolled	Remarks.
		1847.	
Stalts, William	Alton, Ill.	Aug. 28	
Shelby, James	"	"	
Staggs, Pleasant	"	"	
Staggs, Thomas	"	"	
Tongate, John T.	"	"	Resigned from 1st Sergeant Oct. 26, 1847
Tillotson, Willard	"	"	
Tindall, Lewis W.	"	"	
Turpin, Calohill	"	"	
Taylor, Jack R.	"	"	
Taylor, Jeffrey M.			
Thompson, Daniel E.	City of Mexi'o	Feb., '48	Re-enlisted in Mexico
Vestal, Jesse	Alton, Ill.	Aug., '47	
Vanhouton, John S.	"	"	
Wells, Isaac L.	"	"	
Woods, Hiram D.	"	"	
Webb, William W.	"	"	
Washburn, Coleman	"	"	
Woods, George W.	"	"	
Woods, John	"	"	
Weir, Gerd	"	"	

Died:

		1847.	
Sergeant. Isaiah Tetrick	Alton, Ill.	Aug. 28	Died near Memphis, July, 1848
Corporal. Jonathan G. Smith	"	"	Died at Rio Frio, Feb. 27, 1848
Blacksm'h & Farrier. John Murphy	"	"	Died Dec. 2, 1847, at Jalapa, of wounds
Privates.			
Barrow, James	"	"	Died on Gulf of Mexico, June 25, 1848
Cameron, Joseph	"	"	Died at Puebla, Dec. 16, 1847
Judd, Corben C.	"	"	" Dec. 27, 1847
Jones, William T.	"	"	" Rio Frio, Jan. 1, 1848
Kuhn, Herman	"	"	" Alton, July 19, 1848
McWain, William, 2d	"	"	" New Orleans, Oct. 29, 1847
Odoll, Allen	"	"	" Vera Cruz, Nov. 17, 1847
Stone, Thomas	N. Orleans, La	Nov. 8	Killed by guerrillas, Nov. 20, 1847
Sullivan, Jerry	Alton, Ill.	Aug. 28	Drowned in the Mississippi, Nov. 3, 1847
Schmidt, Hartman	"	"	Died at Camp Encerro, June 16, 1848
Wells, John E.	"	"	" Rio Frio, Feb. 12, 1848

Deserted:

		1847.	
Charles Durand	N. Orleans, La	Oct. 28	Absent without leave from Jan. 6, 1848

Discharged:

		1847.	
Corporal. Charles H. Cowden	Alton, Ill.	Aug. 28	Discharged on Surg. certificate, April 1, 1848.
Privates. Cork, Henry	"	"	Discharged on Surg. certificate, Mar. 1, 1848.
Davis, William	"	"	" " "
Fleming, David	N. Orleans, La	Oct. 28	" " " April 6, 1848.
Kuykendall, Peter	Alton, Ill.	Aug. 28	" " " April 4, 1848.
Payne, Charles E.	"	"	" " "
Taylor, Henry	"	"	" " " Jan. 15, 1848.

This company was discharged at Alton, Ill., July 25, 1848.

REGULAR ENLISTMENTS.

The following rolls of enlisted men were furnished this office by the War Department at Washington, D. C., being of men recruited in the State of Illinois, under the act of Congress, known as "the ten regiment bill." Nothing is known of the particulars of their service further than is already given in the "Historical Memoranda," in the earlier pages of this book. The Adjutant-General of the army, when applied to for data as to the killed, wounded, discharged, etc., stated: "I have the honor to inform you, by direction of the Secretary of War, that the request cannot be complied with, it being contrary to the well established practice of the office, and not consistent with the interests of the public service."

An application was made at the same time for the names of commissioned officers, but the War Department, for some unexplained reason, failed to furnish those also.

14TH U. S. INFANTRY.

Muster roll of the enlisted men of Co. "E," 14th U. S. Infantry, during the Mexican War, who were enlisted in the State of Illinois:

First Sergeants.
William Y. Dillard,
Harrison Q. Roberts.

Sergeants.
Alexander K. Hams,
Benjamin R. Johnson,
William H. Leeper,
Jackson Rushing,
William Willett,
William Waymond.

Corporals.
Reuben Davis,
Robert Green,
John W. Harvey,
Bethnel Hitch,
Henry Irvin,
Lewis Varner.

Drummer.
Thomas Gilbert.

Privates.
Allen, Wm. M,
Barnsfield, William,
Baronett, Zadoch C.,
Baronett, Wm. H.,
Broad, David P.,
Burton, James,
Boyles, Absolem,
Blevens, Warden P.,
Bolerjack, Albert G.,
Culpepper, Joel,
Clubb, Edward A.,
Carbaugh, Simon,
Cowan, Andrew J.,
Davis, Robert,
Dobbs, Elijah,
Durham, James I.,
Dorherty, John P.,
Doyer, Antoine,
French, Hansford,
Franklin, William E.,
Harris, Hardin,
Hoffard, Adam,
Holt, Jesse,
Hilt, Wm. I.,
Hewitt, Samuel R.,
Hutchinson, Phillip S.,
Hopkins, Carley,
Hawks, William E.,
Irick, George,
Irvin, William,
Johnson, William E.,
Jacobs, Bernard,
Jackson, James H.,
Jolleff, Aaron,
Kinnard, Wm. H.,
Kinnard, Simon,
King, James,
King, Robert,
Kelley, William, 1st.,
Kelley, William, 2d.,
Knap, Andrew W.,
Laflure, Ralph,
Lowery, Wm. I.,
Leslie, Wm. W.,
Metcalf, Jackson,
Myers, Wm. C.,
Melton, Joel S.,
Morgan, John S.,
Miller, Arch,
Morris, Jesse C.,
Matthews, Nichols,
Penington, Geo. W.,
Phelan, Gideon I.,
Plunkett, Patrick,
Pate William,
Richey, John,
Rabstock, Anton,
Robinson, George,
Rosser, Peter,
Roswell, Henry C.,
Sharp, John W.,
Stephen, James,
Simes, Thomas M.,
Southworth, Perry,
Smith, John O.,
Swards, David,
Stoker, Gabriel,
Southworth, James,
Trout, Joseph,
Trout, Erasmus,
Trout, John H.,
Turner, Fielding C.,
Thomas, Augustus,
Underwood, Edward,
Williams, Henry M.,
Williams, Reece,
Warren, John,
Williamson, Vincent P.,
Waymond, Edward,
Williams, George,
Withrow, William,
Witzel, Frederick,
Woodsworth, Richard I.,
White, Adam M.,
Wilson, Aaron,
Winter, Geo. W.

16TH U. S. INFANTRY.

Muster roll of the enlisted men of Co. "A," 16th U. S. Infantry, during the Mexican War, who were enlisted in the State of Illinois:

First Sergeants.
Benjamin F. Keys,
Robert B. McDowell.

Q. M. Sergeant.
William F. Peck.

Sergeants.
Charles S. Bagg,
Gilbert W. Dean,
Andrew G. Price,
E. C. Bennett.

Corporals.
Benjamin F. Clark,
Abram Courtright,
Jason Pattee,
Lorence Kern.

Musicians.
Stephen F. W. Lord,
John Van Arnum.

Privates.
Abbott, Henry,
Allen, Andrew,
Anderson, Andrew,
Adderly, John,
Brown, Ephraim,
Boker, John B.,
Bradley, A. St. John,
Benson, A. F.,
Bailey, William,
Bentley, Geo. W.,
Brown, Wm. S.,
Barton, George,
Burger, Robert,
Barber, William,
Bryant, Edward W.,
Bemus, Geo. W.,
Brierton, Sylvester,
Branch, Wheeler,
Boggs, Wm. J.,
Brown, Henry,
Congdonge, Thomas,
Curtis, Jackson,
Crampton, Eli,
Cooper, Thomas L.,
Cole, Samuel C.,
Courtwright, Christopher,
Cottera, Charles,
Charterton, John M.,
Crim, James,
Cunningham, John,
Downs, E. A.,
Davis, Ransom B.,
Doty, Cornelius,
Daley, Edwin,
Ducey, Patrick B.,
Dewitt, Almond T.,
Evans, C. W.,
Estell, John W.,
Edmunds, William,
Flucord, John E.,
Foley, John P.,
Fry, Christian,
Fisher, Hezekiah,
Fager, Henry,
Guthrie, James W.,
Gilbert, Charles M.,
Gordon, Morrison,
Goodwin, Robert,
Hunter, Robert,
Hart, Warren R.,
Hull, Joseph L.,
Heaton, James A.,
Higgins, James H.,
Hoslie, Henry,
Huston, George,
Hicks, Theodore E.,
Hood, Thomas A.,
Johnson, Joseph,
Jackson, Samuel B.,
Klinetop, Walton,
Lyslo, Matthew,
Miller, Orson H.,
Mahone, Thomas,
Miller, Isaac S.,
Moses, Byron,
McNealey, Levi,
McCarthy, Charles F.,
McConnell, John,
Mitts, William H.
Maserip, William L.,
Mitchell, Joseph B.,
McChesney, John,
Mix, George,
Newcomer, Martin E.
Osterhoudt, Charles H.
Otterson, James,
Peacock, Francis J.,
Phillips, Christian Y.,
Patterson, William,
Roberts, Thomas,
Rosebrook, Lyman,
Read, George D.,
Reed, Elias,
Ramsey, John,
Sherman, A. D.,
Scofield, James,
Steward, Isaac,
Sternes, Daniel A.,
Stacy, Martin C.,
Slaymaker, Wm. A.,
Scott, Jerome,
Secord, George,
Smith, Orange P.,
Stanover, Frederick,
Taylor, William,
Thatcher, John,
Townsend, Philomen,
Taylor, John,
Van Horn, P. H.,
Vest, Wm. H.,
Wright, Pharris,
Whelply, Mangle R.,
Willard, James,
Waddle, Joseph,
Ware, Levi,
Watterbury, James W.,
Wiley, William H.,
Wause, David,
Wilkinson, Thomas H.,
Williams, Cornelius,
Youngeourt, Theodore.

Muster roll of the enlisted men of Co. "G," 16th U. S. Infantry, during the Mexican War, who were enlisted in the State of Illinois:

First Sergeant.
Daniel Gregg.

Sergeants.
John C. Parks,
Edwin A. Partridge,
Myron Whipple,
Richard Hudunt.

Corporals.
James S. Porter,
George Watrod,
Levi R. Smith,
John E. Kimberly.

316 MEXICAN WAR.

Fifer.
Edwin H. Fay.

Drummer.
Henry E. VanDyke.

Privates.
Amidon, Henry,
Adkin, Valentine,
Butler, Geo. H.
Bennett, William,
Bennett, Elijah C.,
Benson, Bradford,
Blackwell, Geo. W.,
Brown, David T.,
Brown, Edward,
Brown, Henry,
Branch, John F.,
Brockbuler, John,
Babcock, Benjamin K.,
Bowen, David T.,
Birch, Marcellas,
Beecher, Geo. M.,
Bartley, John,
Burnes, Charles B.,
Baldy, Geo. W.,
Beaurgardt, Mathias,
Clark, Lewis P.,
Cecil, George,
Coates, John,
Colburn, William,
Cook, David,
Cluney, James,
Chapman, Bola J.,
Childers, Calvin,
Clark, Geo. W.,
Clasby, Dandridge B.,
Deane, Josiah,
Dewitt, Martin,
Duter, Anthony,
Daskem, William H.,
Dickson, John A.,
Devore, Nicholas,
Dymond, John,
Domback, Godfrey,
Duncan, Joseph W.,
Durell, Charles W.,
Fearrow, William,
Fielding, James E.,
Filley, Timothy,
Fitzsimmons, Hugh D. K.,
Fowler, James,
Fury, William,
Gates, John E.,
Green, Herman,
Godfrey, Scott C.,
Goodman, Thomas F.,
Getzler, Charles H.,
Ghuntley, Andrew,
Haskill, Charles H.,
Hawley, Edward G.,
Horr, John A.,
Holdridge, Luther,
Hefty, Samuel,
Israel, Peter,
Jeffords, Sidney H.,
Johnson, Arthur D.,
Johnson, Ashel C.,
Joslin, Almond,
Link, Anthony,
Lansing, Henry,
Leutz, Geo. F.,
Lake, Nelson P.,
Loe, Fielding,
McAllister, Hugh,
McCombs, John M.,
McDonald, Edward,
McWain, Clark,
May, John,
Martlett, Richard D.,
Morris, John,
Miler, Sylvester,
Murray, John
Nash, Isaac,
Northcutt, Wm. W.,
Owen, Evan,
Otis, Charles,
Power, Patrick,
Perry, James,
Perry, John,
Plastridge, Francis,
Pfister, George,
Rogers, John W.,
Rogers, Wm. J.,
Skinner, Dempsey,
Smith, Samuel M.,
Smith, Henry,
Smith, Jacob F.,
Synot, Marcus,
Spies, Andrew,
Simpson, James M.,
Sammis, Benj. N.,
Styne, Levi,
Teele, John W.,
Ules, Frederick,
Vogt, Jacob,
Walton, Nicholas,
Wilder, James,
Wickham, Isaac J.,
Wheeler, John L.,
Williams, Ruel,
Wise, Frederick,
Walton, Mark,
Wilson, William A.,
Walls, William R.,
Walker, Henry.

APPENDIX.

WAR OF 1810-'13.

CONTENTS OF APPENDIX.

	PAGE.
Ensign Whitesides Company	319
Massacre of Chicago	320
Captain William Alexander's Company, 1811	320
Campaign of 1812	321
Destruction of Peoria	322

MUSTER ROLLS—1812.

Capt. Thomas E. Craig's Company	323
Capt. Samuel Whiteside's Company	324
Capt. Jacob Short's (first) Company	326
Capt. John Scotts' Company	326
Capt. Samuel Judy or Henry Cooks' Company	327
Capt. William Hargraves Company	328
Capt. Samuel Judy's Spy Company	328
Capt. Absolem Cox's Company	329
Capt. James B. Moore's 1st Company	330
Capt. James B. Moore's 2d Company	330
Capt. Philip Tramell's Company	331
Capt. Dudley Williams Company	332
Field and Staff Roll	333
Campaign of 1813	334

MUSTER ROLLS—1813.

Capt. James B. Moore's (3d) Company	334
Capt. Jacob Short's Company	335
Capt. William Jones' Company	336
Sergt. James N. Fox's Detachment	337
Lieut. Daniel G. Moore's Company	338
Capt. Nathan Chamber's Company	398
Regimental Field and Staff, 1813	339
Capt. James B. Moore's (4th) Company	339
Campaign of 1814	840

APPENDIX.

A RECORD OF THE SERVICES OF THE ILLINOIS MILITIA, RIFLEMEN AND VOLUNTEERS, IN THE INDIAN WARS, 1810 to 1813.

In 1810 a series of massacres and depredations were committed by the Indians of Illinois Territory, upon citizens of Louisiana Territory, which led to a long correspondence between the Governor of Louisiana Territory and Governor Edwards of Illinois Territory. The most daring of these, and which caused great excitement at the time, was committed at Portage du Sioux, on July 19th, which resulted in the killing of four white men and the serious wounding of a fifth. After some correspondence, in which it was made evident to Governor Edwards that the Pottawotamies were guilty of the outrage, and a requisition having been made on him for the murderers, Capt. Samuel Levering, on the 24th of July, 1811, was commissioned by Gov. Edwards to visit the tribes on the Illinois River, and demand of them, the author of the murders which had been committed. (Edwards Ill.)

Of this expedition, Ninian W. Edwards (in his History of Illinois,) says: "Capt Levering departed on that day (July 24, 1811), from Kaskaskia, and arrived at Mr. Jarrot's, in the village of Cahokia, on the next day at 11 P. M. Capt. Ebert had engaged part of the crew for the boat, and on the 25th of July, the boat having been furnished by Governor Clark with the necessary equipments, provisions, etc., they left in the boat for Peoria, with the crew, consisting of Capt. Levering, Capt. Hebert, Henry Swearingen, N. Rector, a Frenchman (who passed as an interpreter but was intended for a spy), a Pottawotamie Indian named Wish-ha, and eight oarsmen, each armed with a gun. The names of the boatmen were, Pierre St. John, Pierre La Parche, Joseph Trotier, Francis Pensoneau, Louis Bevanno, Thomas Hull (alias Woods) Pierre Voedre and Joseph Grammason, all of whom signed the articles of agreement as boatmen and soldiers of the expedition." (Edwards' History Illinois, p. 38). This expedition was met at Portage du Sioux three days afterward by Captain Whiteside and his men, "who had just arrived from a blockhouse near the mouth of the Illinois river."

Of Captain Whitesides company the records of this office show a muster roll of the date of Nov. 13th, 1812. We publish this roll complete.

A muster roll of a detachment of mounted riflemen commanded by Ensign Samuel Whitesides, of St. Clair county, Illinois Territory. By order of his Excellency, Ninian Edwards, Governor of Illinois Territory. From August 7th to August 22, 1812:

Ensign.
Samuel Whitesides.

Privates.
Titus Gragg,
John Swigert,
Henry Taylor,
Azor Gragg,
Abram Howard,
Wm. Pursley,
John Pursley,
Jos. Borough,
Matthew Roach,
John La y,
David Porter,
John Howard,
Abram Vanhoozer,
Roland Hewitt,
Alexander Biram,
John Davison,
Jacob Smelcer,
David Gragg,
Charles Kitchens,
John Gragg.

The record in Edwards' History continues: "On the morning of the 29th day of July, they arrived at Prairie Marcot, about nineteen miles above the mouth of the Illinois river, where Lieut. John Campbell was stationed, with seventeen men." The records in this office contain no roll of these men.

On the arrival of the party at Peoria a parley was held between Capt. Levering and a chief named Gomo, of the Pottawotamies. After several conferences Gomo gave up two stolen horses which he found in the possession of his men, but claimed that he could not find the murderers. Little Chief promised to deliver two more horses to Capt. Heald at Chicago, and Gomo promised to deliver the murderers when they could be found. At this conference it was ascertained that the Missouri murderers were near Prophet's town,—Tippecanoe—and hopes were entertained of catching them in the fall. By exposure incurred and disease contracted on this expedition, Capt. Levering died soon after his return to Kaskaskia.

Throughout the whole summer of 1811 the English emissaries kept up, industriously the dastardly work of setting the Indians on the white settlers. Encouraged by their promises, Tecumseh had conceived the plan of combining the Southern tribes into a league with the Northern Indians to make war on the United States until their lands were restored to them.

His attack on General Harrison with a force of over 700 men, under cover of darkness, and his ultimate defeat and flight, with a serious loss of killed and wounded, is a part of the history of our country which concerns us only, as our Illinois troops participated in the victory. This battle, which took place on the 6th day of November, 1811, cost the lives of 37 killed outright and 25 mortally wounded who afterward died, and these were the very flower of the young settlers of Indiana and Illinois Territories. Among the killed in this battle was Capt. Isaac White (for whom White county was afterward named), who commanded a company of Illinois troops raised in Saline county, of which we possess no roll. Here also fell Major Joe Daviess, whose name is also perpetuated in the county of that name; and of the others whose names are not recorded—nor have they be en perpetuated—we can only say they did their duty bravely, and the sacrifice of their own lives saved those of hundreds of women and children who might otherwise have fallen ready victims to the cruelty of the victorious savages.

The rolls of companies of rangers mustered into the United States service during the summer and fall of 1811, are no doubt preserved at the War Department. Of the militia who from time to time were called out by Governor Edwards, there are but few of the rolls preserved. We find, however, a pay roll of militia from July 4th, to July 29th, 1811, as follows:

CAPT. WM. ALEXANDER'S COMPANY.

Pay roll of company of militia commanded by Captain William Alexander, of the county of Randolph, Illinois Territory, by order of Ninian Edwards, Governor of said Territory.

Captain.
William Alexander.

Lieutenant.
Wm. McBride.

Sergeants.
Amos Chaffin,
David Everett,
George Wilson,
John Anderson.

Corporals.
Adam McDonald,
William Dees,
George Cochran,
Joseph Robinson.

Privates.
Joseph Vassume,
George Martin,
James Curry,
James Murtry,
Calvin Laurence,
Idmer Patton,
Drury Stephens,
Leonard St. John,
John Hill,
John McBride,
John Lively, (see campaign 1813)
Daniel Hull,
James McNabb,
Jean B. Iondrow,
Joseph Conway,
Robert Robinson,
Alexander Camudy,
Joseph Petoin,
John Pillers,
Joseph Miller,
Daniel Winn,
Jerome F. Pure,
John F. White,
Arch. Snodgrass,
Amos Robinson,
Edward Lay,
John Crawford,
Daniel Bilderback,
Robert Haggins,
Israel Bailey,
William Welch,
George Creath,
John May,
James Gill,
Robert McDonald,
Edward Rolls,
John Fisher,
John Baptiste Pera,
Joseph Butea,
Louis Dore,
William Bilderback,
Joseph Eberman,
Henry Null,
James White,
Simeon Brundage,
Eli Lankford,
James Eden,

During the winter of 1811-12 the Indians on the upper Mississippi were very hostile, and committed many murders.

Gov. Reynolds charges in his "Own Times" that the British agent at Prairie-du-Chien —it was reported by Indian traders—"had engaged all the warriors of that region to descend the Mississippi and exterminate the settlements on both sides of the river."

A few marauding parties penetrated far down in the State, killing Andrew Moore and his son on the middle fork of Big Muddy (Moore's Prairie, in Jefferson county, was named for him). Later in the same year they attacked Hill's fort, and were repulsed.

In view of the troubled state of affairs Gov. Edwards, in March, 1812, dispatched Capt. Edward Hebert as a friendly messenger to the Indians living on the Illinois river, inviting them to a counsel, which met on the 16th day of April, at Cahokia, and in which all the tribes in the State were represented. After protracted speech making, in which the Indians rather had the advantage, they came away loaded with substantial presents. Reynolds says:

"The wild men exercised the most diplomacy, and made the Governor believe that the Indians were for peace, and that the whites need dread nothing from them. They promised enough to obtain presents, and went off laughing at the credulity of the whites."

Some of the same Indians who participated in this council were engaged in the Chicago massacre the August following.

The Indians of the North-west, however, did not desire peace. They had been kept stirred up and excited by the British agents, so that when Congress, on the 19th day of June, 1812, declared war against Great Britain, they were ready to take advantage of the fact and throw their aid with the enemy in a general warfare against the settlers on the whole American frontier. In Illinois the militia was thoroughly organized in anticipation of the outbreak, and additional forts were built, one near the mouth of Little Wabash, and another at the mouth of La Motte creek.

MASSACRE AT CHICAGO.

The greatest massacre ever committed in the State occurred on the 15th day of August, 1812, near the site of the present city of Chicago. In 1804 the General Government had erected Fort Dearborn at the mouth of Chicago river, on the site of an old fort built by the French in the 17th century, and maintained in it a small garrison, usually consisting of 50 men and three pieces of artillery. Under this precarious protection there had gathered quite a number of Indian traders, and their families, and a few settlers had established their homes in the immediate vicinity. For the eight years of the existence of the fort the history of the garrison had been free from incident. The relations of the officers, the soldiers, and even of the settlers and traders, with the savages were supposed to be of the most cordial nature. At the time of the massacre the garrison consisted of 75 men, few of whom were effective soldiers. The officers were Capt. Heald, Lieut. Helm, Ensign Ronan and Surgeon Voorhees.

On the 7th of August Capt. Heald received an order from Governor Hull, commander-in-chief, to evacuate the fort. The captain and Lieut. Helm, as well as John Kinzie, the principal trader, had families there, and their condition was all the more critical. Mr. Kinzie, who was seconded strongly by the sagacious chief who brought the order, Winnemeg, strongly advised against the evacuation, not believing it to be safe to leave the protection of the block-houses. But the commander, impressed more with his duty of obedience than of fear of danger, which he did not consider imminent, without consultation with his subordinates gave the order to evacuate the following morning. The other officers immediately added their remonstrances, and urged the improbability of being able to make a successful retreat with so small a force to so great a distance as Fort Wayne, through the country of so vigilant and hostile a foe.

The publication of this order for a week previous to the intended evacuation, no doubt added much to the danger.

Capt. Heald called together the Pottawotamies in council on the 12th, and promised them the goods belonging to the government, and in return they promised him to escort his force to Fort Wayne.

Capt. Heald, when too late, found that it was indiscreet to give the ammunition and whiskey to the Indians, so on the night of the 13th he destroyed all the ammunition by throwing it in a well, broke the extra guns and stove the whiskey barrels to prevent them falling into the hands of the Indians. A council of the savages held on the 14th expressed great indignation at this breach of faith on the part of the whites. Notice of the unfriendly attitude of the Indians was given during this day by Black Partridge, but Capt. Wells with 15 friendly Miamis having arrived from Fort Wayne, the despondency of the whites was somewhat dispelled. Capt. Wells was a brother of Mrs. Heald, and hearing of the intended evacuation, had hastened to strengthen the escort with the few men he could command at a short notice.

The reserved ammunition, 25 rounds to the man, was issued, and the baggage wagons for the sick, and women and children, made ready, and on the morning of the 15th of August, notwithstanding another message from a friendly Indian to Mr. Kinzie, warning them of danger, they started on their ill-advised journey, leaving the fort at 9 in the morning, headed by a band of martial music; about a mile and a half from the fort, they encountered the Indians, hid behind the sand-hills which follow the course of the beach of Lake Michigan. The troops fought bravely, but were overborne by numbers; only 28 out of 66 surrendered. Capt. Heald in his report gives them at 54 regulars and 12 militia, of which 26 regulars and all the militia were killed—all the other officers, including Capt. Wells, except the Capt. and Lieut. Helm, and most of the women and children were killed outright, one savage tomahawking 12 children in one wagon alone.

Of all who started out on the fatal morning, was left the Capt., 1st Lieut., 25 enlisted men, and 11 women and children, fortunately including among the latter the brave wife of Lieut. Helm, who herself and Mrs. Heald, who although seriously wounded, escaped most fortunately with her life.

A most notable incident of this massacre was the fact that Mr. Kinzie and family were unharmed, and restored to their house the next day, with the loss of but a small part of their goods; they however ran a close chance of destruction on the day following by a party of Wabash Pottawotamies, who arrived too late for the main attack, and were only saved by the presence of mind of Billy Caldwell, a half-breed Wyandott, who placated them with good speeches in recommendation of Mr. Kinsie's kindness to the Indians, and friendship for them.

CAMPAIGN OF 1812.

In the meantime Governor Edwards had not been idle. Anticipating for some months the action of the General Government, he had, on his individual credit, thoroughly organized and equipped the militia of the territory, built forts, and made every possible effort.

—21

General Hull having surrendered at Detroit on the 16th day of August, the British and Indians had full sway in the whole northwest, with the exception of Forts Wayne and Harrison. This emboldened them to penetrate further and further into the interior, even encroaching on the settlements in Southern Illinois. The British had descended the Mississippi to Rock Island and were distributing goods to the Indians through their notorious agent, Samuel Girty.

In the latter part of August, General Harrison superseded General Hull in the command of the Northwest.

The State of Kentucky had raised a force of 7,000 men, a portion of which, under the command of General Hopkins and Col. William Russell, was directed to the aid of Indiana and Illinois. On the 11th day of October, Col. Russell with two companies started from Vincennes to join Governor Edwards in an expedition then fitting out at Camp Russell. These companies were commanded by Captains Perry and Modrell. General Hopkins, in command at Vincennes with over 2,000 of the Kentuckians, was to move off the Wabash to Ft. Harrison, pass over into Illinois, march across the prairies on the headwaters of the Sangamon and Vermillion rivers, destroying the Indian villages in the course of his march, and to finally effect a junction with Edwards and Russell on the Illinois, and, combined, to sweep the Indians from the whole length of that river.

Governor Hopkins and his branch of the expedition succeeded very well in their plans, and about the middle of October crossed the Wabash at Ft. Harrison, but the men began to show symptoms of discontent, which on the 20th had assumed so violent a form that the generals were forced to return after having penetrated from 80 to 90 miles into the heart of the Indian country.

In the meantime Gov. Edwards had collected 350 men of the Illinois militia at Camp Russell, by the time Col. Russell had arrived with the U. S. Rangers, as the regular troops were then called. These he divided in two small regiments, commanded respectively by Colonels Elias Rector and Benjamin Stephenson. (Rolls of a portion of these companies are yet preserved, and are published complete in the following pages).

DESTRUCTION OF PEORIA.

It having been reported to Governor Edwards that the French settlers at Peoria were inciting the Indians to attacks on the settlers, he dispatched Capt. Thomas E. Craig, of Shawneetown, with his company (see roll) in advance of the expedition, with two boats on the Illinois river, one boat loaded with provisions, and tools to build a fort, the others armed with blunderbusses and a swivel, as a sort of a gun boat, while both were "fortified so that the enemies bullets could not enter their sides." Craig was to wait at Peoria for further orders from the commander-in-chief, and was to make offensive war on the French inhabitants of that town. The latter instruction was carried out fully, by burning the place and taking prisoners the white inhabitants, who were afterwards sent as prisoners to Camp Russell and from there sent to St. Louis, and discharged some months afterwards. Governor Coles, in a report made to the Secretary of the Treasury, several years afterward, gives the names of these settlers as, Thomas Forsythe, Jacques Mette, P. Larasier, (alias Chamberlain), Antonie Le Claire, Michael La Croix, Francis Racine, Sr., Francis Racine, Jr., Felix Fontaine, Hypolyte Maillet, Francis Banche, heirs of Charles La Belle, Antonie La Pance, Antoine Barbonne and Louis Poncennau. The above list does not include women and children, the number of prisoners in the aggregate numbering 75.

GOVERNOR EDWARDS' CAMPAIGN, 1812.

On the 18th day of October, Governor Edwards and his army took up their march. Their route was up the west side of Cahokia creek, thence to the Macoupin, which they crossed near the present town of Carlinville, thence in a northeast direction, they crossed the Sangamon below the junction of the north and south forks east of the present city of Springfield; passing thence east of Elkhart Grove, they crossed Salt creek near the site of the present city of Lincoln; from thence marching still northward, they came upon a deserted Kickapoo village on Sugar creek, which they set on fire and destroyed. After this, their course was directed to the head of Peoria Lake, where was located the village of Black Partridge, a chief of the Pattawotamies. Having approached within a few miles of the town, Thomas Carlin, (afterwards Governor of the State) and Robert Stephen and Davis Whitesides were sent to reconnoiter the enemy, which they successfully accomplished by passing through and over the town in the night without discovery.

Early on the following morning, the army, with Capt. Judy and his spy company in advance, under the cover of a dense fog moved upon the village, but the troops becoming entangled in the swamps, the Indians were apprised of their approach and fled without fighting or encountering any serious loss. Following the fleeing Indians for several miles across the yielding swamps, a small Indian town was reached and burned. The Indians having all made good their escape, and no news having been received from Governor Hopkins, and a rainy season having set in, the Governor deemed it prudent to retire. As Governor Reynolds quaintly observes in his "Own Times," "Our army returned home with all convenient speed."

MUSTER ROLLS OF VOLUNTEERS—1812.

Capt. Thomas E. Craig's Company.

A muster roll of a company of Volunteer riflemen, raised in Illinois Territory, under the command of Capt. Thomas E. Craig in the service of the United States, by order of His Excellency Ninian Edwards, Governor of said Territory. From the 5th September to the 2d December, 1812.

In column headed "date of appointment or engagement," all appear to have been enlisted Sept 5th and all were discharged December 2, 1812.

Captain.
Thomas E. Craig.

Lieutenant.
John Forrester.

Ensign.
Harrison Wilson.

Sergeants.
Walker Skantlin,
Charles Hill,
John G. Wilson,
Phil. Buckner.

Corporals,
Robert Preston,
Joseph Lepan.
Joseph Gordon,
Willis Wheeler.

Music.
John Ormsby, drummer,
Nat. Reeves, fifer.

Privates.
Elias Hubbard
Thomas Hatfield,
Jacob Yocum,
Stephen Fowler,
Moses Rawlings
John Hazelton,
John Woods,
Robert Harris,
William Corn,
Charles Druyer,
Henry Jenna,
Arthur Owens,
James Drake,

Samuel Kimberly,
Richard Hayden,
Robert Cox,
Hiram Higgins,
Randall Davis,
William Gable,
Lewis Young,
Edward Farely,
Sampson Dunn,
David Stanly,
James Wright,
Enoch Brown,
Edmond Stokes,
Jacob Willis,
Elisha Livingston,
John Powell,
Samuel Green,
Dennis Clay,
Russel E. Haycock,
David Johnston,
John Clendenin,
Joel Crane,
Squire Crane,
Alex. Barbour,
Spencer Adkins,
Amos Paxton
John Farney,
George Glun,
Michael Burris,
John Lard,
Lasadore Gander,
Inlam Bart,
Peter Bono,
George Conner,
Richard Hazle,
John Campbell,
David Sipley,
George T. Woods,
Antoine Sander,
Lewis Freedom,
John B. Genam,
Edward Miller,

Although Governor Edwards had several times during the years of 1811 and 1812 recommended to the Secretary of War the enlistment of one or more companies of "Rangers," to protect the frontier, and Congress having, in 1811, passed an act authorizing the organization of ten companies of rangers, which were afterward organized as the 17th United States Regiment, under Col. William Russell, of Kentucky, an Indian fighter of bravery and experience, it does not appear that more than one Company was recruited in the Illinois Territory. Davidson and Stuve say in their History, in reference to this force: "Four companies were allotted to the defense of Illinois, whose respective Captains were Samuel and William B. Whitesides, James B. Moore and Jacob Short. Independent Cavalry Companies were also organized for the protection of the remote settlements in the lower Wabash country, of which Willis Hargrave, William McHenry, Nathaniel Journey, Capt. Craig, at Shawneetown, and William Boon, on Big Muddy, were respectively commanders, ready, on short notice of Indian outrages, to make pursuit of the depredators." (D. and S. Hist. Ill., p. 249.) We are, however, of the opinion that there must have been some mistake about the fact alleged of four Companies of the 17th Regiment being from Illinois, as, of the Captains mentioned, we have evidence that Samuel Whitesides, James B. Moore and Jacob Short were commanding Companies of Militia at the time, in the service of the Governor of Territory, all belonging to the Regiment which William Whiteside, as Lieutenant Colonel, was then commanding, (the 2d Regiment Ter. Militia.) The organization and size of this command appear from a regimental return, on file in this office, bearing date Sept. 16, 1812, which was no doubt made out at Camp Russell, signed by Lieut. Col. William Whiteside, Commanding, and Elihu Mather, Adjutant, and is as follows:

1st Battalion—Major John Murdock.

	Total.
Capt. Jacob Short	80
Capt. John Scott	75
Capt. Abraham Stallions	55
Capt. Edward Ebart	91
Capt. James B. Moore	71
Total, 1st Battalion	372

2d Battalion—Major Samuel Judy.

	Total.
Capt. Amos Squires	64
Capt. Samuel Whiteside	56
Capt. Solomon Pruitt	60
Capt. Henry Cook	79
Capt. Cale Jourango	..
Total, 2d Battalion	259

3d Battalion—Major William Pruitt.

	Total.
Capt. Valentine Brazil	..
Capt. Isaac Griffin	30
Capt. Nathaniel Journey	39
Shoal Creek Company	..
Total, 3d Battalion	69
Aggregate	700

In a morning report, also made at Camp Russell, dated Sept. 12, 1812, "of the troops under the command of Major Benjamin Stephenson," we find companies under the command of Captains James B. Moore, W. B. Whiteside, Absolem Cox, Jacob Short, Willis Hargraves, Samuel Whiteside, Nathaniel Journey and Amos Squires, giving an aggregate of 570 men. Two companies on this return, viz: Absolem Cox's and William Hargraves' were probably independent companies or belonged to another regiment, and were reported because present at the same post. These returns were both made out and signed by A. Whitney, Sergeant-Major, and a penman of no mean ability.

In another morning report of "troops under the command of Lt.-Col. Whiteside," dated Oct. 10, 1812,—and also made out by A. Whitney, Sergeant-Major—their appears companies under the command of Captain N Ramsey, Thomas E. Craig, Willis Hargraves, Absolem Cox and James Trousdale, showing present an aggregate of 316 men. A "staff" return on the same blank shows present 1 surgeon, 1 surgeon-mate, 1 Adjutant, 1 Sergeant-Major, and 1 Judge Advocate. At the bottom of this return is the following: "N. B.—Six company on command, Capt. Moore, S. Whitsid, Short. Whitsid, N. Journey, Squires," Of these companies mentioned in these returns we have rolls of a part only. Those we will now give:

Captain Samuel Whitesides' Company.

A muster roll of a volunteer company of mounted riflemen commanded by Captain Samuel Whitesides, of St. Clair county, Illinois Territory, by order of His Excellency Ninian Edwards, Governor of said Territory. Date of enlistment, Aug. 22;—enlisted to Nov. 13, 1812.

Names.	Remarks.
Captain.	
Samuel Whitesides	
First Lieutenant.	
Titus Gragg (or Greig)	
Second Lieutenant.	
John Swigert	

APPENDIX.

Names.	Remarks.
Ensign,	
Henry Taylor.	
Sergeants.	
Jesse Creek, 1st.	Reduced to the ranks Oct. 10, 1812.
Azor Gragg (or Greig).	
Abram Howard.	Reduced to the ranks Oct. 18, 1812.
Wm. Simpson.	Reduced to the ranks Oct. 13, 1812.
Corporals.	
John Pursley.	Made Sergeant Oct. 18, 1812.
John Waggoner.	
William Pursley.	Made Sergeant Oct. 18, 1812.
Harmon Gragg.	Absented himself without leave Aug. 23, 1812.
Privates.	
Aaron Armstrong.	
Benjamin Bishop.	
Wm. Burgess.	
Jos. Borough.	Made 1st Sergeant Oct. 10, 1812.
John Brisco.	One horse lost, $30.
Jonas Bradshaw.	
Simeon Brundage.	
George Barnsback.	
Louis Baimmie.	
Daniel Cornelius.	
William Chelton.	
David Carter.	
Samuel Davis.	
Huber Delorme.	One horse lost, $30.
John Ferguson.	
John Fulmore.	
Joseph Ferguson.	
John Gragg.	
Wm. Howard.	
John Howard.	Made Corporal 18th Oct., 1812.
Roland Hewitt.	
Matthias Hanlon.	
George Hewitt.	
John Higens.	
Philip Hawk.	
George Harmon.	
John Jacobs.	
James Johnson.	
George Kinder.	
Charles Kitchens.	
John Lacey.	
Samuel Lee.	
Joseph Lee.	
Raphael Langlue.	
Batees Labrau.	
Walter McFarling.	
James Marney.	
James McFadgin.	
Jesse Million.	
Joseph Myars.	
Jacob Ogle.	
Jubilee Posey.	
Pierce Plant.	
Wm. Phillips.	
John Pixley.	
John Powell.	
James Pullum.	
John Paine.	
Wm. Pruitt.	
David Porter.	
Daniel Pierce.	
Matthew Roach.	
Wm. Right.	
Samuel Stockton.	
David Sampler.	
Jacob Smelcer.	
Robert Stockton.	
Moses Sweeten.	Deserted.
Thomas Smith.	Discharged.
James Tolley.	
John Teeter.	
Toussant Tramble.	
Napees Tuckee.	
John Turner.	

Names.	Remarks.
Abram Vanhooser	
Joseph Williams	
William Groats	
Joshua Patterson	
Joel Whitesides	
Isaac Lecount	
Joshua Lamotte	
Allan Bridges	
Ellsworth Bayne	One horse lost, $40.
Benjamin Samples	
Benjamin Warren	

I do certify on honor that the foregoing statement is correct, and exhibits a true account of the men under my command. This 13th day of November, 1812.

SAMUEL WHITESIDES, Captain.

CAPT. JACOB SHORT'S FIRST COMPANY.

Muster roll of the mounted riflemen detached from the 2d Regiment of militia, Illinois Territory, for a three months' tour, by order of the Commander-in-Chief, March 3, 1812.

Captain.
Jacob Short.

First Lieutenant.
John Murdoch.

Ensign.
Henry Carr.

Sergeants.
Robert Middleton,
Alexander Scott,
George Mitchell,
William Arundel.

Privates.
Adam Clover,
David Kenedy,
Thomas Marney,
Wm. Quigley,
Thomas Porter,
James Hendricks,
Jacob Borrier,
John B. Wisser,
Isaac Carmack,
Daniel Guyee,
Zachariah Hayse,
Samuel Scott,
William Philips,

John Walker,
David Eckman,
Elijah Hoake,
William Ritenhouse,
James Wilderman,
Henry Stout,
Peter Hill,
Peter Wills,
John Bier,
George Wilderman,
Fulden Jarvic,
Hiram Tidwell,
John Brigance,
Daniel McKinney,
John Brigham,
William Steele,
Charles Radcliff,
Henry Walker,
William Middleton,
John Waddle,
Robert Middleton,
Jeptha D. Williams,
Hubard Short,
Peter Risenbough,
William Walker,
Jacob Wilderman,
John Cooper,
John Eastes,
John Myers,
Sam'l Shook,
Andrew Bankston.

Mustered and inspected by me, Elihu Mather, Adjutant 2d Regiment Militia, Illinois Territory.

CAPT. JOHN SCOTT'S COMPANY.

A list of the third Company detached from Colonel Whiteside's Regiment, the 3d of March, 1812, as infantry.

Captain.
John Scott.

Lieutenant.
Titus Gragg.

Ensign.
Phillip Roder.

Sergeants.
John Mitchell,
Jacob Randleman,
William Cerns.

Corporals.
Birdett Green,

Christopher Halterman,
James Porter,
John Stallions.

Privates.
Asyl Jerome,
Prior Hogan,
Thomas Todd,
Alexander Wells,
John Robins,
Alexander Jamison,
Daniel Sink,
Jacob Trout,
Geo. Atchison,
Jacob Clover,
Leonard Carr,
Charles Goldsmith,
Joseph Fry,

John Huffman,
Martin Jones,
Patrick Cullin,
Robert Patton,
John Winters,
Isaac Toland,
Absolem Bradshaw,
Jacob Clark,
Abraham Miller,
James Bradshaw,
Thomas Ramey,
James Johnston,

James Whaley,
Robert Hawk,
Jacob Eyman,
George Ramey,
Baker Whaley,
John Moore,
John Porter,
David Whiteside,
Enoch Moore,
John L. Whiteside,
Phillip Cramer,
William Mears.

Mustered and inspected by me, Elihu Mather, Adjutant 2d Regiment Militia, Illinois Territory.

CAPT. SAMUEL JUDY'S COMPANY,
OTHERWISE KNOWN AS
CAPT. HENRY COOK'S COMPANY.

A list of the first Company detached from the 2d Regiment of Militia, Illinois Territory, for a three months tour, by order of the Commander-in-Chief, 3d March, 1812. Inspected at Cohakia.

Captain.
Samuel Judy.

Lieutenant.
Henry Cook.

Ensign.
Christopher Barnhart.

Sergeants.
Samuel Gillham,
Wm. Bradshaw,
Charles Gillham,
Thomas Kitchell.

Drummer.
Hiram Beck.

Fifer.
Bolin Shepherd.

Privates.
Thomas Cox,
David Moon,
Jonas Bradshaw,
Henry Rogers,
Field Bradshaw,
J. Clemont Gillham,
John Hawks,
John Kirkpatrick,
Aaron Linvill,
George Fuse,
John Finley,
Meril Ledbetter,
Jesse Bill,
Thomas Rendell,
Joseph Luster,
Thomas Downing,
Abraham Vanhoofer,
Benjamin Samples,

David Samples,
John Talbott,
Ezra Gragg,
James Wilson,
Hardin Wardin,
James McFadgin,
Absolem Wodams,
Wm. Gillham,
John Starkey,
John Arons,
Jacob Linder,
Thomas Blankenship,
Wm. Prewitt,
John Vickery,
Royal Green,
Joseph Ogle,
Davis Waddle,
John McDow,
George Hewitt,
Robert Anderson,
John Adkins,
Willey Willbanks,
Alexander Elliott,
Richard Ackles,
Samuel Hutten,
Robert Whiteside,
Th. Andrew,
Justis Kick,
Jonathan Graham,
Andrew Emert,
John Newman,
Bird Lockhart,
Joshua Diliplain,
Samuel Quigley,
Michael Dodd,
Uton Smith,
John Newman, Jr.,
Wm. Ryons,
John Johnston,
Charles Kitchens,
Jacob Whiteside.

Mustered and inspected by me, Elihu Mather, Adjutant 2d Regiment Militia, Illinois Territory

CAPT. WILLIS HARGRAVE'S COMPANY.

We, the undersigned, being formed into a Company of Mounted Volunteers, under the command of Willis Hargrave as Captain, tender to your Excellency our services, to perform a tour of duty against the Indians on the frontiers of Illinois Territory, and hold ourselves in readiness to march at a minute's warning to any point you may direct.

Captain.
Willis Hargrave.

First Lieutenant.
Wm. McHenry.

Second Lieutenant.
John Graves.

Ensign.
Thomas Berry.

Enlisted Men.
James Long,
William Maxwell,
David Trammel (a spy),
James Wilson,
Thomas McKinney,
John Smith,
Taylor Maulding,
Jeremiah Lisanbee,
James Small,
Thomas Trammel,
James Hannah,
Charles Slocomb,
Edward Covington,
Nathan Young,
Joseph Upton,
James Garrison,
Robt. D. Cates,
Dickason Garratt,
Thomas Boatwright,
Richard Moulding (spy),
Aaron Williams,
John Summers,
Seth Hargrave,
James Trammel,
Lee Moulding,
Morris May,
David Milch,

Henry Wheeler,
Joel Berry,
David Whooley,
Thomas McAllister,
John Love,
James Davenport,
Thomas Stovery,
James Carr,
Daniel Battenhouse,
Gillam Harris,
Abner Howard,
Josiah Dunnell,
Ely Stewart,
Philip Sturn,
Neadham Standlee,
Charles Stewart,
John Lawton,
Alexander Hamilton,
David Snodgrass,
Philip Fleming,
John Morris,
George Morris,
Thomas Upton,
Martin Whitford,
Joseph Lane,
John Dover,
Simon Cannon,
John Mitchell,
James McDaniel,
Adam Winkler,
William Wheeler,
John Bradberry,
Michel Deckers,
Thomas Williams,
Barnabas Chambers,
Ephriam Blackford,
Reubin Blackford,
Rial Potter,
Frederick Buck,
Charles Sparks,
William McCormick,
William Fowler.

CAPT. SAMUEL JUDY'S SPY COMPANY.

Captain.
Samuel Judy.

Privates.
Henry Cook,
Isaac Gilham,
Calvin Adams,
Alexander Waddle,
Ambrose Nix,
Samuel Gilham,
George Moore,
Toliver Right,

Thomas Smith,
Pierre Crossey,
Joseph Newman,
William Griffin,
John Adkins,
Davis Stockdon,
Thomas Cox,
William Going,
William Radcliff,
John Reynolds,
Edward Clark,
Robert Frazure,
Patrick Larner.

CAPT. ABSOLEM COX'S COMPANY.

Muster roll and inspection return of a detachment of the 1st Regiment of Illinois militia, under the command of Capt. Absolem Cox, at Kaskaskia, the 3d of September, 1812.

(This detachment did not go to Peoria, but was no doubt left behind to protect the settlers.)

FROM CAPT. COX'S COMPANY.

Captain.
Absolem Cox.

Lieutenant.
Thomas Roberts.

Ensign.
Adam Wobrick.

Sergeants.
Robert Foster,
William McDonald,
*Richard Robinson,
Samuel Reiner.

Corporals.
John Irwin,
Shadrach Lively,
Amos Lively,
Edward Clark.

Privates.
William Thompson,
William Little,
James Patterson,
James McFarland,
Shadrach Lively,
John McClinton,
John Beatty,
John Smyth,
James Clark,
Thomas McBride,
George Baggs,
John Willson,
Reuben Lively,
Archibald Steel,
John Miller,
Solomon Allen,
John Pillere,
Andrew Ross,
Robert Thompson.

FROM CAPT. ALEXANDER'S COMPANY.

Jesse Boggs,
Matthew Jarvis,
Hugh Robston,
Seth Chalfin,

Wm. McLaughlin,
George Conner,
John Worley,
Chester Marvel.

FROM CAPT. HENRY LEVON'S COMPANY.

George Glenn,
Patrick Lamer,
Benjamin Vermillion,

James Adkins,
Abraham McMurtry.

FROM CAPT. JOHN COCHRAN'S COMPANY.

Jonathan Bowman,
James Steele,
David Johnston.

William May,
John Clendenon,
Squire Crain.

FROM CAPT. M'DINEY'S COMPANY.

James Sleter,
Cyrus Fulton,
Thomas Beson,
Adam Wingate,
Alexander Barber,
James Bail.

William Garver,
Samuel Lard,
Charles Garner,
William Hall,
George Belsher,
David Petel.

APPENDIX.

FROM CAPT. GREENUP'S COMPANY.

Ralph Lee,
Joseph Curry,
Francis Toulouse,
James D. Mitchell,
Amos Paxton,
Pascal Lessauree,
Louis Segar,
Jean B. Gendeon,
B. Lachasspell,
N. Beatt,
Louis Lemiene,

George Baker,
Robert St. Pierre,
Manuel Troupa,
J. Chinia,
Alexis Beauvais,
Louis Beatt,
Andrew Charleville,
B. Montrow,
Francis Deproet,
Alexis Beatt,
James Smyth.

FROM CAPT. GABRIEL DECOCHE'S COMPANY.

Francis Tongue,
Joseph Tongue,
Andre Barboure,
Alexis Godere,
Andre Roy,
Joseph Godere,

Joseph Vassure,
Ettienne Louglore,
Joseph Piluer,
Jean Marie Gidier,
Francis Louglore,
August Alter,

Signed: DAVID ANDERSON, Inspector,
Adjutant 1st Ill. Militia.

CAPT. JAMES B. MOORE'S COMPANY.

1ST COMPANY—April 15 to May 3, 1812.

Captain.
James B. Moore,

First Lieutenant.
Jacob Ogle,

Second Lieutenant.
John Vaugn,

Ensign.
Simon Wheelock,

Sergeants.
John T. Lusk,
Septemus Mace,
Thomas Piper,
Jesse Miller,

Privates.
J. Milton Moore,
William Biggs,
John Rutherford,
Thomas Talbott,

David Robinson,
James Kirkpatrick,
Henry Mace,
Richard Wright,
Isaac Biggs,
John Davidson,
Israel Robinson,
Cath Wilson,
Aaron Shook,
William Lemon,
Samuel Bonham,
Joseph Bear,
Philip Teter,
Charles T. Walker,
Joseph Ogle,
Francis Kirkpatrick,
John Bloom,
Isham Gillham,
Simeon Vanarsdale,
William Gillham,
Hiram Badgely,
Arthur Morgan,
Joshua Talbott,
Pleasant Goings,
William Goings.

CAPT. JAMES B. MOORE'S (2ND) COMPANY.

A muster roll of a volunteer company of Cavalry, commanded by Capt. James B. Moore of St. Clair county, Illinois Territory. By order of His Excellency Ninian Edwards, Governor of Illinois Territory. From July 27, 1812, to Aug. 11, 1812.

Captain.
James B. Moore.

First Lieutenant.
Jacob Ogle.

Second Lieutenant.
Joshua Vaughn.

Cornet.
Simeon Wheelock.

APPENDIX.   331

Sergeants.
John T. Lusk, 1st,
Septemus Mace,
Thomas Piper,
Jem Miller,

Corporals.
Wm. Reed,
James McKinney,
John Davidson,
Pleasant Goings,

Privates.
James Kirkpatrick,
Isham Gillham,
Charles P. Walker,
Aaron Shook,
J. Milton Moore,
David Robinson,
Israel Robinson,
Francis Kirkpatrick,
Daniel G. Moore,
Samuel Bonham,
Philip Teter,
Henry Mace,
Isaac Biggs,
Cath Wilson,
Wm. C. Davidson,
Richard Wright,
Thomas Randle,
Jesse Bell,
John Good,

Wm. Briggs, Jr.,
Thomas W. Talbott,
Ezekial Gillham,
Simon Vadarsdal,
Moses Quick,
Matthew J. Cox,
Arthur Morgan,
Hardy Wilbanks,
Charles R. Matheny,
John L. Whiteside,
George Sanders,
Joseph Ogle (son of B. Ogle)
Isaiah Dunnigan,
Thos. Blankinship,
Bennet Nowlan,
Wm. Talbott,
John Crocker,
William Otwell,
Clement Gillham,
John Deleplain,
Absolem Bradshaw,
Anthony Foucher,
Isaac Clark,
Isham Wright,
Zachariah Hays,
William Porter,
Fielding Jervis,
David Ackerman,
Aaron Whitney,
Guy Beck,
John Huitt,
Charles Gillham,
Wm. Gillham.

CAPT PHILIP TRAMELL'S COMPANY.

Muster roll of a detachment of Mounted Militia, called into the service of the United States, under the orders of His Excellency Governor Edwards, to guard military stores from Shawneetown to Camp Russell, under the command of Philip Tramell, Lieut.-Col. of the 4th Regt. Illinois Militia, acting as Capt. From the 12th day of October to the 31st day of October, 1812.

Captain.
Philip Tramell.

Sergeant.
Morton Ewbanks.

Privates.
James McFarland,
John Murphy,

James Lee,
William Cumins,
Covington Wilson,
John Gillard,
Isaac Sibley,
Wm. Wheeler,
John Campbell,
David Sibley,
Solomon Blue,
James Inman,
Pompey, servant to Philip Tramell.

I do certify that the within muster roll exhibits a true statement of the detachment for the purpose mentioned therein, and that James Ratcliff furnished a wagon and team for the purpose of transporting military stores from Shawneetown to Camp Russell, which was employed in the United States service from the 5th day of October until the 31st; the same month with Adam Croach, wagoner. William Morrison furnished wagon, team and driver, for the same purpose, from the 9th October to the 31st of same month. Meed Laughlin and Davis Gillard each furnished wagon, and team, and driver, for the above purpose, from the 31st of same month

PHILIP TRAMELL, Lieut.-Col., 4th Illinois Militia,
now acting as Capt., in place of Leonard White.

CAPT DUDLEY WILLIAMS' COMPANY OF THE 4TH REGIMENT MILITIA.

A muster roll of a Volunteer company of Mounted Riflemen, called into service of the United States, agreeable to an order of His Excellency Ninian Edwards, Commander-in-Chief of the Illinois Militia (against the late invasions of the hostile Indians), commanded by Capt. Dudley Williams. From October 14th to November 5th, 1812.

Captain.
Dudley Williams.

Lieutenant.
David Moore.

Ensign.
Reuben Linn.

Cornet.
Alfred Linsey.

Sergeants.
Joseph Ferguson,
John Reed,
Henry Griffin,
James Moor.

Corporals.
Wm. Megee,
James Brown,
Thomas Armstrong,
John Jarrat.

Privates.
Henry Fuel,
John Walker,
Asher Davis,
John Neal,
John Hallin,
Daniel Calhoun,
Allen Barnes,
Furnas Harrison,
Hiram Dikerson,
Matthew Thomas,
Thomas Futral,
Andrew Hallin,
John Show,
Isaac Davis,
Micajah Fort,
Jesse Rascow,
William Cravens,
Elijah Ladd,
Thomas Casten,
Samuel Reas,
Redden Wolf,
Wilbourn Futral,
Joseph Bridges,
Samuel Walker,
William Mathias,
Ezekiel Stevens,
Robert Cain,
Jeremiah Mitchell,
James Woolf,
Hiram Griffith,
Samuel Jennings,
John Matthews,
Richard Clark,
Daniel Coshler,
Joseph Williams,
John Ferguson,
Charles Brownfield,
James Blasingham,
William Armstrong,
John Mabury,
James Randolph,
James Cook,
Harvey Bramlett,
Thomas White.

I certify that the foregoing is a correct muster roll of my company, and that they were mustered into service of the United States Saline, on the 14th day of October, 1812.

Examined and approved,
B. STEPHENSON, Brigade Major.

DUDLEY WILLIAMS, Capt.

Also endorsed by a certificate of Philip Tramell, Lieut.-Col. of the 4th Regiment Illinois Militia: "That this company found their own provisions from Christian county to the United States Saline and back again, which going and coming may be considered 160 miles."

The foregoing comprises all the rolls of Companies which have been preserved in this office of those who enlisted during and prior to year 1812. As the rolls of many of these Companies of Rangers are no doubt preserved in the archives of the War Department at Washington, and their publication would add much to the resources of the early history of the State, it is to be hoped that the General Assembly may see fit to take some steps to have them transcribed and published.

As to the other most common means of security for families of the settlers in these early days, these consisted of block-house forts, a number of which were built extending from the Illinois river to the Kaskaskia, thence to United States Salines, near the present town of Equality, and up the Ohio and Wabash rivers, and in nearly all settlements in Illinois. Some of those forts were situated as follows: One at the site of the present town of Carlyle, one a short distance above the town of Winston, and two on east side of Shoal Creek, known as Hills and Jones; all these in the limits of the present county of Clinton. One on the west side of Looking Glass Prairie, a few miles southeast of the present town of Lebanon, was known as Chambers' Fort. On the Kaskaskia river were Middleton's and Going's Forts; one on Doza creek, a few miles from its mouth, known as Nat. Hills,; two in the Jourdan settlement, in the eastern part of Franklin county, on the road from the Kaskaskia settlements to the salt works; one at the mouth of the Illinois river, and later John Campbell, an United States officer, erected a small block-house on the west bank of the Illinois river (at Prairie Marcot), 19 miles above its mouth. Larger forts than these were erected opposite the mouth of the Missouri river, to guard the river; and on Silver creek, near Troy. The main fort, however, and military depot of the territory, was at Camp Russell, a mile and a half northwest of the present town of Edwardsville, in Madison county, in honor of the Colonel, the commander of the Regiment of Rangers. (D. and S. Hist. Ill., pp. 249-250.) This fort was protected by the cannon from old Fort Chartres, and under the guns of Louis XIV., under whose protecting muzzles the Territorial Governor was wont to organize his expeditions, gather his military stores, and rendezvous his recruits under the various calls which the necessities of a desultory Indian warfare, of several years' duration, made it obligatory on his Excellency to make.

At this fort, besides the rangers and riflemen mentioned in the various rolls above given, was also a small company of regular troops, under Capt. N. Ramsey, as the return

APPENDIX. 333

of Lieutenant-Colonel Whiteside on the 10th of October, 1832, hereinbefore published, shows to have contained a total of 33 men. This company was the only company of regular troops in Illinois Territory, during the war of 1812, which reached the headquarters of Governor Edwards, or tested the hospitalities of his fort.

Among these old rolls we find one of perhaps the most interest, in an historical point of view, of any small paper connected with the history of the State. It reads as follows:

GENERAL STAFF.

Muster roll of general and staff officers of a detachment of militia of Illinois Territory, ordered into the actual service of the United States, and commanded by his Excellency Ninian Edwards, Governor and Commander-in-Chief of the Territory aforesaid:

No.	Names.	Rank.	Commencement of Service.	Expiration of Service.	Remarks.
1.	Ninian Edwards	Comm'nder-in-Chief	Sept. 2, 1812.	Nov. 10, 1812.	
2.	Elias Rector	Adjutant-General	Sept. 10, 1812	" "	
3.	Benjamin Stephenson	Brigade Major	Sept. 2, 1812.	" "	
4.	Nath. Pope	1st Aid	Sept. 20, 1812	" "	
5.	William Rector	2d Aid	Oct. 10, 1812.	" "	
6.	Nelson Rector,	Volunteer Aids	Oct. 18, 1812.	" "	
7.	Robert Todd,				

On the back of this roll is the following endorsement:

"NOVEMBER 23, 1812.

"Examined, approved, certified and returned by me according to law, to the Commander-in-Chief. "ELIAS RECTOR,

"Adjutant General I. T."

CAMPAIGN OF 1813.

Early in this year, the country was put in as good state of defense as circumstances would allow. The forts and blockhouses were strengthened and the settlers in remote and weakly garrisoned blockhouses removed to those that were stronger. New companies of rangers were enlisted and stationed so as to cover the settlements. In addition to the regular forts, from the present city of Alton to Kaskaskia, were twenty-two family forts, scattered along. These precautions, however, did not prevent numerous depredations by the savages. Of these, the following appear to be the most important: In Washington county, four miles southeast of Covington (then the county seat) on the Kaskaskia river, the family of John Lively, an old ranger (see Alexander's company) were attacked ane five persons killed, including Mr. Lively. The bodies of all were shockingly mutilated. The Indians who perpetrated this outrage were supposed to be Kickapoos, and were followed by Capt. Boon and his company, (see roll) but having four days the start, made good their escape. Near the present town of Carlyle a Mr. Young and a minister by the name of McLean were attacked by the savages. Young was killed, and McLean made an almost miraculous escape by swimming the Kaskaskia river, losing his horse and the greater part of his clothing.

Murders were also committed on Cache river within the present limits of Alexander county. Near Fort LaMotte, about 30 miles above Vincennes, Mrs. Houston and four children were killed. In a small prairie near Albion in Edwards county, Mr. Boltinghouse was killed. This prairie was afterwards named for him.

Notwithstanding these, and many other outrages, the general government had provided no means for the support of the rangers and militia, and those in the service, in Illinois, were discharged on the 9th day of June by the Governor.

From a "daily and weekly report of a detachment of rangers of the Illinois Territory, under the command of Benjamin Stephenson, Brigade Major, April 17, 1813," we find that the following companies were included in his command: Capt. B. Whiteside's, Capt. James B. Moore's (3d company), Capt. Samuel Whiteside's, Capt. Jacob Short's, and Capt. Nicholas Jarrott's. Rolls of Moore's and Short's companies at that time, are as follows:

Capt. James B. Moore's (3d) Company.

Captain.
James B. Moore.

First Lieutenant.
David Robinson.

Second Lieutenant.
Arthur Morgan.

Ensign.
John Duitt.

Sergeants.
Thomas Jordan,
Jacob Young,
Benjamin Marney,
James Hutton.

Corporals.
Isaac Basey,
James Talbott,
Henry Randleman,
John Crawford.

Privates.
Enoch Moore,
Jesse Miller,
Joseph Miller,
David Miller,
Abraham Miller,
John Enoch,
Jonathan Knox,
Anthony B. Conner,
Samuel McFarland,
George Lary,
Thomas Johnston,
Hugh Roylston,
Marcus Pelham,
Peter Wills,
Thomas Marney,
Solomon Strong,
Amos Shook,
Francis Pelham,
Fielding Porter,
John Ryan,
Stephen Lacy,
Elihu Axely,
William Ryan,
Joh Stallings,
David Porter,
John Waddle,
John Briscoe,
John Moore,
Jacob Clark,
John Clover,
William Harrington,
David Moore,
Thomas J. Mattingly,
Willy Harrington,
Felix Clark,
Stephen Rector,
Joshua Vaughn,
Charles Gillham,
George Richardson,
William Griffin,
Pleasant Going,

APPENDIX.   335

William Forgason,
Hiram Huitt,
Joseph Forgason,
Ornan Beman,
John Finley,
Fleming Cox,
Aaron Whitney,
Martin Wood,
Bennett Newlin,
Henry Mace,
Isaac Smith,
Daniel Winn,
Roland Huitt,
Edward Crouch,
Isaac Carmack,
William Going,
Elisha Taylor,
Andrew Robinson,
William Hogan,
Prior Hogan,

Bartley Cox,
Richard Windsor,
Alexander Biron,
Jude Converse,
George Hawk,
John Hogan,
Eli Langford,
William Chance,
Jacob Luntzford,
Josiah Langford,
John Marney,
John Collins,
Thomas Marney,
Daniel Converse,
John Ferguson,
Robert Hawke,
Benjamin Edwards,
Janus Marney,
Jesse Harrison.

Examined and approved.

B. STEPHENSON,
Brigade-Major.

Capt. Jacob Short's Company.

Muster roll of a company of mounted rangers commanded by Captain Jacob Short, called into the actual service of the United States, by his Excellency, Ninian Edwards, Governor and Commander-in-Chief,—from the 27th day of February, 1813, to the 31st day of May, 1813, inclusive.

Captain.
Jacob Short.

First Lieutenant.
Nathaniel Journey.

Second Lieutenants.
Andrew Bankston.

Ensign.
John Journey.

Sergeants.
John Brigance,
Alexander Scott,
George Mitchell,
James Wyett,
Robert Thomas.

Corporals.
Richard Ackless,
Robert Lynn,
George Soy,
Nicholas Darter,
George Wise,
Samuel Ware.

Privates.
Robert Anderson,
William Adair,
Solomon Allen,
Hugh Alexander,
Elijah Bankson,
Ellsworth Barnes,
Jacob Brimberry,
John Boucher,
Preston Brickey,
Abraham Bateman,
Taphney Brooks,
William Burgess,
Benjamin Cox,
Isaac Clark,
John Corathers,
Jacob Drocker,
Thomas Drocker,
Janus Clark,
Squire Craine,
Isaac Darneal,
John Duncan, Sr.,
John Duncan, Jr.,
James W. Davidson,

Stanley Dodge,
Matthias Edes,
William Edes,
Joseph Fray,
Cyrus Fulton,
Robert Gaston,
Jacob Gragg,
John Hopton,
Nathaniel Hill,
Jesse Hill,
Burrill Hill,
Martial Hawkins,
Robert Huse,
William Journey,
David Johnston,
Jacob Kerns,
David Loyd,
Samuel Lee, Sr.,
Samuel Lee, Jr.,
John Linley,
John Lively,
John Lard,
Rueben Lively,
James Lard, Jr.,
Alex. Mattocks,
Daniel McKinney,
James Moore,
Thomas Morris,
William Moore,
William McElroy,
Edward Miller,
Abel McNeal,
Henry Neele,
William O'Neal,
Aden Posey,
Samuel Patterson,
Field Pruitt,
Joseph Pruitt,
Jacob Pritchard,
John Rutherford,
Francis Scott,
Henry Sealey,
George Swigart,
John Swigart,
Hubbard Short,
John Stout,
John Scott,
Moses Short,
William Stout,
Abraham Smalley,
Abraham Thomas,
William Tilford,
William Virgin,

Charles Wakefield,
George Wakefield,
Henry Watley,
John Woods,
Jacob Wilderman,
John Walker,
John A. Wakefield.

William Walker,
Peter Wright,
Andrew White,
John Whitley,
Mills Whitley,
David White,
Adam Winghart,

Examined and approved.

B. STEPHENSON,
Brigade-Major.

Besides the above which were included in the return quoted, we find the following, which appear to have been under the same command, about the same time, all of which are endorsed as the two foregoing.
"Examined and approved."

B. STEPHENSON,
Brigade-Major.

These following, as well as the two preceding, were evidently the rolls on which these companies were musterd out of the service on June 9th, 1813.

CAPT. WILLIAM JONES' COMPANY.

A muster roll of a company of volunteer infantry, commanded by Captain William Jones, ordered into the service by his Excellency, Ninian Edwards, Governor of the Illinois Territory, May 9, 1813, to June 9th, 1813.

Captain.
William Jones.

Lieutenant.
John Springer.

Ensign.
Thomas Finley.

Sergeants.
Edward Reavis,
John Whitley, Sr.,
David White,
Robert Brazel.

Corporals.
Solomon Pruitt,
Jacob Gragg,
David Smelson,
Andrew Lockhart.

Privates.
Simon Lindley, Sr.,
Simon Lindley, Jr.,
Joseph Lindley,
Benjamin Henson,
John Henson,
William Stubblefield,
Easley Stubblefield,
John Lindley,
John Green,
Ephraim Cox,
John Finley,
James Finley,
Howard Finley,
Moses Finley,
Fields Pruitt,
Martin Jones,
John Jones,
William Roberts,
Abraham Bateman,
William Bateman,

Samuel Lindley,
Mills Whitley,
John Whitley, Jr.,
Randolph Whitley,
Elisha Whitley,
Andrew Robert,
Charles Tetricks,
Valentine Brazel,
Abraham Tetricks,
William Brazel,
Jacob Tetricks,
Richard Brazel,
Peter Tetricks,
Robert White,
David S. White,
John Holt,
James Anderson, Sr.,
James Anderson, Jr.,
Abraham Howard,
James Chilton, Sr.,
William Chilton,
John Giger,
William Howard,
Mathias Chilton,
Isaac Ferguson,
John Higgins,
Aquilla Dallarhide,
Harmon Smelser,
Joshua Chilton,
James Chilton, Jr.,
Byrd Lockhart, Sr.,
George Tayes,
George Hutton, Sr.,
Henry Green, Sr.,
William Lockhart,
George Hutton, Jr.,
Henry Green, Jr.,
John Green,
Bartlett Tayes,
Abraham Van Hoozer,
Jacob Neely,
Joseph St. John,
William Davis,
Henry Walker,
Henry Cox.

SERGEANT JAMES N. FOX'S DETACHMENT.

Muster roll of a detachment of rangers, on the frontier of Johnson county, under the command of Sergeant James N. Fox from February 17th, 1813, to March 1st, 1813. This detachment being called into service by order of his Excellency, Ninian Edwards, Governor of said Territory.

Sergeant.
James N. Fox.

Privates.
William Edwards,
James Flanery,
Buckner Harris,
James Buchan,
George Deason,
Daniel Griffin,
Moas Blanc,
John F. Norton,
Shadrack Rawlison,
William Rawlison,
John Davis.

CAPTAIN WILLIAM BOON'S COMPANY.

Muster roll of a company of mounted volunteers of Randolph county, Illinois Territory, commanded by Captain William Boon, and called into service by his Excellency, Ninian Edwards, Governor of said Territory, from the 6th day of March, 1813, to the 5th day of June, 1813.

Captain.
William Boon.

First Lieutenant.
John Lacy.

Second Lieutenant.
William Bilderback.

Ensign.
John Bilderback.

Sergeants.
Robert Gaston,
Louis La Chapelle,
Michael Buyat,
Amos Chaffin.

Corporals.
Joseph French,
Adam Wolrick,
Zephue Brooks,
Henry Barbeau.

Privates.
James Lee,
Charles Garner,
William Tilford,
David Bailey,
Peter Dolin,
Archibald Snodgrass,
Ellis Chaffin,
John Drury,
Erne Godier,
Joseph La Franbris,
Louis Dory,
William Gaston,
John Young,
Adam Winghart,
Stace McDonough,
Gregone DeGognie,
Henry Teubeau,
Charles Bilberback,
William Barnett,
Robert Thompson,
George Cochran,
Elias Roberts,
Andre Roy,
John Gudier,
Levi French,
Samuel French,
Ralph Davis,
John Wootan,
Isaac Glenn,
Thomas Glenn,
Jacob Bowerman,
Francis Garner,
John Robinson,
George Creath,
Jacob Philhart,
Joel Craine,
John Roberts,
Daniel Bilderback,
William Fisher,
Robert Alexander,
James Hughes,
William Garner,
Thomas Wadley,
John Maclain,
Benjamin Buyat,
Baptiste Gendron,
Julian Bart,
Francis Montroy,
Peter Pillet,
Henry Conner,
Peter Cossy,
Isadore Godier,
Antoine Barbeau,
Jacob May,
Archibald Steele,
Jacob Honnan,
James Robinson,
Daniel Hull,
Shadrock Lively,
Alexander Clarke,
John Clyne,
Posio,
Levi Tamaraoa,
Cola,
Poscal,
John Babtiste Tamaraoa,
Jabez Leone,
Jacob Lazadder,

—22

LIEUTENANT DANIEL G. MOORE'S COMPANY.

Muster roll of a company of volunteer infantry commanded by Lieutenant Daniel G. Moore, and called into service by his Excellency, Ninian Edwards, Governor of Illinois Territory, from May 9th, 1813, to June 9th, 1813.

Lieutenant.
Daniel G. Moore.

Sergeants.
Martin Jones,
William P. Bowdon,
Benjamin Stidman,
Zadoch Newman.

Corporals.
George Moore,
James Beaman,
John Russell,
Eli Savadge.

Privates.
John Bows,
John Beck,
John Kirkpatrick,
Thomas Kirkpatrick,
Harrison Kirkpatrick,
Henry B. Riggor,
Joseph Newman,
William Jones,
John Newman,
Jesse Starkey,
Abel Moore,
Jesse Ennis,
William Ennis,
James Beck,
John Braman,
John Fullmore,
Hezekiah Cosby,
William Bartlett,
Burrill Hill,
James Hill,
John Lorton.

CAPT. NATHAN CHAMBERS' COMPANY.

A muster roll of a company of militia in the Illinois Territory, under the command of Captain Nathan Chambers, as foot men. Called into the United States service by his Excellency, Ninian Edwards, from the 12th day of April to the 12th day of May, 1813.

Captain.
Nathan Chambers.

Ensign.
John Savage.

Sergeants.
Henry Carr,
John Nichols,
James Bankson,
Joseph Duncan.

Corporals.
William Scott,
James Crocker,
Charles Cox,
Henry White.

Privates.
George Nichols,
Pleasant Nichols,
Abraham Baker,
Abram Minson,
Francis Swann,
Malcom Johnson,
William Dunkin,
John Broom,
Robert Farrar,
Thomas Nichols,
Leven Maddox,
William Armstrong,
James Chambers,
Samuel Scott,
Abraham Fike,
Nathan Langston,
Joseph Holcomb,
John Robertson,
Daniel Peck,
Bond Bernett,
Benjamin Hagerman,
Robert Middleton,
Reuben Middleton,
Robert Abernathey,
Miles Abernathey,
Robert Moore,
Arthur Crocker,
William Crocker,
Job Vanwinkle,
Simeon Wakefield,
Henry Hutton,
Jonathan Hill,
Patton Bankson,
John Pea,
John Journey, Sr.,
Robert Dunkin, Sr.,
James McCracken,
Barnet Bone,
Robert Dunkin, Jr.,
James Petty,
Bryant Mooney,
John Crocker,
Hugh Gilbreath,
Paul Gasgill,
Jonathan Gasgill,
William Wakefield.

Following is a Muster roll of regimental and staff officers ordered into service by his Excellency, Ninian Edwards, Governor and Commander-in-Chief of the Illinois Territory, from the 18th day of February, to the 16th day of June, 1813:

APPENDIX.

Names.	Rank.
B. Stephenson	Major
Philip Trample	Major
Nathaniel Jurney	Adjutant
George Fisher	Surgeon
William Reynolds	Surgeon's Mate
Daniel G. Moore	Quartermaster
Aaron Whitney	Sergeant Major

I do certify that the foregoing muster roll exhibits a just statement of the regiment and staff officers as above stated, this 16th day of June, 1813.

B. STEPHENSON,
Brigade-Major.

CAPT. JAMES B. MOORE'S COMPANY (4th COMPANY.)

A muster roll of Capt. James B. Moore's company of mounted rangers of the Illinois Territory, under the command of Major Benjamin Stephenson, from the first day of June to the sixteenth day of the same month, 1813—by order of his Excellency, Ninian Edwards, Governor, etc.

Captain.
James B. Moore.

First Lieutenant.
David Robinson.

Second Lieutenant.
Arthur Morgan.

Ensign.
John Hewitt.

Sergeants.
Daniel Converse,
Jacob Young,
Benjamin Marney,
James Hutton.

Corporals.
Isaac Basey,
James Talbott,
Henry Randleman,
John Crawford.

Privates.
Thomas Jordin,
Enoch Moore,
Jesse Miller,
Joseph Miller,
David Miller,
John Enochs,
Jonathan Knox,
Anthony B. Conner,
Samuel McFarland,
George Lary,
Thomas Johnston,
Hugh Royalston,
Marcus Pelham,
Peter Wills,
Francis Pelham,
Abraham Miller,
Thomas Marney,
Solomon Strong,
Amos Shook,
Fielding Porter,
John Ryan,
Stephen Lacy,
Elisha Axley,
William Ryan,
John Stallings,
David Porter,
John Waddle,
John Brisco,
John Moore,
Jacob Clark,
John Clover,
William Harrington,
David Moore,
Thomas G. Mattingly,
Wylie Harrington,
Felix Clark,
Stephen Rector,
Joshua Vaughn,
Charles Gilham,
George Richardson,
William Griffin,
Pleasant Goings,
William Ferguson,
Hiram Huitt,
Joseph Ferguson,
Orman Beoman,
John Finley,
Fleming Cox,
Martin Wood,
Bennett Nowlin,
Roland Huitt,
Henry Mace,
Isaac Smith,
Daniel Winn,
Edward Crouch,
Isaac Carmack,
William Going,
Elisha Taylor,
Andrew Robinson,
William Hogan,
Prior Hogan,
Bartlett Cox,
Richard Windsor,
Alexander Biron,
Jude Converse,
George Hawk,
John Hogan,
Eli Lankford,
Josiah Lankford,
William Chance,
Jacob Luntzford,
John Marney,
John Collins,
Thomas Ramey,
John Ferguson,
Robert Hawks,
Benjamin Edwards,
James Marney,
Jesse Harrison,
George Glenn,
Simon Vanarsdall,
Samuel D. Davidson,
Elias Roberts,
Aaron Whitney,

The foregoing company was, no doubt, temporarily called into service to hold the forts and protect the government property from the Indians until some more definite arrangement should be made by the War Department to sustain a military force. The following letter from Governor Edwards to the Secretary of War, will shed some light on the subject:

ELVIRADE, Randolph County, Illinois Territory, May 4, 1813.

SIR: A short time ago I received a letter from Colonel Bond, informing me that you had authorized him to request me to raise and organize three additional companies of rangers. I immediately wrote you, that I supposed what had been done would be sufficient, and that those three companies who, through me, tendered the President their services as rangers, would be accepted.

They have been notified by me that they have been accepted, but lest some accident may have prevented my letters from reaching you, I will here give the names of these officers—all of whom have been chosen by their companies and approved by me:

James B. Moore, Captain.
David Robinson, 1st Lieutenant.
Arthur Morgan, 2d Lieutenant.
John Huitt, Ensign.

Samuel Whiteside, Captain.
Joseph Borough, 1st Lieutenant.
Samuel Gilbaur, 2d Lieutenant.
Arthur Armstrong, Ensign.

Jacob Short, Captain.
Nathaniel Journey, 1st Lieutenant.
Andrew Bankston, 2d Lieutenant.
John Journey, Ensign.

These officers and those of the companies raised here last year, are all exceedingly anxious to be commanded by Benjamin Stephenson as their major, with the exception of an ensign and a lieutenant, who were absent at the time. They have unanimously petitioned me on this subject. The privates comprising the battalion are equally desirous of it, and I can most conscientiously say, that, in my opinion, the territory does not admit of a better choice.

The Legislature of this Territory, at its last session, by the solicitations of certain individuals, was induced to ask for this force and to recommend John Murdock to be authorized to raise and command it.

But I beg leave to observe that the force I have raised has been upon a different plan altogether. Murdock has not raised a man, and has endeavored to throw every impediment in my way. He is not qualified, either by his knowledge or experience, for the command, and those who have recommended him will not pretend to say that his habits do not form a most important objection.

I have the honor to be,

Your obedient servant
N. EDWARDS.

(Edwards' History of Illinois, pp. 347-8.)

SECOND CAMPAIGN 1813.

Large numbers of hostile Indians having gathered among the Kickapoos and Potawotamies at their villages on Lake Peoria, and marauding parties from these being frequently sent out to harass, rout and kill the settlers on the frontiers of both Illinois and Missouri, a joint expedition was projected of the militia of both territories, to disperse them from their convenient location. An army of 900 men was collected and placed under the command of Gen. Howard, who had resigned the position of Territorial Governor of Missouri, for that purpose. The Illinois contingent was ordered to rendezvous at Camp Russell.

One company, however, was ordered to a point on the Mississippi called Piasa, where they remained several weeks and suffered seriously from sickness.

The organization of the Illinois troops at Camp Russell was as follows: Colonel, Benjamin Stephenson, Randolph county; W. B. Whitesides and John Murdock, Majors, and Joseph Phillips, Samuel Judy, Nathaniel Journey, and Samuel Whitesides, Captains. The Missouri contingent was commanded by Colonel McNair, afterward Governor of that State. Both regiments marched up on their respective sides of the Mississippi river, without any adventure, except a slight skirmish by the Illinois troops with straggling Indians in search of wild honey in the present limits of Calhoun county. A junction was formed by the Missourians crossing the river at Ft. Mason, 100 miles above the mouth of the Illinois river, when General Howard took the principal command of the expedition. Passing a recently deserted Indian village on the site of the present city of Quincy, they struck out eastward and reached the Illinois river at the mouth of Spoon river, not far from the present town of Havana, in Mason county.

Here the provision boats arrived and took on board their sick. The march was continued up the Illinois river to Peoria, where there was a small stockade in charge of Capt. Nicholas of the U. S. Army, on which the Indians had two days before made an attack, but were repulsed. But the Indians gaining knowledge of the advance of this force, had, with their usual cunning, fled northward. Of the conclusion of this expedition Davidson and Stuvé, say:

"The army was marched up the lake to Goma's village, the present site of Chilicotho, and finding that the enemy had ascended the Illinois, two deserted villages were demolished under the shock of its onset, and burned, when it took up its retrograde march. At the outlet of the lake, the present site of Peoria, the troops remained in camp several weeks, building Fort Clark, named in honor of Gen. George Rogers Clark. Major Christy in the meantime, was dispatched with a force, in charge of two fortified keel boats, up the river (Mississippi) to the foot of the rapids, to chastise and rout such of the enemy as might have lodged in that region. Major Boone was sent with a force to scour the Spoon river country, towards Rock river. Both expeditions returned without other discoveries than signs of alarm on the part of the enemy, and his retreat into the interior. The army returned by a direct route to Camp Russell, where the volunteers and militia were disbanded, October 22, 1813. (D. and S., History Illinois, p. 277.)

1814.

The year 1814 was prolific with horrible deeds of savage butchery. The Indians were incited by British agents and were active all along the line of the advancing frontier. Illinois with her large line of explored settlements suffered severely. We will mention only a few of the most aggravated of their outrages. Compiled from Reynolds Times, and Stuve's History of Illinois:

In July, a Mrs. Reagan, living in the Wood River settlement six miles east of the present city of Alton, with her six children, were murdered by the Indians, who were pursued by Capt. Samuel Whiteside and his company of rangers, to the Sangamon river, where all escaped except the leader, who was shot out of a tree top by Capt. Whiteside, with the scalp of Mrs. Reagan fastened to his belt.

In August, Capt. Short's rangers, who were encamped at the Lively cabins in Washington county, discovered the trail of 7 Indians with 14 stolen horses. Capt. Short with 30 men followed them overtaking them on a fork of the little Wabash, near the east line of Fayette county, and killed them all. The whites lost but one man, William O'Neal, who was killed by an adversary quicker than himself.

The military expeditions in which Illinois participated in this year were by water on the Mississippi. The first was that of Governor Clark (in the absence of General Howard) which left St. Louis on the 1st of May, composed of 200 men, in five barges destined for Prairie de Chien.

Dickson, a British agent, had recruited at that place, a short time previously, a force of 300 Indians for the British army, which he had conducted to Canada, leaving a small garrison of "Macinoc Fencibles" under the command of a British officer to hold the post until his return. These Governor Clark had no difficulty in putting to flight, and quartering his troops in the house of the Mackaw Fur Company, erected a fort which he called Ft. Shelby, and returned in June to St. Louis. But in July a large force of British and Indians under Col. Mackey, coming by water from Mackinaw, via Green Bay, and the Wisconsin river, after a short siege captured the entire garrison, which they paroled, thus leaving the British the gainers of all the material advantages of the expedition.

General Howard having returned to his post in St. Louis in the meantime, and believing it desirable to strengthen the fort at Prairie du Chien, to this end sent 108 men in charge of Lieutenant Campbell of the regular army, in three keel boats up the river, as reinforcements. Of this force 66 men were Illinois rangers under the command of Capt. Stephen Rector and Capt. Riggs, who occupied two of the boats. The remainder of the force with Campbell occupied the other boat. They passed as far as Rock Island, where they laid up for a night without molestation. At the rapids great numbers of the Sac and Fox Indians visited the boats with professions of friendship, yet gave hints to some of the French boatmen, who accompanied the expedition, that all was not right. Lieut. Campbell, however, disregarded these hints, and allowed his force to become scattered, when a gale blew his boat, which was two miles in the rear, over towards the Illinois shore to a small island, when it was attacked by a large force of the Indians from the shore, under the command of Black Hawk.

The strong gale prevented the return of the boats which had gone ahead, and the force on Campbell's boat had been mostly killed and wounded. When Rector, throwing overboard all provisions, with a gallantry deserving of commemoration, came to the rescue of the imperiled men and rescued the survivors, and removed the dying and all to their vessel, leaving Campbell's barge to the enemy, the contents of which furnished them material for a feast as unusual as it was enjoyable.

Riggs' boat was for a time surrounded by the enemy, but toward evening the wind having become somewhat allayed, the boat, under cover of the approaching darkness, and the crew made good their escape without the loss of a single man.

After the two foregoing disasters still another expedition was projected this season for the Upper Mississippi. This latter was fitted up at Cape au Gris, an old French hamlet on the left bank of the Mississippi, a few miles above the mouth of the Illinois. It consisted of 334 men (forty of whom were regulars) in command of Major Zacury Taylor, Nelson Rector and Samuel Whitesides and Captain Hempstead being each in command of a boat. Their principal instruction was to penetrate well up in the Indian country and returning to destroy the corn growing within reach on both banks of the river down to Rock Island, where they intended to establish a fort and leave a permanent garrison.

The expedition passed up as far as Rock Island unmolested, although the country swarmed with the enemy who were aided by the English, who were then in command, with a detachment of regulars and artillery. On the 2d day of August, 1814, the boats were attacked by the combined force of the Indians and English, and turning about began to descend the rapids, fighting with great gallantry, the enemy pouring in a hot fire into their flanks from both sides of the river. A little way above the mouth of the Rock river, near some willow islands. Major Taylor anchored his fleet out in the river out of reach of the rifles, but during the night the English planted a battery of six pieces of artillery at the water's edge, and landed a considerable force of the red skins on the island, to supplement the attack they expected to make. But early in the morning Major Taylor, with all his force except 20 men left in charge of the boats, with great gallantry charged on the savages and drove them with considerable loss from the upper island to the lower one. The fire of the artillery had become to be a serious matter with the boats and they dropped out of range down the stream. After an ineffectual, though partially successful attempt on the part of Capt. Rector to clear the other island of savages, the expedition, with a total loss of 11 men wounded—of whom 3 afterwards died—continued its retreat down the river. On the site of the present town of Warsaw, in Hancock county, they erected a fort, which consisted of a rough stockade, and blockhouses of unhewn logs, which they named for Governor Edwards. This fort, like Ft. Madison on the opposite bank of the river a little higher up, was a few weeks after (in October) considered untenable—the troops being out of provisions—and was evacuated and burnt, and the expedition continued its retreat to Cape au Gris.

Thus ended the third and last of these ill-fated expeditions, like its predecessors, in defeat and disaster. The rangers and volunteers were discharged Oct. 18, 1814.

With the approach of winter the Indian depredations became fewer, and finally ceased altogether with the peace of Ghent, which closed the war December 24, 1814.

We subjoin a muster roll of a company of mounted rangers, called into service in September, 1814, and which is remarkable as the last body of men enlisted in this State for the war of 1812.

Muster roll of Captain Daniel Boultinghouse's company of mounted volunteers, called into the service of the United States by order of his Excellency, Governor Edwards, Commander-in-Chief of the Illinois militia, to repel the invasions of the hostile Indians. From Sept. 8, to Dec. 8, 1814, inclusive:

Captain.
Daniel Boultinghouse.

First Lieutenant.
John Graves.

Second Lieutenant.
Robert Tavery.

Third Lieutenant.
John Morris.

Ensign.
Thomas Tavery.

Sergeants.
William Nash,
Stephen Stanley,
James Boyd,
James Hopkins,
Tira Robinson.

Corporals.
John Wilson,
Robert Boyd,
David Haney,
William Cummins,
Asa Ross,
Robert Clark.

Privates.
Real Porter,
Edward Potter,
James Dunlap,
William Trask,
Rolen Lane,
Benj. Kirkendall,
Hiram Jones,
Daniel McHenry,
John Dover,
James Hencely,
Jesse Kirkendall,
George Stumm,
John Morris,
George Martin,
John Burney,
Needham Stanley,
Charles Hencely,
James Paton,
Jonathan Steward,
John Brown,

Eli Solph,
James Boultinghouse,
Charles Burney,
Daniel Boultinghouse,
George Morris,
David Daniel,
John Daniel,
David Brown,
Irvan Wilson,
Charles Steward,
William Vaughn,
John Dennis,
Philip Steward,
John Buckels,
James Corn,
Archibald Clayton,
Nathan Young,
Nathan Harris,
Thomas Pool,
William Moriday,
John Moor,
John Lucus,
William Burney,
Joseph Daniels,
Jesse Boman,
Jarrard Tramell,
Seth Hargrave,
Daniel Snodgrass,
Joseph Lawry,
William Adkins,
James Devenport,
James Wilson,
Robert Stafford,
John Martin,
Robert D. Cates,
Henry Coley,
John Beck,
Moses Sweeton,
Charles Dickerson,
Hugh Collins,
Edward Meloy,
James Hix,
Willis Chambers,
Jesse Adkins,
Wyatt Adkins,
Thomas Chambers,
Joseph Culbertson,
Arvin Wilson,
William Read,
William Chambers,
John Ferret,
Edward Michel,
John Poley,
Thomas McCallister,

Alden Henry,
James Martin,
Archibald Rowan,
Joel Metcalf,
Elijah Reede,
Henry Wheeler,
Samuel Davidson,
Moses Lamb,
William McCormick,
Ezekial Hide,
John Gastin,
Charles Lezenby,
James Morris,
Robert Gastin,
Merritt Taylor,
Nimrod Taylor,
Edmond Starks,
William McGehee,

Thomas Gastin,
John McGahan,
William Clark,
Jonathan Hampton,
John Walls,
William McCoy,
John Perry,
Elias Chaffin,
Brice Hannah,
Thomas Wilson,
John McCallister,
Reuben Walden,
James Gastin,
John Heart,
Henry Stumm,
John Whitaker,
George McCann,
James Haynes,

www.ingramcontent.com/pod-product-compliance
Lightning Source LLC
Chambersburg PA
CBHW021942240426
43668CB00037B/371